FIGHTING WORDS

FIGHTING WORDS

COMPETING VOICES FROM THE CRUSADES

Andrew Holt & James Muldoon

Greenwood World Publishing
Oxford / Westport Connecticut
2008

First published in 2008 by Greenwood World Publishing

1 2 3 4 5 6 7 8 9 10

Copyright © Greenwood Publishing Group 2008

This book is sold subject to the condition that it shall not, by way of trade or otherwise, be lent, resold, hired out, or otherwise circulated without the publisher's prior consent in any form of binding or cover other than that in which it is published and without a similar condition being imposed on the subsequent publisher

Greenwood World Publishing
Wilkinson House
Jordan Hill
Oxford OX2 8EJ
An imprint of Greenwood Publishing Group, Inc
www.greenwood.com

British Library Cataloguing-in-Publication Data: a catalogue record for this book is available from the British Library

Library of Congress Cataloging-in-Publication Data

Competing voices from the Crusades : fighting words / edited by Andrew Holt and James Muldoon.
    p. cm. – (Fighting words)
 Includes bibliographical references and index.
 ISBN 978-1-84645-011-2 (alk. paper)
   1. Crusades–Sources. I. Holt, Andrew (Andrew P.) II. Muldoon, James, 1935–

D151.C73 2008
909.07–dc22

                      2008010072

ISBN 978-1-84645-011-2 (hardback)

Designed by Fraser Muggeridge studio
Typeset by TexTech International
Printed and bound by South China Printing Company

Andrew dedicates his efforts to his two young daughters, Isabella and Claire, while Jim dedicates this work to all his grandchildren

CONTENTS

ix
SERIES FOREWORD

xi
PREFACE

xiii
INTRODUCTION

1
CHAPTER ONE
POPE URBAN II'S CALLING OF THE FIRST CRUSADE, 1095

23
CHAPTER TWO
ATTACKS ON THE JEWS DURING THE FIRST CRUSADE, 1096

39
CHAPTER THREE
CRUSADER MASSACRE OF THE INHABITANTS OF JERUSALEM, 1099

55
CHAPTER FOUR
THE SIEGE OF DAMASCUS DURING THE SECOND CRUSADE, 1148

73
CHAPTER FIVE
THE FAILURE OF THE SECOND CRUSADE

87
CHAPTER SIX
THE BATTLE OF HATTIN, 1187

107
CHAPTER SEVEN
SALADIN'S CONQUEST OF JERUSALEM, 1187

121
CHAPTER EIGHT
THE SACK OF CONSTANTINOPLE, 1204

139
CHAPTER NINE
THE CRUSADE OF FREDERICK II, 1228–1229

163
CHAPTER TEN
THE CRUSADE OF LOUIS IX, 1248–1249

193
CHAPTER ELEVEN
THE FALL OF ACRE, 1291

207
CHAPTER TWELVE
LIFE ON A CRUSADE, 1095–1270

235
CHAPTER THIRTEEN
LIFE IN THE CRUSADER STATES, 1098–1291

259
CHAPTER FOURTEEN
CRUSADES AND THE CANON LAW

275
ENDMATTER

SERIES FOREWORD

Fighting Words: Competing Voices from the Crusades is a unique new series aimed at a broad audience, from college-level professors and undergraduates to high school teachers, students and the general reader. Each volume in this series focuses on a unique historical controversy, told through first-hand accounts from the diverse perspectives of both the victors and the vanquished. The series is designed to introduce readers to a broad range of competing narratives about the past, giving voices to those often left silent in the secondary literature.

Each volume offers competing perspectives through relatively short primary documents, such as newspaper articles, contemporary chronicles, excerpts from participants' letters or memoirs, as well as other carefully selected sources; brief introductions provide the necessary background information and context to help guide readers through the disparate accounts. Where necessary, key documents are reproduced in their entirety. Most of the documents are brief in nature, and sharp in content, which will help to promote general classroom discussion and debate. The inclusion of vivid and colourful accounts from the participants themselves, combined with other primary sources from all sides, give the series an exciting and engaging flavour.

The *Fighting Words* series is designed to promote meaningful discussion and debate about the past. Furthermore, the volumes in this series encourage readers to think critically about the evidence that historians use, or ignore, to reconstruct an understanding of that past. Each volume will challenge accepted assumptions about the topics covered, and readers will question the nature of primary sources, the motivations, agenda and perspectives of the authors, and the silences inherent in all of the sources. Ultimately, readers will be left to ponder the question: whose history is this?

J. Michael Francis

ABOUT THE SERIES EDITOR

Dr J. Michael Francis received his PhD in 1998 from the University of Cambridge, where he specialised in colonial Latin American history. Since then, he has taught at the University of North Florida, where he is an associate professor of history. He has written numerous articles on the history of early-colonial New Granada (Colombia). In 2006, he edited a three-volume reference work called *Iberia and the Americas: Culture, Politics, and History* (ABC-CLIO). His most recent book, *Invading Colombia: Spanish Accounts of the Gonzalo Jiménez de Quesada Expedition of Conquest*, was published in 2007 by Penn State University Press.

Dr Francis serves as Book Review editor for the journal *Ethnohistory*, and series co-editor for *Latin American Originals* (Penn State University Press). He is also a member of the advisory board of the University Press of Florida. In 2007, Dr Francis was appointed Research Associate at the American Museum of Natural History in New York. At present, he is completing a manuscript entitled *Politics, Murder, and Martyrdom in Spanish Florida: Don Juan and the Guale Uprising of 1597*, which will be published in 2009 by the American Museum of Natural History Press.

PREFACE

This volume seeks to highlight the most important and controversial events of the crusading movement by providing competing eyewitness or contemporary accounts of each event. By having access to first-hand accounts from both sides of an event, readers will be able to determine for themselves how such events were interpreted and understood by the participants. While acknowledging a broader crusading movement against Muslims in the Iberian Peninsula, pagans in northern Europe and political opponents and heretics in southern Europe, the editors have focused their efforts on the well-known crusades to the East. They have done so because the theological, cultural and judicial developments of the broader crusading movement were, in many ways, primarily based on the key events and experiences that took place during those crusades that sought the conquest of the Holy Land as their ultimate goal. Additionally, rather than devoting limited space to a broad overview of the larger crusading movement, the editors have sought to focus more narrowly on crusading efforts in the East to allow for a more substantial and in-depth review of the key events and sources.

There are a number of people that the editors wish to thank, including series editor Michael Francis of the University of North Florida, whose patience, encouragement and conceptual guidance were invaluable in the creation of this book. The editors would also like to thank Charles Glasheen and David Sheffler, both of the University of North Florida, and Nina Caputo and Andrea Sterk, both of the University of Florida, for reading various parts of this manuscript and suggesting many valuable improvements. The editors also extend their thanks to William C. Jordan of Princeton University, who upon becoming aware of this project, referred the editors to one another and suggested their partnership. Finally, Andrew Holt would also like to thank his family, especially his wife, Michele, his brother, Michael, and his mother, Anita, as well as his advisor, Florin Curta of the University of Florida, for providing various forms of sometimes crucial support and encouragement for this project, from its inception to its conclusion.

Andrew Holt
James Muldoon

INTRODUCTION

Understood by participants at once as a statement of Christian charity, religious devotion and godly savagery, the 'wars of the cross' helped fashion for adherents a shared sense of belonging to a Christian society, *societas Christiana*, Christendom, and contributed to setting its human and geographic frontiers.
In these ways, the crusades helped define the nature of Europe.
– Christopher Tyerman[1]

The crusading movement involved peoples of varying religious and cultural backgrounds engaged in a violent struggle that spanned several centuries and took place on three continents. The crusades were so broad in scope that diverse sections of modern society continue to exhibit an affinity with the various religious and cultural groups that took part. This is perhaps best demonstrated by the large number of modern-day petitioners demanding papal recognition of wrongdoing during the crusades. The petitioners include, or have included, a number of influential Muslim clerics who decry the crusades as a brutal invasion of Muslim lands, a modern Knights Templar association in Great Britain concerned over the scandal surrounding the dissolution of the order in the early fourteenth century and Eastern Orthodox Christians, who eight centuries later still lament the sacking of the Byzantine capital of Constantinople in 1204.[2]

In response, there has been no shortage of remorse from many modern Westerners who, although several centuries removed from the crusading era, are willing to offer passionate apologies for the deeds of their spiritual or cultural ancestors. In 1996 a group of evangelical Protestant Christians belonging to the so-called Reconciliation Walk movement went on a walking tour through parts of Europe and the Muslim world. It was their mission, 900 years after the launching of the First Crusade, to apologise for the crusades, and while doing so, they wrote off the entire crusading movement as one fuelled by fear, greed and hatred. Nearly as enthusiastic in his willingness to express sorrow for abuses committed during the crusades was Pope John Paul II. While never apologising for the principle of crusading itself, or the broader crusading movement, the Pope showed little hesitation in apologising for specific abuses committed by some crusaders in the service of the Church. Among the Pope's various apologies was one made during a visit to Greece in 2001 for the crusaders' sack of Constantinople in 1204. Three years later, Ecumenical Patriarch Bartholomew I, the spiritual leader of the world's 300 million Orthodox Christians, finally accepted the Pope's apology on the 800th anniversary of the event.

That crusading is generally held in such low esteem is unsurprising when considering the basis for popular understandings of the crusades. Commentators regularly express contempt for the crusaders in films, in print and on television. In reference to the efforts of modern Christians to apologise for the crusades, the well-known attorney and Harvard Law School professor Allen Dershowitz has written, 'Now that good Christians have taken the lead in renouncing the Crusades and in seeking atonement for their butchery, the time has come to correct history and to eliminate all positive references to the Crusades.'[3] Representative of many popular critics of the crusades, the novelist and regular History Channel commentator Tariq Ali has on multiple occasions claimed that the crusaders were motivated by greed, noting that their goal was 'to loot as much wealth as available and bring it back to Europe'.[4] In April 2002, the popular news magazine *U.S. News and World Report* implied that the history of military conflict and bad relations began with the clash of the first crusader armies against the forces of Islam. Its headline read: 'During the Crusades, East and West first met – on the battlefield.'[5] Later that year the History Channel television special, *Inside Islam*, also cited the crusades as the first violent struggle between Christendom and the Islamic world. The implication of such claims was that the history of bad relations between Islam and the West originated with the attack of the crusaders on the Muslim world.

SCHOLARLY PERSPECTIVES OF THE CRUSADES

While popular perspectives of the crusades are often dominated by hostility and suspicion, scholarly perceptions are considerably more restrained. This divide between scholarly and popular perceptions finds its origins in the latter half of the twentieth century when crusades historians began to argue for new understandings of the crusading movement. Although scholars debated a number of matters concerning the crusades, including the origins of crusading and the motivations of the crusaders, the fundamental issue of simply defining a crusade was, until recently, among the areas of greatest disagreement. Historians have essentially divided into two camps on the issue, those known as traditionalists and those known as pluralists.[6]

Traditionalists have emphasised the well-known and often-popularised crusading efforts in the East, which took place from the end of the eleventh century to the end of the thirteenth century, as the embodiment of the crusading movement. In this case, the purpose of a crusade is either to assist eastern Christians or to liberate Jerusalem and the Holy Sepulchre.[7] Pluralists, as opposed to the traditionalists, cite papal authorisation as the defining feature of a crusade, regardless of against whom or where it is directed. Consequently, the pluralists' definition of a crusade provides for a broad expansion of the crusading movement to include expeditions against religious dissenters, pagans, political opponents and Muslims in Europe. Perhaps the most well known and influential of the pluralists is Cambridge University historian Jonathan Riley-Smith. In 1977, he defined a crusade as 'a holy war authorised by the pope, who proclaimed it in the name of God or Christ...a defensive reaction to injury or aggression or as an attempt to recover Christian territories lost to the infidels, it answered the needs of the whole church or all of Christendom...rather than those of a particular nation'.[8]

In contrast to popular understandings of the crusades, which generally attribute the crusading movement to base motives like greed or a desire for violence, both the pluralist and traditionalist definitions of crusading maintain that crusades were formally called to aid suffering Christians, to liberate Christian holy places, or even as a defensive reaction to outside aggression. While there is no doubt that some early crusaders headed East with the hope of acquiring land or riches,[9] scholars have largely concluded that most crusaders were primarily motivated by genuine religious convictions, even concepts of charity, rather than greed.[10] The crusaders were troubled by stories of recent Muslim aggression against Christians and holy places in the East as many were aware that enormous Christian territories had been conquered by Muslim armies since the rise of Islam in the seventh century. Among those formerly Christian areas lost to Islamic armies were large portions of Spain, southern Italy, North Africa, the Levant and Asia Minor. As a result, crusades preachers and contemporary source authors portrayed recent Turkish aggression in the East as an extension of a historic assault of Islam against the Christian world, in a successful effort to win the sympathy of their audience.

The new conclusions of crusades scholars over the last four decades have inspired a backlash against popular perceptions of the crusades. In response to those who attribute baser motives to the crusaders, a number of prominent historians, including Jonathan Riley-Smith, have argued that the crusades can be viewed as defensive in nature.[11] Few historians have argued this as forcefully as St. Louis University historian Thomas Madden, who has noted that the crusades were 'the West's belated response to the Muslim conquest of fully two-thirds of the Christian world'.[12] In the light of such views, it is not surprising that a number of prominent crusades scholars have expressed varying levels of contempt for the value of modern apologies for the crusades.[13] Contrary to the claims of some popular commentators, scholars are quite correct in pointing out that the history of military conflict between Christians and Muslims began long before the crusades. Major conflicts had taken place between both Eastern and Western Christians and the emerging, but quickly powerful, Muslim dynasties for centuries before the crusades in eastern and southern Europe, western Asia and throughout northern Africa. They began nearly as early as the era of the Prophet Muhammad and continued with varying degrees of intensity until the calling of the First Crusade at the end of the eleventh century.

THE DEVELOPMENT OF MILITANT CHRISTIANITY AND MILITANT ISLAM

Because Christianity was born during the height of the Roman Empire's power, its early minority status ensured that violence on the part of Christians would bring disaster on the new faith. Yet Christian opinions on the legitimacy of the use of violence began to change during the fourth and fifth centuries as they found themselves in positions of authority. During this period, Christians recognised that the duties of the Roman state required the maintenance and effective use of armies to preserve and protect the empire. Consequently, later-patristic-era writers increasingly noted distinctions between killing in war and the sin of murder.[14] St. Augustine of Hippo, for example, justified as appropriate the use of force by the state against heretics who were disturbing the peace of the countryside.[15] Christian writers often supported such arguments with reference to their Holy Scriptures, which contained numerous instances of divinely sanctioned warfare against the opponents of God's people, the Israelites.

It would be more than three centuries before Christians found themselves in a position of leadership, with the accompanying responsibilities; however, Islam had, nearly from its inception, found itself in a position of political authority. There was never a serious question over the acceptability of the use of force in the preservation and expansion of Islamic religious and political ideals. Even during the lifetime of the Prophet Muhammad, numerous military conflicts took place between the nascent Muslim community and various tribes of the Arabian Peninsula who were hostile to the new faith. In the wake of a number of important early Islamic military victories, as well as the power vacuum created by the collapse of the Persian Empire, the religious unification and political consolidation of numerous Arab tribes quickly took place. This early good fortune seemed to prove the divine sanction of Islam and allowed the Islamic world and its armies to turn their attention to lands and peoples beyond the Arabian Peninsula.

CONFLICT BETWEEN ISLAM AND EASTERN CHRISTIANITY BEFORE THE CRUSADES

In hindsight, an eventual clash between Christian and Islamic forces, both confident in their special relationship with God, seemed inevitable. Yet the speed and scope with which these conflicts developed remain surprising. The Islamic conquests that took place from the time of Muhammad (d.632) to the year 750 were so explosive in their speed and effectiveness that in roughly 120 years, Muslim armies laid claim to enough conquered lands to challenge the size of the Roman Empire at its height. From the Atlantic coast of modern-day Portugal to the Hindu Kush, Islamic armies took control of enormous territories, many of which were formerly ruled by Christian kings or emperors.

The Christian Byzantine Empire, what remained of the Roman Empire in the East after its counterpart's decline in the West, had experienced numerous military conflicts with the Persian Empire (Sassanid Empire) in the centuries leading to the rise of Islam. The final outbreak of war, and perhaps the most significant for the future of both empires, began in 602 and finally ended with a Byzantine victory in 628. This war with Persia was in one way similar to a crusade in that it was promoted by Byzantine leaders as a holy war between Christianity and Zoroastrianism (the dominant religion of the Persians). The seriousness of the Persian threat to the Byzantine Empire during this period was perhaps best demonstrated by the sack of the Byzantine-controlled city of Jerusalem in 614 and the nearly successful conquest of the Byzantine capital of Constantinople in 625. This conflict ultimately exhausted both the Byzantines and the Persians economically, militarily and psychologically, and as a result, neither was well prepared to deal with the rise of Islam in the decades that followed. Early Islamic armies had an especially devastating impact on the Persians, as they conquered and consolidated the Persian Empire under the Islamic caliphate by the middle of the seventh century.

The earliest military conflicts between Byzantium and Islam began within a few years after the death of the Prophet Muhammad in 632. In addition to the conquest of lands previously held by the Persian Empire, including Jerusalem in 638, Islamic forces began their assault on Christian-controlled territories with the conquest of Egypt in 642 and then engaged in an unsuccessful siege of Constantinople in 678, which would be repeated in 716. Significant portions of the Byzantine Empire came under the control of Islamic armies, who also swept across North Africa and devastated both Coptic and Catholic Christianity. A factor that possibly contributed to the success of Islamic armies during this period was that some of the newly conquered peoples seemed to have been quite content with their new rulers. Theological and political differences dating back to the fifth century resulted in the view of many Byzantine authorities that Syrian and Egyptians Christians were heretics. Additionally, non-Christians (Jews and Pagans) were often subjected to varying levels of discriminatory treatment. Consequently, life under Byzantine rule for religious minorities was often difficult, and some viewed Islamic rule, which did not force religious conversion, as a welcome relief from Byzantine imperial and ecclesiastical oppression.[16]

Throughout the remainder of the eighth, ninth and early tenth centuries, Muslim forces consolidated their numerous gains, stabilising the new frontier between those areas under Christian control and those areas under Islamic control. Yet in the latter half of the tenth century, during a period of strife and division within the Muslim world, a reinvigorated Byzantine Empire briefly went on the offensive against Islam. Byzantine forces successfully recaptured some of their most important Christian cities[17] and pushed into northern Syria. Yet with the rise of the Seljuk Turks in the eleventh century, the Byzantine Empire again found itself on the defensive. The Seljuk

Turks originated on the borders of the Turkish steppe, east of the Aral Sea, and had converted to Islam in the tenth century. As zealous new converts, they quickly became a threat to both Eastern Christians and their co-religionists, as during the early eleventh century, they turned their attention to the conquest of Western lands controlled by Christians and those Muslims whom they considered to be impious. In contrast, the Byzantines during this period, unlike in their earlier wars with the Persian Empire, do not seem to have viewed the advancing Turks as enemies in religious terms (unlike Latin Christians), but only as a competing and growing empire.

During the later part of the eleventh century, Turkish attacks on Eastern Christian lands intensified and prompted significant concerns about the vulnerability of the Byzantine Empire. Few events during this period reportedly caused as much concern as the humiliating defeat of a Byzantine army by the Seljuk Turks at Mantzikert in 1071. It was then that the Byzantine army led by Emperor Romanus IV Diogenes engaged a force under the command of Sultan Alp Arslan. The sultan was in the middle of a campaign to consolidate his frontier, during which he captured several Christian places that prompted the Byzantine response. The Turks not only defeated the Byzantine army, but also took Emperor Romanus IV as a prisoner. While the emperor, as an extremely valuable prisoner, was treated well by his Turkish captors and quickly ransomed, the effect of the battle was to hasten the transfer of large parts of Asia Minor to Turkish control.

Such consequences contributed to later Byzantine appeals to the West for aid. In fact only three years after the events at Mantzikert, Pope Gregory VII responded to an appeal for military aid from the Byzantine Emperor Michael VII Dukas by calling for an armed expedition to go to the aid of Eastern Christians. Gregory VII went so far as to propose personally leading an army of 50,000 against the Turks.[18] Had Gregory's efforts been successful, he would have held the distinction of being the first pope to launch a crusade. Yet a power struggle between secular and ecclesiastical authorities in medieval Europe, the so-called Investiture Controversy (discussed later in this chapter), ensured that Gregory VII's efforts never developed beyond the proposal stage.

Other significant Turkish military victories quickly followed their success at Mantzikert. Among the more notable included the conquest of the ancient Christian cities of Nicaea and Antioch. Nicaea, as the site of two important early ecumenical Church councils, had a long and respected history as a Christian city. It was while in attendance at the First Council of Nicaea in 325 that Christian bishops had developed the so-called Nicene Creed, and then later in 787, the Second Nicean Council responded to the Iconoclasm Controversy by officially approving the honour and use of icons in Christian worship. Consequently, there was great alarm when the Turks captured Nicaea in 1075 and made it their capital in Anatolia. Antioch was equally as important to Christians, because according to the Book of Acts (11:26), Antioch's converts were the first to be called 'Christians'. As one of the four original Eastern patriarchates, Antioch had flourished in its early prominence under Byzantine rule until it was captured by Arab forces in 638. Antioch remained under Muslim control for more than 300 years until being retaken by Byzantine forces in 969, but the city was lost once again in 1084 to the Turks.

CONFLICT BETWEEN ISLAM AND WESTERN CHRISTIANITY BEFORE THE CRUSADES

The citizens of the Byzantine Empire were not the only Christians faced with the challenge of a thriving and growing Islamic world. Due to the massive expansion that took place during the early Islamic conquests, Christians in the West soon found themselves facing Muslim armies in Italy, Spain, France and the various islands of the western Mediterranean. The successful Islamic conquest of Spain began in the early eighth century with the crossing of the straits of Gibraltar by North African Muslim armies in 711. Within a few short years, the majority of the Iberian Peninsula came under Muslim control. The rapid success of the Muslim armies in Spain was facilitated by the chaotic state of the Catholic Visigothic Kingdom at the time of the conquest, which in some areas had been suffering from famine prior to the invasion.

As the new Muslim leaders of Spain consolidated their victories, some began to turn their attention to the North. In a battle that has been interpreted as among the most significant early victories for Western Christians against their new foes, Muslim and Christian forces clashed at the battle of Tours in central-western France. It was in Tours in 732 that the Carolingian leader Charles Martel led his Christian forces to victory and halted the further advance of Muslim armies into Europe. As a result of the battle, and in contrast to some more recent scholarship, some historians have traditionally credited Charles Martel as the cause of Europe's continued status as a Christian continent.[19] Whether the Christian victory at Tours prevented the ultimate conquest of Europe by Muslims is ultimately unknowable, but it is possible that the outcome of the battle denied Muslim armies an overland base for military operations against regions in northern Italy.

The ninth and tenth centuries saw no cessation in hostilities between Christians and Muslims in the West. In the early part of the century (c.832), Muslim forces captured the Byzantine-controlled island of Sicily and maintained a significant presence until the thirteenth century. The eternal city of Rome was sacked, and its most important churches were looted by a Muslim army in 846. In the wake of such events, increasingly assertive popes advocated a greater response and proclaimed spiritual benefits for those willing to combat the various enemies of the Church. Ninth-century popes – including Leo IV (847–855), who made extensive efforts to fortify Rome following the attack on the city in 846, and John VIII, who during his reign (872–882) dealt with both domestic and external threats – issued bold calls for Christians to wage war on the Church's behalf. They declared that those who participated in such a cause would be fighting for no less than the preservation of their faith, their homelands and their fellow Christians. Under such circumstances, those Christian warriors who fell in combat could be assured of the forgiveness of their sins and would be rewarded with entry into the Kingdom of Heaven.

For the early-tenth-century Christian leaders, the Muslim presence in Italy was a constant source of concern. Pope John X (r.914–928) was so heavily involved in efforts to eradicate the Muslim presence in Italy that in 916, he personally led an army against Italian Islamic forces. The efforts of John X contributed to the end of any significant Muslim occupation of mainland bases, but pirates based in North Africa and various islands in the Mediterranean remained a threat to European ships on the Italian coasts until around the year 1000. It was then that Italian fleets finally put an end to such threats.

As in Italy during the tenth century, Christian forces in Spain went on the offensive against Islam during the early eleventh century. While Christian armies had some notable successes against Muslim forces as early as the beginning of the ninth century, the so-called Reconquista, the Christian reconquest of the Iberian Peninsula, began in earnest only in the early eleventh century. The disunity that affected Muslim Spain in the wake of the collapse of the once-powerful Cordoba caliphate in 1031 provided Christian armies an opportunity to go on the offensive. With varying degrees of intensity, this offensive would last intermittently for nearly five centuries as Iberian and French Christians – through a series of wars, alliances and truces with each other and sometimes their Muslim opponents – waged war in Spain.[20]

WESTERN INTERNAL REFORM AND THE RISE OF CRUSADING

While the threat posed by external enemies to Christian Europe was considerably reduced in the mid-eleventh century, internal problems prevented Western leaders from becoming significantly involved with issues beyond their borders. Indeed, during this period, medieval Europe was in many ways defined by an internal struggle for authority between lay rulers and reformed ecclesiastical leaders in what became known as the Investiture Controversy. The reformers and their views were the product of the so-called Gregorian Reform movement, which during this time sought to reclaim authority over ecclesiastical matters from the lay lords and eliminate the corruption that prevailed among its clergy. Although technically the Investiture Controversy was over whether kings or popes had the right to invest bishops with the symbols of their authority, it was in reality a reflection of the broader tensions that resulted from the rise of an increasingly powerful and assertive papacy and the extent of its power in relation to secular rulers.[21]

The disputes of the Investiture Controversy served as a distraction from events in the East. While Pope Gregory VII, for example, had wished to lead a crusade in 1074 to the aid of the Byzantine Empire, his ongoing dispute with the Holy Roman Emperor Henry IV prevented his doing so. Yet while the Investiture Controversy delayed any major papal involvement in the affairs of the East, Western leaders nevertheless kept track of events in the Holy Land during this period.[22] For centuries before the crusading era, news about events in the East had been carried to the West by Christians returning from pilgrimages. The Holy Land, particularly Jerusalem, had long held a special significance for Christians as it was the site of Jesus' ministry, Crucifixion, burial and later, as Christians believed, his resurrection. Consequently, the recent Turkish conquests of much of Anatolia and the invasion of Palestine were a cause for alarm.

While the rise of papal authority and concerns over Turkish abuses in the Holy Land were foundational to the rise of the crusading movement, they were, by themselves, not enough to bring about its birth. A third element, resulting from the increased authority and prestige of the clergy during this time, was the Church's effort to appropriate and sanctify warfare. Indeed, clerics during this period increasingly argued that there were occasions when fighting was more than simply justified, but even a positive good that under the right circumstances was pleasing to God.[23] That such thinking developed during the era of the so-called Peace and Truce of God movements is not as curious as it might initially appear. Through the Peace and Truce of God movements, the Church sought to limit violence within Latin Christendom by the imposition of various spiritual penalties on those who harmed non-combatants or fought on particular holy days.[24] The reduction of violence among Western Christians would ideally lead to a unified and stronger Christendom. The Church's efforts to appropriate and sanctify war worked in favour of the goals of the Peace and Truce of God movements in two important ways. The Church would only express its approval for warfare under certain conditions, generally those that furthered the goals of the Church or Christendom on the whole. By extension, this brought considerable scrutiny to all warfare in eleventh-century Europe and led Christian warriors to become more discriminating in their choice of victims.[25] Because the Church was seeking to reduce intra-Christian violence in the West, the Church could also use its new authority to channel violence in what it considered appropriate directions. Indeed, warriors became more habituated to the idea that clerics were empowered to tell them where, when and against whom they could fight.[26] Such a policy had two major benefits: it contributed to the expansion of the culture, institutions and faith of Christendom[27] and such wars could redirect violence away from Christians to non-Christians, including Muslims and, later, pagans and heretics.[28]

In the light of the enhanced authority of the papacy and its goal of controlling and sanctifying warfare, it is not surprising that this period, under the pontificate of Pope Urban II, witnessed the birth of the crusading movement. Like Gregory VII and other popes before him, Urban II initially had to deal with problems in Europe before he could focus more fully on the East. While Urban began his pontificate in exile, he worked hard to win support from powerful allies so that he could return to Rome in 1094. In the following year, the Council of Piacenza was held to settle a number of issues resulting from the Investiture Controversy.[29] The Council was attended by a large number of bishops and representatives of secular powers. Perhaps the most important representative to attend was that of the Byzantine Emperor Alexius I Comnenus. The Byzantine ambassador was there with the express purpose of asking for aid in their increasingly dangerous conflict with the Turks, who by then controlled most of Asia Minor and were considered a serious threat to the Byzantine capital of Constantinople. The Byzantine ambassador's appeal for aid at Piacenza set in motion events that would become fully realised only later that year at the Council of Clermont. It was then, in November 1095, that Pope Urban II gave a speech calling for what later became known as the First Crusade.

The First Crusade nearly perfectly addressed the Church's new thinking on holy war. It was perhaps the ultimate manifestation of holy war as the combatants were technically pilgrims taking part in no less than an armed penitential pilgrimage. Indeed, 'pilgrim' was the common term throughout the twelfth century to describe those who took part in crusades, with the term 'crusader' only much later becoming the normative term.[30] The anticipated hardships of the First Crusade were promoted by clerical leaders as a type of redemptive suffering for those formerly sinful knights who might now employ their skills with God's favour on behalf of suffering Christians. During Urban's speech at Clermont, he reportedly focused his listeners' attention on the abuses of Christians and important Christian holy places in the East. In an effort to stir his audience, Urban described in vivid detail the rape and torture of Christians at the hands of their Muslim persecutors. He also described the desecration of the most important holy places in the Christian world, including the Church of the Holy Sepulchre. Urban then insisted that his listeners had a moral obligation to go to the defence of Christians in the East and that God would reward them for the love and charity they expressed in doing so. It was warfare with a holy purpose, according to the Pope, who contrasted the nature of the proposed crusade with the sinful wars Western knights had fought until this point. Cleric Guibert of Nogent, for example, noted that Urban II warned his listeners that previously they had 'waged wrongful wars' for which they 'deserved only eternal death and damnation'.[31] Yet with the calling of the First Crusade, the knightly class now had the opportunity to fight in 'battles which offer the gift of glorious martyrdom' and the potential to win them eternal praise.[32] Urban's listeners responded to his powerful words with enormous enthusiasm, and it was amid their shouts of 'God wills it!' that the crusading movement was born.

CHAPTER ONE
POPE URBAN II'S CALLING OF THE FIRST CRUSADE, 1095

9
LETTER OF ALEXIUS TO COUNT ROBERT OF FLANDERS, c.1088–1099

12
FULCHER OF CHARTRES, c.1101

14
ROBERT THE MONK, c.1107

16
BALDRIC OF DOL, c.1107

19
GUIBERT OF NOGENT, c.1109

Whatever Urban said in the fields on the 27th of November, the enthusiasm of his auditors certainly surpassed all expectations, as they stamped the ground and shouted 'God wills it!', some in tears.

– Ronald C. Finucane[1]

For knights steeped in a culture of militant Christianity, these were stories to make the blood boil. The shouts of Europe's fighting men, filled with righteous anger, rang out across the land: 'God wills it! God wills it!'

– Thomas Madden[2]

GOD WILLS IT

In November, 1095 at the French town of Clermont, a council was held to deal with issues of ecclesiastical reform. In the last session, however, laypersons were admitted to listen to Pope Urban II (r.1088–1099) speak about events in the East. Reportedly, the Pope roused his listeners with tales of Christian suffering and the desecration of Christian holy places by the Turks. Urban promised that those who were willing to go to the rescue of the Holy Land and its Christian inhabitants would receive no less than the full remission of the penalty owed for their sins. As the Pope finished speaking, several rushed forward, vowing to go to the Holy Land amid enthusiastic cheers of 'God wills it!'[3] Although the events were momentous, it is unlikely that the Pope understood the full significance of his speech that day. His words were the ultimate fighting words, which sparked a new crusading ideology that would dominate the mindset and actions of European Christians for centuries to come.

Although the precise content of the Pope's speech is not known, few events of the crusading movement have received as much scholarly and popular attention. The modern fascination with Urban's speech is understandable in the light of the events that followed. Tens of thousands of men, and some women, from various parts of Latin Christendom, began to make preparations for what amounted to an armed pilgrimage to the Holy Land. These armed pilgrims, only later known as 'crusaders', realised that there would be great hardships suffered at home in their absence. Farms and businesses would, in many cases, have to be maintained and managed by wives, elderly relatives and younger children, while husbands, sons, brothers and fathers would be in the East. Yet, in spite of these concerns, there was an enormous level of popular enthusiasm for the crusade as demonstrated by the estimated 50,000 to 90,000 who participated.[4] In the following months, thousands of patrimonies, family lands and various other possessions were sold or mortgaged to provide for their expenses.[5] Indeed, recent estimates suggest that a knight needed to raise five times his annual income just to cover the expenses of crusading to include equipment, supplies, horse and servants.[6]

Historians have long debated the causes of the enthusiastic response to the calling of the First Crusade. A number of potential motivations have been attributed to the crusaders, of which charity and economic gain are among the most common.[7] Although we are inclined to view these explanations as contradictory, the notions of doing good for others while doing well for oneself are not necessarily incompatible and were not considered so in the Middle Ages.[8] An examination of Pope Urban's calling of the First Crusade is an obvious starting place for those considering crusader motivations. Specifically, what in the Pope's speech prompted the enthusiastic response that followed? In addition to the motivation of the crusaders, there has been equal interest in the motivations of the papacy and what Urban II, and those who followed him, hoped to accomplish through crusading.[9]

BACKGROUND TO THE SOURCES

While it is unlikely that any of the source authors, in some cases writing several years after the event, produced an accurate text of the Pope's speech, it is possible that they provide at least some of the substance of his remarks at Clermont.[10] Yet although scholars have found great value in the surviving accounts of Urban's speech, they have also warned of the importance of reading such accounts with caution. Concerns arise from the likelihood that the particulars of their involvement in the crusade, as well as its outcome, influenced the way in which various authors remembered or recorded the Pope's speech. All versions of the speech were written after the capture of Jerusalem, and those involved in the conquest of the Holy City could not have been unaffected by the exciting news of its capture. According to one historian, 'no writer was immune from a general euphoria that bathed the immediate past in an artificial glow'.[11] Additionally, the chroniclers of the First Crusade undoubtedly availed themselves of the customary license in which medieval writers embellished or put words in the mouth of their characters, which was done to give their readers and hearers the flavour of the situations that they were describing.[12] Nor was it uncommon for medieval historians, like their Roman and Greek predecessors, to re-create historical speeches as much to demonstrate their own rhetorical skills as to provide a representation of the speech.[13]

There are also concerns over the striking resemblance of some points in the various surviving accounts of Urban's speech with the text of a letter claiming to be from the Byzantine Emperor Alexius I Comnenus to Count Robert of Flanders (included in this chapter).[14] Such concerns have contributed to controversies about the authenticity and dating of the letter of Alexius, as some scholars argued that it was a forgery based in part on the themes discussed by Urban II at Clermont. However, if the surviving form of the letter of Alexius is based on a genuine original, it is also possible that the Pope drew some of his inspiration for his preaching from the text of the letter. A final possibility is that those authors who claim to provide accounts of Urban's speech used the letter as a source, but if the letter was a source it was used for no more than a few points and does not seem to excessively influence their versions.

The earliest surviving record of Urban's speech at Clermont was written by the French cleric Fulcher of Chartres (1059–1127), who had published the first part of his work no later than 1105.[15] His three-book chronicle, *A History of the Expedition to Jerusalem* [*Historia Iherosolimitana*], began with the preparations that took place under Pope Urban II for the launching of the First Crusade and ended in 1127 when Fulcher died of plague. Fulcher participated in the First Crusade and ultimately completed his pilgrimage vow when he arrived in Jerusalem in 1099. Unlike most crusaders, Fulcher remained in the Holy Land, and in 1115 he became canon of the Church of the Holy Sepulchre.[16] In addition to the likelihood of Fulcher's attendance at Clermont, some historians believe that he had the benefit of a now-lost copy of the decrees of the Council as a source for his version of the Pope's speech.[17] Fulcher's account emphasises the role of the so-called Peace and Truce of God movements in the calling of the First Crusade, which would become a familiar theme in all future accounts of his speech. In doing so, the Pope followed the tradition of papal reform efforts (beginning in the late tenth century) that sought to quell widespread intra-Christian violence in Europe.[18] The Pope noted that the situation in Europe was 'so bad' that in some provinces 'one can hardly go along the road by day or night without being attacked by robbers.' As a result, Urban notes that it is necessary 'to re-enact the truce' and that anyone who breaks the truce will be 'anathematised'. Urban then turns his attention to the sufferings of Christians in the East at the hands of 'Turks and Arabs' who have 'killed and captured many [Christians], and have destroyed the churches and devastated the [Byzantine] empire'. The Pope proclaims that those who go to the aid of Eastern Christians, whether rich or poor, and are willing to 'destroy that vile race [apparently either Turks or Arabs]' will receive the full remission of their sins because 'Christ commands it'. Urban finishes by noting that violence once directed by Christians against other Christians can now instead be directed towards 'infidels' and 'barbarians' in defence of other Christians. Consequently, some historians have argued that Urban was able to implement the Peace and Truce of God movement at home because the First Crusade effectively allowed for an export of violence from Europe to the East.[19]

The monk Robert of Rheims recorded his version of Urban's speech in his *Historia Iherosolimitana,* which was written no later than 1107.[20] Robert attended the Council of Clermont in his capacity as the Abbot of the monastery of Saint-Remi. Because Robert did not participate in the military campaigns of the First Crusade, he largely relied on the *Gesta Francorum et Aliorum Hierosolimitanorum* [The Deeds of the Franks and the Other Pilgrims to Jerusalem], possibly the earliest surviving history of the First Crusade, for many details.[21] As an educated clergyman, Robert criticised the crude account of the *Gesta,* which was probably authored by an anonymous knight, and sought to rewrite it in a more literary form.[22] Perhaps the most valuable aspect of Robert's text is the lengthy eyewitness account of Urban's speech at Clermont, which is nowhere mentioned in the *Gesta.* Robert's account of the speech is undoubtedly the most sensational, as he goes into particularly gruesome detail about the sufferings of Christians at the hands of the Turks. To stir his listeners (or at least Robert's readers), the Pope described how Christians were suffering torture and enslavement at the hands of Muslims, noting that they 'circumcise the Christians, and the blood of the circumcision they either spread upon the altars or pour into the vases of the baptismal font.'[23] There is also mention of the rape of Christian women, but only briefly as 'to speak of it is worse than to be silent'. Urban then reminds his listeners to let the deeds of their ancestors, particularly the Carolingians, 'move' and 'incite' them to 'manly achievements' to put an end to such abuse through the crusade. Also unique to Robert's account is the statement by the Pope that the land of the Franks is 'too narrow' for their 'large population', which implies a sort of colonialism on the part of the crusaders.[24] Yet modern scholars have increasingly debated the connection between modern notions of colonisation and the crusades, as the vast majority of crusaders simply went home once they had fulfilled their vows, and maintaining Christian populations in the later crusader states was always a major problem.[25] Robert's work was apparently very popular as thirty-seven manuscript copies of it have survived from the twelfth century alone, with several dozen more surviving from the centuries that followed.[26]

Robert's account was followed by Baldric of Bourgueil's *Historia Iherosolimitana*, which may have been written as early as 1107. Baldric was a well-known poet and Archbishop of Dol who, like Robert, criticised the *Gesta*, but as a non-participant of the crusade he had to extensively rely on it as a source for events that he had not witnessed. Yet, again like Robert, Baldric claims to have been a witness to the Council of Clermont, and thus his account of Urban's preaching is valuable. Like those of his predecessors, Baldric's account also points to the sufferings of Eastern Christians, the need to stop Christian infighting in the West and the desecration of holy places in the East, especially in Jerusalem and Antioch. Yet Baldric also introduces some new themes and gives greater emphasis to other themes than previous accounts. For one, unlike Fulcher and Robert, Baldric attributes the misfortunes of Eastern Christians solely to the 'base and bastard Turks' rather than Arabs or Persians. Also, even more than the clerical accounts of Fulcher and Robert, Baldric refers to scriptural allusions to justify the legitimacy of Christian violence against their opponents when he cites the Psalms, 'Gird thy sword upon thy thigh O mighty one…' and compares the crusaders' future battles against Turks to the biblical wars of the Israelites against the Amalekites.[27] Moreover, Baldric makes a distinction between the non-combatant role of clerics like himself, for whom he claims it is their duty to pray, and the role of combatants who have the duty to fight. 'Like Moses', Baldric notes, 'we shall extend unwearied hands in prayer to Heaven, while you go forth and brandish the sword… against Amalek.'[28] This distinction of clerics as non-combatants was an important aspect of the Peace and Truce of God movements. Like in Robert's account, Baldric's account also records the Pope as emphasising the potential for material gains when he notes that the possessions of their enemies will be theirs if they are successful. Yet equally, and not necessarily in contradiction, the Pope also reminds the crusaders that to risk their lives for Eastern Christians is true charity. Finally, while all the accounts portray Eastern Christians in sympathetic terms, Baldric's account is perhaps the most explicit, in that he refers to them as 'brothers' and 'blood brothers' who are 'sons of the same Christ and the same Church'.

Finally, Guibert, the Abbot of Nogent, recorded his version of the Pope's speech in his *Gesta Dei per Francos* [The Deeds of God through the Franks], which was written no later than 1109. While Guibert used Fulcher's account of the First Crusade for the later portions of his history, it is likely that he was present at the Council of Clermont and would have relied on his memory for his version of the Pope's speech. Like earlier versions, Guibert's account refers to the need to stop violence among Christians in the West and focus such energies on aiding Christians in the East. Yet the *Gesta* also emphasises the special importance of the Holy Land, particularly Jerusalem, and cites the Pope's concern over the 'pollution' of the Holy City by the Turks. Urban then compares the crusaders' actions to end such pollution to the efforts of the Maccabees.[29] Even more so, biblical prophecy dominates Guibert's account, as he frames the crusaders' efforts as a fulfilment of biblical prophecy. Also unique to Guibert's account is the emphasis on the sufferings of pilgrims in the Holy Land, for whom the Pope stirs up sympathy through the telling of various abuses committed against them by the Turks. Finally, and perhaps most interesting, is the claim by Urban that 'Egypt, Africa, and Ethiopia' have 'withdrawn from the communion' of their Christian belief, which indicates a historical awareness on the part of the Pope (or at least Guibert) of the conquests by Islam of these formerly Christian lands and thus perhaps frames the First Crusade as only part of a larger clash between the two faiths.

In addition to these four versions of Urban's speech at Clermont, there survive several other twelfth-century accounts of the Pope's preaching of the First Crusade.[30] These accounts are of comparatively less value as they are based on the earlier histories examined here, sometimes more limited in scope, recorded decades later or, at worst, completely fictitious.[31] There is the possibility that some of the later accounts are based on additional eyewitness reports that do not survive, but there is no way of being certain. Yet the fact that so many later twelfth-century writers saw the need to include the speech in their narratives suggests that they viewed Urban's efforts at Clermont as essential for understanding the origins of the crusading movement and the context in which it developed.

THE SOURCES

Letter of Alexius to Count Robert of Flanders, c.1088–1099[32]

Some historians have viewed the supposed letter of the Byzantine Emperor Alexius to Count Robert of Flanders as either having influenced the crusading sermons of Pope Urban II or, if a forgery, having been influenced by the Pope's sermons. In either case, there is a suspicious resemblance of some portions of the letter and the various accounts of Urban's preaching, making it likely that these sources are in some way dependent on each other. Historian Dana Carleton Munro notes that most historians date the letter to anywhere from 1088 to 1099, but other historians have given a later date. Although some have claimed that the letter was genuine, the surviving form of the letter that has been passed down to the present is almost certainly a forgery that was, at best, based on a real document.

To Robert, lord and glorious count of the Flemings, and to all the Princes in the entire realm, lovers of the Christian faith, laymen as well as clerics, the Constantinopolitan emperor [extends] greeting and peace in our same Lord Jesus Christ and His Father and the Holy Spirit.

O most Illustrious count and especial comforter of the Christian faith! I wish to make known you prudence how the most sacred empire of the Greek Christians is being sorely distressed by the Patzinaks and the Turks, who daily ravage it and intermittently seize [its territory]; and there is promiscuous slaughter and indescribable killing and derision of the Christians. But since the evil things they do are many and, as we have said, indescribable, we will mention but a few of the many, which nevertheless are horrible to hear and disturb even the air itself.

For they circumcise the boys and youths of the Christians over the Christian baptismal fonts, and in contempt of Christ they pour the blood from the circumcision into the said baptismal fonts and compel them to void urine [sic] thereon; and thereafter they violently drag them around in the church, compelling them to blaspheme the name of the Holy Trinity and the belief therein.[33] But those who refuse to do these things they punish in diverse ways and ultimately they kill them. Noble matrons and their daughters whom they have robbed [of their possessions] they, one after another like animals, defile in adultery. Some, indeed, in their corrupting shamelessly place virgins before the faces of their mothers and compel them to sing wicked and obscene songs, until they have finished their own wicked acts.

Thus, we read, it was done also against God's people in antiquity, to whom the impious Babylonians, after making sport of them in diverse ways, said: 'Sing us one of the songs of Zion.' Likewise, at the dishonouring of their daughters, the mothers are in turn compelled to sing wicked songs, [though] their voices sound forth not a song but rather, we believe, a plaint, as is written concerning the death of the innocents: 'A voice was heard in Ramah, Weeping and great mourning, Rachel weeping for her children; and she would not be comforted, because they are not.'

However, even if the mothers of the innocents, who are figured by Rachel, could not be comforted for the death of their children, yet they could derive comfort from the salvation of their souls; but these [mothers] are in worse plight, for they cannot be comforted at all, because they perish in both body and soul. But what further? Let us come to matters of greater depravity. Men of every age and order i.e. boys, adolescents, youths, old men, nobles, serfs, and, what is worse and more shameless, clergymen and monks, and alas and alack, what from the beginning has never been said or heard, bishops! – they defile with the sin of sodomy and now they are also trumpeting abroad that one bishop has succumbed to this abominable sin.

The holy places they desecrate and destroy in numberless ways, and they threaten them with worse treatment. And who does not lament over these things? Who has not compassion? Who is not horrified? Who does not pray? For almost the entire land from Jerusalem to Greece, and the whole of Greece with its upper regions, which are Cappadocia Minor, Cappadocia Major, Phrygia, Bithynia, Lesser Phrygia (i.e. the Troad), Pontus, Galatia, Lydia, Pamphylia, Isauria, Lycia, and the principal islands Chios and Mytilene, and many other regions and islands which we cannot even enumerate, as far as Thrace, have already been invaded by them, and now almost nothing remains except Constantinople, which they are threatening to snatch away from us very soon, unless the aid of God and the faithful Latin Christians should reach us speedily.

For even the Propontis, which is also called the Avidus and which flows out of the Pontus near Constantinople into the Great Sea, they have invaded with two hundred ships, which the Greeks robbed by them had built; and they are launching them with their rowers, willy nilly, and they are threatening, as we have said, speedily to capture Constantinople by land as well as by way of the Propontis. These few among the innumerable evil things which this most impious people is doing we have mentioned and written to you, count of the Flemings, lover of the Christian faith. The rest, indeed, let us omit in order not to disgust the readers. Accordingly, for love of God and out of sympathy for all Christian Greeks, we beg that you lead hither to my aid and that of the Christian Greeks whatever faithful warriors of Christ you may be able to enlist in your land – those of major as well as those of minor and middle condition: and as they in the past year liberated Galicia and other kingdoms of the Westerners somewhat from the yoke of the pagans, 'so also may they now, for the salvation of their souls, endeavour to liberate the Kingdom of the Greeks; since I, albeit I am emperor, can find no remedy or suitable counsel, but am always fleeing from the face of the Turks and Patzinaks: and I remain in a particular city only until I perceive that their arrival is imminent. And I think it is better to be subjected to your Latins than to the abominations of the pagans. Therefore, before Constantinople is captured by them, you most certainly ought to fight with all your strength so that you may joyfully receive in heaven a glorious and ineffable reward.

For it is better that you should have Constantinople than the pagans because in that city are the most precious relics of the Lord, to wit: the pillar to which he was bound: the lash with which he was scourged: the scarlet robe in which he was arrayed: the crown of thorns with which he was crowned: the reed he held in his hands, in place of sceptre: the garments of which he was despoiled before the cross: the larger part of the wood of the cross in which he was crucified: the nails with which he was affixed: the linen clothes found in the sepulchre after his resurrection: the twelve baskets of remnants from the five loaves and the two fishes: the entire head of St. John the Baptist with the hair and the beard: the relics or bodies of many of the innocents, of certain prophets and apostles, of martyrs and, especially, of the protomartyr St. Stephen, and of confessors and virgins, these latter being of such great number that we have omitted writing each about them individually.

Yet all the aforesaid the Christians rather than the pagans ought to possess: and it will be a great monument for all Christians if they retain possession of all these, but it will be to their detriment and doom if they should lose them. However, if they should be unwilling to fight for the sake of these relics, and if their love of gold is greater, they will find more of it there than in all the world; for the treasure vaults of the churches of Constantinople abound in silver, gold, gems, and precious stones, and silken garments, i.e. vestments, which could suffice for all the churches in the world. But the inestimable treasure of the mother church, namely St. Sophia,[34] the Wisdom of God, surpasses the treasures of all other churches and without doubt, equals the treasures of the Temple of Solomon. Again, what shall I say of the infinite treasures of the nobles, when no one can estimate the treasure of the common merchants? What is contained in the treasures of the former emperors? I say for certain that no tongue can tell it; because not only the treasure of the Constantinopolitian emperors is there contained, but the treasure of all the ancient Roman emperors has been brought thither and hidden in the palaces. What more shall I say? Certainly, what is exposed to men's eyes is as nothing compared with that which lies hidden.

Hasten, therefore, with your entire people and fight with all your strength, lest such treasure fall into the hands of the Turks and Patzinaks: because, while they are infinite, just now sixty thousand are daily expected, and I fear that by means of this treasure they gradually will seduce our covetous soldiers, as did formerly Julius Caesar who by reason of avarice invaded the kingdom of the Franks and as antichrist will do at the end of the world after he has captured the whole earth. Therefore, lest you should lose the kingdom of the Christians and, what is greater, the Lord's Sepulchre, act while you still have time; and then you will have not doom, but a reward in heaven.

Fulcher of Chartres, c.1101[35]

In the *Historia Iherosolimitana* written by the cleric Fulcher of Chartres around the year 1101, we find the earliest known account of Pope Urban II's preaching at Clermont. It is likely that Fulcher was either present for the speech or had access to a now-lost copy of the decrees of the Council. Of particular interest are Fulcher's comments on the Pope's efforts to implement the Peace and Truce of God to make possible the crusade, followed by details on the abuse of Christians and Christian holy places by Muslims in the East.

Most beloved brethren: Urged by necessity, I, Urban, by the permission of God chief bishop and prelate over the whole world, have come into these parts as an ambassador with a divine admonition to you, the servants of God. I hoped to find you as faithful and as zealous in the service of God as I had supposed you to be. But if there is in you any deformity or crookedness contrary to God's law, with divine help I will do my best to remove it…

If you wish to be the friends of God, gladly do the things which you know will please Him. You must especially let all matters that pertain to the church be controlled by the law of the church. And be careful that simony does not take root among you, lest both those who buy and those who sell [church offices] be beaten with the scourges of the Lord through narrow streets and driven into the place of destruction and confusion. Keep the church and the clergy in all its grades entirely free from the secular power. See that the tithes that belong to God are faithfully paid from all the produce of the land; let them not be sold or withheld. If anyone seizes a bishop let him be treated as an outlaw. If anyone seizes or robs monks, or clergymen, or nuns, or their servants, or pilgrims, or merchants, let him be anathema. Let robbers and incendiaries and all their accomplices be expelled from the church and anathematized. If a man who does not give a part of his goods as alms is punished with the damnation of hell, how should he be punished who robs another of his goods? For thus it happened to the rich man in the gospel; he was not punished because he had stolen the goods of another, but because he had not used well the things which were his.[36]

You have seen for a long time the great disorder in the world caused by these crimes. It is so bad in some of your provinces, I am told, and you are so weak in the administration of justice, that one can hardly go along the road by day or night without being attacked by robbers; and whether at home or abroad one is in danger of being despoiled either by force or fraud. Therefore it is necessary to re-enact the truce, as it is commonly called, which was proclaimed a long time ago by our holy fathers.[37] I exhort and demand that you, each, try hard to have the truce kept in your diocese. And if anyone shall be led by his cupidity or arrogance to break this truce, by the authority of God and with the sanction of this council he shall be anathematized. After these and various other matters had been attended to, all who were present, clergy and people, gave thanks to God and agreed to the pope's proposition. They all faithfully promised to keep the decrees. Then the pope said that in another part of the world Christianity was suffering from a state of affairs that was worse than the one just mentioned. He continued:

Although, O sons of God, you have promised more firmly than ever to keep the peace among yourselves and to preserve the rights of the church, there remains still an important work for you to do. Freshly quickened by the divine correction, you must apply the strength of your righteousness to another matter which concerns you as well as God. For your brethren who live in the east are in urgent need of your help, and you must hasten to give them the aid which has often been promised them. For, as the most of you have heard, the Turks and Arabs have attacked them and have conquered the territory of Romania [the Greek empire] as far west as the shore of the Mediterranean and the Hellespont, which is called the Arm of St. George. They have occupied more and more of the lands of those Christians, and have overcome them in seven battles.[38] They have killed and captured many, and have destroyed the churches and devastated the empire. If you permit them to continue thus for awhile with impurity, the faithful of God will be much more widely attacked by them. On this account I, or rather the Lord, beseech you as Christ's heralds to publish this everywhere and to persuade all people of whatever rank, foot-soldiers and knights, poor and rich, to carry aid promptly to those Christians and to destroy that vile race from the lands of our friends. I say this to those who are present, it meant also for those who are absent. Moreover, Christ commands it.

All who die by the way, whether by land or by sea, or in battle against the pagans, shall have immediate remission of sins. This I grant them through the power of God with which I am invested. O what a disgrace if such a despised and base race, which worships demons, should conquer a people which has the faith of omnipotent God and is made glorious with the name of Christ! With what reproaches will the Lord overwhelm us if you do not aid those who, with us, profess the Christian religion! Let those who have been accustomed unjustly to wage private warfare against the faithful now go against the infidels and end with victory this war which should have been begun long ago. Let those who for a long time, have been robbers, now become knights. Let those who have been fighting against their brothers and relatives now fight in a proper way against the barbarians. Let those who have been serving as mercenaries for small pay now obtain the eternal reward. Let those who have been wearing themselves out in both body and soul now work for a double honour.

Robert the Monk, c.1107[39]

The following eyewitness account of Urban's speech at Clermont is taken from Robert the Monk's *Historia Iherosolimitana* written around the year 1107. Robert's account is undoubtedly the most sensational and graphic of all versions of the speech because of its graphic depiction of the abuse Christians suffered at the hands of their Muslim opponents.

Oh, race of Franks, race from across the mountains, race chosen and beloved by God as shines forth in very many of your works set apart from all nations by the situation of your country, as well as by your catholic faith and the honour of the holy church! To you our discourse is addressed and for you our exhortation is intended. We wish you to know what a grievous cause has led us to your country, what peril threatening you and all the faithful has brought us.

From the confines of Jerusalem and the city of Constantinople a horrible tale has gone forth and very frequently has been brought to our ears, namely, that a race from the kingdom of the Persians, an accursed race, a race utterly alienated from God, a generation forsooth which has not directed its heart and has not entrusted its spirit to God, has invaded the lands of those Christians and has depopulated them by the sword, pillage and fire; it has led away a part of the captives into its own country, and a part it has destroyed by cruel tortures; it has either entirely destroyed the churches of God or appropriated them for the rites of its own religion. They destroy the altars, after having defiled them with their uncleanness. They circumcise the Christians, and the blood of the circumcision they either spread upon the altars or pour into the vases of the baptismal font.[40] When they wish to torture people by a base death, they perforate their navels, and dragging forth the extremity of the intestines, bind it to a stake; then with flogging they lead the victim around until the viscera having gushed forth the victim falls prostrate upon the ground. Others they bind to a post and pierce with arrows. Others they compel to extend their necks and then, attacking them with naked swords, attempt to cut through the neck with a single blow. What shall I say of the abominable rape of the women? To speak of it is worse than to be silent. The kingdom of the Greeks [the Byzantine Empire] is now dismembered by them and deprived of territory so vast in extent that it cannot be traversed in a march of two months. On whom therefore is the labour of avenging these wrongs and of recovering this territory incumbent, if not upon you? You, upon whom above other nations God has conferred remarkable glory in arms, great courage, bodily activity, and strength to humble the hairy scalp of those who resist you.

Let the deeds of your ancestors move you and incite your minds to manly achievements; the glory and greatness of King Charles the Great, and of his son Louis, and of your other kings, who have destroyed the kingdoms of the pagans, and have extended in these lands the territory of the holy church.[41] Let the holy sepulchre of the Lord our Saviour, which is possessed by unclean nations, especially incite you, and the holy places which are now treated with ignominy and irreverently polluted with their filthiness. Oh, most valiant soldiers and descendants of invincible ancestors, be not degenerate, but recall the valour of your progenitors.

But if you are hindered by love of children, parents and wives, remember what the Lord says in the Gospel, 'He that loveth father or mother more than me, is not worthy of me.' 'Every one that hath forsaken houses, or brethren, or sisters, or father, or mother, or wife, or children, or lands for my name's sake shall receive an hundredfold and shall inherit everlasting life.'[42] Let none of your possessions detain you, no solicitude for your family affairs, since this land which you inhabit, shut in on all sides by the seas and surrounded by the mountain peaks, is too narrow for your large population; nor does it abound in wealth; and it furnishes scarcely food enough for its cultivators. Hence it is that you murder one another, that you wage war, and that frequently you perish by mutual wounds. Let therefore hatred depart from among you, let your quarrels end, let wars cease, and let all dissension and controversies slumber. Enter upon the road to the Holy Sepulchre; wrest that land from the wicked race, and subject it to yourselves. That land which as the Scripture says 'floweth with milk and honey,' was given by God into the possession of the children of Israel.[43]

Jerusalem is the navel of the world; the land is fruitful above others, like another paradise of delights. This the Redeemer of the human race has made illustrious by His advent, has beautified by residence, has consecrated by suffering, has redeemed by death, has glorified by burial. This royal city, therefore, situated at the centre of the world,[44] is now held captive by His enemies, and is in subjection to those who do not know God, to the worship of the heathens. She seeks therefore and desires to be liberated, and does not cease to implore you to come to her aid. From you especially she asks succour, because, as we have already said, God has conferred upon you above all nations' great glory in arms. Accordingly undertake this journey for the remission of your sins, with the assurance of the imperishable glory of the kingdom of heaven. When Pope Urban had said these and very many similar things in his urbane discourse, he so influenced to one purpose the desires of all who were present that they cried out, 'It is the will of God! It is the will of God!'

Baldric of Dol, c.1107[45]

Like those of his predecessors, Baldric's possible eyewitness account of Urban's speech points to the sufferings of Eastern Christians, the need to stop intra-Christian warfare in the West and the desecration of holy places in the East, especially in Jerusalem and in Antioch. Yet Baldric's account also emphasises the Pope's use of scripture to justify the violence of the crusades and makes a sharp distinction between the role of the clergy as non-combatants and the role of knights and others as combatants.

…We have heard, most beloved brethren, and you have heard what we cannot recount without deep sorrow how, with great hurt and dire sufferings our Christian brothers, members in Christ, are scourged, oppressed, and injured in Jerusalem, in Antioch, and the other cities of the East. Your own blood brothers, your companions, your associates (for you are sons of the same Christ and the same Church) are either subjected in their inherited homes to other masters, or are driven from them, or they come as beggars among us; or, which is far worse, they are flogged and exiled as slaves for sale in their own land. Christian blood, redeemed by the blood of Christ, has been shed, and Christian flesh, akin to the flesh of Christ, has been subjected to unspeakable degradation and servitude. Everywhere in those cities there is sorrow, everywhere misery, everywhere groaning (I say it with a sigh). The churches in which divine mysteries were celebrated in olden times are now, to our sorrow, used as stables for the animals of these people! Holy men do not possess those cities; nay, base and bastard Turks hold sway over our brothers. The blessed Peter first presided as Bishop at Antioch; behold, in his own church the Gentiles have established their superstitions, and the Christian religion, which they ought rather to cherish, they have basely shut out from the hall dedicated to God! The estates given for the support of the saints and the patrimony of nobles set aside for the sustenance of the poor are subject to pagan tyranny, while cruel masters abuse for their own purposes the returns from these lands. The priesthood of God has been ground down into the dust. The sanctuary of God (unspeakable shame!) is everywhere profaned. Whatever Christians still remain in hiding there are sought out with unheard of tortures.

Of holy Jerusalem, brethren, we dare not speak, for we are exceedingly afraid and ashamed to speak of it. This very city, in which, as you all know, Christ Himself suffered for us, because our sins demanded it, has been reduced to the pollution of paganism and, I say it to our disgrace, withdrawn from the service of God. Such is the heap of reproach upon us who have so much deserved it! Who now serves the church of the Blessed Mary in the valley of Josaphat, in which church she herself was buried in body?[46] But why do we pass over the Temple of Solomon, nay of the Lord, in which the barbarous nations placed their idols contrary to law, human and divine? Of the Lord's Sepulchre we have refrained from speaking, since some of you with your own eyes have seen to what abominations it has been given over.[47] The Turks violently took from it the offerings which you brought there for alms in such vast amounts, and, in addition, they scoffed much and often at your religion. And yet in that place (I say only what you already know) rested the Lord; there He died for us; there He was buried.

This, beloved brethren, we shall say, that we may have you as witness of our words. More suffering of our brethren and devastation of churches remains than we can speak of one by one, for we are oppressed by tears and groans, sighs and sobs. We weep and wail, brethren, alas, like the Psalmist, in our inmost heart! We are wretched and unhappy, and in us is that prophecy fulfilled: 'God, the nations are come into thine inheritance; thy holy temple have they defiled; they have laid Jerusalem in heaps; the dead bodies of thy servants have been given to be food for the birds of the heaven, the flesh of thy saints unto the beasts of the earth. Their blood have they shed like water round about Jerusalem, and there was none to bury them.'[48] Woe unto us, brethren! We who have already become a reproach to our neighbours, a scoffing, and derision to them round about us, let us at least with tears condone and have compassion upon our brothers! We who have become the scorn of all peoples, and worse than all, let us bewail the most monstrous devastation of the Holy Land!

What are we saying? Listen and learn! You, girt about with the badge of knighthood, are arrogant with great pride; you rage against your brothers and cut each other in pieces. This is not the (true) soldiery of Christ which rends asunder the sheepfold of the Redeemer. The Holy Church has reserved a soldiery for herself to help her people, but you debase her wickedly to her hurt. Let us confess the truth, whose heralds we ought to be; truly, you are not holding to the way which leads to life. You, the oppressors of children, plunderers of widows; you, guilty of homicide, of sacrilege, robbers of another's rights; you who await the pay of thieves for the shedding of Christian blood – as vultures smell fetid corpses, so do you sense battles from afar and rush to them eagerly. Verily, this is the worst way, for it is utterly removed from God! If, forsooth, you wish to be mindful of your souls, either lay down the girdle of such knighthood, or advance boldly, as knights of Christ, and rush as quickly as you can to the defence of the Eastern Church. For she it is from whom the joys of your whole salvation have come forth, who poured into your mouths the milk of divine wisdom, who set before you the holy teachings of the Gospels. We say this, brethren, that you may restrain your murderous hands from the destruction of your brothers, and in behalf of your relatives in the faith oppose yourselves to the Gentiles.... You should shudder, brethren, you should shudder at raising a violent hand against Christians; it is less wicked to brandish your sword against Saracens. It is the only warfare that is righteous, for it is charity to risk your life for your brothers. That you may not be troubled about the concerns of tomorrow, know that those who fear God want nothing, nor those who cherish Him in truth. The possessions of the enemy, too, will be yours, since you will make spoil of their treasures and return victorious to your own; or empurpled with your own blood, you will have gained everlasting glory.

For such a Commander you ought to fight, for One who lacks neither might nor wealth with which to reward you.

Short is the way, little the labour, which, nevertheless, will repay you with the crown that fadeth not away. Accordingly, we speak with the authority of the prophet: 'Gird thy sword upon thy thigh O mighty one.'[49] Gird yourselves, everyone of you, I say, and be valiant sons; for it is better for you to die in battle than to behold, the sorrows of your race and of your holy places. Let neither property nor the alluring charms of your wives entice you from going; nor let the trials that are to be borne so deter you that you remain here.

And turning to the bishops, he said, 'You, brothers and fellow bishops; you, fellow priests and sharers with us in Christ, make this same announcement through the churches committed to you, and with your whole soul vigorously preach the journey to Jerusalem. When they have confessed the disgrace of their sins, do you, secure in Christ, grant them speedy pardon. Moreover, you who are to go shall have us praying for you; we shall have you fighting for God's people. It is our duty to pray, yours to fight against the Amalekites. With Moses, we shall extend unwearied hands in prayer to Heaven,[50] while you go forth and brandish the sword, like dauntless warriors, against Amalek'.[51]

Guibert of Nogent, c.1109[52]

Like earlier versions, Guibert of Nogent's possible eyewitness account of Urban's speech, written around the year 1109, refers to the need to stop intra-Christian violence in the West and focus such energies on aiding Christians in the East. Guibert's account also emphasises the special religious significance of the Holy Land, particularly Jerusalem, and how the crusaders represent the fulfilment of biblical prophecy.

If in olden times the Maccabees attained to the highest praise of piety because they fought for the ceremonies and the Temple, it is also justly granted you, Christian soldiers, to defend their liberty of your country by armed endeavour. If you, likewise, consider that the abode of the holy apostles and any other saints should be striven for with such effort, why do you refuse to rescue the Cross, the Blood, the Tomb? Why do you refuse to visit them, to spend the price of your lives in rescuing them? You have thus far waged unjust wars, at one time and another; you have brandished mad weapons to your mutual destruction, for no other reason than covetousness and pride, as a result of which you have deserved eternal death and sure damnation. We now hold out to you wars which contain the glorious reward of martyrdom, which will retain that title of praise now and forever.

Let us suppose, for the moment, that Christ was not dead and buried, and had never lived any length of time in Jerusalem. Surely, if all this were lacking, this fact alone ought still to arouse you to go to the aid of the land and city – the fact that 'Out of Zion shall go forth the law and the word of Jehovah from Jerusalem!'[53] If all that there is of Christian preaching has flowed from the fountain of Jerusalem, its streams, whithersoever spread out over the whole world, encircle the hearts of the Catholic multitude, that they may consider wisely what they owe such a well-watered fountain. If rivers return to the place whence they have issued only to flow forth again, according to the saying of Solomon, it ought to seem glorious to you to be able to apply a new cleansing to this place, whence it is certain that you received the cleansing of baptism and the witness of your faith.

And you ought, furthermore, to consider with the utmost deliberation, if by your labours, God working through you, it should occur that the Mother of churches should flourish anew to the worship of Christianity, whether, perchance, He may not wish other regions of the East to be restored to the faith against the approaching time of the Antichrist. For it is clear that Antichrist is to do battle not with the Jews, not with the Gentiles; but, according to the etymology of his name, He will attack Christians. And if Antichrist finds there no Christians (just as at present when scarcely any dwell there), no one will be there to oppose him, or whom he may rightly overcome. According to Daniel[54] and Jerome,[55] the interpreter of Daniel, he is to fix his tents on the Mount of Olives;[56] and it is certain, for the apostle teaches it, that he will sit at Jerusalem in the Temple of the Lord, as though he were God.[57] And according to the same prophet, he will first kill three kings of Egypt, Africa, and Ethiopia, without doubt for their Christian faith: This, indeed, could not at all be done unless Christianity was established where now is paganism. If, therefore, you are zealous in the practice of holy battles, in order that, just as you have received the seed of knowledge of God from Jerusalem, you may in the same way restore the borrowed grace, so that through you the Catholic name may be advanced to oppose the perfidy of the Antichrist and the anti-Christians then, who can not conjecture that God, who has exceeded the hope of all, will consume, in the abundance of your courage and through you as the spark, such a thicket of paganism as to include within His law Egypt, Africa, and Ethiopia, which have withdrawn from the communion of our belief?[58] And the man of sin, the son of perdition, will find some to oppose him. Behold, the Gospel cries out, 'Jerusalem shall be trodden down by the Gentiles until the times of the Gentiles be fulfilled.'[59] 'Times of the Gentiles' can be understood in two ways: Either that they have ruled over the Christians at their pleasure, and have gladly frequented the sloughs of all baseness for the satisfaction of their lusts, and in all this have had no obstacle (for they who have everything according to their wish) are said to have their time; there is that saying: 'My time is not yet come, but your time is always ready,' whence the lustful are wont to say 'you are having your time'.[60] Or, again, 'the times of the Gentiles'[61] are the fullness of time for those Gentiles who shall have entered secretly before Israel shall be saved. These times, most beloved brothers, will now, forsooth, be fulfilled, provided the might of the pagans be repulsed through you, with the cooperation of God. With the end of the world already near, even though the Gentiles fail to be converted the Lord (since according to the apostle there must be a withdrawal from the faith),[62] it is first necessary, according to their prophecy, that the Christian way be renewed in those regions either through you, or others, whom it shall please God to send before the coming of Antichrist, so that the head of all evil, who is to occupy there the throne of the kingdom, shall find some support of the faith to fight against him...

If neither the words of the Scriptures arouse you, nor our admonitions penetrate your minds, at least let the great suffering of those who desired to go to the holy places stir you up. Think of those who made the pilgrimage across the sea![63] Even if they were more wealthy, consider what taxes, what violence they underwent, since they were forced to make payments and tributes almost every mile, to purchase release at every gate of the city, at the entrance of the churches and temples, at every side journey from place to place: also, if any accusation whatsoever were made against them, they were compelled to purchase their release; but if they refused to pay money, the prefects of the Gentiles, according to their custom, urged them fiercely with blows. What shall we say of those who took up the journey without anything more than trust in their barren poverty, since they seemed to have nothing except their bodies to lose? They not only demanded money of them, which is not an unendurable punishment, but also examined the callouses of their heels, cutting them open and folding the skin back, lest, perchance, they had sewed something there. Their unspeakable cruelty was carried on even to the point of giving them scammony to drink until they vomited, or even burst their bowels, because they thought the wretches had swallowed gold or silver; or, horrible to say, they cut their bowels open with a sword and, spreading out the folds of the intestines, with frightful mutilation disclosed whatever nature held there in secret. Remember, I pray, the thousands who have perished vile deaths, and strive for the holy places from which the beginnings of your faith have come. Before you engage in His battles, believe without question that Christ will be your standard-bearer and inseparable forerunner.

CHAPTER TWO

ATTACKS ON THE JEWS DURING THE FIRST CRUSADE, 1096

ALBERT OF AACHEN (AIX) ON THE SLAUGHTER OF THE RHINELAND JEWS, 1096

EKKEHARD OF AURA ON THE SLAUGHTER OF THE RHINELAND JEWS, 1096

SOLOMON BAR SAMSON ON THE SLAUGHTER OF THE RHINELAND JEWS, 1096

BERNARD OF CLAIRVAUX'S LETTER PROMOTING THE SECOND CRUSADE, 1146

BERNARD OF CLAIRVAUX'S PREACHING AGAINST RUDOLPH ACCORDING TO OTTO OF FREISING, 1146

BERNARD OF CLAIRVAUX'S DEFENCE OF THE JEWS RECORDED BY EPHRAIM BAR JACOB, 1146

If we are going to express contrition for the behaviour of the crusaders, it is not so much to the Muslims that we should apologise, but to the Jews and to our fellow Christians.
— Jonathan Riley-Smith[1]

ATTACKS IN THREE WAVES

The First Crusade embarked from Europe in three waves. At a time of near-famine conditions in Europe, the second and third waves heeded the leadership of the Pope and waited until after the robust harvest of 1096 to ensure that they had proper supplies to begin the journey. The impatient members of the first wave, also known as the People's Crusade, however, set out earlier, expecting to be supplied by local Christian populations along their route.[2] Without question, the most notorious leader of the People's Crusade was Emicho of Flonheim. Based in the Rhineland, Emicho was a well-known robber Baron who held lands near Mainz (Mayence) and Worms, but it was the brutality inflicted by his forces on European Jews that became his legacy.

The earliest crusaders began their march, fired with a passion for battle against infidels in the East, who, as they had been told, brutally mistreated Christians and Christian holy places in the Holy Land. The motive for revenge was high, and for some crusaders it was a relatively easy transition from the hoped-for killing of Muslim infidels in the East to the very real slaughter of Jewish infidels in Europe.[3] That this transition was easy was certainly the case for Emicho and his men, who also happened to be in need of supplies for their journey.[4]

In early May 1096, they marched along the Rhine, attacking Jews nearly everywhere they found them. The first major attack took place in May 1096 in the city of Speyer and resulted in several deaths. From there, Emicho's forces marched to the city of Worms, where the violence was much deadlier than the violence at Speyer. From Worms the crusaders then turned their attention to a third major settlement of German Jews at Mainz. Attacks on Jews in Mainz and the surrounding area continued into early June, and by the time the killing stopped, anywhere from 700 to 1,300 Jews were dead and many others were forced to convert to Christianity. Similar attacks were then directed against Jewish populations in Trier, Metz, Cologne and several neighbouring villages. By the time the attacks were over, around 3,000 Rhineland Jews had been slaughtered.[5]

Attacks on Jews did not begin or end with the so-called People's Crusade and were not limited to the Rhineland. Some earlier and much more limited attacks took place in France shortly after the Council of Clermont. At least two other attacks on Jews were also carried out by other armies of the Peasants' Crusade.[6] Nor were attacks on Jews entirely limited to the First Crusade, as some violence, although much more limited, flared in later crusades. Yet it would be a mistake to assume that the actions of Emicho's crusaders were representative of the larger crusading movement or its goals.[7] Indeed, even during Emicho's attacks in 1096, several Rhineland bishops made a serious effort to protect Jews and in some cases were successful. Additionally, Christian chroniclers of the events of 1096 condemned the actions of Emicho's crusaders.[8] Later ecclesiastical leaders took precautions to prevent similar outbreaks of violence. During the Second Crusade, for example, no less a figure than St. Bernard of Clairvaux (1090–1153), perhaps the dominant Christian voice of the twelfth century, was employed with considerable success to counteract efforts to again stir up violence against Jews.

BACKGROUND TO THE SOURCES

The First Crusade generated an enormous amount of source material by Christian writers, who wished to record and celebrate the accomplishments of the crusaders. Yet any failures or shortcomings were usually downplayed and given little emphasis by source authors. This was certainly the case with the attacks on Jews by Emicho and his crusaders. Indeed, they were seen by some as an embarrassment, who had contributed nothing to the success of the crusade, and their extremism had sullied the accomplishments of other far more successful crusaders.[9] Additionally, the First Crusade included no formal anti-Jewish objectives and most Christians saw no basis for attacking Jews in relation to crusading and even less reason for glorifying such violence.[10] As a result, there are few Christian sources from the First Crusade that even cite the events of 1096, much less provide any useful level of detail.

Two major Christian sources that do refer to the attacks on Jews are those of the clerics Albert of Aachen (c.1080) and Ekkehard of Aura (d.1126). Our knowledge of Albert is derived entirely from his lengthy history of the First Crusade and the early Latin Kingdom of Jerusalem.[11] Although he did not participate in the Crusade, he based his work on several written and oral eyewitness accounts and covered events beginning with the Council of Clermont and ending around the year 1120.[12] The fact that Albert gave any coverage at all to the crusaders' deeds in the Rhineland, unlike so many other Christian sources, may stem from his extensive personal knowledge of the area, as his hometown of Aachen (or *Aix-la-Chapelle* in French) is located in the region.[13] As seen in the selection provided later in this chapter,

Albert clearly views the actions of Emicho's crusaders with disdain, as he condemns their excessive 'cruelty' while ascribing their motivations to a combination of misguided piety and greed. In doing so, Albert is exceptional among Christian authors, as his sense of outrage is only surpassed by the Hebrew authors. Additionally, it is not insignificant that Albert equates the crusaders' [pilgrims'] killing of Jews with those who have sinned by excessive impurity and fornication, which were among the chief concerns of clerics during the crusades.[14]

Of particular interest are Albert's comments on the forced conversion efforts of the crusaders, in which he declares, 'The Lord is a just judge and orders no one unwillingly, or under compulsion, to come under the yoke of the Catholic faith.'

The other Christian account to provide a short summary of the slaughter of the Jews during the First Crusade comes from the German Benedictine chronicler Ekkehard of Aura (d.1126). Unlike Albert, he participated in the First Crusade as a member of the third wave, which, combined with his residence in Germany during the attacks on Jews, well positioned him to record both the events of 1096 in the Rhineland and a larger narrative of the First Crusade. Ekkehard's short account of the violence of 1096 is harsh on Emicho, noting that he was a man of 'ill repute' and that he lived a 'tyrannical mode of life'. Yet he is more sympathetic to the crusaders as he attributes their attacks primarily to religious zealotry.

While there are three major Hebrew source accounts of the crusaders's attacks on Jews, the account of Solomon bar Samson is the lengthiest and most detailed. A second account attributed to the twelfth-century Hebrew-poet Rabbi Eliezer bar Nathan is believed to be a derivative of Solomon bar Samson's account, while what survives of a third account attributed to an anonymous writer from Mainz is perhaps the most polished, although incomplete, source.[15] For these reasons, a selection from Solomon bar Samson's account detailing the crusaders' attack on the Jews of Mainz is presented in this chapter.

Solomon bar Samson, of whom we know very little, recorded his account of the crusaders' actions in the Rhineland around 1140, more than forty years later.[16] Yet his account was based on eyewitness oral testimony and written records, thus providing enough detail to make his the lengthiest Hebrew account of the massacre.[17] Unsurprisingly, Emicho is referred to as 'the wicked' and the crusaders, as well as the townspeople who aided them, were 'enemies of the Lord'. According to Solomon, the crusaders justified their attacks on the Jews as retribution for the killing of Christ. Solomon's account of the Bishop of Mainz is a bit more sympathetic as he notes that the Bishop had to flee for his life because, in an effort to prevent the violence, he had 'spoken good things of the Jews'.[18] Yet, ultimately, the efforts of the Bishop were of no avail as his men were among the first to flee. Of particular interest is Solomon's account of the Jews' reaction to the attack. He refers to those killed, whether by the hand of the crusaders or their own, as 'martyrs' who were determined to remain faithful to the bitter end. He also describes how the Jewish defenders were weakened after having fasted in the hope of averting the wrath of the crusaders. Yet Solomon ascribes the massacre to a form of chastisement in which God's displeasure with the sins of the Jews was the cause of their misfortune (a belief common to all three religions of the Book).[19] Solomon also provides a particularly gripping account of the ritual suicides performed by some desperate and besieged Jews (after killing their families), as a form of sanctification, to ensure that they would not abandon their faith out of fear of abuse by the crusaders.

Finally, this chapter also provides three short selections reflective of efforts by the Christian leaders to prevent a repeat of anti-Jewish violence in the early stages of the Second Crusade. All three sources claim to record the arguments Bernard made in his efforts to prevent such violence from flaring again during the Second Crusade. In the first source – a letter promoting the Second Crusade – Bernard cites the traditional justifications for the toleration of Jews in Christian societies, noting that the Jews serve as 'living signs…representing the Lord's passion', and reminds his readers that if the Jews were 'trampled down', then they would not be able to convert. In the second source, Bernard orates against a popular German monk Rudolph, who was preaching violence against Rhineland Jews during preparations for the Second Crusade. The effectiveness of Rudolph's preaching best demonstrated by the thousands of people he reportedly convinced to join the crusade. Consequently, when Rudolph preached against the Jews, the local bishop, concerned about a repeat of violence as happened during the First Crusade, called for immediate aid from Bernard, perhaps the only clerical figure of greater repute in the Rhineland, to help quell any potential trouble. The third and final source is a short selection from a Jewish history written during the later twelfth century by the German Talmudist and poet Ephraim bar Jacob. The source claims to re-create the preaching and arguments used by Bernard as he sought to suppress violence against Rhineland Jews.

THE SOURCES

Albert of Aachen (AIX) on the Slaughter of the Rhineland Jews, 1096[20]

The following source selection is taken from Albert of Aachen's *Historia Ierosolimitana* [History of the Journey to Jerusalem] and is based on several written and oral eyewitness accounts. Albert of Aachen begins with the crusaders' attacks on the Jews of Cologne but later devotes the majority of his account to events in Mainz. He briefly, but graphically, describes the efforts of the Jews to die by their own hands rather than abandon their faith or suffer the abuse of the crusaders. His account ends with the dissolution of Emicho's crusaders in Hungary, where local authorities did not allow them to pass.

At the beginning of summer in the same year in which Peter, and Gottschalk, after collecting an army, had set out, there assembled in like fashion a large and innumerable host of Christians from diverse kingdoms and lands; namely, from the realms of France, England, Flanders, and Lorraine....I know not whether by a judgement of the Lord, or by some error of mind; they rose in a spirit of cruelty against the Jewish people scattered throughout these cities and slaughtered them without mercy, especially in the Kingdom of Lorraine,[21] asserting it to be the beginning of their expedition and their duty against the enemies of the Christian faith. This slaughter of Jews was done first by citizens of Cologne. These suddenly fell upon a small band of Jews and severely wounded and killed many; they destroyed the houses and synagogues of the Jews and divided among themselves a very large, amount of money. When the Jews saw this cruelty, about two hundred in the silence of the night began flight by boat to Neuss.[22] The pilgrims and crusaders discovered them, and after taking away all their possessions, inflicted on them similar slaughter, leaving not even one alive.

Not long after this, they started upon their journey, as they had vowed, and arrived in a great multitude at the city of Mainz. There Count Emico [Emicho], a nobleman, a very mighty man in this region, was awaiting, with a large band of Teutons, the arrival of the pilgrims who were coming thither from diverse lands by the King's highway.

The Jews of this city, knowing of the slaughter of their brethren, and that they themselves could not escape the hands of so many, fled in hope of safety to Bishop Rothard.[23] They put an infinite treasure in his guard and trust, having much faith in his protection, because he was Bishop of the city. Then that excellent Bishop of the city cautiously set aside the incredible amount of money received from them. He placed the Jews in the very spacious hall of his own house, away from the sight of Count Emico and his followers, that they might remain safe and sound in a very secure and strong place.

But Emico and the rest of his band held a council and, after sunrise, attacked the Jews in the hall with arrows and lances. Breaking the bolts and doors, they killed the Jews, about seven hundred in number, who in vain resisted the force and attack of so many thousands. They killed the women, also, and with their swords pierced tender children of whatever age and sex. The Jews, seeing that their Christian enemies were attacking them and their children, and that they were sparing no age, likewise fell upon one another, brother, children, wives, and sisters, and thus they perished at each other's hands. Horrible to say, mothers cut the throats of nursing children with knives and stabbed others, preferring them to perish thus by their own hands rather than to be killed by the weapons of the uncircumcised.

From this cruel slaughter of the Jews a few escaped; and a few because of fear, rather than because of love of the Christian faith, were baptised. With very great spoils taken from these people, Count Emico, Clarebold, Thomas, and all that intolerable company of men and women then continued on their way to Jerusalem, directing their course towards the Kingdom of Hungary, where passage along the royal highway was usually not denied the pilgrims. But on arriving at Wieselburg, the fortress of the king, which the rivers Danube and Leytha protect with marshes, the bridge and gate of the fortress were found closed by command of the King of Hungary, for great fear had entered all the Hungarians because of the slaughter which had happened to their brethren....

But while almost everything had turned out favourably for the Christians, and while they had penetrated the walls with great openings, by some chance or misfortune, I know not what, such great fear entered the whole army that they turned in flight, just as sheep are scattered and alarmed when wolves rush upon them.[24] And seeking a refuge here and there, they forgot their companions....

Emico and some of his followers continued in their flight along the way by which they had come. Thomas, Clarebold, and several of their men escaped in flight towards Carinthia and Italy. So the hand of the Lord is believed to have been against the pilgrim who had sinned by excessive impurity and fornication, and who had slaughtered the exiled Jews through greed of money, rather than for the sake of God's justice, although the Jews were opposed to Christ. The Lord is a just judge and orders no one unwillingly, or under compulsion, to come under the yoke of the Catholic faith.

Ekkehard of Aura on the Slaughter of the Rhineland Jews, 1096[25]

The following selection is by the German Benedictine monk Ekkehard of Aura and represents one of only two Christian accounts from the era referring to the attacks on Jews in 1096. Although Ekkehard was not an eyewitness to the attacks, he lived in the region at the time and could have had access to first-hand information.

Just at that time, there appeared a certain soldier, Emico, Count of the lands around the Rhine, a man long of very ill repute on account of his tyrannical mode of life. Called by divine revelation, like another Saul, as he maintained, to the practise of religion of this kind, he usurped to himself the command of almost twelve thousand cross bearers. As they were led through the cities of the Rhine and the Main and also the Danube, they either utterly destroyed the execrable race of the Jews wherever they found them (being even in this matter zealously devoted to the Christian religion) or forced them into the bosom of the Church.

Solomon bar Samson on the Slaughter of the Rhineland Jews, 1096[26]

Provided here is a selection on the events of 1096 from the Hebrew account of Solomon bar Samson, written around the year 1140. He provides the lengthiest and most detailed account, Christian or Hebrew, of the crusaders' actions in Mainz (Mayence). His account graphically details the crusaders' brutality and the efforts of the Jews to resist at first, ultimately sacrificing their families and themselves. Solomon based his account on eyewitness oral testimony and written records.

It was on the third of Sivan[27]...at noon, that Emico the wicked, the enemy of the Jews, came with his whole army against the city gate, and the citizens opened it up for him. Then the enemies of the Lord said to each other: 'look! They have opened up the gate for us. Now let us avenge the blood of 'the hanged one'.[28] The children of the holy covenant who were there, martyrs who feared the Most High, although they saw the great multitude, an army numerous as the sand on the shore of the sea, still clung to their Creator. Then young and old donned their armour and girded on their weapons and at their head was Rabbi Kalonymus ben Meshullam, the chief of the community. Yet because of the many troubles and the fasts which they had observed they had no strength to stand up against the enemy. Then came gangs and bands, sweeping through like a flood until Mayence [Mainz] was filled from end to end.

The foe Emico proclaimed in the hearing of the community that the enemy be driven from the city and be put to flight. Panic was great in the town. Each Jew in the inner court of the bishop girded on his weapons, and all moved towards the palace gate to fight the crusaders and the citizens. They fought each other up to the very gate, but the sins of the Jews brought it about that the enemy overcame them and took the gate.

The hand of the Lord was heavy against His people. All the Gentiles were gathered together against the Jews in the courtyard to blot out their name, and the strength of our people weakened when they saw the wicked Edomites [Christians] overpowering them.[29] The bishop's men, who had promised to help them, were the very first to flee, thus delivering the Jews into the hands of the enemy. They were indeed a poor support; even the bishop himself fled from his church for it was thought to kill him also because he had spoken good things of the Jews....

When the children of the covenant saw that the heavenly decree of death had been issued and that the enemy had conquered them and had entered the courtyard, then all of them – old men and young, virgins and children, servants and maids – cried out together to their Father in heaven and, weeping for themselves and for their lives, accepted as just the sentence of God. One to another they said: 'Let us be strong and let us bear the yoke of the holy religion, for only in this world can the enemy kill us – and the easiest of the four deaths is by the sword.'[30] But we, our souls in paradise, shall continue to live eternally, in the great shining reflection [of the divine glory].

With a whole heart and with a willing soul they spoke: 'After all it is not right to criticise the acts of God – blessed be He and blessed be His name – who has given to us His Torah and a command to put ourselves to death, to kill ourselves for the unity of His holy name. Happy are we if we do His will. Happy is anyone who is killed or slaughtered, who dies for the unity of His name so that he is ready to enter the World to come, to dwell in the heavenly camp with the righteous – with Rabbi Akiba and his companions, the pillars of the universe, who were killed for His name's sake.[31] Not only this; but he exchanges the world of darkness for the world of light, the world of trouble for the world of joy, and the world that passes away for the world that lasts for all eternity. Then all of them, to a man, cried out with a loud voice: 'Now we must delay no longer for the enemy are already upon us. Let us hasten and offer ourselves as a sacrifice to the Lord. Let him who has a knife examine it that it not be nicked, and let him come and slaughter us for the sanctification of the Only One, the Everlasting and then let him cut his own throat or plunge the knife into his own body.'[32]

As soon as the enemy came into the courtyard they found some of the very pious there with our brilliant master, Isaac ben Moses. He stretched out his neck, and his head they cut off first. The others, wrapped by their fringed praying shawls, sat by themselves in the courtyard, eager to do the will of their Creator. They did not care to flee into the chamber to save themselves for this temporal life, but out of love they received upon themselves the sentence of God. The enemy showered stones and arrows upon them, but they did not care to flee, and 'with the stroke of the sword, and with slaughter, and destruction' the foe killed all of those whom they found there.[33] When those in the chambers saw the deed of these righteous ones, how the enemy had already come upon them, they then cried out, all of them: 'There is nothing better than for us to offer our lives as a sacrifice.'

The women there girded their loins with strength and slew their sons and their daughters and then themselves. Many men, too, plucked up courage and killed their wives, their sons, their infants. The tender and delicate mother slaughtered the babe she had played with, all of them, men and women arose and slaughtered one another. The maidens and the young brides and grooms looked out of the Windows and in a loud voice cried: 'Look and see, O our God, what we do for the sanctification of Thy great name in order not to exchange you for a hanged and crucified one....'

Thus were the precious children of Zion, the Jews of Mayence, tried with ten trials like Abraham, our father, and like Hananiah, Mishael and Azariah.[34] They tied their sons as Abraham tied Isaac his son, and they received upon themselves with a willing soul the yoke of the fear of God, the King of the Kings of Kings, the Holy One, blessed be He, rather than deny and exchange the religion of our King 'an abhorred offshoot [Jesus]....'[35] They stretched out their necks to the slaughter and they, delivered their pure souls to their Father in heaven. Righteous and pious women bared their throats to each other, offering to be sacrificed for the unity of the Name. A father turning to his son or brother, a brother to his sister, a woman to her son or daughter, neighbour to a neighbour or a friend, a groom to a bride, a fiancé to fiancée, would kill and would be killed, and blood touched blood, the blood of the men mingled with their wives', the blood of the fathers with their children's, the blood of the brothers with the sisters, the blood of the teachers with their disciples', the blood of the grooms with their brides', the blood of the leaders with the cantors', the blood of the judges with their scribes', and the blood of infants and sucklings with their mothers'. For the unity of the honoured and awe inspiring Name were they killed and slaughtered.

The ears of him who hears these things will tingle, for who has ever heard anything like this? Inquire now and look about, was there ever such an abundant sacrifice as this since the days of the primeval Adam? Were there ever eleven hundred offerings on one day, each one of them like the sacrifice of Isaac, the son of Abraham?

For the sake of Isaac who was ready to be sacrificed on Mount Moriah, the world shook, as it is said: 'Behold their valiant ones cry without; [the angels of peace weep bitterly]'[36] and 'the heavens grow dark'.[37] Yet see what these martyrs did! Why did the heavens not grow dark and the stars not withdraw their brightness? Why did not the moon and the sun grow dark in their heavens when on one day, on the third of Sivan, on a Tuesday eleven hundred souls were killed and slaughtered, among them so many infants and sucklings who had not transgressed nor sinned, many poor, innocent souls? Wilt Thou, despite this, still restrain Thyself, O Lord? For thy sake it was that these numberless souls were killed. Avenge quickly the blood of Thy servants which was spilt in our days and in our sight. Amen.

Now I shall recount and tell of the most unusual deeds that were done on that day by these righteous ones.... Who has ever seen anything like this? Who has ever heard of a deed like that which was performed by this righteous and pious woman, the young Rachel, the daughter of Rabbi Isaac ben Asher, the wife of rabbi Judah? For she said to her friends: 'I have four children. Do not spare even them, lest the Christians come, take them alive, and bring them up in their false religion. Through them, too, sanctify the name of the Holy God.'

So one of her companions came and picked up a knife to slaughter her son. But when the mother of the children saw the knife, she let out a loud and bitter lament and she beat her face and breast, crying: 'Where are Thy mercies, O God?' In the bitterness of her soul she said to her friend: 'Do not slay Isaac in the presence of his brother Aaron lest Aaron see his brother's death and run away.' The woman then took the lad Isaac, who was small and very pretty, and she slaughtered him while the mother spread out her sleeves to receive the blood, catching it in her garment instead of a basin. When the child Aaron saw that his brother Isaac was slain, he screamed again and again: 'Mother, mother, do not butcher me', and ran and hid under a chest.

She had two daughters also who still lived at home, Bella and Matrona, beautiful young girls, the children of her husband Rabbi Judah. The girls took the knife and sharpened it themselves that it should not be nicked. Then the woman bared their necks and sacrificed them to the Lord God of Hosts who has commanded us not to change His pure religion but to be perfect with Him, as it is written: 'Perfect shall you be with the Lord your God.'[38]

When this righteous woman had made an end of sacrificing her three children to their Creator, she then raised her voice and called out to her son Aaron: 'Aaron, where are you? You also I will not spare nor will I have any mercy.' Then she dragged him out by his foot from under the chest where he had hidden himself, and she sacrificed him before God, the high and exalted. She put her children next to her body, two on each side, covering them with her two sleeves, and there they lay struggling in the agony of death. When the enemy seized the room they found her sitting and wailing over them 'Show us the money that is under your sleeves,' they said to her. But when it was the slaughtered children they saw, they struck her and killed her, upon her children, and her spirit flew away and her soul found peace at last. To her applied the Biblical verse: 'The mother was dashed in pieces with her children'.....[39]

When the father saw the death of his four beautiful, lovely children, he cried aloud, weeping and wailing, and threw him upon the sword in his hand so that his bowels came out, and wallowed in blood on the road together with the dying who were convulsed, rolling in their life's blood. The enemy killed all that who were left in the room and then stripped them naked; 'See, O Lord, and behold, how abject I am become.'[40] Then the crusaders began to give thanks in the name of 'the hanged one' because they had done what they wanted with all those in the room of the bishop so that not a soul escaped.

Bernard of Clairvaux's Letter Promoting the Second Crusade, 1146[41]

Provided here is the partial text of a letter written in 1146 by Bernard of Clairvaux to promote the Second Crusade. This selection from the letter reflects Bernard's concern over the potential for violence against Jews during the Second Crusade and represents his early efforts to prevent it. Of particular interest are the two traditional arguments Bernard makes in favour of the toleration of Jews in Christian societies. Specifically, he notes that Jews serve as 'living signs… representing the Lord's passion' and that they are not to be harmed in hopes of their eventual conversion.

…Besides, brethren, I warn you, and not only I, but God's apostle, 'Believe not every spirit.'[42] We have heard and rejoice that the zeal of God abounds in you, but it behoves no mind to be wanting in wisdom. The Jews must not be persecuted, slaughtered, nor even driven out. Inquire of the pages of Holy Writ. I know what is written in the Psalms as prophecy about the Jews. 'God hath commanded me', says the Church, 'Slay them not, lest my people forget.'[43]

They are living signs to use, representing the Lord's passion.[44] For this reason they are dispersed into all regions, that now they may pay the just penalty of so great a crime, and that they may be witnesses of our redemption. Wherefore the Church, speaking in the same Psalm, says, 'Scatter them by thy power; and bring them down, O Lord, our shield.'[45] So has it been. They have been dispersed, cast down. They undergo a hard captivity under Christian princes. Yet they shall be converted at even time, and remembrance of them shall be made in due season. Finally, when the multitude of the Gentiles shall have entered in, then, 'all Israel shall be saved', saith the apostle.[46] Meanwhile he who dies remains in death. I do not enlarge on the lamentable fact that where there are no Jews there Christian men *judaize* even worse than they in extorting usury, – if, indeed, we may call them Christians and not rather baptised Jews. Moreover, if the Jews be utterly trampled down, how shall the promised salvation or conversion profit them in the end?

Bernard of Clairvaux's Preaching against Rudolph according to Otto of Freising, 1146[47]

Provided here is a selection from Otto of Freising's *The Deeds of Frederick Barbarossa*. Otto refers to the efforts of Bernard of Clairvaux against the popular German monk Rudolph who, prior to the Second Crusade, was attempting to stir the German populace to attack Jews in a manner similar to that of the First Crusade.

The aforesaid Abbot of Clairvaux, teaching them to avoid that propaganda, directed messengers or letters to the people of Gaul and Germany in which he skilfully demonstrated from the authority of the Sacred Page that the Jews ought not to die in consequence of the immensity of their crimes,[48] but rather to suffer the Diaspora…And when he came to Mayence, there he found Rudolph, dwelling, and enjoying the greatest popularity. Still, having summoned him and admonished him that he ought not, against the rule of monks, presume to preach the Word, wandering over the globe, on his own authority, with the result that he induced this fellow [Rudolph] having promised obedience, to go back to his monastery, even though the people were highly indignant, even ready to start a rebellion, had they not been restrained by the consideration of his [Bernard's] sanctity.

Bernard of Clairvaux's Defence of the Jews Recorded by Ephraim bar Jacob, 1146[49]

The Rabbi Ephraim bar Jacob of Bonn was a survivor of the attacks of 1096, having been a boy of the age of thirteen in Cologne at the time.[50] The following selection is taken from his *Book of Remembrance*. Here Ephraim claims to provide a short account of the arguments Bernard of Clairvaux used in an effort to prevent similar violence during the Second Crusade.

[Bernard asked] It is noble of you to wish to go forth against the Ishmaelites;[51] still, whoever touches a Jew so as to lay hands on his life, does something as sinful as if he laid hands on Jesus himself! My disciple, Rudolph, who has spoken against them to exterminate them, has preached only unrighteousness, for, concerning them it stands written in the Books of Psalms: 'Do not kill them, let my people not be forgotten!'[52]

CHAPTER THREE
CRUSADER MASSACRE OF THE INHABITANTS OF JERUSALEM, 1099

44
THE *GESTA FRANCORUM* ON THE CRUSADERS'
VICTORY AT JERUSALEM IN 1099

46
RAYMOND D'AGUILIERS ON THE CRUSADERS'
CAPTURE OF JERUSALEM IN 1099

50
IBN AL-QALANISI ON THE CRUSADERS' CAPTURE
OF JERUSALEM IN 1099

51
IBN AL-ALTHIR ON THE CRUSADERS' CONQUEST
OF JERUSALEM IN 1099

52
LETTER OF MANASSES TO LAMBERT

The contemporaneous descriptions of the event describe soldiers walking on the Temple mound, a holy place to Christians, with blood running up to their knees. I can tell you that that story is still being told today in the Middle East and we are still paying for it.
— Former U.S. President Bill Clinton[1]

As for those streets of blood, no historian accepts them as anything other than a literary convention. Jerusalem is a big town. The amount of blood necessary to fill the streets to a continuous and running three-inch depth would require many more people than lived in the region, let alone the city.
— Thomas Madden[2]

THE IMPORTANCE OF JERUSALEM TO THE CRUSADERS

Since the eleventh century, an enormous amount of attention has been paid to events that took place in Jerusalem during the First Crusade. This is partly because of the importance of the city to all three of the Abrahamic faiths. The Jews have the oldest claim to a special significance of the city for their faith, as it was the spiritual capital of the Jewish kingdoms of Israel and Judea during both the first and second Temple periods. Christians and Muslims, who both have traditionally viewed themselves as the successors of the Jewish faith, also attach a special significance to Jerusalem. Muslims believe that it was from Jerusalem that the Prophet Muhammad ascended to heaven, while Christians have traditionally believed that Jesus was crucified and buried in Jerusalem before his resurrection. As a result, Jerusalem's conquest was an especially appealing proposition for crusade leaders. Indeed, Pope Urban II emphasised the desecration of Christian sites in the city by the Turks to successfully stir audiences during his preaching of the First Crusade.[3] Certainly, the goal of reaching Jerusalem contributed to the pilgrimage as many crusaders had taken vows to pray in the Church of the Holy Sepulchre upon their arrival in the Holy Land.

THE BATTLE FOR JERUSALEM

Unlike the first wave of crusaders, who never made it past Asia Minor (see Chapter 2), the second wave would take the Holy Land by storm. Crusaders of the second wave began to set out from Europe for the East in August 1096. Before arriving at Jerusalem, they experienced several military successes, including important victories at Nicaea, Dorylaeum and Antioch. It was in the wake of these successes, nearly three years after leaving Europe, that the crusaders first approached the Holy City in early June 1099.

Camped outside the city, the crusaders realised that Jerusalem was too large to be surrounded by their limited forces. They decided on a plan in which the bulk of their forces would focus on the western section of the northern wall of the city.[4] These forces were under the control of the nobles Robert of Normandy, Robert of Flanders, Godfrey of Bouillon and Tancred of Taranto, while the remaining forces were placed in the south under the control of Raymond of

St. Gilles.⁵ Once all their forces were in position, the crusaders began their assault on Jerusalem during which they employed siege towers, a battering ram and catapults. Yet, even with such resources, their initial efforts met with little success and to make matters worse, the crusaders became aware of an Egyptian army that was making its way to Jerusalem to aid the city's defenders.

On 8 July the weary crusaders were called together by their leaders in a penitential procession to visit the holy places outside the walls of the city and listen to sermons on the Mount of Olives. The crusaders hoped that their efforts would win God's favour and inspire them with greater confidence. Perhaps it worked, because shortly afterwards the crusaders began to make substantial progress, and by 15 July, forces under the command of Godfrey of Bouillon successfully forced their way into the city. The defending forces fell into disarray and, in the confusion, crusaders poured over and through the walls and captured the ultimate prize, Jerusalem.

BACKGROUND TO THE SOURCES

For Latin Christians, the capture and possession of Jerusalem in 1099 was undoubtedly the high point of the crusading movement. In the wake of the victory, letters were sent to Europe to encourage other would-be crusaders to hurry to the East. Christians in Europe rejoiced upon hearing the news, while poets and chroniclers made accounts of the event that glorified the crusaders.⁶ Some eyewitness accounts, including those of the anonymously authored *Gesta Francorum*⁷ and Raymond d'Aguiliers' *Historia Francorum qui Ceperunt Iherusalem* [The History of the Franks who Captured Jerusalem],⁸ also provide detailed descriptions of the crusaders' treatment of the inhabitants of Jerusalem in the immediate aftermath of the conquest. Such accounts became a source of controversy as they recorded what amounted to a massacre of the city's population by the euphoric crusaders. The *Gesta Francorum* describes the killing as so extensive that the Temple of Solomon was covered with blood. Both Christian and Muslim sources claim that tens of thousands were massacred at Jerusalem. One later Muslim source by Ibn al-Athir notes that as many as 70,000 were slain by the crusaders. The author of the *Gesta Francorum* notes that the slaughter was so great that the crusaders waded in blood up to their ankles, while the account of Raymond d'Aguiliers notes that men rode in blood up to their knees and horses' bridle reins.⁹

While it is true that both Muslim and Christian sources for the crusaders' conquest of Jerusalem in 1099 portray the event as exceptional in its violence, recent scholarship has given historians a different perspective. To begin with, the reported high numbers of those slain by the crusaders at Jerusalem have been convincingly challenged to the point that no scholar accepts them. This scepticism is based on four counts. First, a recently discovered source puts the total number of those slain at 3,000, a more realistic number.[10] Second, the practical impossibility of the sensational events described in the sources has always been a problem for sober-minded historians.[11] Third, it is unlikely that any chroniclers, including the eyewitnesses, would have been able to take an accurate count of the dead.[12] Finally, scholars have developed a better understanding of the literary conventions of the source authors, as both Christian and Muslim writers were motivated to inflate the numbers of those slain based on their rhetorical goals.

For Christians, the high numbers of enemies slain served as evidence that God was on their side. In such a case, the destruction of tens of thousands of those who opposed the crusaders and, by extension, the work of God would have bathed the crusaders' efforts in a more heroic light. The Christian accounts support such a motive as they clearly associate these high figures they give with a sign of the greatness of the victory. Some of the earliest Muslim accounts, which report even higher numbers of those slain by the crusaders, were composed during the era of the Second and Third Crusades when jihadist ideology was approaching or at its zenith. There is little doubt that reports of the mass slaughter of tens of thousands of Muslims during the First Crusade were used to inspire Muslims to join in a jihad against the crusaders.[13]

Finally, recent scholarship has also argued that the actions of the crusaders during the siege of Jerusalem were not necessarily exceptional in their brutality and, in contrast, were within commonly accepted standards for siege warfare at the time.[14] Both Muslim and Christian armies, whether in the East or West, waged siege warfare by similar rules which dictated that if a city resisted capture, then everything that was in the city, including its people, were the property of the conquerers.[15] As a result, every population under siege had to carefully consider whether they should continue to fight or negotiate terms of surrender. The Islamic rulers of Jerusalem refused to surrender believing that they could hold out against the crusaders until the arrival of a relief force from Egypt. They miscalculated. So when the city fell to the crusaders, it was predictably sacked.

THE SOURCES

The *Gesta Francorum* on the Crusaders' Victory at Jerusalem in 1099[16]

The following source by the anonymous author of the *Gesta Francorum* provides one of the earliest Latin eyewitness accounts of the attack on Jerusalem.[17] It was written by a participant of the First Crusade, who composed his account during the crusade and completed it no later than a year or two after the event (c.1100 or 1101). Although the author provides some insights into the planning of the crusade leadership and the strategic adjustments the leaders made as the battle evolved, as well as their sufferings during the siege from a lack of water, perhaps the most interesting commentary deals with the massacre that took place during and after the crusaders' capture of the city. As crusaders poured into the city, the battle continued to rage, eventually reaching the Temple of Solomon where the Muslims had gathered in force. This explains why so many were slain in and around the Temple area, as this is where the Muslim defenders made their strongest stand.

At length, our leaders decided to beleaguer the city with siege machines, so that we might enter and worship the Saviour at the Holy Sepulchre. They constructed wooden towers and many other siege machines.[18] Duke Godfrey made a wooden tower and other siege devices, and Count Raymond did the same, although it was necessary to bring wood from a considerable distance. However, when the Saracens saw our men engaged in this work, they greatly strengthened the fortifications of the city and increased the height of the turrets at night. On a certain Sabbath night, the leaders, after having decided which parts of the wall were weakest, dragged the tower and the machines to the eastern side of the city. Moreover, we set up the tower at earliest dawn and equipped and covered it on the first, second, and third days of the week. The Count of St. Gilles erected his tower on the plain to the south of the city.

While all this was going on, our water supply was so limited that no one could buy enough water for one denarius to satisfy or quench his thirst.[19] Both day and night, on the fourth and fifth days of the week, we made a determined attack on the city from all sides. However, before we made this assault on the city, the bishops and priests persuaded all, by exhorting and preaching, to honour the Lord by marching around Jerusalem in a great procession, and to prepare for battle by prayer, fasting, and almsgiving. Early on the sixth day of the week we again attacked the city on all sides, but as the assault was unsuccessful, we were all astounded and fearful. However, when the hour approached on which our Lord Jesus Christ deigned to suffer on the Cross for us, our knights began to fight bravely in one of the towers – namely, the party with Duke Godfrey and his brother, Count Eustace. One of our knights, named Lethold, clambered up the wall of the city, and no sooner had he ascended than the defenders fled from the walls and through the city. Our men followed, killing and slaying even to the Temple of Solomon, where the slaughter was so great that our men waded in blood up to their ankles....

Count Raymond brought his army and his tower up near the wall from the south, but between the tower and the wall there was a very deep ditch. Then our men took counsel how they might fill it, and had it proclaimed by heralds that anyone who carried three stones to the ditch would receive one *denarius*. The work of filling it required three days and three nights, and when at length the ditch was filled, they moved the tower up to the wall, but the men defending this portion of the wall fought desperately with stones and fire. When the count heard that the Franks were already in the city, he said to his men, 'Why do you loiter? Lo, the Franks are even now within the city.' The Emir who commanded the Tower of St. David[20] surrendered to the count and opened that gate at which the pilgrims had always been accustomed to pay tribute. But this time the pilgrims entered the city, pursuing and killing the Saracens up to the Temple of Solomon,[21] where the enemy gathered in force. The battle raged throughout the day, so that the Temple was covered with their blood. When the pagans had been overcome, our men seized great numbers, both men and women, either killing them or keeping them captive, as they wished. On the roof of the Temple a great number of pagans of both sexes had assembled, and these were taken under the protection of Tancred and Gaston of Beert. Afterwards, the army scattered throughout the city and took possession of the gold and silver, the horses and mules, and the houses filled with goods of all kinds.

Later, all of our people went to the Sepulchre of our Lord, rejoicing and weeping for joy, and they rendered up the offering that they owed. In the morning, some of our men cautiously ascended to the roof of the Temple and attacked the Saracens; both men and women, beheading them with naked swords; the remainder sought death by jumping down into the temple. When Tancred heard of this, he was filled with anger.[22]

Raymond d'Aguiliers on the Crusaders' Capture of Jerusalem in 1099[23]

The following description of the crusaders' capture of Jerusalem is found in the *Historia Francorum* by Raymond d'Aguiliers. Raymond's eyewitness account of the crusaders' victory at Jerusalem is lengthier, or more detailed and much more graphic than the account in the *Gesta Francorum*. Raymond notes, for example, that in Solomon's Temple the slaughter by the crusaders was so intense that men rode in blood up to their knees and horses' bridal reins, rather than just to their ankles, as described in the *Gesta Francorum*. Raymond d'Aguiliers' claim of blood rising up to the bridle reins of the crusaders' horses almost certainly reflected more of Raymond's familiarity with Scripture than any reality during the siege of Jerusalem. The biblical verse found in Revelation 14:20 uses similar language and would have been known to Raymond, who was a clergyman.[24]

The Duke and the Counts of Normandy and Flanders placed Gaston of Beert in charge of the workmen who constructed machines. They built mantlets and towers with which to attack the wall.[25] The direction of this work was assigned to Gaston by the princes because he was a most noble lord, respected by all for his skill and reputation. He very cleverly hastened matters by dividing the work. The princes busied themselves with obtaining the material, while Gaston supervised the construction. Likewise, Count Raymond made William Ricau superintendent of the work on Mount Zion and placed the Bishop of Albara in charge of the Saracens and others who brought in the timber. The count's men had taken many Saracen castles and villages and forced the Saracens to work, as though they were their serfs. Thus for the construction of machines at Jerusalem fifty or sixty men carried on their shoulders a great beam that could not have been dragged by four pair of oxen. What more shall I say? All worked with a singleness of purpose, no one was slothful, and no hands were idle. All worked without wages, except the artisans, who were paid from a collection taken from the people. However, Count Raymond paid his workmen from his own treasury. Surely the hand of the Lord was with us and aided those who were working!

When our efforts were ended and the machines completed, the princes held a council and announced: 'Let all prepare themselves for a battle on Thursday; in the meantime, let us pray, fast, and give alms. Hand over your animals and your boys to the artisans and carpenters, that they may bring in beams, poles, stakes, and branches to make mantlets. Two knights should make one mantlet and one scaling ladder. Do not hesitate to work for the Lord, for your labours will soon be ended.' This was willingly done by all. Then it was decided what part of the city each leader should attack and where his machines should be located.

Meanwhile, the Saracens in the city, noting the great number of machines that we had constructed, strengthened the weaker parts of the wall, so that it seemed that they could be taken only by the most desperate efforts. Because the Saracens had made so many and such strong fortifications to oppose our machines, the Duke, the Count of Flanders, and the Count of Normandy spent the night before the day set for the attack moving their machines, mantlets, and platforms to that side of the city which is between the church of St. Stephen and the valley of Josaphat.[26] You who read this must not think that this was a light undertaking, for the machines were carried in parts almost a mile to the place where they were to be set up. When morning came and the Saracens saw that all the machinery and tents had been moved during the night, they were amazed. Not only the Saracens were astonished, but our people as well, for they recognised that the hand of the Lord was with us. The change was made because the new point chosen for attack was more level, and thus suitable for moving the machines up to the walls, which cannot be done unless the ground is level; and also because that part of the city seemed to be weaker having remained unfortified, as it was some distance from our camp. This part of the city is on the north.

Count Raymond and his men worked equally hard on Mount Zion,[27] but they had much assistance from William Embriaco, and the Genoese sailors, who, although they had lost their ships at Joppa, as we have already related, had been able, nevertheless, to save ropes, mallets, spikes, axes, and hatchets, which were very necessary to us. But why delay the story? The appointed day arrived and the attack began. However, I want to say this first, that, according to our estimate and that of many others, there were sixty thousand fighting men within the city, not counting the women and those unable to bear arms, and there were not many of these. At the most we did not have more than twelve thousand able to bear arms, for there were many poor people and many sick. There were twelve or thirteen hundred knights in our army, as I reckon it, not more. I say this that you may realize that nothing, whether great or small, which is undertaken in the name of the Lord can fail, as the following pages show.

Our men began to undermine the towers and walls. From every side stones were hurled from the *tormenti* and the *petrahae,* and so many arrows that they fell like hail. The servants of God bore this patiently, sustained by the premises of their faith, whether they should be killed or should presently prevail over their enemies. The battle showed no indication of victory, but when the machines were drawn nearer to the walls, they hurled not only stones and arrows, but also burning wood and straw. The wood was dipped in pitch, wax, and sulphur; then straw and tow were fastened on by an iron band, and, when lighted, these firebrands were shot from the machines. (They were) all bound together by an iron band, I say, so that wherever they fell, the whole mass held together and continued to burn. Such missiles, burning as they shot upward, could not be resisted by swords or by high walls; it was not even possible for the defenders to find safety down behind the walls. Thus the fight continued from the rising to the setting sun in such splendid fashion that it is difficult to believe anything more glorious was ever done. Then we called on Almighty God, our Leader and Guide, confident in His mercy. Night brought fear to both sides. The Saracens feared that we would take the city during the night or on the next day for the outer works were broken through and the ditch was filled so that it was possible to make an entrance through the wall very quickly. On our part, we feared only that the Saracens would set fire to the machines that were moved close to the walls, and thus improve their situation. So on both sides it was a night of watchfulness, labour, and sleepless caution: on one side, most certain hope, on the other doubtful fear. We gladly laboured to capture the city for the glory of God, they less willingly strove to resist our efforts for the sake of the laws of Mohammed.[28] It is hard to believe how great were the efforts made on both sides during the night.

When the morning came, our men eagerly rushed to the walls and dragged the machines forward, but the Saracens had constructed so many machines that for each one of ours they now had nine or ten. Thus they greatly interfered with our efforts. This was the ninth day, on which the priest had said that we would capture the city. But why do I delay so long? Our machines were now shaken apart by the blows of many stones, and our men lagged because they were very weary. However, there remained the mercy of the Lord which is never overcome nor conquered, but is always a source of support in times of adversity. One incident must not be omitted. Two women tried to bewitch one of the hurling machines, but a stone struck and crushed them, as well as three slaves, so that their lives were extinguished and the evil incantations averted.[29]

By noon our men were greatly discouraged. They were weary and at the end of their resources. There were still many of the enemy opposing each one of our men; the walls were very high and strong, and the great resources and skill that the enemy exhibited in repairing their defences seemed too great for us to overcome. But, while we hesitated, irresolute, and the enemy exulted in our discomfiture, the healing mercy of God inspired us and turned our sorrow into joy, for the Lord did not forsake us. While a council was being held to decide whether or not our machines should be withdrawn, for some were burned and the rest badly shaken to pieces, a knight on the Mount of Olives began to wave his shield to those who were with the count and others, signalling them to advance. Who this knight was we have been unable to find out. At this signal our men began to take heart, and some began to batter down the wall, while others began to ascend by means of scaling ladders and ropes. Our archers shot burning firebrands, and in this way checked the attack that the Saracens were making upon the wooden towers of the Duke and the two Counts. These firebrands, moreover, were wrapped in cotton. This shower of fire drove the defenders from the walls. Then the count quickly released the long drawbridge which had protected the side of the wooden tower next to the wall, and it swung down from the top, being fastened to the middle of the tower, making a bridge over which the men began to enter Jerusalem bravely and fearlessly. Among those who entered first were Tancred and the Duke of Lorraine, and the amount of blood that they shed on that day is incredible. All ascended after them, and the Saracens now began to suffer.

Strange to relate, however, at this very time when the city was practically captured by the Franks, the Saracens were still fighting on the other side, where the count was attacking the wall as though the city should never be captured. But now that our men had possession of the walls and towers, wonderful sights were to be seen. Some of our men (and this was more merciful) cut off the heads of their enemies; others shot them with arrows, so that they fell from the towers; others tortured them longer by casting them into the flames. Piles of heads, hands, and feet were to be seen in the streets of the city. It was necessary to pick one's way over the bodies of men and horses. But these were small matters compared to what happened at the Temple of Solomon, a place where religious services are ordinarily chanted. What happened there? If I tell the truth, it will exceed your powers of belief. So let it suffice to say this much, at least, that in the Temple and porch of Solomon, men rode in blood up to their knees and bridle reins.[30] Indeed, it was a just and splendid judgement of God that this place should be filled with the blood of the unbelievers, since it had suffered so long from their blasphemies.[31] The city was filled with corpses and blood. Some of the enemy took refuge in the Tower of David, and, petitioning Count Raymond for protection, surrendered the Tower into his hands.

Now that the city was taken, it was well worth all our previous labours and hardships to see the devotion of the pilgrims at the Holy Sepulchre.[32]

How they rejoiced and exulted and sang a new song to the Lord! For their hearts offered prayers of praise to God, victorious and triumphant, which cannot be told in words. A new day, new joy, new and perpetual gladness, the consummation of our labour and devotion, drew forth from all new words and new songs. This day, I say, will be famous in all future ages, for it turned our labours and sorrows into joy and exultation; this day, I say, marks the justification of all Christianity, the humiliation of paganism, and the renewal of our faith. 'This is the day which the Lord hath made, let us rejoice and be glad in it,' for on this day the Lord revealed Himself to His people and blessed them.

On this day, the Ides of July,[33] Lord Adhemar, Bishop of Puy, was seen in the city by many people. Many also testified that he was the first to scale the wall, and that he summoned the knights and people to follow him. On this day, moreover, the apostles were cast forth from Jerusalem and scattered over the whole world. On this same day, the children of the apostles regained the city and fatherland for God and the fathers. This day, the Ides of July, shall be celebrated to the praise and glory of the name of God, who, answering the prayers of His Church, gave in trust and benediction to His children the city and fatherland which He had promised to the fathers. On this day we chanted the Office of the Resurrection, since on that day He, who by His virtue arose from the dead, revived us through His grace. So much is to be said of this.

Ibn al-Qalanisi on the Crusaders' Capture of Jerusalem in 1099[34]

Arab historian Ibn al-Qalanisi (d.1160) was a twelfth-century resident of Damascus, whose sole surviving work, the *Damascus Chronicle*, ranks among the most important of all Muslim accounts of the crusades. Although al-Qalanisi was a contemporary of the First Crusade, it is not certain that he was involved in or witnessed any of the events he describes. Yet he almost certainly would have had access to first-hand information as he composed his account.[35] Provided here is his brief, but intense, account of the crusaders' siege and conquest of Jerusalem.

Thereafter they [the crusaders] proceeded towards Jerusalem, at the end of Rajab (middle of June) of this year, and the people fled in panic from their abodes before them. They descended first upon al-Ramla, and captured it after the ripening of the crops. Thence they marched to

Jerusalem, the inhabitants of which they engaged and blockaded, and having set up the tower against the city they brought it forward to the wall. At length news reached them that al-Afdal was on his way from Egypt with a mighty army to engage in the Holy War against them, and to destroy them, and to succour and protect the city against them. They therefore attacked the city with increased vigour, and prolonged the battle that day until the daylight faded, then withdrew from it, after promising the inhabitants to renew the attack upon them on the morrow. The townsfolk descended from the wall at sunset, whereupon the Franks renewed their assault upon it, climbed up the tower, and gained a footing on the city wall. The defenders were driven down, and the Franks stormed the town and gained possession of it. A number of the townsfolk fled to the sanctuary [of David], and a great host were killed. The Jews assembled in the synagogue, and the Franks burned it over their heads.[36] The sanctuary was surrendered to them on guarantee of safety on the 22nd of Sha'ban (14th July) of this year, and they destroyed the shrines and the tomb of Abraham.

Ibn al-Althir on the Crusaders' Conquest of Jerusalem in 1099[37]

Arab historian Ibn al-Athir (1160–1233) wrote much later than Ibn al-Qalanisi, whose account he most probably used as a source. His account of the crusaders' sack of Jerusalem is unique, in that he claims that as many as 70,000 Muslims were slaughtered. As he was an eyewitness of the Third Crusade and contemporary of Saladin, his numbers could be a reflection of the age in which he lived, roughly a century later, during a period when calls for Jihad against the crusaders were experiencing great success. Consequently, his use of sensational numbers was possibly intended as a means of inspiring participation in Jihad against the crusaders in his era, which saw the return of Jerusalem to Muslim control (see Chapters 7 and 8).[38]

After their vain attempt to take Acre by siege,[39] the Franks moved on to Jerusalem and besieged it for more than six weeks. They built two towers, one of which, near Sion, the Muslims burnt down, killing everyone inside it. It had scarcely ceased to burn before a messenger arrived to ask for help and to bring the news that the other side of the city had fallen. In fact Jerusalem was taken from the north on the morning of Friday 22 shaban 492/15 July 1099. The population was put to the sword by the Franks, who pillaged the area for a week. A band of Muslims barricaded themselves into the oratory of David and fought on for several days. They were granted their lives in return for surrendering. The Franks honoured their word, and the group left by night for Ascalon.[40] In the Masjid al-Aqsa the Franks slaughtered more than 70,000 people, among them a large number of Imams and Muslim scholars, devout and ascetic men who had left their homelands to live lives of pious seclusion in the Holy Place. The Franks stripped the Dome of the Rock[41] of more than forty silver candelabra, each of them weighing 3,600 drams, and a great silver lamp weighing forty-four Syrian pounds, as well as a hundred and fifty smaller silver candelabra and more than twenty gold ones, and a great deal more booty. Refugees from Syria reached Baghdad in Ramadan,[42] among them the qadi Abu Sa'd al-Harawi. They told the Caliph's ministers a story that wrung their hearts and brought tears to their eyes. On Friday they went to the Cathedral mosque and begged for help, weeping so that their hearers wept with them as they described the sufferings of the Muslims in that Holy City; the men killed, the women and children taken prisoner, the homes pillaged. Because of the terrible hardships they had suffered, they were allowed to break the fast.[43]

Letter of Manasses to Lambert[44]

The following letter is by Manasses (r.1096–1106), the Archbishop of Reims, and is addressed to the Bishop of Arras.[45] It demonstrates the jubilation experienced by some in the West upon hearing the news of the crusaders' successful capture of Jerusalem and the zeal with which such news was spread.

Manasses, by grace of God Archbishop of Reims, to Lambert, his brother, Bishop of Arras; greeting in Jesus Christ.

Be it known to you, dearest brother that a true and joyful rumour has recently come to our ears, which we believe to have come down not from human knowledge, but from the Divine Majesty – to wit: Jerusalem stands on high with joy and gladness which it has so gloriously received from God in our times. Jerusalem, the city of our redemption and glory, delights with inconceivable joy, because through the effort and incomparable might of the sons of God it has been liberated from most cruel pagan servitude. And let us also be joyful, whose Christian faith in such times as these has been placed in a mirror of eternal clarity.

We, therefore, admonished, summoned, and compelled, not only through the letters of Lord Pope Paschal,[46] but, also, through the most humble prayers of Duke Godfrey, whom the army of Christ by divine direction elevated as king,[47] as well as through the mellifluous entreaties of Lord Arnulf, whom they have unanimously chosen as Patriarch of the see of Jerusalem – we command with equal affection that you have every one of your parish churches, without fail, pray with fasts and almsgiving that the King of Kings and the Lord of Lords crown the King of the Christians with victory against the enemy, and the Patriarch with religion and wisdom against the sects and deceptions of heretics. We command, likewise, and admonish, through your obedience, that you constrain by threat all who vowed to go on the expedition and took the sign of the cross upon themselves to set out for Jerusalem, if they are vigorous of body and have the means to accomplish the journey.[48] As for the others, however, do not cease skilfully and most devoutly to admonish them not to neglect aiding the people of God, so that not only the first, but likewise the last, may receive the shilling which is promised to those labouring in the vineyard. Farewell.

Pray for the Bishop of Puy, for the Bishop of Orange, for Anselm, of Ribemont, and for all the others who lie at rest, crowned with so glorious a martyrdom.[49]

CHAPTER FOUR
THE SIEGE OF DAMASCUS DURING THE SECOND CRUSADE, 1148

61
EUGENIUS III – CALLING OF THE SECOND CRUSADE, 1 DECEMBER 1145

63
WILLIAM OF TYRE – THE FIASCO AT DAMASCUS IN 1148

68
IBN AL-QALANISI – THE MUSLIM DEFEAT OF THE CRUSADERS AT DAMASCUS IN 1148

The disaster led to bitter recriminations and accusations of treachery that scandalised the West, casting the whole idea of such expeditions in doubt.

– Christopher Tyerman[1]

THE CONSEQUENCES OF THE SECOND CRUSADE

The unimaginable success of the First Crusade brought fame to many of its participants. The nobles who led the crusade became the rulers of the Holy Land, and their deeds were celebrated by medieval chroniclers and poets. Consequently, the Second Crusade represented an opportunity for the nobility and monarchs of Europe. Both kings and saints lent their reputations to the expedition, as they were confident of divine approval and the success that was sure to follow. When the crusaders finally set out for the Holy Land, little did they know that their efforts would end in a military disaster at Damascus which would call into question the future legitimacy of the crusading movement.

THE EVENTS OF THE SECOND CRUSADE UNTIL THE SIEGE OF DAMASCUS

On Christmas Eve of 1144, the Turkish leader Imad ad-Din assaulted and captured the Latin Christian county of Edessa. Upon hearing the news, Muslims rejoiced, while Christians were stunned.[2] In November 1145 an embassy of the Latin East officially delivered to the papal court the troubling news of Edessa's fall. Pope Eugenius III wasted little time in responding, as he issued the crusading encyclical, *Quantum Praedecessores,* on 1 December 1145.[3] The Pope also employed the considerable skills of St. Bernard of Clairvaux to preach the crusade. Bernard, as perhaps the most influential cleric in Christendom at this time, had enormous success in stirring recruits to take crusading vows. Indeed, Bernard was instrumental in convincing the French King Louis VII and the German King Conrad III to lead the crusade.

In May 1147 the crusading army of King Conrad III was the first to set out for the Holy Land, with plans to meet up later with the forces of Louis VII. In October 1147, while watering their horses near Dorylaeum, Conrad's forces were ambushed by the Turks, resulting in the killing or enslaving of the majority of Conrad's forces and in a disaster for the crusaders. Conrad and the remainder of his forces then retreated to the safety of Nicaea, where in November, they finally linked up with the forces of Louis VII. As the crusaders made their way from Nicaea to Antioch, they received little assistance from local populations and were continually attacked by the Turks, resulting in enormous losses by the time they reached Antioch in mid-March.[4] In Antioch, the crusaders reorganised their depleted forces before travelling on to Jerusalem, where, with local rulers, they organised for a major council in Acre on June 24. It was at this council that the local leadership and the crusaders, in seeking to provide greater security for the Latin Kingdom of Jerusalem, made the fateful decision to attack the Syrian city of Damascus.[5]

THE ATTACK ON DAMASCUS

In mid-July the largest crusading army to date assembled at Tiberius under the combined leadership of King Louis VII, King Conrad III and King Baldwin III of Jerusalem. The crusaders' initial strategy called for an attack on Damascus from the west. This strategy was based on the reasoning that they would have access to local orchards for supplies.[6] They successfully pushed into the area, driving back Muslim resistance, and settled into a promising location from which to launch an assault. Shortly after the crusaders had established this position, they discovered that the inhabitants of Damascus had sought military aid from Nur ad-Din and his brother (sons of Imad ad-Din). As a result, the crusaders worried that they might not have the time for a prolonged siege of the better-fortified western part of the city and gambled that the less-fortified eastern walls of the city could be breached more quickly. On 27 July, apparently at the urging of local Jerusalemites who accompanied the crusaders, they moved their camp to an exposed site on the eastern side of the city that provided no water and little food.[7] It was this change that would prove to be a strategic blunder.[8] As the crusaders relocated to the eastern side of the city, Muslim forces reoccupied the western side ensuring that there would be no going back for the crusaders. At this point, everything hinged on the belief of the crusaders that the eastern walls would not hold for very long. Yet the city's Muslim defenders were indeed able to hold the eastern walls, which ultimately forced the stunned and demoralised crusaders to withdraw the siege. This withdrawal effectively marked the end of the Second Crusade and became the symbol of its failure.

BACKGROUND TO THE SOURCES

The first source provided here is Pope Eugenius III's initial draft of the crusading encyclical *Quantum Praedecessores,* as it was issued on 1 December 1945. Minor revisions were made, and the document was released a second time in March 1146. It is provided here to give the reader some sense of the expectations of the crusading leadership, if not the crusaders themselves, as they eventually rallied around the cause of the Second Crusade. The success of the First Crusade figures prominently in Eugenius' account, as he cites the esteem won by the first crusaders and advises potential recruits for a Second Crusade that they have both the opportunity to win similar glory for themselves and the duty to uphold the honour of their forerunners. Citing Pope Urban II's grant of indulgences to the participants of the First Crusade, Eugenius announces that those willing to set out on crusade with a pure heart will win equal spiritual rewards, including the remission of their sins. Also of interest is the Pope's careful delineation of crusading privileges, both legal and financial, that set a benchmark for later crusades.[9]

Although the failure of the crusaders stunned the Christian West, there are curiously few contemporary Latin Christian accounts of the Second Crusade, much less specific accounts of the disastrous siege of Damascus. The lack of success in the Second Crusade stood in stark contrast to the achievements of the First Crusade, and this discouraged Latin Christians from writing about the expedition.[10] The only major exception is Odo of Deuil's *The Journey of Louis VII to the East*, which is the best eyewitness source for the Second Crusade.[11] Yet Odo's surviving account makes only a brief reference to the disastrous events at Damascus.[12] Whether Odo's otherwise detailed work was never finished or the last part of it was lost has never been determined.[13] Likewise, Otto of Freising's account, *The Deeds of Frederick Barbarossa*, which documents Frederick's participation in the Second Crusade prior to his becoming Holy Roman Emperor in 1152, glosses over the failure of the siege of Damascus, noting only that its details were 'related elsewhere…by others'.[14] In referring the reader elsewhere concerning the events of the siege of Damascus, Otto suggests his disgust with the 'royal pride' to which he attributes the crusaders' misfortunes by his refusal to discuss it any further.[15] Consequently, the best Latin Christian source covering events at Damascus is found in William of Tyre's *Historia rerum in partibus transmarinis gestarum* [*History of Deeds Done beyond the Sea*].

William of Tyre (1130–1185) was perhaps the most prolific historian of the Latin East. He composed his *History* over a period of several years, beginning in the 1160s and ending only with his death around 1185. During the time of the Second Crusade, William was a teenager living in the Holy Land, and the crusade undoubtedly left a lasting impression on him.[16] In his later life, William had access to important documents and oral testimony by virtue of his positions as Archbishop of Tyre and Chancellor of Jerusalem. As a talented historian with knowledge of Latin, French, Arabic, Greek, and even some Hebrew and Persian, William was able to put such information to good use in constructing his lengthy history of the crusades.[17] Indeed, William's account provides one of the most detailed existing descriptions of the process and reasoning leading up to the crusade leadership's decision to attack Damascus as well as the poor decisions and events that led to their failure. He notes that things were going quite well for the crusaders as they occupied strategic orchards that provided the army with supplies. It was only at that point that things began to go wrong as, according to William, the Muslims were able to bribe some of the crusade leadership to push for a change in strategy. These leaders, whom William compared to Judas, effectively lobbied to have the army shift its forces to the eastern wall of Damascus, arguing that the wall was weak and would fall quickly.[18] This of course was not the case and resulted in a disaster for the crusaders. Consequently, William ascribes the failure of the crusaders at Damascus to greed and treachery.

The earliest and most detailed Muslim account of the crusaders' defeat at Damascus is by Ibn al-Qalanisi (d.1160).[19] Although he may have been quite elderly and almost certainly did not participate in any fighting during the Second Crusade, he was well positioned to gather information from the Muslim perspective for his treatment of the events at Damascus in 1148. He seems to have had a general awareness, perhaps through later discussions with Christian sources, of the decision-making of the crusade leadership prior to and during the siege of Damascus. He notes the efforts of the besieged Muslim defenders to call for reinforcements and that, as a result, cavalry and bowmen were steadily arriving and adding to the strength of the Muslim forces. He then describes the concern this caused to the crusaders in and cites this concern as the cause of their retreat from Damascus. He nowhere mentions the specific strategic blunder of the crusaders in repositioning their forces from the orchards to the eastern wall of the city, instead attributing victory only to the military prowess of the Muslim forces.

THE SOURCES

Eugenius III – Calling of the Second Crusade, 1 December 1145[20]

The following selection is from Pope Eugenius III's encyclical *Quantum Praedecessores*, as it was issued on 1 December 1145. It represents his first formal call for the Second Crusade. While the Pope emphasises the success of the First Crusade and the spiritual rewards that will benefit those willing to take up the cross, it also clearly lays out the economic and legal protections that would become standard in later crusades.

Bishop Eugene, servant of the servants of God, to his most beloved son in Christ, Louis, the illustrious King of the French, and to his beloved sons, the princes, and to all the faithful ones of God who are established throughout Gaul – greeting and apostolic benediction.

How much our predecessors the Roman pontiffs did labour for the deliverance of the oriental church, we have learned from the accounts of the ancients and have found it written in their acts. For our predecessor of blessed memory, Pope Urban,[21] did sound, as it were, a celestial trump and did take care to arouse for its deliverance the sons of the holy Roman church from the different parts of the earth. At his voice, indeed, those beyond the mountain and especially the bravest and strongest warriors of the French kingdom, and also those of Italy, inflamed by the ardour of love did come together, and, congregating a very great army,[22] not without much shedding of their own blood, the divine aid being with them, did free from the filth of the pagans that city[23] where our Saviour willed to suffer for us, and where He left His glorious sepulchre to us as a memorial of His passion, and many others which, avoiding prolixity, we refrain from mentioning.

Which, by the grace of God, and the zeal of your fathers, who at intervals of time have striven to the extent of their power to defend them and to spread the name of Christ in those parts, have been retained by the Christians up to this day; and other cities of the infidels have by them been manfully stormed. But now, our sins and those of the people themselves requiring it, a thing which we can not relate without great grief and wailing, the city of Edessa which in our tongue is called Rohais, which also, as is said, once when the whole land in the east was held by the pagans, alone by herself served God under the power of the Christians – has been taken and many of the castles of the Christians occupied by them (the pagans). The archbishop, moreover, of this same city, together with his clergy and many other Christians, have there been slain, and the relics of the saints have been given over to the trampling under foot of the infidels, and dispersed. Whereby how great a danger threatens the church of God and the whole of Christianity, we both know ourselves and do not believe it to be hid from your prudence. For it is known that it will be the greatest proof of nobility and probity, if those things which the bravery of your fathers acquired be bravely defended by you the sons. But if it should happen otherwise, which God forbid, the valour of the fathers will be found to have diminished in the case of the sons.

We exhort therefore all of you in God, we ask and command, and, for the remission of sins enjoin: that those who are of God, and, above all, the greater men and the nobles do manfully gird themselves; and that you strive so to oppose the multitude of the infidels, who rejoice at the time in a victory gained over us, and so to defend the oriental church – freed from their tyranny by so great an outpouring of the blood of your fathers, as we have said, – and to snatch many thousands of your captive brothers from their hands, that the dignity of the Christian name may be increased in your time, and that your valour which is praised throughout the whole world, may remain intact and unshaken. May that good Matthias be an example to you, who, to preserve the laws of his fathers, did not in the least doubt to expose himself with his sons and relations to death, and to leave whatever he possessed in the world; and who at length, by the help of the divine aid, after many labours however, did, as well as his progeny, manfully triumph over his enemies.

We, moreover, providing with paternal solicitude for your tranquillity and for the destitution of that same church, do grant and confirm by the authority conceded to us of God, to those who by the promptings of devotion do decide to undertake and to carry through so holy and so necessary a work and labour, that remission of sins which our aforesaid predecessor Pope Urban did institute; and do decree that their wives and sons, their goods also and possessions shall remain under the protection of our selves and of the archbishops, bishops and other prelates of the church of God. By the apostolic authority, moreover, we forbid that, in the case of any thing, which they possessed in peace, when they took the cross, any suit be brought hereafter until most certain news has been obtained concerning their return or their death. Moreover since those who war for the Lord should by no means prepare themselves with precious garments, nor with provision for their personal appearance,[24] nor with dogs or hawks, other things which portend licentiousness: we exhort your prudence in the Lord that those who have decided to undertake so holy a work shall not strive after these things, but shall show zeal and diligence with all their strength in the matter of arms, horses and other things with which they may fight the infidels. But those who are oppressed by debt and begin so holy a journey with a pure heart, shall not pay interest for the time past....It is allowed to them also when their relations, being warned, or the lords to whose fee they belong, are either unwilling or unable to advance them the money, to freely pledge without any reclamation, their lands or other possessions to churches, or ecclesiastical persons, or to any other of the faithful. According to the institution of our aforesaid predecessor, by the authority of almighty God and by that of St. Peter the chief of the apostles, conceded to us by God, we grant such remission and absolution of sins, that he who shall devoutly begin so sacred a journey and shall accomplish it, or shall die during it, shall obtain absolution for all his sins which with a humble and contrite heart he shall confess,[25] and shall receive the fruit of eternal retribution from the Remunerator of all.

Given at Vetralle on the Calends of December.

William of Tyre – The Fiasco at Damascus in 1148[26]

The following source selection is taken from William of Tyre's *History of Deeds Done beyond the Sea*. Although William wrote several years after the crusaders' defeat at Damascus, he undoubtedly had access to important documents and oral testimony from eyewitnesses as he composed his account. Consequently, he provides the most detailed description of the process and reasoning leading up to the crusade leadership's decision to attack Damascus as well as a detailed analysis of their poor decisions, consequent events and ultimate failure.

Damascus is the largest city of lesser Syria and is its metropolis, for as it is said, 'Damascus is the head of Syria.'[27] The city is also known as the Phoenicia of Lebanon and is named after a certain servant of Abraham who is believed to have founded it. The name means 'bloody' or 'dripping with gore'. The city is located on a plain in a land which is barren and arid, save where it is irrigated by waters brought down for its benefit through ancient canals. A stream descends from a nearby mountain ridge in the highlands of that area and is channelled through the various lower sections of the region so as to fertilise the barren fields.

Since there is an abundance of water, the surplus is used to nourish the orchards of fruit trees which are located on either side of the stream. The stream flows along the eastern wall of the city. When the kings came to the place which had been agreed upon, namely Daria, which was close to Damascus, they organised their lines for battle and settled the order of battle for their legions lest, if they went ahead in disorderly fashion, quarrels should break out among them and hinder their common task.

By the common decision of the princes it was agreed that the King of Jerusalem[28] and his men were to go first, principally because they were supposed to be familiar with the lay of the land. They were supposed to open the way for the rest who were following them. The French King and the men of his expedition were ordered to take the second, or centre, place, so that, if necessary, they could assist those ahead of them. The emperor,[29] by the same token, was ordered to keep in the third and last place, so that he would be ready to resist the enemy if perchance they should attack from the rear. He was thus to make the forces ahead secure from behind. When the three armies had been placed in proper order, they moved the camp forward and attempted to approach the city.

On the western side of Damascus from which our troops approached, and on the northern side, too, the city is enclosed far and wide by orchards which are like dense woods or a shady forest, extending five miles or more towards Lebanon. These orchards are enclosed by mud walls – rock is not plentiful in that region – so that their ownership will not be in doubt and also to keep out trespassers. The orchards are, therefore, enclosed by defensive walls in such a way that each man's possessions are identified. Paths and public roads, though they are narrow, are left open so that the gardeners and those who have charge of the orchards can make their way to the city with the animals which carry the fruit. These orchards are the city's greatest protection. Because of their density, because of the number of the trees, and because of the narrowness of the roads, it seemed difficult – indeed, almost impossible – for those who wished to approach Damascus to do so from that side. From the beginning, however, our princes had decided to bring the army in through this area to gain access to the city. There was a double reason for this: on the one hand, it was done so that after the most securely guarded areas in which the Damascenes had the greatest faith had been occupied, what remained would seem easy and would be more readily accomplished. On the other hand, the approach was made in this way so that the army would not be deprived of the benefits of food and water. The King of Jerusalem, therefore, sent his fighting formations in first through those narrow orchard paths. The army could scarcely make headway and did so with great difficulty, both because it was hemmed in by the narrow roads and also because it was hindered by the ambushes of the men who were hidden in the thickets. Also, the army had sometimes to engage the enemies who appeared and seized the circuitous paths.

All the people of Damascus came out together and descended upon the aforesaid orchards in order to block the army's passage both by stealth and by open attack. There were, furthermore, walls and large, tall houses among the orchards. These were defended by soldiers whose possessions lay nearby. They defended the orchard walls by shooting arrows and other missiles and allowed no one to approach them, while the arrows shot from on high made the public roads exceedingly dangerous for those who wished to pass through them. Nor were our men beset with formidable obstacles only on one side. Rather, on every side there was equal peril for the unwary and danger of sudden and unforeseen death. There were, moreover, men with lances hiding inside of the walls. When these men saw our men passing by, they would stab them as they passed, through little peepholes in the walls which were cleverly designed for this purpose, so that those hiding inside could scarcely be seen. Many are said to have perished miserably that day in this way. Countless other kinds of danger, too, faced those who wished to pass through those narrow paths.

As our men became aware of this, they pushed on more fiercely. When they had broken down the barricades in the orchards, they occupied them eagerly. Those whom they discovered within the walls or in the houses, they pierced with their swords or threw into chains as captives. When the townsmen who had come out to defend the orchards heard this, they feared that they would perish as the others had. They left the orchards and returned to the city in droves. Thus, when the defenders either had been slaughtered or had been turned to flight, a free path forward lay open to our men.

The cavalry forces of the townsmen and of those who had come to their assistance realised that our army was coming through the orchards in order to besiege the city and they accordingly approached the stream which flowed by the town. This they did with their bows and ballistas[30] so that they could fight off the Latin army, which was fatigued by its journey and also so that they could prevent the thirsty men from reaching the river and the water which was so necessary for them. Our men hurried to the river, which they had heard was nearby, in order to relieve their thirst, which had grown intense from the difficulties of their labours and the dense clouds of dust which were raised by the feet of horses and men. There they saw such a multitude of the enemy that they halted for a time. After a while they collected their men. They were given strength and hardiness by necessity. Once and then again they strove to get to the water, but in vain. While the King of Jerusalem and his men struggled vainly, the emperor, who commanded the formations in the rear, demanded to know why the army was not moving forward. He was told that the enemy had seized the river and that they were blocking the progress of our men. When he learned of this, the emperor was angered and, together with his lieutenants, he speedily made his way through the French King's ranks to the place where the fight for the river was going on. They dismounted from their horses and became infantrymen – as the Germans are accustomed to do in the crisis of battle. With shields in hand they fought the enemy hand-to-hand with swords. The enemy, who had earlier resisted valiantly, were unable to withstand the attack. They relinquished the river bank and fled at full speed to the city.

In this combat the Lord Emperor is said to have performed a feat which will be remembered through the ages. It is related that one of the enemy was resisting manfully and vigorously and that the emperor with one blow cut off this enemy soldier's head and neck with the left shoulder and arm attached, together with part of his side – despite the fact that the foe was wearing a cuirass. At this deed the citizens, both those who witnessed it and those who learned of it from others, were thrown into such a fright that they despaired of resisting and even of life itself.

When the river had been won and its banks had been freely yielded, the Crusaders camped far and wide around the city, with the advantage of using freely the orchards, for which they had so strenuously fought, as well as the river. The townsmen were astonished both at the amazing number of our troops and at their courage. They began to be troubled about their own men and whether they could withstand us. They feared a sudden attack by us and counted nothing safe when they considered what kind of men they had discovered us to be in the previous day's battles. They conferred, therefore, and with the ingenuity which is characteristic of those suffering misery and adversity, they had recourse to desperate devices. In all the sections of the city which faced our camps they heaped up huge, tall beams, for they could only hope that while our men were working to tear down these barriers they might be able to flee in the opposite direction with their wives and children. It seemed evident to our men that if the divine favour was with us the city would soon be taken by the Christians. But it seemed otherwise to Him Who is 'terrible in his judgements of the sons of men'.[31] The city, as we have said, was in despair and its citizens held no hope of resisting or of being saved, but rather they were packing their bags and preparing to leave. At this point, for our sins, they began to work on the greed of our men. Using money, they attempted to conquer the hearts of those whose bodies they could not overcome. With consummate skill they proposed a variety of arguments to some of our princes and they promised and delivered a stupendous sum of money to them so that the princes would strive and labour to lift the siege. They persuaded these princes to assume the role of the traitor Judas. Corrupted by gifts and promises, led on by greed, the root of all evil, these princes fell in with the crime. By impious suggestions they persuaded the kings and the leaders of the pilgrims, who trusted their good faith and industry, to leave the orchards and to lead the army to the opposite side of the city. To camouflage their plot they alleged that on the opposite side of Damascus, which faced south and west, there were neither orchards to strengthen the city nor any moat or river to hinder their approach to the walls. The wall, they said, was low and was made of sun-baked bricks and it would scarcely withstand the first attack. There, they asserted, neither engines nor any great force would be needed. In the first attack the wall could immediately be torn down by hand and it would not be difficult to break into the city....

The kings and all the leaders of the army believed them and they deserted the places which they had earlier won with so much sweat and at the cost of the lives of so many of their men. They transferred all of their formations and, under the leadership of the traitors, they camped on the opposite side of the city. There they found themselves located far from access to water, deprived of the abundance of fruit, and lacking almost all supplies. They were saddened and they discovered, all too late, that they had maliciously been led to move from a region of abundance.

The food supply in the camp began to run out. Before the men had set out on the expedition, they had been persuaded to believe that the city would be quickly taken and they had brought along provisions for only a few days. This was especially true for the pilgrims, nor could they be blamed for it, since they were unfamiliar with the country. They had been persuaded, too, that the city would be taken at once in the initial attacks and they were assured that in the meantime a large army could be fed on the fruit supply which they could get for nothing, even if all other food were lacking.

The doubtful men deliberated publicly and privately as to what they were to do. To return to the places they had left seemed hard, even impossible, for, when our men had left, the enemy saw that what they desired had been accomplished. They had entered those places more strongly than before and had barricaded the roads by which our men had earlier entered. They had blocked them by piling up beams and large rocks and had sent in an immense company of archers who made access impossible. To attack the city from the area where the camps were now located would, on the other hand, involve delay; but the lack of food supplies would not allow a long respite. The pilgrim princes consulted one another. Seeing the manifest discomfort of the men whose spiritual care and whose Crusade had been confided to them and knowing that they could make no headway, they decided to return, despising the false pretences of the men who had betrayed them.

Thus a company of kings and princes such as we have not read of through all the ages had gathered and, for our sins, had been forced to return, covered with shame and disgrace, with their mission unfulfilled. They returned to the kingdom by the same route over which they had come. Henceforth, so long as they remained in the East, they regarded the ways of our princes with suspicion. With good reason they turned down all their wicked plans and henceforth the leaders of the Crusade were lukewarm in the service of the Kingdom.[32] Even after they had returned to their own lands they constantly remembered the injuries they had suffered and detested our princes as wicked men.[33] Nor were they alone affected. For they also caused others who had not been there to neglect the care of the kingdom, so that henceforth those who undertook the pilgrimages were fewer and less fervent. Even today those who come are careful lest they fall into a trap and they strive to return home as soon as possible.

Ibn al-Qalanisi – The Muslim Defeat of the Crusaders at Damascus in 1148[34]

The following selection from Ibn al-Qalanisi represents the earliest and most detailed surviving Muslim account of the crusaders' defeat at Damascus. He omits any reference to the strategic blunder of the crusaders' relocating their siege position away from the orchards and, instead, ascribes their defeat to the ultimate military prowess of the Muslim army. He was, perhaps, quite elderly at the time of the siege of Damascus and almost certainly did not participate in any fighting during the Second Crusade. Yet as a respected member of the Muslim community, he was well positioned to gather first-hand information from the Muslim perspective while composing his account.

There was a divergence of views amongst them as to which of the lands of Islam and Syrian cities they should proceed to attack, but at length they came to an agreed decision to attack the city of Damascus, and their malicious hearts were so confident of capturing it that they already planned out the division of its estates and districts. This news arrived in a series of reports, and the governor of the city, the amir Mu'in al-Din Unur, set about making ready equipment and preparing to engage them and to counter their malice, fortifying the places where their attack was feared, setting men to guard the roads and passes, cutting off the movement of supplies to their stations, filling up the wells, and effacing the watering places.

The Franks directed their march towards Damascus with their host, their might and their armoury, in numbers estimated at fifty thousand horse and foot, and accompanied by such quantities of baggage train, camels and cattle, as swelled their forces to a surpassing number. They approached the city and made for the site known as Manazil al-Asakir, but finding no water there, since the supply had been cut off from it, they proceeded to al-Mizza, owing to its proximity to water, and advanced on the town with their cavalry and foot soldiers. The Muslims drew up in face [sic] of them on Saturday, 6th First Rabi (24th July) and battle was joined between the two forces. A great multitude joined in the struggle with them, composed of the levies and the death dealing Turks, the town hands, volunteers and ghazis, and death was scattered abroad among them. The infidels gained the upper hand over the Muslims owing to the superiority of their numbers and equipment. They gained control of the water, spread throughout the orchards, and encamped in them. They moved close up to the town and occupied a section of it which no troops either in ancient or recent times had succeeded in holding. On this day the Malikite jurisconsult and imam Yusuf al-Findalawi (God's mercy upon him) found martyrdom by the water near al-Rabwa, owing to his stand in face of the Franks and refusal to retire before them, in steadfast obedience to the commands of God in his Holy Book. A similar fate befell the ascetic 'Abd al-Rahman al-Halhull (God's mercy upon him).

The Franks now set about cutting down trees and building stockades with them, and destroying the enclosures. The night passed in this wise, with all the people discouraged and straitened in spirit through fear because of the horror of what they had witnessed. They made a sortie against the Franks early on the following morning, which was Sunday, and after charges by each side against the other, the Muslims gained the upper hand over them and multiplied death and wounds amongst them. The amir Mu'in al-Din distinguished himself in combat with them, and displayed a valour, steadfastness and gallantry such as was never seen in any other, never wearying in repelling them nor taking respite from the struggle against them. The mill of war ceased not to grind between them, with the infidel horsemen ever delaying to make their famous onslaught until the opportunity should be offered them, until at length the sun inclined to its setting, night drew nigh, and men's souls sought for rest. Each side returned to its own place, but the regular troops passed the night in the field facing the Franks, and the citizens in watch and sentry duty on their walls, with the enemy in full view close to them.

Meanwhile letters had been dispatched to the governors of the outlying districts with appeals for assistance and reinforcement. Parties of Turkmen cavalry and of footmen from the outskirts were constantly arriving and [next morning] the Muslims made an early attack upon the Franks, with their confidence renewed and their fears dissipated. They held their ground in face of the Franks and discharged upon them shafts of fate and arrows of wounding, which fell without intermission upon footman or knight, horse or camel, in their camp. During this day there arrived from the Biqa and elsewhere large numbers of bowmen, by whom the numerical strength [of the Muslims] was increased and their military equipment redoubled. Each side separated from the other and retired to the position which it had established [at the end of] this day. In the early morning of the following day, Tuesday, the Muslims advanced to attack them with the swiftness of hawks swooping on mountain partridges, and having encompassed them in their camp and surrounded their sleeping quarters, they made havoc of the barricades which they had constructed with trees from the orchards, by a hail of arrows and bombardment of stones. The Franks on their part declined to come out, in fear and discouragement, and not one man of them showed himself. It was thought that they were planning a ruse and preparing a stratagem. None of them appeared save a few horsemen and foot soldiers by way of skirmishing and keeping off the enemy in case the latter should attack before they found either a clear field for their own charge or some device to secure their escape. Not a man of them could approach [the Muslims] without being thrown prostrate by a shower of arrows or a lance thrust. A large number of foot soldiers of the town bands and men of the villages became emboldened against them, and made a practice of lying in wait for them on the roads, when they suspected no danger, and killing all those whom they captured, and bringing in their heads to claim rewards for them. A large number of heads were brought in.

Meanwhile reports reached the Franks from several quarters of the rapid advance of the Islamic armies to engage in the Holy War against them and of their eagerness to exterminate them, and they became convinced of their own destruction and of the imminence of disaster. Having taken counsel of one another, they found no way of escape from the net into which they had fallen and the abyss into which they had cast themselves save to retreat in disorder at dawn on the Wednesday, the following day, and to flee, broken and forsaken. When the Muslims learned this, and the signs of the retreat of the Franks became clear to them, they moved out to attack them on the morning of the same day and hastened towards them, pursuing them with arrows, so that they slew a large number of men, horses, and other animals in their rear files. In the remains of their camps, moreover, and along their highroads there were found such uncountable quantities of burial pits of their slain and of their magnificent horses, that there were stenches from their corpses that almost overcame the birds of the air. They had also burned down al-Rabwa and al-Qubba al-Mamdudiya during that night. The people rejoiced at this mercy which God had bountifully bestowed upon them, and multiplied their thanks to Him for having vouchsafed to them an answer to the prayers which they had offered up without ceasing during the days of this distress, and to God be praise and thanks therefore.

CHAPTER FIVE
THE FAILURE OF THE SECOND CRUSADE

ODO OF DEUIL ON THE PROBLEM OF NON-COMBATANTS DURING THE SECOND CRUSADE — 77

THE ANONYMOUS ANNALIST OF WURZBURG ON THE IMPIOUS MOTIVATIONS OF OPPORTUNISTS, THE INDEBTED, AND THE POOR DURING THE SECOND CRUSADE — 77

ODO OF DEUIL ON THE TREACHERY OF MANUEL I COMNENUS DURING THE SECOND CRUSADE — 79

ODO OF DEUIL OF THE BETRAYAL OF THE BYZANTINES DURING THE SECOND CRUSADE — 79

CONRAD III – SECOND LETTER TO WIBALD, ABBOT OF CORVEY, ON THE FAILURE OF THE CRUSADERS' SIEGE OF DAMASCUS, 1148 — 81

CRITICISM OF THE CLERICAL ADVOCATES OF THE SECOND CRUSADE BY THE ANONYMOUS ANNALIST OF WURZBURG — 83

GEOFFREY OF CLAIRVAUX'S DEFENCE OF BERNARD OF CLAIRVAUX — 83

BERNARD OF CLAIRVAUX'S *APOLOGIA* FOR THE SECOND CRUSADE — 86

The disappointment was, of course, correspondingly deep.
This is clear from the many attempts which were made to explain
the failure.

– Hans Eberhard Meyer[1]

THE SEARCH FOR ANSWERS

Since Urban II's calling of the First Crusade, popes and preachers had assured crusaders that they acted with divine sanction and, as a result, that God would grant them significant spiritual rewards for their efforts. Pope Eugenius III and his preachers used the same formula in their preaching of the Second Crusade, announcing that those willing to take the cross would win no less than the full remission of their sins. Thousands responded to Eugenius III's call and headed for the Holy Land confident of God's support. Yet few were prepared for the disastrous events that followed, which witnessed the nearly total destruction of King Conrad III's army and the ignoble withdrawal of the crusaders from the siege of Damascus. Once the demoralising results of the crusade became known, disillusioned Christians began to seek answers for the failure of warriors, who, as they had been assured by their priests, fought on God's behalf. It was not long before the search for answers turned to criticism of nearly all involved with the crusade.

CRITICISM OF NON-COMBATANTS

The First Crusade had developed in the context of a pilgrimage with papal promises of spiritual benefits for those who participated. Although Pope Urban II had discouraged non-combatants from participating in the crusade, it was not strictly forbidden and women, children, the sick and the elderly all took part.[2] When problems were encountered during the First Crusade, including starvation, thirst and immorality in the camps, non-combatants were often blamed. Following the Second Crusade, when the pragmatic causes of the crusaders' failure were examined, the presence of non-combatants again became a source of criticism. Theorists and strategists concluded that crusading armies needed to be more professionalised, with less popular participation.[3] Rather than dealing with the logistical problems of providing provisions and security for large numbers of poorly supplied and unruly non-combatants, later crusades preaching efforts focused more on the recruitment of disciplined men of fighting age and select members of the nobility to lead them. In England, France and Germany, official measures were implemented to prevent those who were unable to bear arms or support themselves from going to the East, which excluded the vast majority of the population of these countries from taking part in future crusading efforts.

Provided in this chapter are two selections from the works of Latin Christian authors condemning the presence of non-combatants. The first excerpt is from Odo of Deuil's eyewitness account of the Second Crusade. This account emphasises the main problems created for the leaders of the Second Crusade by the presence of weak and poorly equipped non-combatants, whom he describes as 'a burden to their comrades and a source of prey to their enemies'. The second account is taken from the *Annales Herbipolenses* of the Anonymous Annalist of Wurzburg (written shortly after the Second Crusade). The author emphasises the various undesirable goals and motivations of many of those who took part in the crusade, noting that some went seeking novelties and to learn about new lands, while others were motivated by poverty at home, seeking new opportunities in the East. As a result, with few exceptions, the Annalist argued that the crusaders' motivations were impious.

THE SOURCES

Odo of Deuil on the Problem of Non-Combatants during the Second Crusade[4]

In the following short selection from Odo of Deuil's eyewitness account of the Second Crusade, the author emphasises the problems created for the leaders of the Second Crusade by the presence of weak and poorly equipped non-combatants.

But, would that he [Pope Eugenius III] had instructed the infantry in the same way and, keeping the weak at home, had equipped all the strong with the sword instead of the wallet and the bow instead of the [pilgrim's] staff; for the weak and helpless are always a burden to their comrades and a source of prey to their enemies.

The Anonymous Annalist of Wurzburg on the Impious Motivations of Opportunists, the Indebted, and the Poor during the Second Crusade[5]

The following account is taken from the *Annales Herbipolenses* of the Anonymous Annalist of Wurzburg (written shortly after the Second Crusade). The author emphasises the various undesirable goals and motivations of many of those who joined the Second Crusade only to flee poverty or avoid debt.

The intentions of the various men were different. Some, indeed, lusted after novelties and went in order to learn about new lands. Others there were who were driven by poverty, who were in hard straits at home; these men went to fight, not only against the enemies of Christ's cross, but even against the friends of the Christian name, wherever opportunity appeared, in order to relieve their poverty. There were others who were oppressed by debts to other men or who sought to escape the service due to their lords, or who were even awaiting the punishment merited by their shameful deeds. Such men simulated a zeal for God and hastened chiefly in order to escape from such troubles and anxieties. A few could, with difficulty, be found who had not bowed their knees to Baal,[6] who were directed by a holy and wholesome purpose, and who were kindled by love of the divine majesty to fight earnestly and even to shed their blood for the holy of holies.[7]

CRITICISM OF BYZANTIUM

Latin Christian writers had also attributed setbacks during the First Crusade to Byzantine duplicity.[8] Yet such criticism was little in comparison with the criticism in the aftermath of the Second Crusade. Odo of Deuil was reflective of Western writers, who considered Byzantine treachery as fundamental to the cause of the crusaders' failure. He claimed that the 'idol of Constantinople', the Byzantine Emperor Manuel Comnenus, had given the crusaders inadequate supplies and provided them with a 'treacherous guide' whose goal was to 'prostrate the Christian faith, strengthen paganism, encourage the timid pagans, and cool our ardour'.[9] Odo also accused the Byzantines of bad faith for failing to provide previously-agreed-upon ships to transport the crusaders from Antalya to Antioch during the crusade. This failure resulted in a long and dangerous land march for the crusaders, who along the way suffered several attacks from the Turks and received little assistance from local populations. Two brief selections of Odo of Deuil's account of the Second Crusade are provided in this section. In each account, he describes these and other hardships suffered by the crusaders, which he attributes to Byzantine duplicity.

THE SOURCES

Odo of Deuil on the Treachery of Manuel I Comnenus during the Second Crusade[10]

The two following selections by Odo of Deuil are representative of the criticism that those who participated in the Second Crusade directed at Byzantium after its failure. Here Odo blames the Byzantine Emperor for failing to supply the crusaders during their journey.

On meeting, therefore, they [the representatives of King Louis and Emperor Manuel] first set forth the agreements, that is, that the king should not take from the emperor any stronghold or town which was under his jurisdiction. This reasonable and modest request was followed by an equally generous, but false promise; for in order to grant a favour which would form a counterpart to the king's agreement of peace the emperor added that two or three of his chief barons should go along to guide the king on the right route and to furnish a suitable market everywhere. When a market should be unavailable, however, he would willingly allow them to plunder castles and seize cities, if, when the spoils had been taken, the land should remain unoccupied.... Finally homage had been exacted from the barons, when the king and the barons had been honoured with gifts which were imperial in their generosity, Louis hastened after his army. The impious emperor, sullied with a new breach of faith, but relieved from fear, stayed behind, procuring for only a few days the market which was needed for a long time and never sending the guides which he had promised.

On that day the sun saw a crime which it could not endure, but, so that this crime should not seem equal to the betrayal of the Lord, half of the sun gave light to the world and only half hid itself. Thus, when the army was proceeding without the king and saw the sun shaped like half a loaf of bread for most of the day, it feared that the king, who above all others shown with faith, glowed with charity, and attained celestial heights because of hope, had been deprived of some part of his light by the treachery of the Greeks.

Odo of Deuil on the Betrayal of the Byzantines during the Second Crusade[11]

In the following selection, Odo of Deuil directly blames the deaths of many crusaders on the duplicity of the Byzantine Emperor and questions if it would not be 'easier to endure the Turk's sword than the treachery of these natives'.

…but how will a just judge, either God or man, spare the Greek Emperor, who by cunning cruelty killed so many Christians in both the German and Frankish armies? Thus, when the host of new paupers [crusaders in Antalya], succumbing to tedium, robbed of their money, and wasted with disease, learned that the Greeks had lied about the ships, they came to the king and set forth their will and their poverty to him in these words and others like them: 'O Lord King, in the presence of your majesty, we stand confused, as is right, but we dare to come because we put our trust in your goodness; for when we did not wish to march with you by land, because we believed in the Greeks, we were both lazy and deluded. But because we now feel the compulsion of poverty, we wish to make the march without our leader. We are rushing to meet death, but, if God wills us to prevail, we can avoid the death which threatens us. Perhaps it will be easier to endure the Turk's sword than the treachery of these natives after your departure. With his usual compassion the king [Louis VII] sympathised with them, and he provided for their needs with such generous largesse that you would have thought he had spent nothing heretofore…Since he wanted his subjects to be safe during their journey….'

CRITICISM OF THE CRUSADING LEADERSHIP

Unsurprisingly, the leaders of the failed Second Crusade also became the subject of criticism. The German monk and theologian Gerhoh of Reichersberg, for example, primarily blamed avarice for the failure of the Second Crusade, noting that the Christian leadership in the Holy Land had sought financial assistance from the West only to amass gold and silver, rather than to secure peace.[12] Members of the crusade leadership also blamed each other. In a letter written to the Abbot Wibald in 1148 while heading home from the Second Crusade, Conrad III attributed the failure of the crusaders to poor decisions and inaction by other members of the crusade leadership, especially local Jerusalemites.[13] The later work of William of Tyre also criticised the local leadership of the Second Crusade,[14] noting that through their strategic blunders, some had even assumed 'the role of the traitor Judas'.

THE SOURCES

Conrad III – Second Letter to Wibald, Abbot of Corvey, on the Failure of the Crusaders' Siege of Damascus, 1148[15]

The following source is a letter written by King Conrad III to the Abbot Wibald in 1148 while on his way home from the Second Crusade. Here Conrad blames the failure of the expedition on local Latin Christian rulers who were involved with the leadership of the Second Crusade.

Conrad, by the grace of God, august King of the Romans, to venerable Wibald, abbot of Corvey, his most kind greeting.

Because we know that you especially desire to hear from us and to learn the state of our prosperity, we think it fitting first to tell you of this. By God's mercy we are in good health and we have embarked in our ships to return on the festival of the blessed Virgin in September, after having accomplished in these lands all that God willed and the people of the country permitted.

Let us now speak of our troops. When following the advice of the common council we had gone to Damascus and after a great deal of trouble had pitched our camps before the gate of the city, it was certainly near being taken. But certain ones, whom we least suspected, treasonably asserted that the city was impregnable on that side and hastily led us to another position where no water could be supplied for the troops and where access was impossible to any one. And thus all, equally indignant grieved, returned, leaving the undertaking uncompleted. Nevertheless, they all promised unanimously that they would make an expedition against Ascalon, and they set the place and time. Having arrived there according to agreement, we found scarcely anyone. In vain we waited eight days for the troops. Deceived a second time, we turned to our own affairs.

In brief therefore, God willing, we shall return to you. We render to you the gratitude which you deserve for your care of our son and for the very great fidelity which you have shown to us, and with the full intention of worthily rewarding your services; we ask you to continue the same.

CRITICISM OF CRUSADES PREACHERS

Critics also targeted the clergy that supported and preached the Second Crusade. The Anonymous Annalist of Wurzburg was particularly aggressive in condemning the advocates of the expedition. Writing shortly after the failure of the Second Crusade, he referred to the preachers as 'pseudo prophets, sons of Belial, and witnesses of anti-Christ' and complained that they had 'seduced the Christians with empty words'. He noted that the effect of this preaching was 'so enormously influential that the inhabitants of nearly every region, by common vows, offered themselves freely for common destruction'. Such words might have been especially troubling for Bernard of Clairvaux, the Christian preacher most associated with the Second Crusade. His popularity and reputation for piety before the crusade did not shield him from criticism after its failure. Bernard had once stirred his listeners with powerful exhortations to take up the cross, yet once the Second Crusade had been deemed a failure, he found it necessary to defend his advocacy of the crusade. In response, the monk Geoffrey of Clairvaux, a disciple of Bernard's who had accompanied him during his preaching of the Second Crusade, wrote a spirited defence of Bernard's preaching. Geoffrey accused Bernard's critics of 'ignorance or malignity' and argued that Bernard was not the primary cause of the crusade. Geoffrey noted that Bernard had been 'commanded' by the Pope and 'urged' by the King of France to preach the crusade and prior to that he had 'refused to speak or to give his advice in the matter'. Selections from both accounts are provided here.

THE SOURCES

Criticism of the Clerical Advocates of the Second Crusade by the Anonymous Annalist of Wurzburg[16]

The comments of the Anonymous Annalist of Wurzburg in his *Annales Herbipolenses* are representative of many Western European Christians, who, in the wake of the Second Crusade, were disillusioned and embittered by its failure. Specifically, he argues that those who had preached the Second Crusade were 'witnesses of anti-Christ' and were responsible for the 'destruction' of the crusaders.

God allowed the Western church, on account of its sins, to be cast down. There arose, indeed, certain pseudo prophets, sons of Belial, and witnesses of anti-Christ, who seduced the Christians with empty words. They constrained all sorts of men, by vain preaching, to set out against the Saracens in order to liberate Jerusalem. The preaching of these men was so enormously influential that the inhabitants of nearly every region, by common vows, offered themselves freely for common destruction. Not only the ordinary people, but kings, dukes, marquises and other powerful men of this world as well, believed that they thus showed their allegiance to God. The bishops, archbishops, abbots, and other ministers and prelates of the church joined in this error, throwing themselves headlong into it to the great peril of bodies and souls....

Geoffrey of Clairvaux's Defence of Bernard of Clairvaux[17]

The following selection is a response to the type of criticism directed at preachers of the Second Crusade by the Annalist of Wurzburg and others. Specifically, in this account, Geoffrey of Clairvaux, student of Bernard of Clairvaux, provides a defence of Bernard's preaching and promotion of the Second Crusade.

We ought not to conceal the fact that certain men, through ignorance or malignity, took offence because Bernard had by his preaching stimulated the expedition for the deliverance of Jerusalem, which had such an unfortunate issue. Nevertheless we can confidently affirm that he was not the first mover in the matter. Even after the report of the unfortunate situation had already deeply stirred the souls of many, and he had been repeatedly urged by the King of France, and he had also been pressed by apostolic letters, he still refused to speak or to give his advice in the matter until the sovereign pontiff himself, in a general letter to all the faithful, had commanded him, as the natural interpreter of the Roman Church, to set forth to the peoples and their rulers the necessity of the crusade. The tenor of this letter was that both people and princes should, for the purpose of penance and the remission of their sins, betake themselves to Jerusalem, where they would either deliver their brethren or sacrifice their lives for them.

Bernard accordingly preached the expedition in the most convincing manner, with the aid of the Lord, who confirmed the truth of his servant's words by miracles. So many were the miracles, and so great, that it would be difficult to enumerate, still more to narrate them. At one time an effort was made to write them out, but the number of the prodigies to report exceeded the strength of the writer, and the grandeur of the subject, the faculties of him who had undertaken to treat it.

In short, as many as twenty sick folk, and even more, were cured of diverse ills in a single day, and hardly a day passed that similar miracles were not performed. In a word, at this time Christ permitted his servant, by his touch and his prayers, to restore sight to men who had been blind from their birth, to cause the lame to walk, to cure the paralytic, to make the deaf to hear and the dumb to speak. All these were restored to a perfection of health truly remarkable in view of that which they had previously enjoyed.

The Eastern Church was not, it is true, granted the happiness of being delivered by the expedition of which we are speaking; but at least the heavenly Church was filled thereby with pious souls and may therefore rightly rejoice. If, on this occasion, it pleased the Lord, instead of saving the bodies of eastern people from the pagans, to snatch the souls of many of the western from sin, who shall say, 'Wherefore, Lord, dost thou so?'

It happened that at the moment when the first news of the lamentable rout of the crusaders' army reached France a father came to present his blind son to the servant of God, that the boy's sight must be restored. After he had succeeded, by many prayers, in overcoming the reluctance of Bernard, the saint, laying his hands upon the child, addressed the Lord, saying that, if it were truly his word that Bernard had spread abroad when he preached the crusade, and if the Holy Spirit had really inspired him when he preached, the Most High might deign to prove this by opening the light the eyes of this blind child. While after this prayer they awaited the outcome, the child cried out, 'And what shall I do now, for I can see?' Immediately a great stir arose among those present, including not only a great number of monks, but secular persons also, who, realising that the little child could see, were greatly consoled and rendered thanks to God.

CRITICISM OF THE MORALITY OF THE CRUSADERS

In addition to the disapproval of crusading as an institution, the crusaders were also subjected to personal criticism. Crusades preachers, perhaps seeking to deflect criticism of their earlier preaching of failed crusades, pointed to the sins of the crusaders and other Christians as the source of failure. This did not begin or end with the Second Crusade, as clerical sources in the first and later crusades consistently listed sins of the crusaders among the causes of failure.[18] This position offered a twofold advantage for clerical leaders because such an argument not only offered the hope of future victory to demoralised crusaders, who through repentance could win back God's favour, but also provided a convenient explanation for failures that appeared to contradict earlier clerical claims of divine sanction for the crusade. Bernard of Clairvaux had resorted to such an explanation in his *Apologia* for the Second Crusade when he argued that God had not abandoned the crusaders; rather, the crusaders had abandoned God through their 'iniquity'.

THE SOURCES

Bernard of Clairvaux's *Apologia* for the Second Crusade[19]

The criticism of crusades preachers in the wake of the failed Second Crusade was intense enough to warrant a defiant response from Bernard of Clairvaux. Bernard was, after all, the preacher most closely associated with the promotion of the expedition. He argued that the failure of the Second Crusade was not his fault; it was instead the 'inequity' and 'evil' of other Christians that were responsible. The following selection is taken from Bernard's *De Consideration*, written in 1148.

I remember, most Holy Father Eugene, My promises made to you long ago,[20] and at long last I shall acquit myself. The delay, were I aware that it proceeded from carelessness or contempt, should cause me shame. It is not thus, however. As you know, we have fallen upon grave times, which seemed about to bring to an end not only my studies but my very life, for the Lord, provoked by our sins, gave the appearance of having judged the world prematurely,[21] with justice, indeed, but forgetful of his mercy. He spared neither his people nor his name. Do not the heathen say: 'Where is their God?' Nor do I wonder, for the sons of the Church, those who bear the label, 'Christian', have been laid low in the desert and have either been slain by the sword or consumed by famine....

We said 'Peace, and there is no peace'; we promised good things, 'and behold, trouble'. It might seem, in fact, that we acted rashly in this affair [i.e. The Second Crusade] or had 'used lightness'.[22] But, 'I did not run my course like a man in doubt of his goal',[23] for I acted on your orders, or rather on God's orders given through you....The judgements of the Lord are true indeed. Who does not know that? This judgement, however, 'is a great deep',[24] so much so, that it seems to me not unwarranted to call him blessed who is not scandalised thereat [sic]'.

How, then, does human rashness dare reprove what it can scarcely understand? Let us put down some judgements from on high, which are 'from everlasting', for there may, perhaps, be consolation in them....I speak of a matter which is unknown to no one, but of which no one now seems to be aware. Such is the human heart, indeed, that what we know when we need it not, is lost to us when it is required.

When Moses was going to lead the people out of the land of Egypt, he promised them a better land. Otherwise, would that people, who knew only earthly things, ever have followed him? He led them away – but he did not lead them into the land which he had promised them. The sad and unexpected outcome, however, cannot be laid to the rashness of the leader, for he did everything at the Lord's command, with 'the Lord aiding them and attesting his word by the miracles that went with them'.[25] But, you may say, they were a stiff-necked race,[26] forever contending against the Lord and Moses his servant. Very well, they were rebellious and unbelieving; but what about these other people [i.e. Crusaders]? Ask them. Why should it be my task to speak of what they have done? One thing I shall say: How could they make progress when they were always looking backwards as they walked? Was there a time in the whole journey when they were not in their hearts returning to Egypt? But if the Jews were vanquished and 'perished because their iniquity', is it any wonder that those who did likewise suffered a similar fate? Would anyone say that the fate of the former was contrary to God's promise? Neither, therefore, was the fate of the latter....

These few things have been said by way of apology, so that your conscience may have something from me, whereby you can hold yourself and me excused, if not in the eyes of those who judge causes from their results, then at least in your own eyes. The perfect and final apology for any man is the testimony of his own conscience. As for myself, I take it to be a small matter to be judged by those 'who call evil good, and good evil, whose darkness is light, whose light darkness'.[27]

If one or the other must be done, *I* would rather that men murmur against us than against God. It would be well for me if he deigns to use me for his shield.... I shall not refuse to be made ignominious, so long as God's glory is not attacked.

REDUCED ENTHUSIASM FOR CRUSADING

The debate over the causes of failure for the Second Crusade was itself a major cause of the decline in popular support for future crusading efforts. The success of the First Crusade had unquestionably set a favourable precedent for the calling of the Second Crusade. Pope Eugenius III had extensively cited the accomplishments of the First Crusade, in his crusading encyclical *Quantum Praedecessores* (see Chapter 4), and many crusaders joined the Second Crusade in hopes of following in their successful ancestors' footsteps. Yet the failure of the Second Crusade reversed this formula. Now the precedent for future crusades was one of failure. Popular support for crusading activities was considerably limited in the decades that followed.[28] This was through no fault of the papacy, which issued numerous crusading encyclicals during this period that received lacklustre responses.[29] It would not be until the shocking news of Saladin's successes in the Holy Land that support for a crusade would again approach the levels witnessed after the calling of the First and Second Crusades (see Chapters 6 and 7).

CHAPTER SIX
THE BATTLE OF HATTIN, 1187

95
DE EXPUGATIONE: SALADIN'S VICTORY AT HATTIN IN 1187

99
LETTER TO ARCHUMBALD ON HATTIN, 1187

101
LETTER OF PATRIARCH ERACLIUS OF JERUSALEM TO POPE URBAN III ON HATTIN, 1187

102
IBN AL-ATHIR – HOW THE SUFFERING FRANKS ENDED UP AT HATTIN IN 1187

104
BEHA ED-DIN – ACCOUNT OF THE BATTLE OF HATTIN IN 1187

The Horns of Hattin marked the greatest defeat in crusading history.... In one disastrous battle, the Kingdom of Jerusalem had lost not only its ability to wage war but also its power to defend itself.

– Thomas Madden[1]

THE SIGNIFICANCE OF THE CRUSADERS' LOSS AT HATTIN

Modern historians uniformly point to the victory of the battle of Hattin as one of the most important Muslim victories of the crusading era. It was then that a force under the leadership of Saladin annihilated the Christian army of Jerusalem. In the immediate wake of the battle, Christians feared for the fate of Jerusalem, as now little would stand in Saladin's way when he turned his attention to the Holy City. Their concerns proved valid as only four months later, the Christian leadership of Jerusalem surrendered the city to Saladin.[2]

BACKGROUND TO THE BATTLE OF HATTIN

In the years leading up to the battle of Hattin on July 4, 1187, Latin Christians in the Holy Land were no longer focused on expansion, but instead on protecting those places under their control. They received little support from the West following the demoralising failure of the Second Crusade.[3] Nor was the Christian Byzantine Empire of much help to Latin Christians, as at this point, the two sides were openly hostile to each other.[4] As a result, Latin Christians in the Holy Land were effectively alone in facing the growing threat of increasingly powerful Islamic armies united by the ideology of jihad. For their defence, Latin Christians in the East turned primarily to the dedicated and powerful military orders. The two most important orders were the Knights Templar and the Knights Hospitallers, who by the time of the battle of Hattin had won great respect for their fighting abilities, from friend and foe alike. Indeed, few had greater concerns about their effectiveness in battle than the Sultan Salah al-Din Yusuf, better known to the crusaders as Saladin.

Although of Kurdish origins, Saladin had controlled both Egypt and Damascus since 1174, which ensured that the divisions that had plagued the Muslim world during the First Crusade no longer crippled their military efforts.[5] Consequently, Saladin could increasingly focus on expelling the crusaders from the Holy Land and held the conquest of the Holy City of Jerusalem as among his chief goals.[6] Saladin's primary Christian opponents at the time of the battle of Hattin included the Christian noble Raynald of Chatillon and Guy de Lusignan, the King of Jerusalem. When Guy came to power, Saladin was at the zenith of his career and was looking for a reason to invalidate an earlier truce he had made with Christians during a devastating drought in 1185. Raynald of Chatillon gave such an opportunity when he attacked a large Muslim caravan headed for Egypt in 1187. Saladin viewed this provocation as a justification to resume his quest to conquer Jerusalem. In doing so he devised and executed a plan for an offensive on the Christian stronghold of Tiberius, which he hoped would draw the otherwise careful army of Jerusalem to their aid. His plan was successful, as Christians under the command of Guy de Lusignan soon marched to relieve Tiberius. As was customary, they brought their most precious relic, a fragment of the true cross discovered in Jerusalem in 1099.

THE BATTLE OF HATTIN

Saladin divided his roughly 30 thousand troops and deployed the smaller division to attack Tiberius on 2 July 1187, but held back the bulk of his forces six miles away at Kafr Sabt to await the Christian forces who would began their march the next day. Tiberius fell quickly, while elements of Saladin's main force moved into position behind the approaching Christian army. This proved to be an important strategic move as the Christian army was then cut off from any water supply and unable to retreat. The Christians finally took up a defensive position on a hill with two peaks known as the Horns of Hattin. The Muslims then attacked the hill from all sides, while the demoralised defenders, weakened by their thirst, fought with little spirit. Some of the Christian rearguard, including its leader Balian of Ibelin (see Chapter 7), was able to escape, but the vast majority of the exhausted Christian army was captured after surrendering on July 4.

The most important Latin Christian army in the region had been devastated. Of the roughly 20,000 Christians that fought at Hattin, perhaps only a few thousand evaded capture or death. Saladin captured King Guy, as well as the masters of the Templars and Hospitallers. He had the defeated Christian leadership brought before him and offered a cup of cooled and sweetened water to King Guy.[7] Yet when Guy passed the cup to Raynald of Chatillon, a man Saladin had sworn to kill, Raynald was immediately executed, possibly by Saladin himself. Then Saladin dipped his hands into Raynald's blood and smeared it on his face as a sign that he had taken his vengeance.[8] Two days later, hundreds of captive Templars and Hospitallers were presented with the choice of conversion to Islam or death. Almost all of the defenceless knights chose death.[9]

BACKGROUND TO THE SOURCES

Because of his access to first-hand accounts, the anonymous author of *De Expugatione Terrae Sanctae per Saladinum* provides what at least one modern historian has suggested is the 'single most important' Christian account of the battle at Hattin.[10] He lived in the Holy Land and claims to have been present at Jerusalem when it fell under siege by Saladin's forces. As a result, the author was well positioned to know of the events at Hattin, as news of the loss was quickly brought by Christian survivors to the terrified residents of Jerusalem. Recognising the significance of the destruction of the main Christian army at Hattin, the citizens of Jerusalem immediately began to prepare for a defence of the Holy City. The *De Expugatione* provides abundant details about the leadership of the Christian army at Hattin and the key events leading to its defeat. The author ultimately attributes the Christians' loss to poor decisions by the Christian leadership that allowed Saladin's forces to outmanoeuvre them and prevent the army from reaching water, which of course left the thirsting crusaders with little choice but to surrender. Of particular interest is the author's fascination with the fate of the relic of the 'true cross' that the crusaders carried into battle with them and was lost to Saladin. This is presented in such a way that it seems to be nearly as great a tragedy as the destruction of the army.

Immediately following Saladin's victory at Hattin, news of the loss of Christians was spread by letters in the Holy Land and Europe, many of which sought help from the West. One anonymous letter addressed to Archumbald, master of the Hospitallers in Italy, provides considerable details of the battle and appears to have been written before news of the surrender of Ascalon in early September 1187.[11] The author inflates the size of Saladin's army to 80,000, as opposed to only 30,000 (other estimates are around 20,000) Christian soldiers and alludes to the sufferings of the poorly provisioned crusaders from the heat of fires set around their camp by their Muslim opponents. He describes how this was the cause of betrayal by six Christian knights who sought relief from their sufferings by renouncing their faith and informing Saladin of the pitiful state of the Christian army. Another letter written by Eraclius (1128–1191), the Latin Patriarch of Jerusalem, to Pope Urban III conveys a much greater sense of fear for the future of Latin Christians in the Holy Land, following the disastrous events at Hattin. The author's primary concern is for the fate of Jerusalem and implores the Pope to stir sympathy in the West for the plight of Latin Christians in the East in hopes of procuring immediate aid. The letter was written sometime between 5 September and 20 September 1187.[12]

Finally, there are two valuable Arab accounts of the battle of Hattin. The first is by the historian Ibn al-Athir (1160–1233), who may even have served under Saladin during the Third Crusade as he was only 27 years old at the time of the battle of Hattin and at an appropriate age for military service.[13] His account details the sufferings of the Franks from thirst, their efforts to reach water and how they ended up trapped on the hills of Hattin, where they made their final stand. Also of interest is Ibn al-Athir's comment on the Muslim capture of the true cross. Like the anonymous author of the *De Expugatione*, he stresses the demoralising effect the capture of the true cross seemed to have had on the Christians and notes that this capture was 'one of the heaviest blows that could be inflicted on them and made their death and destruction certain'. The second Arab account is by Beha ad Din Ibn Shaddad (1145–1234), who began his service under Saladin in 1188 and remained a faithful member of Saladin's court until Saladin's death in 1193. As a result, Beha ad Din was exceptionally well positioned as a source on Saladin and the Muslim perspective of the Third Crusade and the events that led to it. Consequently, his work, *The Rare and Excellent History of Saladin*, is perhaps the best contemporary source on the life of Saladin. The selection provided here gives the most detailed Muslim account of the tactics used to defeat the Christian army at Hattin, as well as the enslavement of thousands of surviving Christian prisoners. Of particular interest is his description of Saladin's treatment of the captive Christian leadership, especially King Guy and his sworn enemy Raynald of Chatillon.

THE SOURCES

De Expugatione: Saladin's Victory at Hattin in 1187[14]

The following selection is from the anonymous Christian author of the *De Expugatione Terrae Sanctae per Saladinum*. The author lived in the Holy Land at the time of Saladin's victory at Hattin and was present in Jerusalem when it was captured in 1187. As a result, he would have had access to first-hand accounts of events at Hattin from survivors streaming into Jerusalem after the battle. He ultimately attributes the Muslim victory to poor decisions by the Christian leadership that allowed Saladin's forces to outmanoeuvre them and prevent them from reaching water.

In the year of the Lord's incarnation 1187, the King of Syria[15] gathered together an army as numerous as the sands of the seashore in order to wage war on the land of Juda. He came up to the Jaulan, across the [Jordan] River, and there made camp.

The King of Jerusalem[16] also gathered his army from all of Judea and Samaria. They assembled and pitched camp near the springs at Saffuriyah. The Templars and Hospitallers also assembled many people from all their castles and came to the camp. The Count of Tripoli[17] likewise rose up with all his people, whom he collected from Tripoli and Galilee and came into the encampment. Prince Reginald of Montreal[18] also came with his people, as did Balian of Naples[19] with his, Reginald of Sidon[20] with his, and the lord of Caesarea in Palestine[21] with his. Not a man fit for war remained in the cities, towns, or castles without being urged to leave by the King's order. Nor was this host sufficient. Indeed, the King of England's treasure was opened up and they gave a fee to everyone who could bear a lance or bow into battle.[22] The army was quite large: 1,200 knights, innumerable Turcopoles,[23] and 18,000 or more infantry. They gloried in their multitude of men, the trappings of their horses, in their breastplates, helmets, lances, and golden shields, but they did not believe in God, nor did they hope in the salvation of him who is the protector and saviour of Israel. Rather, they were taken up with their own thoughts and became vain.

They sent to Jerusalem to ask the Patriarch to bring the Holy Cross with him to the camp…so that they might become bearers and keepers of the Lord's cross.…[24] Meanwhile, the Syrians crossed the Jordan. They overran and laid waste the area around the springs of Cresson, from Tiberias to Bethany...up to Nazareth and around Mount Tabor. Since they found the region deserted by men, who had fled out of fear of them, they set fire to the threshing floors and put everything they found into the flames. The whole region flamed in front of them like a ball of fire. Not satisfied even with this, they ascended the holy mount to the sacred spot on which our Saviour, after the appearance of Moses and Elias, showed his disciples Peter, James, and John the glory of the future resurrection in his transfiguration. The Saracens defiled this place....

After these advance parties had wrought their destruction, Saladin and his whole army crossed the river. Saladin ordered his forces to push on to Tiberias and besiege it. On Thursday, July 2, the city was surrounded by archers and the battle was joined. The Countess[25] and the Galileans, since the city was not fortified, sent messengers to the count and king with the news: 'The Turks have surrounded the city. In the fighting, they have pierced the walls and are just now entering against us. Send help at once or we shall be taken and made captive.'

The Syrians fought and won. When the Galileans saw they could not hold out, they yielded the ramparts and the city. They fled before the pagans into the castle, though the city was taken and burned. But since the King of Egypt [Saladin] heard that the Christian army was approaching against him, he was unable to besiege the castle. He said: 'So be it! They are my prisoners.'

Towards evening on Thursday, July 2, the King of Jerusalem, after he had heard the Galileans' letter, called together all the leaders of the army so that they might give council concerning the action to be taken. They all advised that at dawn they should march out, accompanied by the Lord's cross, ready to fight the enemy, with all the men armed and arrayed in battle formation. Thus arrayed they would relieve the city of Tiberias. The Count of Tripoli, when he heard this, spoke: 'Tiberias is my city and my wife is there. None of you is so fiercely attached, save to Christianity, as I am to the city. None of you is so desirous as I am to succour or aid Tiberias. We and the King, however, should not move away from water, food, and other necessities to lead such a multitude of men to death from solitude, hunger, thirst and scorching heat. You are well aware that since the heat is searing and the number of people is large, they could not survive half a day without an abundance of water. Furthermore, they could not reach the enemy without suffering a great shortage of water, accompanied by the destruction of men and of beasts. Stay, therefore, at this midway point, close to food and water, for certainly the Saracens have risen to such heights of pride that when they have taken the city, they will not turn aside to left or right, but will head straight through the vast solitude to us and challenge us to battle. Then our men, refreshed and filled with bread and water, will cheerfully set out from camp for the fray. We and our horses will be fresh; we will be aided and protected by the Lord's cross. Thus we will fight mightily against an unbelieving people who will be wearied by thirst and who will have no place to refresh themselves. Thus you see that if, in truth, the grace of Jesus Christ remains with us, the enemies of Christ's cross, before they can get to the sea or return to the river, will be taken captive or else killed by sword, by lance, or by thirst. But if, which God forbid, things were perchance to go against us, we have our ramparts here to which we could flee....' But the saying of wisdom: 'Woe to the land whose King is a child and whose citizens dine in the morning' was fulfilled in them.[26] For our young King followed youthful counsel, while our citizens, in hatred and jealousy, ate their neighbours' meat. They departed from the advice which would have saved them and others. Because of their foolishness and simple-mindedness they lost land, people, and selves.

On Friday, July 3, therefore, they marched out by troops, leaving behind the necessities of life. The Count of Tripoli was in the first rank, as befitted his dignity. The others followed on his left or right, according to the custom of the realm. The royal battalion and the battalion of the Holy Cross followed and, because of the lay of the land, the Templars came last, for they were the army's rearguard. They marched to Saffuriyah so that, as was said before, they could go on to Tiberias. Three miles from the city, they came to a hamlet called Marescallia. At this place they were so constrained by enemy attacks and by thirst that they wished to go no further.

They were going to pass through a confined, rocky area in order to reach the Sea of Galilee, which was a mile away. For this reason the count sent word to the King: 'We must hurry and pass through this area, so that we and our men may be safe near the water. Otherwise we will be in danger of making camp at a waterless spot.' The King replied: 'We will pass through at once.'

The Turks were meanwhile attacking the army's rear, so that the Templars and the others in the rear were barely able to struggle on. Suddenly the King (a punishment for sin) ordered the tents to be pitched. Thus were we betrayed to our death. The count, when he looked back and saw the tents pitched, exclaimed: 'Alas, Lord God, the battle is over! We have been betrayed unto death. The Kingdom is finished!' And so, in sorrow and anguish, they camped on a dry site where, during the night, there flowed more blood than water. The sons of Esau [the Muslim army] surrounded the people of God and set fire to the desert [brush] round about them. Throughout the night the hungry and thirsty men were harassed further by arrows and by the fire's heat and flames.... That night God indeed gave them the bread of tears to eat and the wine of compunction to drink.

At length...after the clouds of death had opened, light dawned on a day of sorrow and tribulation, of grief and destruction. When day had dawned, the King of Syria forsook the city of Tiberias and with his whole army came up to the camping ground to give battle to the Christians. He now prepared to attack our men. Our men formed their battle lines and hurried to pass through this region in the hope that when they had regained a watering place and had refreshed themselves, they could attack and fight the foe more vigorously. The count moved out to take the spot which the Turks had already begun to approach.

When our men were arrayed and grouped in battle formation, the infantry were ordered to take positions facing the enemy's arrows, so that the infantry would be protected from an enemy charge by the knights' lances. Thus, with each providing protection for the other, they would both be safe. By this time the Saracens had already arrived. The infantry, banded together in a single wedge shaped formation, clambered at full speed to the very summit of a high mountain, leaving the army to its fate. The King, the Bishop and others sent word, begging them to return to defend the Lord's cross, the heritage of the Crucified, the Lord's army and themselves. They replied: 'We are not coming because we are dying of thirst and we will not fight.' Again the command was given, and again they persisted in their refusal.

The Templars, Hospitallers and Turcopoles, meanwhile, were engaged in a fierce rearguard action. They could not win, however, because enemies sprang up on every side, shooting arrows and wounding Christians. When they had gone on for a little bit, they shouted to the King, asking for some help. The King and the others saw that the infantry were not going to return and that they themselves could not hold out against the Turkish arrows without the sergeants. Accordingly, by the grace of the Lord's cross, they ordered the tents to be put up, in order to block the Saracen charges and so that they could hold out more easily. The battle formations were, therefore, broken up. The units gathered around the Holy Cross, where they were confused and intermixed here and there. The men who were with the Count of Tripoli in the first group saw that the King, the Hospitallers, the Templars and everyone else were jumbled together and mingled with the Turks. They also saw that there was a multitude of the barbarians between themselves and the King, so that they could not get through to return to the Lord's cross. They cried out: 'Those who can get through may go, since the battle is not going in our favour. We have now lost even the chance to flee.' Meanwhile, thousands and thousands of Syrians were charging at the Christians, shooting arrows and killing them.

In the meantime, the Bishop of Acre, the bearer of the Lord's cross, was mortally wounded. He passed on the task of bearing the cross to the Bishop of Lydda. A large group of pagans charged on the infantry and pitched them from the top of the steep mountain to whose summit they had previously fled. They destroyed the rest, taking some captive and killing others....

Upon seeing this, the count and his men, who had been riding onwards, together with Balian of Naples, Reginald of Sidon and the other half-castes, turned back. The speed of their horses in this confined space trampled down the Christians and made a kind of bridge, giving the riders a level path. In this manner they got out of that narrow place by fleeing over their own men, over the Turks, and over the cross. Thus it was that they escaped with only their lives.

The Saracens gathered around the Lord's wooden cross, the King, and the rest, and destroyed the church. What more can be said? The Saracens triumphed over the Christians and did with them as they pleased.... What can I say? It would be more fitting to weep and wail than to say anything. Alas! Should I describe with impure lips how the precious wood of the Lord, our redeemer, was seized by the damnable hands of the damned? Woe to me that in the days of my miserable life I should be forced to see such things....

The next day Prince Reginald of Montreal was killed. The Templars and Hospitallers were ransomed from the other Turks and were killed. Saladin gave orders that the Countess and the men who were in the citadel of Tiberias might leave the fort and that, having accepted the security of life, they might go in peace where they wished. Thus it was done. The city was relinquished. Saladin moved in. After the citadel had been fortified, he went to Saffuriyah. On the site where the Christian army had formerly camped, the King of Syria ordered his tents to be pitched.... He remained there for several days, gleefully celebrating the victory. He divided the heritage of the Crucified, not among the heirs, but rather among his execrable emirs and leaders, giving to each his proper portion.

Letter to Archumbald on Hattin, 1187[27]

Immediately following Saladin's victory at Hattin, news of the loss was spread by letters in the Holy Land and Europe. Provided here is the text of one such letter by an anonymous author addressed to Archumbald, master of the Hospitallers in Italy. Based on the details of the letter, the author was likely an eyewitness to at least some of the events he describes or had access to first-hand information.

We shall tell you, Lord Archumbald, master of the Hospitallers of Italy and the brothers about everything that has taken place in the lands beyond the seas.

You must know that the King of Jerusalem was at Saffuriya around the feast of the Apostles Peter and Paul (29 June) with a huge army of at least 30,000 men. He had been properly reconciled with the count of Tripoli, and the count was with him in the army. And behold, Saladin, the pagan king, came against Tiberias with 80,000 cavalry and captured it. The King of Jerusalem was informed, and he moved from Saffuriya and went with his men against Saladin. Saladin attacked them at Meskenah on the Friday after the feast of the Apostles Peter and Paul (3 July). Battle was joined, and for the whole day they fought bitterly. But night put an end to the strife. With the coming of night, the King of Jerusalem pitched his tents near Lubiyah, and next day – the Saturday – he set off with his army. At around the third hour the master of the Temple charged with all his brothers. They received no assistance, and God allowed most of them to be lost. After that the king with his army forced his way with great difficulty to a point about a league from Nimrin, and there the count of Tripoli came to him and had him pitch his tents near a mountain that is like a castle. They could only get three tents up. Once the Turks saw them marking out their defences, they lit fires round the king's army, and so great was the heat that the roasting horses could neither eat nor drink. At this point Baldwin of Fatinor, Bachaberboeus of Tiberias and Leisius, with three other companions, separated themselves from the army and went to Saladin and, sad to say, renounced their faith. They surrendered themselves and told him the situation in the King of Jerusalem's army and its dire condition. Thereupon Saladin sent Taqi al-Din against us with 20,000 chosen knights. They charged at the Christian army, and from nones until vespers the fighting was most bitter. As a consequence of our sins many of our men were killed, and the Christians were defeated. The king was captured and the Holy Cross. So too were Count Gabula, Miles of Colaverdo, Humphrey the Younger [of Toron], Prince Reynald who was captured and killed, Walter of Arsur, Hugh of Jubail, the lord of Botron and the lord of Maraclea. A thousand more of the better men were captured and killed, with the result that no more than 200 of the knights or foot soldiers escaped.

Letter of Patriarch Eraclius of Jerusalem to Pope Urban III on Hattin, 1187[28]

Provided here is a letter written by Eraclius, the Latin Patriarch of Jerusalem, to Pope Urban III, seeking aid for Latin Christians in the Holy Land after the battle of Hattin. It conveys the author's sense of fear for Latin Christian settlements in the Holy Land, especially the Holy City of Jerusalem, in the wake of Saladin's success at Hattin. Eraclius no doubt based his account on what he had learned from survivors of the battle of Hattin, many of whom had fled to Jerusalem in the wake of their defeat.

To his most holy lord and father, Urban, supreme pontiff of the most holy Roman church and universal pope. Eraclius, by the permission of God, miserable patriarch of the Church of the Holy Resurrection of Christ, greetings and most dutiful service in due subjection.

The enormity of our lamentations and sorrow, Reverend Father, we are scarcely able to convey to your piety's ears. It has fallen to us to see in our days the oppression of our people, the doleful and lamentable desolation of the holy church of Jerusalem and that which is holy given unto dogs. Truly, Holy Father, the anger of the Lord has come upon us and His terrors have put us to confusion. His displeasure drains my spirit, while He has added sorrow to our sorrow. He has allowed the most holy and life giving cross, once and only given for our salvation, to be captured by the Turks, and our venerable brothers, the bishops of Lydda and Acre who were in its service, the one to be captured, the other to die on the field of battle. Also He has given over our king and the whole Christian army into the hand of pagans, and of all those who were in the battle, some have fallen by the sword, some have been led off into captivity and just a few have escaped by means of flight. Nor are these things enough to satiate the barbarity of the enemies of the cross of Christ. Indeed, striving to blot out the Christian name from under heave, they have captured and brought under their dominion the cities and castles of the Holy Land, namely Jubail, Beirut, Sidon, Acre, Tiberias, Nazareth, Sebastea, Nablus, Haifa, Caesarea, Arsur, Jaffa, Ascalon, Lydda, Ibelin, Toron, Mirabel, Bethlehem and Hebron, and have killed almost all the inhabitants by the edge of the sword. Alas, alas, O Reverend Father, that the Holy Land, the inheritance of the Crucified, should be given into the hands of pagans. Alas, alas that the Lord has thrown away His inheritance and has not spared it, withholding His mercy behind his anger. Your piety should consider and see whether there is any sorrow like unto our sorrow, and should grieve for the love of the Crucified one and ourselves in accordance with the magnitude of our grief. For the Holy City of Jerusalem, which formerly was wont to have dominion far and wide over the neighbouring lands, now allows unrestricted exit beyond the walls to none of its inhabitants, as it and Tyre alone remain. But now that we find ourselves in this final and dreaded moment of our need, unless the Day-spring from on high according to the multitude of His mercies shall have visited us, and unless your fatherhood shall have compassion and, through the sending of letters and your own envoys, shall have stirred all the princes of the west to bring aid speedily to the Holy Land, we despair of being able to defend these cities at all by ourselves for half a year. Your holiness may know for certain that if the Turks, having now recently won the battle, were to come to the Holy City, they would find it devoid of all human defence. Therefore, although there remains no other refuge for us apart from God, we have recourse to bring our afflictions and intolerable miseries tearfully to the feet of your holiness, like sons to their father, like the shipwrecked to a haven, that out of your paternal affection your heart may be roused on our behalf and on behalf of the Holy City of Jerusalem. By this your supporting protection may the Lord be appeased for his inheritance, and may He redeem our life from death. By your counsel and aid may the Lord send us quickly what is to be sent to alleviate the needs of His land and to destroy the persecutions of the enemy that most violently afflicts it. Now Saladin in overrunning the whole land is near Jerusalem, and daily we are expecting him to come and lay siege to it. He has occupied all the archbishoprics and bishoprics of our patriarchate apart from Tyre and Petra.

Ibn al-Athir – How the Suffering Franks Ended Up at Hattin in 1187[29]

The following selection is from the Arab historian Ibn al-Athir's account of the battle at Hattin. As a young man, the author served under Saladin at the time and thus provides extensive details of the sufferings of the Franks from thirst, their efforts to reach water and how they ended up trapped on the hills of Hattin where they made their final stand amid the taunts of their Muslim opponents.

When Saladin received the news he ordered his army to withdraw from its position near Tiberias; his only reason for besieging Tiberias was to make the Franks abandon their position and offer battle. The Muslims went down to the water (of the lake). The water was blazingly hot and the Franks, who were suffering greatly from thirst, were prevented by the Muslims from reaching the water. They had drained all the local cisterns, but could not turn back for fear of the Muslims. So they passed that night tormented with thirst. The Muslims for their part had lost their first fear of the enemy and were in high spirits, and spent the night inciting one another to battle. They could smell victory in the air, and the more they saw of the unexpectedly low morale of the Franks the more aggressive and daring they became; throughout the night the cries Allah akbar (God is great) and 'there is no God but Allah' rose up to heaven. Meanwhile the sultan was deploying the vanguard of archers and distributing the arrows.

On Saturday 24 rabi' II/4 July 1187 Saladin and the Muslims mounted their horses and advanced on the Franks. They too were mounted, and the two armies came to blows. The Franks were suffering badly from thirst, and had lost confidence. The battle raged furiously, both sides putting up a tenacious resistance. The Muslim archers sent up clouds of arrows like thick swarms of locusts, killing many of the Frankish horses. The Franks, surrounding themselves with their infantry, tried to fight their way towards Tiberias in the hope of reaching water, but Saladin realised their objective and forestalled them by planting himself and his army in the way. He himself rode up and down the Muslim lines encouraging and restraining his troops where necessary. The whole army obeyed his commands and respected his prohibitions. One of his young mamluks led a terrifying charge on the Franks and performed prodigious feats of valour until he was overwhelmed by numbers and killed, when all the Muslims charged the enemy lines and almost broke through, slaying many Franks in the process. The count saw that the situation was desperate and realised that he could not withstand the Muslim army, so by agreement with his companions he charged the lines before him. The commander of that section of the Muslim army was Taqi ad-Din 'Umar, Saladin's nephew. When he saw that the Franks charging his lines were desperate and that they were going to try to break through, he sent orders for a passage to be made for them through the ranks.

One of the volunteers had set fire to the dry grass that covered the ground; it took fire and the wind carried the heat and smoke down on to the enemy. They had to endure thirst, the summer's heat, the blazing fire and smoke and the fury of battle. When the count fled the Franks lost heart and were on the verge of surrender, but seeing that the only way to save their lives was to defy death they made a series of charges that almost dislodged the Muslims from their position in spite of their numbers, had not the grace of God been with them. As each wave of attackers fell back they left their dead behind them; their numbers diminished rapidly, while the Muslims were all around them like a circle about its diameter. The surviving Franks made for a hill near Hittin [a town near the hills of Hattin], where they hoped to pitch their tents and defend themselves. They were vigorously attacked from all sides and prevented from pitching more than one tent, that of the King. The Muslims captured their great cross, called the 'True Cross', in which they say is a piece of the wood upon which, according to them, the Messiah was crucified. This was one of the heaviest blows that could be inflicted on them and made their death and destruction certain. Large numbers of their cavalry and infantry were killed or captured. The King stayed on the hillside with five hundred of the most gallant and famous knights.

Beha ed-Din – Account of the Battle of Hattin in 1187[30]

The following selection by Beha ed-Din provides the most detailed Muslim account of the tactics used to defeat Christian army at Hattin as well as the enslavement of thousands of surviving Christian prisoners. Also of interest is his description of Saladin's treatment of the captive Christian leadership, especially King Guy and his sworn enemy Raynald of Chatillon. Although Beha ed-Din did not begin his service under Saladin until a year after the events at Hattin, he was a member of the sultan's court and had extensive access to first-hand information.

The sultan believed that it was his duty, above all things, to devote his whole strength to fulfil the command we have received to war against the infidels, in recognition of God's mercy in establishing his dominion, in making him master of so many lands, and granting him the obedience and devotion of his people. Therefore he sent an order to all his troops to join him at Ashtera. When he had mustered and reviewed them…he made his dispositions, and marched full speed upon the enemy's territory – may God confound their hopes! – on the 17th of the month Rabi'a II (June 26, 1187). He used always to attack the enemy on a Friday, at the hour of prayer, believing that the prayers that the preachers were offering from their pulpits at that time would bring him good luck, because their petitions that day were generally granted. At this hour, then, he began his march, holding his army in readiness to fight. He heard that the Franks, having received intelligence of his mustering of troops, had assembled in the plain of Seffuria, in the territory of Acre, and meant to come out and meet him and give him battle. He therefore took up a position close to the Sea of Tiberias, hard by a village called es-Sennabra. He next encamped on the top of the hill that lies to the west of Tiberias. There he remained ready for battle, thinking that the Franks would advance and attack him as soon as they had ascertained his movements; but they did not stir from their position. It was on Wednesday, the 21st of this same month (June 30th, 1187), that the sultan pitched his camp there.

Seeing that the enemy [was] not moving, he left his infantry drawn up opposite the enemy and went down to Tiberias with troops of light cavalry. He attacked that city and carried it by assault within an hour, devoting it to slaughter, burning, and sacking. All that were left of the inhabitants were taken prisoner. The castle alone held out. When the enemy heard the fate of Tiberias, they were forced to break through their policy of inaction, to satisfy this call upon their honour, and they set out for Tiberias forthwith to drive the invaders back. The pickets of the Moslem army discerned their movement, and sent an express to inform the sultan. When he received this message he detached a sufficient force to blockade the castle, and then rejoined the army with his suite. The two armies met on the summit of the hill to the west of Tiberias. This was on the evening of Thursday, the 22nd of the same month. Darkness separated the combatants, who passed the night under arms in order of battle, until the following day, Friday, the 23rd (July 2, 1187). Then the warriors of both armies mounted their steeds and charged their opponents; the soldiers in the vanguard discharged their arrows; and the infantry came into action and fought furiously. This took place in the territory belonging to a village called Lubia. The Franks saw they must bite the dust, and came on as though driven to certain death; before them lay disaster and ruin, and they were convinced that the next day would find them numbered amongst the dead. The fight raged obstinately; every horseman hurled himself against his opponent until victory was secured, and destruction fell upon the infidels. Night with its blackness put an end to the battle.

Terrible encounters took place that day; never in the history of the generations that haves gone have such feats of arms been told. The night had been spent under arms, each side thinking every moment that they would be attacked. The Muslims, knowing that behind them lay the Jordan, and in front the territory of the enemy, felt that God alone was able to save them. God, having granted His aid to the Muslims, gave them success, and sent them victory according to His decree. Their infantry charged from all sides; the centre came on like one man, uttering a mighty cry; |God filled the hearts of the infidels with terror (for He has said), 'Due from Us it was to help the believers.' The count (Raymond of Tripoli), the most intelligent man of that race, and famous for his keenness of perception, seeing signs of the catastrophe impending over his brothers in religion, was not prevented by thoughts of honour from taking measures for his personal safety. He fled in the beginning of the action, before the fighting had become serious, and set out in the direction of Tyre. Several Muslims started in pursuit of him, but he succeeded in evading them; true believers had nothing thereafter to fear from his cunning.

The upholders of Islam surrounded the upholders of infidelity and impiety on every side, overwhelming them with arrows and harassing them with their swords. One body of the enemy took to flight, but they were pursued by the Moslem warriors, and not one of the fugitives escaped. Another band climbed Hattin hill, so called from the name of a village, near which is the tomb of the holy patriarch Shu'aib (Jethro). The Muslims hemmed them in, and lighted fires all around them, so that, tortured by thirst and reduced to the last extremity, they gave themselves up to escape death. Their leaders were taken captive, and the rest were killed or made prisoners. Among the leaders who surrendered were King Guy,[31] the King's brother, Raynald of Chatillon,[32] Lord of el-Kerak, and of esh-Shobek, the son of el-Honferi,[33] the son of the Lord of Tiberias,[34] the chief of the Templars, the Lord of Jibeil, and the chief of the Hospitallers. The others who were missing had met their death; and as to the common people, some were killed and others taken captive. Of their whole army, none remained alive, except the prisoners. More than one of their chief leaders accepted captivity to save his life. A man, whom I believe to be reliable, told me that he saw one soldier in the Hauran leading more than thirty prisoners, tied together with a tent cord. He had taken them all himself, so great had been the panic caused by their defeat.

We will here narrate the fate of those leaders who escaped with their lives. The count, who had fled, reached Tripoli, and was there, by the grace of God, carried off by pleurisy. The Hospitallers and Templars the sultan resolved to execute, and he spared not a single one. Salah ed-Din had sworn to put Raynald of Chatillon to death if he ever fell into his hands, and the reason he took that oath is this: A caravan coming from Egypt, and taking advantage of the truce, went quite close to esh-Shobek, where the prince then happened to be. Thinking there was nothing to fear, they halted in the neighbourhood of the place; but this man set upon them, in defiance of his oath, and killed (a number) of them. The travellers in vain besought him for mercy in the name of God, telling him there was a treaty of peace between him and the Muslims. He only answered by insulting the Holy Prophet. When the sultan heard what he had done, he was compelled by the Faith and by his determination to protect his people to swear to take this man's life whenever he should fall into his power.

After God had granted him this victory, he stayed at the entrance of his tent (for the tent itself was not yet set up), and there he sat to receive his soldiers, who came to win his approval of their services, bringing the prisoners they had made and the leaders they had found. As soon as the tent was pitched the sultan went to sit within, full of joy and gratitude for the favour which God had just granted him. He then commanded King Guy, and his brother, and Raynald of Chatillon, to be brought. He gave a bowl of sherbet made with iced rose-water to the King, who was suffering severely from thirst. Geoffrey drank part of it, and then offered the bowl to Raynald of Chatillon. The sultan said to the interpreter: 'Tell the King that it is he, and not I, who is giving this man to drink.' He had adopted the admirable and generous custom of the Arabs, who grant life to the captive who has eaten or drunk of their viands. He then ordered his men to take them to a place prepared for their reception, and, after they had eaten, he summoned them again to his presence. He had only a few servants at that time in his tent. He seated the King at the entrance, then summoned the prince [Raynald], and reminded him of what he had said, adding: 'Behold, I will support Muhammad against thee!' He then called upon him to embrace Islam, and, on his refusal, drew his sabre and struck him a blow which severed his arm from the shoulder. Those who were present quickly dispatched the prisoner, and God hurled his soul into hell. The corpse was dragged out and thrown down at the entrance of the tent. When the King saw the way in which his fellow-captive had been treated, he thought he was to be the second victim; but the sultan had him brought into the tent and calmed his fears. 'It is not the want of kings,' said he, 'to kill kings; but that man had transgressed all bounds, and therefore did I treat him thus.' The conquerors spent that night in rejoicings; every voice chanted praise to God, and on all sides rose cries of 'Allah Akbar!'[35] and 'La ilalha il Allah!'[36] till dawn.

CHAPTER SEVEN
SALADIN'S CONQUEST OF JERUSALEM, 1187

113
THE LETTER OF TERRICIUS, MASTER OF THE TEMPLE, ON THE CAPTURE OF THE LAND OF JERUSALEM

114
DE EXPUGATIONE: SALADIN'S SIEGE OF JERUSALEM IN 1187

117
BEHA ED-DIN – SALADIN'S SIEGE OF JERUSALEM IN 1187

119
IBN AL-ATHIR – NEGOTIATIONS FOR THE SURRENDER OF JERUSALEM, SEPTEMBER 1187

The news of the catastrophe at Hattin and the fall of Jerusalem reached the West in the early autumn of 1187. The old pope, Urban III, died, it was said of grief....

– Jonathan Riley-Smith[1]

THE SIEGE AND CONQUEST OF JERUSALEM

Only a few days after their victory at Hattin, Saladin's envoys began successful negotiations for the surrender of the crusader stronghold of Acre and the release of 4,000 Muslim slaves.[2] In the weeks that followed, Saladin's forces also took control of the various outlying provinces of the Latin Kingdom of Jerusalem, often with the help of local Muslims and Jews, who rose in revolt against local Christian authorities.[3] By the end of the campaign, more than 20,000 Muslim slaves or prisoners had been set free while Saladin's men took a much greater number of Latin Christians captive.[4] In August, Saladin's forces swept through southern Palestine and took control of the remaining Latin towns and fortifications they encountered on their way to Jerusalem.

The Christian inhabitants knew that Saladin was coming and had plenty of time to consider their options before his arrival.[5] They essentially had three options. First, they could flee the city before Saladin's forces arrived. Second, they could surrender the city in the hope of favourable terms. Third, they could fight to defend the city. In one sense, they chose all three options, as many of those who could flee the city before the attack did so, while those who remained behind fought hard enough in defending the city to win favourable terms for its surrender. Indeed, those who remained scoured the region for supplies as they awaited Saladin's approach. The Patriarch Heraclius and Queen Sibylla were in charge of the Holy City, but they knew little about fighting much less defending a city under siege. Yet Christian spirits were no doubt raised with the arrival of the noble Balian of Ibelin. He initially planned only to collect his family members and leave, but he was urged by the city's residents to take command of the defence, to which he ultimately agreed.[6] Balian organised what forces he had, which were mostly composed of refugees, while the women of the city shaved their heads as a form of penance.[7]

Saladin's forces first arrived outside the walls of Jerusalem on 20 September and began the siege the next day at the north-western corner of the city.[8] The Christian defenders fought hard, and Muslim losses were surprisingly high. After four days of intense fighting with little progress, in what must have seemed at least a minor victory to Jerusalem's defenders, Saladin called off the attack to reorganise his forces. Yet the next day, Saladin's forces reappeared at the North of Jerusalem and the siege began again, resulting in some success, as by September they caused a breach in the wall. In response, Balian went to Saladin's camp the next day to negotiate with the Sultan. There he announced, in what may have been a last desperate gamble, that the Christian defenders of the city were prepared to wage a total war, in which they were willing to kill their own families, their animals and the 5,000 Muslim prisoners in their control. They would also destroy Muslim holy places, including the Dome of the Rock and Aqsa Mosque before marching out to meet Saladin's troops to die gloriously on the battlefield.[9] If Balian was only bluffing, it worked, as Saladin wanted no part of what he proposed. A peaceful surrender was negotiated for 2 October, giving Saladin control of the city. Latin Christians could leave the city unmolested and take whatever they could carry in exchange for a ransom of ten dinars for every man, five dinars for every woman and one dinar for every child.[10]

THE AFTERMATH: RENEWED ENTHUSIASM FOR CRUSADING AND THE THIRD CRUSADE

After the conquest of Jerusalem, Saladin engaged in extensive combat to capture almost every Christian town in the region, with the notable exceptions of Antioch, Tripoli and Tyre. Saladin's failure to take these cities proved fatal to his ultimate hope of driving the crusaders into the sea. The cities provided a collective base of operation from which Christians could mount a defence and await reinforcements from the West, the armies of the Third Crusade. The disaster of the loss of Jerusalem had shocked European Christians and spurred them into action, and recruitment for the Third Crusade was strong.[11] The Third Crusade – called *Crusade of Kings* because it was led by Emperor Frederick I Barbarossa, King Richard I Lionheart and King Phillip II of France – could not recapture Jerusalem, but it did put an end to Saladin's unchecked power in the Levant. The fall of Acre to the combined armies of King Guy of Lusignan, who had ultimately been spared by Saladin after being captured at Hattin, Richard I of England and Phillip II of France shattered the myth of Saladin's invincibility and put him on the defensive. Because Saladin was not in a position to continue fighting after his defeat at Acre, he soon signed a peace agreement on 2 September 1192 that guaranteed protection for the crusader states in the Levant and the right of Christians to have unmolested access to Jerusalem, although the Holy City would remain under Islamic control. While Saladin had not achieved his ultimate goal of expelling the crusaders from the Holy Land, he had achieved enormous gains against Latin Christians before he died in March 1193.

BACKGROUND TO THE SOURCES

The first source presented here is a letter written sometime between the battle of Hattin and the siege of Jerusalem. In an appeal for aid from the West, the author gives a sense of the desperation Latin Christians in the Holy Land must have felt as Saladin began racking up victory after victory. The author describes himself as the Master of the Temple. Since other sources tell us that the Master of the Temple was taken captive at Hattin (see Chapter 6) and the knights of the crusading orders suffered a mass execution while in captivity after the battle, it is possible that this Master, as a valuable prisoner, was ransomed or that the author was a newly appointed replacement. The tone of the appeal for aid is urgent. First, the author briefly describes the events that led to Saladin's dominance of the Holy Land, including the massacre of the Templars at Hattin, and the speedy conquests of several Christian towns that followed. Although much of the Kingdom of Jerusalem was captured, he lists the city of Jerusalem as among the four important cities (others being Tyre, Ascalon and Berytus) that remain under Latin Christian control at the time of his writing. Yet the author emphasises that they are under threat and need immediate aid to survive Saladin's onslaught in the region.

Perhaps the best Christian source for Saladin's siege of Jerusalem is the eyewitness account of the anonymous author of the *De Expugatione Terrae Sanctae per Saladinum*.[12] The author was in Jerusalem during the siege, even claiming that he was wounded by an arrow that struck the bridge of his nose. His account provides an understanding of the chaos of siege warfare, as he describes the trumpets and battle cries of the attacking Muslim forces causing a great clamour during the assault. He describes, for example, the devastating effect of the hail of arrows sent into the city by Muslim archers, which kept the city's surgeons working full time to remove them from their victims (including the author). Of particular interest is the author's description of the terms for surrender of the city, which included ransoms for each citizen that greatly concerned the poor who could not afford to pay. A selection from Beha ed-Din's *The Life of Saladin* provides similar details and confirms many of the events related in the *De Expugatione*. Yet, of course, the tone is one of triumph rather than desolation as found in Christian accounts. He approvingly notes, for example, how Saladin's army became 'glutted with pillage and rapine' before marching on Jerusalem and the inspiration Saladin drew from the Koran prior to the siege. He then describes the festivities as Saladin and other Muslims celebrated the capture of the city, at which Saladin remained for about a month before moving on.

Oddly, neither Beha ed-Din nor the author of the *De Expugatione* provides any detailed information on the fascinating negotiations that took place between Saladin and Balian of Ibelin for the surrender of Jerusalem. The author of the *De Expugatione*, for example, only notes that without favourable terms the Christians 'would hold out to the death'. Beha ed-Din only notes that the Christians asked for a treaty, giving no sense of how an agreement was reached. Much better details are provided in the account of the Arab historian Ibn al-Athir, who describes how initially the Sultan had no interest in allowing for the surrender of Jerusalem, seeking instead a conquest along the lines of what the crusaders did in 1099 (see Chapter 3).[13] Yet Balian changed the Sultan's mind with the threat of a total war in which the Christian defenders promised to slaughter their wives and children to prevent them from becoming Saladin's slaves, raze Muslim holy places to the ground, execute 5,000 Muslim prisoners and then fight to the death. Only after Balian's threat did Saladin give serious consideration to terms for surrender, to which he ultimately agreed.

THE SOURCES

The Letter of Terricius, Master of the Temple, on the Capture of the Land of Jerusalem[14]

The following is a letter written sometime after the battle of Hattin, but before the siege of Jerusalem. Its author, the self-described Terricius, Master of the Temple, appeals for aid from the West and in doing so gives an understanding of the desperation Latin Christians in the Holy Land must have felt as Saladin began his onslaught against them after his victory at Hattin.

The brother Terricius, So called Grand Master of the most impoverished house of the Temple, and of all the brethren himself the most impoverished, and that brotherhood all but annihilated, to all commanders and brethren of the Temple to whom these presents shall come, greeting, and may they lift up their sighs to Him at whom the sun and moon are astounded. With how many and how great calamities, our sins so requiring it, the anger of God has lately permitted us to be scourged, we are unable, O sad fate! either in writing or in the language of tears to express. For the Turks, assembling together an immense multitude of their nations, began with bitter hostility to invade the territories of us Christians; and accordingly, uniting the forces of our nation against them, we ventured, before the octave of the Apostles Saint Peter and Saint Paul, to attack them; and for that purpose ventured to direct our march towards Tiberias, which, leaving their camp unprotected, they had taken by storm. After repulsing us among some most dangerous rocks, they attacked us with such vehemence, that after they had captured the Holy Cross and our king, and a whole multitude of us had been slain, and after two hundred and thirty of our brethren, as we verily believe, had been taken by them and beheaded (besides those sixty who had been slain on the first of May), with great difficulty, the lord the earl of Tripolis, the lord Reginald of Sidon, the lord Ballovius, and ourselves, were enabled to make our escape from that dreadful field. After this, the Pagans, revelling in the blood of us Christians, did not delay to press on with all their hosts towards the city of Tyre; and, taking it by storm, spread themselves over nearly the whole of the land, Jerusalem, Tyre, Ascalon and Berytus being alone now left to us and to Christendom. These cities also, as nearly all the citizens have been slain, we shall not be at all able to retain in our hands, unless we speedily receive the Divine assistance, and aid from yourselves. For at the present moment they are besieging Tyre with all their might, and cease not to assault it either night or day, while so vast are their numbers, that they have covered the whole face of the land from Tyre, as far as Jerusalem and Gaza, just like swarms of ants. Deign, therefore, with all possible speed, to bring succour to ourselves and to Christianity, all but ruined in the East, that so through the aid of God and the exalted merits of your brotherhood, supported by your assistance, we may be enabled to save the remainder of those cities. Farewell.

De Expugatione: Saladin's Siege of Jerusalem in 1187[15]

The eyewitness account of the anonymous author of the *De Expugatione Terrae Sanctae per Saladinum* is the most detailed Christian source on Saladin's siege of Jerusalem. His account provides a sense of the chaos of siege warfare and how the terms of surrender, including the payment of substantial ransoms, were a concern for the poor who could not afford them.

The Holy City of Jerusalem was besieged on 20 September. It was surrounded on every side by unbelievers, who shot arrows everywhere into the air. They were accompanied by frightening armaments and, with a great clamour of trumpets, they shrieked and wailed, 'Hai, hai.' The city was aroused by the noise and tumult of the barbarians and, for a time, they all cried out: 'True and Holy Cross! Sepulchre of Jesus Christ's resurrection! Save the city of Jerusalem and its dwellers!'

The battle was then joined and both sides began courageously to fight. But since so much unhappiness was produced through sorrow and sadness, we shall not enumerate all the Turkish attacks and assemblies, by which, for two weeks, the Christians were worn down.... During this time it seemed that God had charge over the city, for who can say why one man who was hit died, while another wounded man escaped? Arrows fell like raindrops, so that one could not show a finger above the ramparts without being hit. There were so many wounded that all the hospitals and physicians in the city were hard put to it just to extract the missiles from their bodies. I myself was wounded in the face by an arrow which struck the bridge of my nose. The wooden shaft has been taken out, but the metal tip has remained there to this day. The inhabitants of Jerusalem fought courageously enough for a week, while the enemy settled down opposite the tower of David.

Saladin saw that he was making no progress and that as things were going he could do no damage to the city. Accordingly, he and his aides began to circle around the city and to examine the city's weak points, in search of a place where he could set up his engines without fear of the Christians and where he could more easily attack the town.... At dawn on a certain day[16] the King of Egypt [Saladin] ordered the camp to be moved without any tumult or commotion. He ordered the tents to be pitched in the Vale of Jehosephat, on the Mount of Olives, and on Mount Joy, and throughout the hills in that region. When morning had come the men of Jerusalem lifted up their eyes and, when the darkness of the clouds had gone, they saw that the Saracens were pulling up their tents as if they were going to leave. The inhabitants of Jerusalem rejoiced greatly and said: 'The King of Syria has fled, because he could not destroy the city as be had planned.' When the turn of the matter was known, however, this rejoicing was quickly turned into grief and lamentation.

The tyrant [Saladin] at once ordered the engines to be constructed and balistas to be put up. He likewise ordered olive branches and branches of other trees to be collected and piled between the city and the engines. That evening he ordered the army to take up arms and the engineers to proceed with their iron tools, so that before the Christians could do anything about it, they would all be prepared at the foot of the walls. The cruellest of tyrants also arrayed up to ten thousand armed knights with bows and lances on horseback, so that if the men of the city attempted a foray they would be blocked. He stationed another ten thousand or more men armed to the teeth with bows for shooting arrows, under cover of shields and targets. He kept the rest with himself and his lieutenants around the engines. When everything was arranged in this fashion, at daybreak they began to break down the corner of the tower and to attack all around the walls. The archers began shooting arrows and those who were at the engines began to fire rocks in earnest.

The men of the city expected nothing of the sort and left the city walls without guard. Tired and worn out, they slept until morning, for unless the Lord watch the city, he labours in vain who guards it. When the sun had risen, those who were sleeping in the towers were startled by the noise of the barbarians. When they saw these things they were terrified and overcome with fear. Like madmen they yelled out through the city: 'Hurry, men of Jerusalem! Hasten! Help! The walls have already been breached! The foreigners are entering!' Aroused, they hastened through the city as bravely as they could, but they were powerless to repulse the Damascenes from the walls, either with spears, lances, arrows, stones or with molten lead and bronze. The Turks unceasingly hurled rocks forcefully against the ramparts. Between the walls and the outer defences they threw rocks and the so-called Greek fire, which burns wood, stone and whatever it touches. Everywhere the archers shot arrows without measure and without ceasing, while the others were boldly smashing the walls.

The men of Jerusalem, meanwhile, were taking counsel. They decided that everyone, with such horses and arms as could be mustered, should leave the city and march steadily through the gate which leads to Jehosephat. Thus, if God allowed it, they would push the enemy back a bit from the walls. They were foiled, however, by the Turkish horsemen and were woefully defeated....

The Chaldeans [Saladin and his army] fought the battle fiercely for a few days and triumphed. The Christians were failing so by this time that scarcely twenty or thirty men appeared to defend the city walls. No man could be found in the whole city who was brave enough to dare keep watch at the defences for a night, even for a fee of a hundred besants. With my own ears I heard the voice of a public crier between the great wall and the outer works proclaiming (on behalf of the lord Patriarch and the other great men of the city) that if fifty strong and brave sergeants could be found who would take up arms voluntarily and keep guard during the night over the corner which had already been destroyed, they would receive five thousand besants. They were not found....

Meanwhile, they sent legates to the King of Syria, begging him to temper his anger toward them and accept them as allies, as he had done for others. He refused and is reported to have given this reply: 'I have frequently heard from our wise men, the *fakih*, [from *al-Fakih*, "a wise man"] that Jerusalem cannot be cleansed, save by Christian blood, and I wish to take counsel with them on this point.' Thus, uncertain, they returned. They sent others, Balian and Ranier of Naples and Thomas Patrick, offering a hundred thousand besants. Saladin would not receive them and, their hopes shattered, they returned. They sent them back again with others, demanding that Saladin himself say what kind of agreement he wanted. If possible they would comply; if not, they would hold out to the death.[17]

Saladin had taken counsel and laid down these ransom terms for the inhabitants of Jerusalem: each male, ten years old and over, was to pay ten besants for his ransom; females, five besants; boys, seven years old and under, one. Those who wished would be freed on these terms and could leave securely with their possessions. The inhabitants of Jerusalem who would not accept these terms, or those who did not have ten besants, were to become booty, to be slain by the army's swords. This agreement pleased the lord Patriarch and the others who had money....

On Friday, October 2, this agreement was read out through the streets of Jerusalem, so that everyone might within forty days provide for himself and pay to Saladin the tribute as aforesaid for his freedom. When they heard these arrangements, the crowds throughout the city wailed in sorrowful tones: 'Woe, woe to us miserable people! We have no gold! What are we to do?... Who would ever have thought that such wickedness would be perpetrated by Christians?'

But, alas, by the hands of wicked Christians Jerusalem was turned over to the wicked. The gates were closed and guards were posted. The *fakihs* and *kadis*,[18] the ministers of the wicked error, who are considered bishops and priests by the Saracens came for prayer and religious purposes first to the Temple of the Lord, which they call Beithhalla and in which they have great faith for salvation. They believed they were cleansing it and with unclean and horrible bellows they defiled the Temple by shouting with polluted lips the Muslim precept: '*Allahu akbar! Allahu akbar!*'...[19]

Our people held the city of Jerusalem for some eighty-nine years....[20] Within a short time, Saladin had conquered almost the whole Kingdom of Jerusalem. He exalted the grandeur of Mohammed's law and showed that, in the event, its might exceeded that of the Christian religion.

Beha ed-Din – Saladin's Siege of Jerusalem in 1187[21]

The following account of Saladin's siege of Jerusalem was written by the Arab historian Beha ed-Din. Although his work provides similar details and confirms many of the events related in the *De Expugatione*, the tone understandably is one of triumph rather than desolation. While it is not known if the author was present at Saladin's conquest of Jerusalem, he later became a member of the sultan's court and had access to first-hand information.

Having taken Ascalon and the districts round Jerusalem (el Kuds), the sultan devoted all his energies to preparations for an expedition against the city. He called together the various detachments of his army there were scattered through the coast-districts, and returned glutted with pillage and rapine; and then marched upon Jerusalem, strong in the hope that God would uphold and direct him. He was anxious to make the most of his opportunities now that the door of success had been opened to him, following the advice of the Holy Prophet, who said:

'He to whom the door of success has been opened must take his opportunity and enter in, for he knows not when the door may be shut upon him.'

It was on Sunday, the 15th of the month of Rejeb in the year 583 [20 September 1187 AD], that he took up his position to the west of the city. The place was teeming with soldiers, both horse and foot, and their numbers, according to the best accounts, exceeded sixty thousand, without reckoning women and children. The sultan shifted his position to the north of the city, thinking this would be best, and directed his mangoneis against the walls. Being very strong in bowmen, he pressed the place so closely by constant assaults and skirmishes that his miners were able to make a breach in one of the northern angles of the wall overlooking the Wadi Jehennum. The enemies of God saw they were menaced by a disaster which they could not escape, and by diverse signs it was revealed to them that the city would fall into the hands of the Muslims. Their hearts were filled with dread when they thought of their bravest warriors slain or taken captive, their strongholds destroyed or captured by the Muslims. Expecting to suffer the same fate as their brothers, and to die by the same sword that had cut them down, they adopted the only alternative, and asked for a treaty, that their lives might be spared.

After messengers had several times passed backwards and forwards between the two parties, a treaty was concluded, and the sultan was put in possession of Jerusalem on Friday, the 27th of Rejeb [2 October 1187], on the anniversary of the night of the ascension (of the Holy Prophet into heaven), an event which is foreshadowed in the glorious Kuran (xvii. 1). What a wonderful coincidence! God allowed the Muslims to take the city as a celebration of the anniversary of their Holy Prophet's midnight journey. Truly this is a sign that this deed was pleasing to Almighty God; and this mighty conquest was a testimony (for the Faith) to a multitude of people – learned men, dervishes and fakirs – who were brought thither by the news of the sultan's victories and successes in the lands on the coast, and by the report that he was going to undertake an expedition against Jerusalem. Therefore all men learned (in the law) came to join the sultan, both from Egypt and from Syria; there was not a single well-known doctor but came to the camp. Every voice was raised in shouts, calling upon God, and proclaiming His unity and power. On the very day of the capitulation Friday's prayer was solemnized in the city, and the khatib delivered the sermon.[22] The huge cross that rose from the dome of the Sakhra was thrown down. In this manner, by means of the sultan, God accorded a magnificent triumph to Islam.

The chief condition stipulated by the treaty was that each man should pay ten Tyrian dinars as his ransom; each woman five; children, both boys and girls, were to pay only one dinar each. Everyone who paid this ransom was to receive his freedom. God in His mercy delivered the Moslem prisoners who were in captivity in the city to the number of more than three thousand. The sultan took possession of the whole of the booty, and distributed it amongst his emirs and soldiers. He also assigned a portion to the jurists, doctors of law, dervishes and other people who had come to the camp. By his orders, all those who had paid their ransom where conducted to their place of refuge – that is to say, to the city of Tyre, I have been told that when the sultan left Jerusalem he retained nothing whatever out of all these treasures, and yet they amounted to nearly two hundred and twenty thousand dinars. He left the city on Friday, the 25th of Sh'aban [30 October].

Ibn al-Athir – Negotiations for the Surrender of Jerusalem, September 1187[23]

The following account of the Arab historian Ibn al-Athir provides fascinating details on the negotiations between Balian of Ibelin and Saladin for the surrender of the Holy City. He was an eyewitness to most of Saladin's career and would have had access to first-hand accounts of the negotiations. Here he provides a description of how it was only Balian's threat of total war that ultimately convinced the Sultan to allow relatively favourable terms of surrender for the besieged Latin Christian inhabitants of Jerusalem.

They sent a deputation of their lords and nobles to ask for terms, but when they spoke of it to Saladin he refused to grant their request. 'We shall deal with you', he said, 'just as you dealt with the population of Jerusalem when you took it in 492/1099, with murder and enslavement and other such savageries!' The messengers returned empty handed. Then Balian Ibn Barzan [Balian of Ibelin] asked for safe conduct for himself so that he might appear before Saladin to discuss developments. Consent was given, and he presented himself and once again began asking for a general amnesty in return for surrender. The sultan still refused his requests and entreaties to show mercy. Finally, despairing of this approach, Balian said: 'Know O sultan, that there are very many of us in this city, God alone knows how many. At the moment we are fighting half-heartedly in the hope of saving our lives, hoping to be spared by you as you have spared others; this is because of our horror of death and our love of life. But if we see that death is inevitable, then by God we shall kill our children and our wives, burn our possessions, so as not to leave you with a dinar or drachma or a single man or woman to enslave. When this is done, we shall pull down the Sanctuary of the Rock and Masjid al-Aqsa and the other sacred places, slaughtering the Muslim prisoners we hold – 5000 of them – and killing every horse and animal we possess. Then we shall come out to fight you like men fighting for their lives, when each man, before he falls dead, kills his equals; we shall die with honour, or win a noble victory!' Then Saladin took counsel with his advisors, all of whom were in favour of his granting the assurances requested by the Franks, without forcing them to take extreme measures whose outcome could not be foreseen.[24]

CHAPTER EIGHT
THE SACK OF CONSTANTINOPLE, 1204

129
WILLIAM OF TYRE – THE MASSACRE OF LATINS LIVING IN CONSTANTINOPLE IN 1182

131
GEOFFREY DE VILLEHARDOUIN – THE PLAN FOR THE DIVISION OF CONSTANTINOPLE

131
ROBERT OF CLARI – SERMONS BEFORE THE ATTACK ON CONSTANTINOPLE

132
NICETAS CHONIATES – THE SACK OF CONSTANTINOPLE

134
NICHOLAS MESARITES – THE SACK OF CONSTANTINOPLE

134
GUNTHER VON PAIRIS – LIST OF RELICS STOLEN BY ABBOT MARTIN

136
POPE INNOCENT III – REPRIMAND OF A PAPAL LEGATE

137
POPE INNOCENT III – COMMAND FOR THE CRUSADERS TO STAY AT CONSTANTINOPLE

Contemporaries and modern historians alike have been fascinated by how a movement that began with the object of reclaiming the Holy Land for Christianity could, in just over a century, develop into a vehicle for the destruction of the most magnificent city in the Christian world.

– Jonathan Phillips[1]

BAD RELATIONS BETWEEN THE EAST AND WEST BEFORE 1204

Bad relations between Latin Christendom and Byzantium did not begin with the crusades. To the contrary, Pope Urban II viewed the First Crusade as an opportunity to heal pre-existing divisions between the Eastern and Western churches.[2] Yet early in the crusading movement, Latin Christians came to suspect the Byzantines of treachery while the Byzantines came to view the crusaders as another imperial power seeking control over their traditional lands.[3] This distrust and suspicion contributed to occasional bouts of violence against Latin Christians living in Constantinople, as seen in the riots of 1182, when thousands of Westerners were slain by its Orthodox residents.[4] These traditional hostilities were manifest during the Fourth Crusade as many of the greatest abuses were committed by local Latin Christians against their former Orthodox neighbours.[5]

EVENTS LEADING TO THE SACK OF CONSTANTINOPLE IN 1204

Regardless of past hostilities, the Fourth Crusade was not conceived by Latin Christians as a way to square historic differences with the Byzantine Empire. The primary target of the crusaders was Egypt, as Christian control of the region would limit the resources of Muslim armies in the Levant and enhance those of Christians.[6] Yet when the crusaders arrived in Venice in 1201, their point of departure for the crusade, they found themselves unable to pay for the newly constructed ships their leadership had contracted to transport the crusaders and their equipment.[7] The Venetians offered to delay the payment in exchange for help in gaining control of the city of Zara, which at the time was under the jurisdiction of the Christian king of Hungary.[8] The crusaders could either abandon the crusade, while still in debt to the Venetians, or accept the offer and continue with the crusade. They chose the latter and began their siege of Zara in November 1202. The city surrendered quickly, and the army camped there during the winter.[9] While at Zara, the crusaders were visited by the ambassadors of Alexius IV, the son of the deposed and imprisoned Byzantine Emperor Isaac II. He had sent his ambassador to request support for his efforts to dethrone Alexius III, the usurper of his father's throne. For doing so, he offered the crusaders money, military support and the unification of the Orthodox and Catholic churches.[10] While money and military support obviously appealed to the crusaders, they hoped that the unification of the churches would be enough to pacify an angry Pope Innocent III.[11] After some debate, the crusaders accepted the deal and arrived in Constantinople in June 1203. The usurper, Alexius III, panicked and fled. Alexius IV's father, Isaac II, was released from prison and both father and son were installed as co-emperors.

All that remained was for Alexius IV to compensate the crusaders as promised. Yet Alexius IV had a problem. The imperial treasuries were empty, leaving him unable to pay the exorbitant amount he had promised.[12] Whereas the crusaders soon became annoyed by Alexius's delay in paying what he owed, things were about to get much more complicated. While the crusaders were camped outside Constantinople, with dwindling food supplies and little money, their patron Alexius IV was strangled to death. The Byzantine nobleman Alexius Ducas Murtzuphlus seized the throne and immediately began fortifying the city's defences in defiance of the crusaders.[13] This turn of events stunned the crusaders. They remained in massive debt and had still done nothing for the liberation of the Holy Land. Now they were even less prepared for an expedition to the East than when they left Venice. Under these circumstances, they saw only one option. They attacked the city in April 1204 with the goal of installing a Latin emperor on the throne. Murtzuphlus soon fled, and the crusaders were victorious.

THE SACK OF CONSTANTINOPLE

What took place after the crusaders captured Constantinople has remained a source of controversy until the present.[14] In contrast to claims that the Byzantines did not have the wealth to pay the crusaders, as Alexius IV had promised, they discovered that Constantinople was indeed among the richest cities in the world. The city's wealth was not in the imperial treasuries, but in the silver and gold that lined its churches, the ancient art and statues that decorated its streets and public buildings and its sacred relics that pilgrims had been visiting for centuries. For three days the crusaders violently plundered and looted anything of value, sacred or otherwise. The sack of the city marked the end of the Fourth Crusade.

Constantinople never became the base of crusading operations as some had hoped, nor did a unification of the Eastern and Western churches ever take place. A Byzantine government in exile was set up in Nicea until 1261 when Constantinople was retaken by the Byzantines and Latin rule ended.

BACKGROUND TO THE SOURCES

The first source presented in this chapter is William of Tyre's graphic account of the massacre of Latin Christians in Constantinople in 1182.[15] Similar attacks against Westerners, mostly Italian merchants and their families living there, took place prior to and after, including immediately before the sack of the city by the crusaders in 1204, but these attacks were not as deadly as the riots of 1182.[16] This source is included in this chapter because some modern authors have made a connection between these traditional hostilities and the events of 1204. They suggest that such violence was the cause of bad blood leading up to the Fourth Crusade and ultimately inspired local Latin Christians, who allied themselves with the crusaders, to commit many of the worst abuses against their former Orthodox tormentors during the sack of Constantinople in 1204.[17]

Political and religious reasons were usually the cause of such violence, as was the case with the massacre of 1182. Byzantine resentment of the pro-Latin policies of Emperor Manuel I Comnenus (d.1180) had resulted in an enormous level of hatred and mistrust of Latin Christians by Orthodox believers in the years before. Soon after Manuel's reign ended, this resentment boiled over during the revolt of Andronicus Comnenus when he enlisted the help of the anti-Latin populace to seize the city. William vividly describes the fear of the Latin Christians as they became aware of the pending danger. Many fled, while others who were unable to flee, 'the aged and infirm', took the brunt of the Greeks' violence, which resulted in thousands of deaths. The Latin clergy also was a special target of the Greek mob. Particularly disturbing is William's description of the fate of a papal legate. The Greeks cut off his head and attached it to the tail of a dog to symbolise their hatred of the papacy. The Greeks also, according to William, sold 4,000 Latin Christians into slavery to the Turks and destroyed Latin religious sites, including several churches and monasteries.[18]

In the light of Greek–Latin hostilities prior to 1204, it is not surprising that similar attacks took place against the Latin residents of Constantinople during the Fourth Crusade. Indeed, the events of 1182 were unique for their intensity, but Greek riots in the Latin Quarter were not unusual when the populace was stirred against Westerners. With the army of the Fourth Crusade camped outside their walls, local Orthodox Christians again attacked local Latin Christians. Embittered by the crusaders' menacing presence and the prospect of ecclesiastical reunion, the Greek mob destroyed Latin churches, homes, hospitals, warehouses and shops.[19] Most Latin Christian residents of Constantinople had little choice but to flee to the camps of the crusaders, where they swelled the army's ranks. They would have their chance for revenge soon enough.

The eyewitness account of Geoffrey de Villehardouin, the marshal of Champaign, is by far the most comprehensive source of the Fourth Crusade.[20] Unfortunately, his description of the sacking of the city is lacking. He sometimes places little emphasis on, or even fails to report, events that would cast the crusade leadership, of which he was a part, in a bad light.[21] Villehardouin was, however, senior enough in the crusade leadership to have had full participation in the councils of the Barons, where all major strategic decisions were made, and he seems to have had the full confidence of the highest ranks.[22] Hence, his source provides excellent details not found elsewhere on the decision-making and planning of the crusaders leading up to the assault on Constantinople.

Included in this chapter is Geoffrey's description of the crusaders' plan for the division of Constantinople and its spoils. Geoffrey notes that the leadership had a 'long and stormy' discussion about such matters but ultimately resolved their differences. The leadership agreed that all booty taken after the conquest of the city should be brought together and distributed 'fairly'. Also, six men would be chosen from the Venetians and six men from the crusaders to elect an emperor. The new emperor would receive certain properties, palaces and a higher division of the spoils (25 per cent), as well as a commitment of feudal service from those who remained in the city. Anyone who failed to keep this compact was to be excommunicated by the clergy. With this agreement in place, the crusaders then focused their efforts on military preparations for their attack on the city.

Following the crusade leadership's decision to attack the city, the Latin clergy made extensive efforts to preach the righteousness of the decision to the army. One of the best sources for these preaching efforts is the eyewitness account of the poor Picard Knight Robert of Clari.[23] Robert's account is valued because it provides the unique perspective of those in the ranks.[24] Robert describes how a clerical council decided that war was righteous since Greeks no longer submitted to 'the law of Rome'. Indeed, to attack the 'disloyal' and schismatic Greeks was promoted as 'an act of great charity'. Robert then describes how the bishops and priests then fanned out to preach the coming attack and commanded the crusaders (pilgrims) to confess their sins and receive communion to prepare for battle. During their preparations all 'evil women' were expelled from the camps, in order to ensure the spiritual purity of the crusaders and reduce the temptation to sin.[25]

The most detailed account of the aftermath of the crusaders' victory, although charged with emotion from the Byzantine perspective, is the eyewitness account of the high-ranking senator Nicetas Choniates.[26] Nicetas was in Constantinople during the events of 1203–1204 and recorded them soon after. His graphic and violent details are not unlike William of Tyre's account of the Greek massacre of Latin Christians in 1182. Nicetas details the defilement of 'virgins consecrated to God' and the 'wounds, rape [and] captivity' of the citizens of Constantinople by the crusading army. Yet even more detailed is his account of the looting of the city, the defilement of its churches and the theft of relics. He notes, for example, in a mockery of Orthodoxy, how 'a certain harlot' was placed in the Patriarch's seat and made to sing an obscene song. He also laments the stripping and looting of the ancient church of Hagia Sophia and refers to the crusaders as 'precursors of Anti-Christ'. This chapter also includes a brief selection by Nicholas Mesarites, the Greek metropolitan of Ephesus, who like Nicetas was an eyewitness to the sacking of Constantinople. Although with far less detail, Nicholas expresses the same emotion as Nicetas in describing the sack. He notes, for example, how the crusaders were 'maddened by war and murderous in spirit' as they desecrated holy places and 'defiled the virgins in the holy chapels'.

Perhaps the best source to give a sense of the sacred objects that were taken during the sack is the account of the monk Gunther von Pairis.[27] Although Gunther did not participate in the Fourth Crusade, he provides a detailed account of the relics that were stolen by his abbot, Martin of Pairis, who was a participant in the sack of Constantinople. His detailed inventory of these items was recorded in 1205 soon after Martin's return from the crusade.

Finally, this chapter contains two selections from the correspondence of Pope Innocent III. The first is a letter of reprimand written by the Pope in 1204 to Peter, a papal legate in Constantinople. The Pope's anger is the most striking aspect of the letter, as he condemns the crusaders' conquest of Constantinople and the treatment of the Orthodox population as an impediment to any potential reunification of the Catholic and Orthodox churches, which had been a goal of his papacy from the beginning.[28] He condemns the legate for the diversion of the crusade to Constantinople and absolving the crusaders from their crusading vows. In doing so, Innocent cites in graphic detail reports that had already made it back to him concerning the crusaders' abuses of the city and its citizens during and after its conquest. Although Innocent was initially furious at the conquest of Constantinople, there was little he could do to alter the outcome and so he made the best of it by eventually recognising and then embracing the new order in Constantinople. In a second letter by Innocent, written in 1205, it becomes clear how Innocent's thinking had evolved on the issue. Innocent exhorts the crusaders to stay in Constantinople because he now believes the 'wonderful transference' of the Byzantine Empire to Latin control is the means by which God will effect the restoration of the Holy Land to Christian control.

THE SOURCES

William of Tyre – The Massacre of Latins Living in Constantinople in 1182[29]

The following source selection is taken from William of Tyre's *History of Deeds Done beyond the Sea*. It provides the most detailed account of one of the most violent episodes in Greek and Latin Christian relations in the years prior to the Fourth Crusade. William describes in detail a brutal massacre of the Latin populace of Constantinople during a revolt inspired by the fiercely anti-Western Andronicus Comnenus in 1182. Such hostilities were reflective of the often tense relations between Orthodox and Latin Christians living in Constantinople in the years leading up to the Fourth Crusade. Such historical bitterness, without any doubt, partly inspired the brutality local Latin Christians later showed towards Greek Christians when they joined forces with the crusaders during the sack of Constantinople in 1204. Although William was not present in Constantinople at the time of the massacre in 1182, he definitely had access to first-hand information from Latin Christian survivors who had fled to the Holy Land.

This change of affairs spread consternation among the Latins, for they feared that the citizens would make sudden attack upon them; in fact they had already received warning of such intention from certain people who had private knowledge of the conspiracy. Those who were able to do so, therefore, fled from the wiles of the Greeks and the death which threatened them. Some embarked on forty-four galleys which chanced to be in the harbour, and others placed all their effects on some of the many other ships there.

The aged and infirm, however, with those who were unable to flee, were left in their homes, and on them fell the wicked rage which the others had escaped. For Andronicus, who had secretly caused ships to be prepared, led his entire force into the city. As soon as they entered the gates these troops, aided by the citizens, rushed to that quarter of the city occupied by the Latins and put to the sword the little remnant who had been either unwilling or unable to flee with the others. Although but few of these were able to fight, yet they resisted for a long time and made the enemy's victory a bloody one.

Regardless of treaties and the many services which our people had rendered to the empire, the Greeks seized all those who appeared capable of resistance, set fire to their houses, and speedily reduced the entire quarter to ashes. Women and children, the aged and the sick, all alike perished in the flames. To vent their rage upon secular buildings alone, however, was far from satisfying their unholy wickedness; they also set fire to churches and venerated places of every description and burned, together with the sacred edifices, those who had fled thither for refuge. No distinction between clergy and laymen, except that greater fury was displayed toward those who wore the honourable habits of high office or religion. Monks and priests were the especial victims of their madness and were put to death under excruciating torture.

Among these latter was a venerable man named John, a subdeacon of the holy Roman church, whom the pope had sent to Constantinople on business relating to the church. They seized him and, cutting off his head, fastened it to the tail of a filthy dog as an insult to the church. In the midst of such frightful sacrilege, worse than parricide, not even the dead, whom impiety itself generally spares, were suffered to rest undisturbed. Corpses were torn from the tombs and dragged through the streets and squares as if the insensate bodies were capable of feeling the indignities offered them.

The vandals then repaired to the hospital of St. John, as it is called, where they put to the sword all the sick they found. Those whose pious duty it should have been to relieve the oppressed, namely the monks and priests, called in footpads and brigands to carry on the slaughter under promise of reward. Accompanied by these miscreants, they sought out the most secluded retreats and the inmost apartments of homes, that none who were hiding there might escape death. When such were discovered, they were dragged out with violence and handed over to the executioners, who, that they might not work without pay, were given the price of blood for the murder of these wretched victims.

Even those who seemed to show more consideration sold into perpetual slavery among the Turks and other infidels the fugitives who had resorted to them and to whom they had given hope of safety. It is said that more than four thousand Latins of various age, sex and condition were delivered thus to barbarous nations for a price. In such fashion did the perfidious Greek nation, a brood of vipers,[30] like a serpent in the bosom or a mouse in the wardrobe evilly requite their guests—those who had not deserved such treatment and were far from anticipating anything of the kind; those to whom they had given their daughters, nieces and sisters as wives and who, by long living together, had become their friends.

Geoffrey de Villehardouin – The Plan for the Division of Constantinople[31]

The following source is taken from Geoffrey de Villehardouin's account of the Fourth Crusade. As a member of the crusade leadership, Geoffrey was well positioned to comment on the planning that took place prior to the siege of Constantinople. Provided here is Geoffrey's report on how the crusaders decided that the spoils of their future conquest would be distributed and the means by which they would elect a new emperor. Geoffrey's account dates to around 1207 when it abruptly ends, suggesting the author's death.[32]

Then the members of the host debated and consulted upon the best course to pursue. The discussion was long and stormy, but the following was the result of the deliberation: If God granted that they should capture the city, all the booty that was taken should be brought together and divided fairly, as was fitting. And, if they captured the city, six men should be chosen from the Franks and six from the Venetians; these were to take oath upon relics that they would elect as emperor him whom they should judge to be the most useful for the good of the land. And he whom they chose as emperor should have one-quarter of all the conquests both in the city and he should have the palace of the Lion's mouth and of Blachern. The other three-quarters should be divided into two parts, one-half for the Venetians and one-half for the crusaders. Then twelve from the wisest of the army of the pilgrims and twelve of the Venetians should be chosen to divide the fiefs and the offices among the men and to define the feudal service which each one owed to the emperor. This compact was guaranteed and sworn to both by the Franks and the Venetians, with the condition that any one who wished could go away within one year from the end of March. Those who remained in the country must perform the feudal service to the emperor, as it might be arranged. Then the compact was made and sworn to and all who should not keep it were excommunicated by the clergy.

Robert of Clari – Sermons Before the Attack on Constantinople[33]

The following selection is taken from the account of the low-ranking knight Robert of Clari. As a participant of the Fourth Crusade, Robert provides the perspective of the men in the ranks on the events leading up to the siege of Constantinople. Included here is his account of the preaching efforts of clerics to stir the crusading army's enthusiasm before their attack on the city. Robert probably recorded his account soon after his return home from the crusade, and several years later in 1216, added an epilogue before its publication.[34]

Meanwhile the bishops and the clergy in the army debated and decided that the war was a righteous one, and that they certainly ought to attack the Greeks. For formerly the inhabitants of the city had been obedient to the law of Rome and now they were disobedient, since they said that the law of Rome was of no account, and called all who believed in it 'dogs'.[35] And the bishop said that for this reason one ought certainly to attack them, and that it was not a sin, but an act of great charity.

Then it was announced to all the host that all the Venetians and every one else should go and hear the sermons on Sunday morning;[36] and they did so. Then the bishops preached to the army, the bishop of Soissons, the bishop of Troyes, the bishop of *Havestaist*,[37] master Jean Faicette and the abbot of Loos, and they showed to the pilgrims that the war was a righteous one; for the Greeks were traitors and murderers, and also disloyal, since they had murdered their rightful lord, and were worse than Jews. Moreover, the bishops said that, by the authority of God and in the name of the pope, they would absolve all who attacked the Greeks. Then the bishops commanded the pilgrims to confess their sins and receive the communion devoutly; and said that they ought not to hesitate to attack the Greeks, for the latter were enemies of God. They also commanded that all the evil women should be sought out and sent away from the army to a distant place. This was done; the evil women were all put on a vessel and were sent very far away from the army.

Nicetas Choniates – The Sack of Constantinople[38]

The following selection is taken from Nicetas Choniates's eyewitness account of the sack of Constantinople. Writing from the Byzantine perspective, Nicetas provides an emotionally charged account with extensive details on the pillage of the city and its inhabitants. Nicetas wrote this account sometime between 1204 and his death around 1215.

…How shall I begin to tell of the deeds wrought by these nefarious men! Alas, the images, which ought to have been adored, were trodden under foot! Alas, the relics of the holy martyrs were thrown into unclean places! Then was seen what one shudders to hear, namely, the divine body and blood of Christ was spilled upon the ground or thrown about.[39] They snatched the precious reliquaries, thrust into their bosoms the ornaments which these contained and used the broken remnants for pans and drinking cups, precursors of Anti-Christ, authors and heralds of his nefarious deeds which we momentarily expect. Manifestly, indeed, by that race then, just as formerly, Christ was robbed and insulted and His garments were divided by lot; only one thing was lacking, that His side, pierced by a spear, should pour rivers of divine blood on the ground.

Nor can the violation of the Great Church [Hagia Sophia] be listened to with equanimity. For the sacred altar, formed of all kinds of precious materials and admired by the whole world, was broken into bits and distributed among the soldiers, as was all the other sacred wealth of so great and infinite splendour.

When the sacred vases and utensils of unsurpassable art and grace and rare material, and the fine silver, wrought with gold, which encircled the screen of the tribunal and the ambo, of admirable workmanship, and the door and many other ornaments, were to be borne away as booty, mules and saddled horses were led to the very sanctuary of the temple. Some of these which were unable to keep their footing on the splendid and slippery pavement, were stabbed when they fell, so that the sacred pavement was polluted with blood and filth.

Nay more, a certain harlot, a sharer in their guilt, a minister of the furies, a servant of the demons, a worker of incantations and poisonings, insulting Christ, sat in the patriarch's seat, singing an obscene song and dancing frequently. Nor, indeed, were these crimes committed and others left undone, on the ground that these were of lesser guilt, the others of greater. But with one consent all the most heinous sins and crimes were committed by all with equal zeal. Could those, who showed so great madness against God Himself, have spared the honourable matrons and maidens or the virgins consecrated to God?

Nothing was more difficult and laborious than to soften by prayers, to render benevolent, these wrathful barbarians, vomiting forth bile at every unpleasing word, so that nothing failed to inflame their fury. Whoever attempted it was derided as insane and a man of intemperate language. Often they drew their daggers against any one who opposed them at all or hindered their demands.

No one was without a share in the grief. In the alleys, in the streets, in the temples, complaints, weeping, lamentations, grief, the groaning of men, the shrieks of women, wounds, rape, captivity, the separation of those most closely united. Nobles wandered about ignominiously, those of venerable age in tears, the rich in poverty. Thus it was in the streets, on the corners, in the temple, in the dens, for no place remained unassailed or defended the suppliants. All places everywhere were filled full of all kinds of crime. Oh, immortal God, how great the afflictions of the men, how great the distress!

Nicholas Mesarites – The Sack of Constantinople[40]

The following short selection by Nicholas Mesarites, the Greek metropolitan of Ephesus, confirms many of the graphic details in Nicetas Choniates's account of the sack of Constantinople. Like Choniates, Nicholas was an eyewitness to the events of 1204 and gave the following description of the attack on the city in a funeral oration for his elder brother.[41]

And so the streets, squares, houses of two and three stories, sacred places, nunneries, houses for nuns and monks, sacred churches, even the Great Church of God and the imperial palace, were filled with men of the enemy, all of them maddened by war and murderous in spirit, all clad in armour and bearing spears, swords and lances, archers and horsemen boasting terribly, barking like Cerberus and exhaling like Charon,[42] as they sacked the sacred places and trampled on the divine things [and] ran riot over the holy vessels.... Moreover, they tore children from their mothers and mothers from their children, and they defiled the virgins in the holy chapels, fearing neither God's anger nor man's vengeance. They searched breasts of women to find out whether some womanly ornament or gold was attached or hidden in the body; hair was loosened and head-coverings removed, and those without homes or money were struck down.

Gunther von Pairis – List of Relics Stolen by Abbot Martin[43]

The following source selection is taken from Gunther von Pairis's catalogue of the relics taken from Constantinople by his abbot, Martin of Pairis. Gunther wrote his account in 1205, shortly after Martin's return from the crusade.[44]

Therefore 'Blessed be the Lord God, who only doeth wondrous things', who in His unspeakable kindness and mercy has looked upon and made glorious His church at Paris [Pairis][45] through certain gifts of His grace, which he deigned to transmit to us through the venerable man, already so frequently mentioned, abbot Martin. In the presence of these the church exults and by their protection any soul faithful to God is aided and assisted. In order that the readers' trust in these may be strengthened, we have determined to give a partial list.

First, of the highest importance and worthy of all veneration: A trace of the blood of our Lord Jesus Christ, which was shed for redemption of all mankind. Second, a piece of the cross of our Lord on which the Son of the Father, the new Adam, sacrificed for us, paid the debt of the old Adam. Third, a not inconsiderable piece of St. John, the forerunner of a Lord. Fourth, the arm of St. James, the Apostle, whose memory is venerated by the whole church. There were also relics of other saints, whose names are as follows:

Christopher, the martyr. George, the martyr. Theodore, the martyr. The foot of St. Cosmas, the martyr. Part of the head of Cyprian, the martyr. Pantaleon, the martyr. A tooth of St. Lawrence Demetrius, the martyr. Stephen, the proto-martyr. Vincentius, Adjutus, Mauritius and his companions. Crisantius and Darius, the martyrs. Gervasius and Protasius, the martyrs. Primus, the martyr. Sergius and Bacchus, the martyrs. Protus, the martyr. John and Paul, the martyrs.

Also relics from the following: the place of the Nativity of our Lord; Calvary; our Lord's sepulchre; the stone rolled away; the place of our Lord's ascension; the stone on which John stood when he baptised the Lord; the spot where Christ raised Lazarus; the stone on which Christ was presented in the Temple; the stone on which Jacob slept; the stone where Christ fasted; the stone where Christ prayed; the table on which Christ ate supper; the place where He was captured; the place where the mother of our Lord died; His grave; the grave of St. Peter, the apostle; the relics of the holy apostles, Andrew and Philip; the place where the Lord gave the law to Moses; the holy patriarchs, Abraham, Isaac and Jacob; St. Nicholas, the bishop; Adelasius, the bishop; Agricius, the bishop; John Chrysostom; John, the almsgiver; the milk of the mother of our Lord; Margaret, the virgin; Perpetua, the virgin; Agatha, the virgin; Agnes, the virgin; Lucia, the virgin; Cecilia, the virgin; Adelgundis and Euphemia, the virgins.

Written and sealed – in this year of our Lord's incarnation, 1205, in the reign of Philip, King of the Roman's, Innocent the supreme pontiff presiding over the holy Roman church – under the direction of the bishops Lutholdus of Basel and Henry of Strassburg.

Pope Innocent III – Reprimand of a Papal Legate[46]

The following source is a letter written in July 1204 by an angry Pope Innocent III to a papal legate with the crusaders in Constantinople. The Pope had recently been made aware of the diversion of the Fourth Crusade to Constantinople and the resulting sack of the city. He was furious, and here he blasts the crusaders and his legate for their actions during the crusade.

To Peter, Cardinal Priest of the Title of St. Marcellus, Legate of the Apostolic See.

We were not a little astonished and disturbed to hear that you and our beloved son the Cardinal Priest of the Title of St. Praxida and Legate of the Apostolic See, in fear of the looming perils of the Holy Land, have left the province of Jerusalem (which, at this point is in such great need) and that you have gone by ship to Constantinople. And now we see that what we dreaded has occurred and what we feared has come to pass.... For you, who ought to have looked for help for the Holy Land, you who should have stirred up others, both by word and by example, to assist the Holy Land – on your own initiative you sailed to Greece, bringing in your footsteps not only the pilgrims, but even the natives of the Holy Land who came to Constantinople, following our venerable brother, the Archbishop of Tyre. When you had deserted it, the Holy Land remained destitute of men, void of strength. Because of you, its last state was worse than the first, for all its friends deserted with you; nor was there any admirer to console it.... We ourselves were not a little agitated and, with reason, we acted against you, since you had fallen in with this counsel and because you had deserted the Land which the Lord consecrated by his presence, the land in which our King marvellously performed the mystery of our redemption....

It was your duty to attend to the business of your legation and to give careful consideration, not to the capture of the Empire of Constantinople, but rather to the defence of what is left of the Holy Land and, with the Lord's leave, the restoration of what has been lost. We made you our representative and we sent you to gain, not temporal, but rather eternal riches. And for this purpose, our brethren provided adequately for your needs.

We have just heard and discovered from your letters that you have absolved from their pilgrimage vows and their crusading obligations all the crusaders who have remained to defend Constantinople from last March to the present. It is impossible not to be moved against you, for you neither should nor could give any such absolution. Whoever suggested such a thing to you and how did they ever lead your mind astray?...

How, indeed, is the Greek church to be brought back into ecclesiastical union and to a devotion for the Apostolic See when she has been beset with so many afflictions and persecutions that she sees in the Latins only an example of perdition and the works of darkness, so that she now, and with reason, detests the Latins more than dogs? As for those who were supposed to be seeking the ends of Jesus Christ, not their own ends, whose swords, which they were supposed to use against the pagans, are now dripping with Christian blood – they have spared neither age nor sex. They have committed incest, adultery and fornication before the eyes of men. They have exposed both matrons and virgins, even those dedicated to God, to the sordid lusts of boys. Not satisfied with breaking open the imperial treasury and plundering the goods of princes and lesser men, they also laid their hands on the treasures of the churches and, what is more serious, on their very possessions. They have even ripped silver plates from the altars and have hacked them to pieces among themselves. They violated the holy places and have carried off crosses and relics.

Furthermore, under what guise can we call upon the other Western peoples for aid to the Holy Land and assistance to the Empire of Constantinople? When the Crusaders, having given up the proposed pilgrimage, return absolved to their homes; when those who plundered the aforesaid Empire turn back and come home with their spoils, free of guilt; will not people then suspect that these things have happened, not because of the crime involved, but because of your deed? Let the Lord's word not be stifled in your mouth. Be not like a dumb dog, unable to bark. Rather, let them speak these things publicly, let them protest before everyone, so that the more they rebuke you before God and on God's account, the more they will find you simply negligent. As for the absolution of the Venetian people being falsely accepted, against ecclesiastical rules, we will not at present argue with you....

Given July 12

Pope Innocent III – Command for the Crusaders to Stay at Constantinople[47]

The following selection is from a later letter written by Pope Innocent III to the crusaders in Constantinople. Here the Pope's perspective on the situation has noticeably changed, as now he seems willing to make the best of Latin control of the city as a means for supporting future crusading in the Holy Land.

To all the clergy and the people in the Christian Army at Constantinople. If the Lord had granted the desires of his humble servants sooner, and had transferred, as He has now done, the Empire of Constantinople from the Greeks to the Latins before the fall of the Holy Land, perhaps Christianity would not be weeping today over the desolation of the land of Jerusalem. Since, therefore, through the wonderful transference of this empire, God has deigned to open to you a way to recover that land, and the detention of this may lead to the restoration of that, we advise and exhort you all, and we enjoin upon you for the remission of your sins, to remain for a year in Romania,[48] in order to strengthen the empire in its devotion to the Apostolic See and to us, and in order to retain it in the power of the Latins; and to give wise advice and efficient aid to Baldwin, our most beloved son in Christ, the illustrious Emperor of Constantinople; unless, perchance, your presence in the Holy Land should be necessary before that time, in which case you ought to hasten to guard it before the year elapses.

CHAPTER NINE
THE CRUSADE OF FREDERICK II, 1228–1229

146
PHILIP DE NOVARE – THE CRUSADE OF FREDERICK II

150
FREDERICK II – LETTER TO KING HENRY III

153
GEROLD OF JERUSALEM – LETTER
TO THE FAITHFUL ON FREDERICK II

156
IBN WASIL – THE HANDOVER OF JERUSALEM
TO THE FRANKS

159
SIBT IBN AL-JAUZI – THE HANDOVER
OF JERUSALEM TO THE FRANKS

The Crusade in Frederick's hands, however, was to be a far different kind of affair from his predecessors....In short, Frederick's objective was the conquest, not of the Moslem held territories of Palestine, but rather of the Crusading states.
– James A. Brundage[1]

FREDERICK II AND TENSIONS WITH THE PAPACY

In the wake of the curious results of the Fourth Crusade, Pope Innocent III had not given up the idea of another crusade to the East. Indeed, in 1213 he released the long-planned crusading encyclical *Quia Maior* as summons to the Fifth Crusade. The most important monarch to take crusading vows in conjunction with the new crusade was Frederick II, King of Norman Sicily and the German Empire. Yet when the time came to embark on the Fifth Crusade, Frederick, concerned about political issues at home, never showed up.[2] Eventually, after a series of lengthy delays based on Frederick's assurances of his pending arrival, the crusaders departed without him. After some initial success, the crusade ultimately ended in disaster in 1221.[3] Frederick's absence did not go unnoticed, and returning crusaders argued that had he and his forces been present on the crusade, the end result probably would have been different.[4]

Undeterred, the papacy almost immediately made plans for another crusade and this time demanded Frederick's participation under threat of excommunication. Frederick met with Pope Honorius III to assure him of his intentions to fulfil his crusading vow and agreed that if he did not take part this time, his excommunication would be proper.[5] Frederick set June 1225, ten years after his initial crusading vow, as the date of his departure. Organisational delays moved the departure date back to August 1227. The papacy made it clear that Frederick would be excommunicated if he delayed again.[6] Frederick delayed again, and on 29 September 1227 Pope Gregory IX, who replaced Pope Honorius III after his death earlier that year, excommunicated the emperor. Under enormous pressure, Frederick finally headed East in June of 1228, but he did so as an excommunicate without papal favour and backing.[7]

FREDERICK II'S CRUSADE

Although criticised for his inaction, Frederick had been engaged in negotiations with al-Kamil, the ruler of Egypt, since 1226. Even though al-Kamil had been victorious during the Fifth Crusade, he then became engaged in a power struggle with his two brothers, who controlled upper Mesopotamia, Syria and Palestine.[8] He offered Frederick Jerusalem and its kingdom if Fredrick was willing to redirect the crusade against Damascus instead of against his kingdom; Damascus was then being ruled by al-Kamil's brother al-Mu'uazzam.[9] Before Frederick could capitalise on this agreement, however, al-Mu'uazzam died in November 1227.

Frederick finally arrived in Acre in September 1228. There were deep divisions in the Holy Land over Frederick's status as an excommunicate and his commitment to the crusade. Indeed, Frederick appears to have been more inspired by the prospect of asserting his control over lands already under Christian control than waging war on Muslims.[10] Pope Gregory had already written to Patriarch Gerold of Jerusalem and others to warn them that Frederick was not a crusader but instead an enemy of the faith. Frederick was not overly concerned because just the presence of a crusading army, regardless of its morale, was a valuable inducement for al-Kamil to negotiate. Indeed, al-Kamil was engaged in a siege of Damascus to expand his authority into Palestine. He did not want Frederick's forces to cause a diversion that would hamper his efforts, so he again negotiated with Frederick to delay any action by the Christian armies until he had accomplished his goals in Syria.[11]

Frederick realised that al-Kamil was stalling, so he turned up the pressure by sending his army to Jaffa to refortify the city's defences for use as a staging ground for an attack on Jerusalem. This got al-Kamil's attention and prompted him to make Frederick an offer that he accepted. The deal stipulated a ten-year truce between Muslims and the Kingdom of Jerusalem, and al-Kamil would give Jerusalem, Bethlehem and Nazareth to Frederick. In exchange, Frederick paid a heavy price by agreeing that Jerusalem would remain defenceless and unfortified. He also agreed that Muslims in Jerusalem would be free to retain their homes and possessions and administer their own justice system; their holy places would be protected and remain under their control. Much more troubling, Frederick agreed to remain neutral in any wars between Muslims and Christians of Tripoli or Antioch and even to fight on the side of Muslims if any Christians broke the truce.[12]

The initial joy of Christians when they heard of Jerusalem's handover turned into anger when they heard the terms. They realised that unfortified Jerusalem would stay in Christian hands only until local Muslim rulers decided otherwise. Indeed, al-Kamil later bragged that he had only conceded the crusaders 'some churches and ruined houses' and he would chase them back out of Jerusalem when he was ready.[13] Frederick was stunned at the poor treatment he received from local Christians. Patriarch Gerold even sought to raise a Christian army against him. Open hostility broke out during Frederick's stay in Acre as clergy who preached against him were publicly flogged and the Templars and Hospitallers were besieged in their homes.[14] On 1 May 1229, Frederick II and his forces finally began their march down the streets of Acre to their ships to return to Europe. The Christian residents of Acre poured out into the streets shouting insults and pelting Frederick and his army with rotten meat.[15] Frederick's long-awaited crusade was over.

BACKGROUND TO THE SOURCES

The knight and chronicler Philip of Novare, who spent his adult life in the Middle East in the service of the Ibelin family, provides the lengthiest contemporary account of Frederick II's crusade.[16] The majority of Philip's work concerning Frederick's crusade focuses on the emperor's efforts to secure control over lands already under Christian control, rather than those under the Muslim control. In this case, Philip reports on an angry discussion that took place on the island of Cyprus when Frederick II demanded from John d'Ibelin, the Lord of Beirut, control of the city of Beirut and the income he had received as regent and ruler of Cyprus for the last ten years. Philip also describes how Frederick seized various fortresses and the royal revenues of several local lords for his use. Such efforts have led historians to speculate that Frederick's real goal was the conquest of the crusading states rather than the Muslim-controlled areas in Palestine.[17] Indeed, Philip devotes very little of his account to the emperor's negotiations with al-Kamil, noting only that Frederick made his truce with the Muslims with 'all particulars as they [Muslims] wished it'.

There also survive some letters by Frederick II in which he gives his view of his efforts in the Holy Land, or at least the perspective that he would like others to have. His letter to the English King Henry III, dated 17 March 1229, provides this perspective and is included in this chapter. In it, Frederick, perhaps in defiance of his earlier excommunication, describes how he came into possession of Jerusalem and other lands by 'a miracle' and 'the hand of the Lord'. Indeed, according to Frederick, God was the cause of Jerusalem's 'surrender' to him and for that reason all Christians should feel blessed. Frederick acknowledges some of the terms of his treaty with al-Kamil but is less than forthright in other instances. For example, he notes that before he leaves Jerusalem, he will be rebuilding the towers and walls of Jerusalem, which was not the case and nor did the treaty permit it.

Also provided in this chapter is a letter from Patriarch Gerold of Jerusalem to Latin Christians in the Holy Land that contrasts sharply with Frederick's claims of divinely inspired success. He warns that Frederick came to the Holy Land with insufficient forces and that his conduct was 'deplorable'. He initially criticises Frederick's poor treatment of other nobles in his efforts to seize their lands and challenges the emperor's claim to the kingship of Jerusalem, noting that it is still in dispute on account of his excommunication. Then Gerold turns his criticism towards the emperor's dealings with al-Kamil. He notes with disdain, for example, the 'long and mysterious conferences' in which Frederick agreed to a treaty with al-Kamil while not bothering to consult other local Christian leaders nor immediately release the terms of their agreement. Yet, by now, Gerold is aware of the terms and laments the 'malice' and 'fraudulent' articles of the truce. He also notes how Frederick had promised to fortify the city of Jerusalem but left for the city of Acre before doing so. Gerold complains that this left the residents of Jerusalem in danger from the Sultan of Damascus, with whom Frederick had not made a treaty. As a result, Gerold and others began raising an army to do what the emperor had not, but Frederick suspected that the army was raised to injure him. Therefore, Frederick dealt roughly with those suspected of having a part in raising the new army, prompting Gerold to comment, 'he never showed as much animosity and hatred against Saracens'. Gerold also notes that it was only after he and other ecclesiastical leaders announced an excommunication of all who aided the emperor against other Christians that Frederick decided to leave Acre. Yet he did so in spite, according to Gerold, by taking many of the 'engines of war' that had been used to defend Acre on his ships with him and sending others to al-Kamil, whom Gerold, with perhaps a touch of sarcasm, describes as 'his dear friend'.

There are also two Arab sources that provide valuable details about the Muslim reaction to Frederick's crusade and the treaty that resulted from it. The account of Ibn Wasil is the lengthier and more valuable of the two, as it extensively details the negotiations between Frederick and al-Kamil and the Sultan's true intentions regarding the treaty. He notes, for example, the Sultan's reasons for agreeing to the treaty, claiming that Jerusalem was indefensible as it was and that once he was in a position to expel the Christians and retake control of the Holy City he would do so. Hence, a temporary truce in which the Franks held a 'disarmed Jerusalem' would pose no threat to their greater plans for the region. He also references the concern and anger of Muslims upon hearing the loss of Jerusalem to Christian control, but this theme receives more coverage in the other Arab account by Sibt Ibn al-Jauzi presented in this chapter. While al-Jauzi confirms many of the details of Ibn Wasil's account, he also seems to confirm the suspicions of Patriarch Gerold over the emperor's commitment to his Christian faith. He notes, for example, that 'it was clear from what he said that he was a materialist and that his Christianity was simply a game to him.'

THE CRUSADE OF FREDERICK II, 1228–1229

THE SOURCES

Philip de Novare – The Crusade of Frederick II[18]

The following selection is taken from the memoirs of the knight Philip de Novare. It is written from the perspective of a man in the service of the Ibelin family, a family which had extensive and hostile interactions with Frederick during his time in the Holy Land and for several years after. As a result, Philip had access to first-hand information concerning the Ibelin's dealings with Frederick and the emperor's efforts to take control of the lands and revenues belonging to John d'Ibelin, the Lord of Beirut.

In the year 1229[19] the Emperor Frederick, at the command of Pope Gregory,[20] crossed the sea to Cyprus. He first landed at the city of Limassol,[21] where he had with him seventy galleys, transports and other ships. Most of his army and his household, together with his marshall and the horses, had already landed at Acre....

The Lord of Beirut[22]... went to the emperor with his children, all his friends and the whole of the Cypriot army, both knights and sergeants. They brought their little lord, King Henry,[23] to the emperor and put themselves completely at his disposal. The emperor received them with a great feast and with the semblance of great joy and it appeared that their enemies had been mistaken. The emperor immediately asked of them a favour, namely that they would put off the black robes which they were still wearing in mourning for the death of Philip d'Ibelin, the Lord of Beirut's brother. For, the emperor said, the joy of his arrival should be greater than their sorrow for the loss of their friend, the Lord of Beirut's brother, who had died, even though he had been a most brave and noble man. They acceded most cheerfully to his command and willingly thanked him. They offered to place their bodies, hearts and goods wholly at his service. The emperor joyfully thanked them, saying that he would repay them amply and richly. The emperor then sent scarlet gowns to those who had worn black and to others he sent jewellery and he gave all of them a verbal invitation to dine with him on the following day. They hastily fixed up their gowns and on the following morning they all appeared, clad in scarlet, before the emperor.

On the previous night, however, the emperor had secretly opened a door in the wall of a room which led into a garden – this was in a gracious house in which my lord Philip had housed him in Limassol.

The emperor had three thousand or more armed men – sergeants, arbalesters and sailors – enter secretly at night through this false postern, so that virtually all the men from his fleet were there. They were stationed throughout the stables and the rooms of the house, behind closed doors, until the dinner hour.

The tables were set and the water poured. The emperor put the Lord of Beirut and the old Lord of Caesarea,[24] who was Constable of Cyprus, at his own table. He placed the King of Cyprus and the King of Salonika[25] at the first place at another long table, together with the Marquis of Lancia[26] and the other barons of Germany and of the Kingdom. He ordered all the Cypriot knights to be seated in such a way that the Lord of Beirut and the others could hear and see him when he spoke. He also arranged for the two sons of the Lord of Beirut to serve him, one with the cup, the other with the bowl, and for the young Lord of Caesarea and the Lord Anceau de Brie to carve before him. The emperor had the four of them don tunics and doublets over their mantles, for such, he said, was the law and custom of the Empire. The young men served him very willingly and nobly and there were many courses and a variety of food. During the last course the armed men emerged from the places where they had been waiting and they took charge of the palace, the rooms and the great court and placed guards there and elsewhere. There were well-armed men in the palace where the emperor was and he had them seated before him with their weapons in their hands some held their swords by the pommel, others grasped their daggers. The Cypriots were well aware of what was going on, but they said not a word and tried to appear at ease.

The emperor turned to the Lord of Beirut and said aloud: 'Sir John, I ask two things of you. You will be wise if you do them agreeably and well.' The Lord of Beirut replied: 'Sire, say what is your pleasure and I shall willingly do what is right, so far as I understand it or as it is understood by honourable men.' 'One of the two things', said the emperor, 'is this: You will give me the city of Beirut, for you do not have it or hold it rightfully. The other thing is this: You will give me the income you have received as regent and ruler of Cyprus since the death of King Hugh, that is the income for the past ten years, for it is mine by right according to the custom of Germany.' The Lord of Beirut replied: 'Sire, I believe that you must be joking and making sport of me, as it may well be. Perchance some evil men who hate me have suggested that you demand these things of me and this is what has prompted you to do it. But, please God, you are such a good and wise lord that you know that we can and will serve you so willingly that you will not trust those evil men.' The emperor placed his hand upon his head and said: 'By this head, which has many times worn a crown, I shall have my way in these two matters which I have mentioned or you will be taken prisoner.' At this the Lord of Beirut rose up and his appearance was striking as he said loudly: 'I have and hold Beirut as my fief by right. My lady, Queen Isabelle [lacuna] who was my sister on my mother's side and a daughter of King Amaury and who is thus the rightful heir of the Kingdom of Jerusalem she and her lord, King Amaury together gave me Beirut in exchange for the constableship, when the Christians had recovered the city all destroyed. The Templars and the Hospitallers and all the barons of Syria had refused the town. I have restored its walls and have maintained it by the alms of Christendom and by my own labours. In it I have invested the income I had from Cyprus and elsewhere.[27] If you maintain that I hold it wrongfully, I will substantiate my reasons and my rights in the court of the Kingdom of Jerusalem. As for the income from the regency and governance of Cyprus which you demand of me, I never had it. My brother got from the regency only the headaches of governing and working for the Kingdom. But my niece, Queen Alice, had the income and did with it as she pleased, as the one who held the rights of regency according to our custom. If you demand this of me, I shall furnish you with proof according to the customs and the court of the Kingdom of Cyprus. And you may be certain that I shall do no more than this out of any fear of death or imprisonment, unless the judgment of the good and loyal court requires me so to do.'

The emperor grew very angry and swore and threatened him. Finally the emperor said: 'I heard and learned a long time ago across the sea that your words were handsome and polite and that you were very discreet and subtle with words, but I shall show you that your wit, your subtlety and your words are worth nothing against my power.'

The Lord of Beirut replied in such a way that those who were present were astounded and all of his friends were much afraid. His reply was: 'Sire, you heard tell long ago of my polite words: I too, have heard often and for long of your deeds. When I planned to come here, my whole council, with one voice, warned me that you would do what you are now doing and worse, and that I was not to trust you in any way. I came under no illusions; I had good advice and I understood it. But I would much rather suffer death or imprisonment than to allow anyone to speak evil of us or to allow the help due to Our Lord, the help due to the conquest of the Holy Land and your service to be hindered by me, my family or my compatriots....' He suddenly stopped and sat down.

The emperor was very angry and changed colour often. People stared at the Lord of Beirut and there were many words and threats. Religious men and other good people intervened to try to reach agreement, but no one could get the Lord of Beirut to alter what he had said he would do. The emperor made many strange and sinister requests. At last they agreed to do what the Lord of Beirut had earlier proposed and he could now be forced to concede no more than this: that he would furnish the emperor with twenty of the most noble vassals of Cyprus as hostages. These men would pledge by their bodies, their belongings and their estates that the Lord of Beirut would serve the emperor, would go to the Court of the Kingdom of Jerusalem and would there prove his rights, and that, when he had appeared in court, the hostages would be freed and released.

...In the year 1229[28] the emperor came to Syria with his whole navy. The King[29] and all the Cypriots, together with the Lord of Beirut, accompanied him. The Lord of Beirut went to Beirut, where he was joyfully received, for never was a lord more warmly loved by his men. He remained there but one day and then followed the emperor to Tyre. The emperor was very well received in Syria where all did homage to him as regent, because he had a little son called King Conrad, who was the rightful heir of the Kingdom of Jerusalem through his mother who was dead. The emperor and his men and all the Syrians left Acre to go to Jaffa. There they held truce conferences with al-Kamil, who was then Sultan of Babylon and Damascus,[30] and who held Jerusalem and the whole country. As a result of their agreement Jerusalem, Nazareth and Lydda were thereby turned over to the emperor.

In this same year,[31] amidst these events, the emperor ordered Count Stephen of Gotron and other Longobards[32] as well, to come to Cyprus. He had all the fortresses and the royal revenues seized for his use. He claimed that he was regent and that this was his right. The Cypriots were much perplexed and had their wives and children placed in religious houses wherever they could. Some of them namely Sir John d'Ibelin, later Count of Jaffa, who was then a child, his sister and other gentle-folk fled in the midst of the winter. It was a bad season and they barely escaped drowning, but, as it so pleased God, they finally arrived at Tortosa. The emperor held Cyprus. The Cypriots who were in his army were very uncomfortable and, had the Lord of Beirut sanctioned it, they would have carried off and kidnapped the young King Henry and would have fled from the emperor's camp.

The emperor was now disliked by all the people of Acre. He was the object of the Templars' special disfavour. There was at that time a very brave Templar, Brother Peter de Montagu, a most valiant and noble man, as was also the master of the Teutonic Knights. The people of the lowlands also had little use for the emperor. The emperor seemed to be delaying. Every day, even in winter, he kept his galleys armed, with the oars in the locks. Many people said that he wished to seize the Lord of Beirut and his children, Sir Anceau de Bries and his other friends, the Master of the Temple and other persons and have them shipped to Apulia. Another said that he wished to have them killed at a council to which he had called and summoned them but that they had been aware of this and went to the council with such forces that he dared not do it.

He made his truce with the Saracens in all particulars as they wished it. He went to Jerusalem and then to Acre. The Lord of Beirut never left him and, though he was often advised to leave, he did not wish to do so. The emperor assembled his people at Acre and had all the people of the city come and there were many who thought well of him....

The emperor secretly prepared to depart. At daybreak on the first of May, he boarded a galley before the Butchers' Street, without notifying anyone. Thus it happened that the butchers and the old people who lived on the street and who were very unfriendly saw his party and pelted him most abusively with tripe and scraps of meat.... Thus the emperor left Acre, cursed, bated and despised.

Frederick II – Letter to King Henry III[33]

The following is a letter written by Frederick II to King Henry III of England during his stay in the city of Jerusalem in March 1229. Frederick, as his own propagandist, casts his achievements regarding his negotiated handover of Jerusalem to his control as no less than a 'miracle' and suggests divine inspiration for the event.

Frederic, by the grace of God, the august Emperor of the Romans, King of Jerusalem and Sicily, to his well-beloved friend, Henry, King of the English, health and sincere affection.

Let all rejoice and exult in the Lord, and let those who are correct in heart glorify Him, who, to make known His power, does not make boast of horses and chariots, but has now gained glory for Himself, in the scarcity of His soldiers, that all may know and understand that He is glorious in His majesty, terrible in His, magnificence and wonderful in His plans on the sons of men, changing seasons at will, and bringing the hearts of different nations together; for in these few days, by a miracle rather than by strength that business has been brought to a conclusion, which for a length of time past many chiefs and rulers of the world amongst the multitude of nations, have never been able till now to accomplish by force, however great, nor by fear.

Not, therefore, to keep you in suspense by a long account, we wish to inform your holiness, that we, firmly putting our trust in God, and believing that Jesus Christ, His Son, in whose service we have so devotedly exposed our bodies and lives, would not abandon us in these unknown and distant countries, but would at least give us wholesome advise and assistance for His honour, praise and glory, boldly in the name set forth from Acre on the fifteenth day of the month of November last past and arrived safely at Joppa, intending to rebuild the castle at that place with proper strength, that afterwards the approach to the Holy City of Jerusalem might be not only easier, but also shorter and more safe for us as well as for all Christians. When, therefore we were, in the confidence of our trust in God, engaged at Joppa, and superintending the building of the castle and the cause of Christ, as necessity required and as was our duty, and whilst all our pilgrims were busily engaged in these matters, several messengers often passed to and fro between us and the Sultan of Babylon; for he and another sultan called Xaphat, his brother, were with a large army at the city of Gaza, distant about one day's journey from us; in another direction, in the city of Sichen, which is commonly called Neapolis, and situated in the plains, the Sultan of Damascus' his nephew, was staying with an immense number of knights and soldiers also about a day's journey from us and the Christians.

And whilst the treaty was in progress between the parties on either side of the restoration of the Holy Land, at length Jesus Christ, the Son of God, beholding from on high our devoted endurance and patient devotion to His cause, in His merciful compassion of us, at length brought it about that the Sultan of Babylon restored to us the Holy City, the place where the feet of Christ trod, and where the true worshippers adore the Father in spirit and in truth. But that we may inform you of the particulars of this surrender each as they happened, be it known to you that not only is the body of the aforesaid city restored to us, but also the whole of the country extending from thence to the seacoast near the castle of Joppa, so that for the future pilgrims will have free passage and a safe return to and from the sepulchre; provided, however, that the Saracens of that part of the country, since they hold the Temple in great veneration, may come there as often as they choose in the character of pilgrims, to worship according to their custom, and that we shall henceforth permit them to come, however, only as many as we may choose to allow, and without arms, nor are they to dwell in the city, but outside, and as soon as they have paid their devotions they are to depart.

Moreover, the city of Bethlehem is restored to us, and all the country between Jerusalem and that city; as also the city of Nazareth, and all the country between Acre and that city; the whole of the district of Turon, which is very extensive, and very advantageous to the Christians; the city of Sidon, too, is given up to us with the whole plain and its appurtenances, which will be the more acceptable to the Christians the more advantageous it has till now appeared to be to the Saracens, especially as there is a good harbour there, and from there great quantities of arms and necessaries might be carried to the city of Damascus and often from Damascus to Babylon. And although according to our treaty we are allowed to rebuild the city of Jerusalem in as good a state as it has ever been, and also the castles of Joppa, Cesarea, Sidon and that of St. Mary of the Teutonic order, which the brothers of that order have begun to build in the mountainous district of Acre, and which it has never been allowed the Christians to do during any former truce; nevertheless the sultan is not allowed, till the end of the truce between him and us, which is agreed on for ten years, to repair or rebuild any fortresses or castles.

And so on Sunday, the eighteenth day of February last past which is the day on which Christ, the Son of God, rose from dead, and which, in memory of His resurrection, is solemnly cherished and kept holy by all Christians in general throughout the world, this treaty of peace was confirmed by oath between us. Truly then on us and on all does that day seem to have shone favourably, in which the angels sing in praise of God, 'Glory to God on high, and on earth peace, and goodwill toward men.' And in acknowledgment of such great kindness and of such an honour, which, beyond our deserts and contrary to the opinion of many, God has mercifully conferred on us, to the lasting renown of His compassion, and that in His holy place we might personally offer to Him the burnt offering of our lips, be it known to you that on the seventeenth day of the month of March of this second indiction, we, in company with all the pilgrims who had with us faithfully followed Christ, the Son of God, entered the Holy City of Jerusalem, and after worshipping at the Holy Sepulchre, we, as being a Catholic emperor, on the following day, wore the crown, which Almighty God provided for us from the throne of His majesty, when of His especial grace, He exalted us on high amongst the princes of the world; so that whilst we have supported the honour of this high dignity, which belongs to us by right of sovereignty, it is more and more evident to all that the hand of the Lord hath done all this; and since His mercies are over all His works, let the worshippers of the orthodox faith henceforth know and relate it far and wide throughout the world, that

He, who is blessed for ever, has visited and redeemed His people, and has raised up the horn of salvation for us in the house of His servant David.

And before we leave the city of Jerusalem, we have determined magnificently to rebuild it, and its towers and walls, and we intend so to arrange matters that, during our absence, there shall be no less care and diligence used in the business, than if we were present in person. In order that this our present letter may be full of exultation throughout, and so a happy end correspond with its happy beginning, and rejoice your royal mind, we wish it to be known to you our ally, that the said sultan is bound to restore to us all those captives whom he did not in accordance with the treaty made between him and the Christians deliver up at the time when he lost Damietta some time since,[34] and also the others who have been since taken.

Given at the Holy City of Jerusalem, on the seventeenth day of the month of March, in the year of our Lord one thousand two hundred and twenty-nine.

Gerold of Jerusalem – Letter to the Faithful on Frederick II[35]

In stark contrast to Frederick's upbeat description of his efforts in the Holy Land, the Patriarch Gerold of Jerusalem, perhaps the emperor's chief nemesis during his time in the Holy Land, describes the emperor's actions as a 'detriment to the cause of Jesus Christ' and a 'great injury' to the Christian faith.

Gerold, patriarch of Jerusalem, to all the faithful – greeting.

If it should be fully known how astonishing, nay, rather deplorable, the conduct of the emperor has been in the eastern lands from beginning to end to the great detriment of the cause of Jesus Christ and to the great injury of the Christian faith, from the sole of his foot to the top of his head no common sense would be found in him. For he came, excommunicated, without money and followed by scarcely forty knights, and hoped to maintain himself by spoiling the inhabitants of Syria. He first came to and there most discourteously seized that noble man J. [John] of Ibelin and his sons, whom he had invited to his table under pretext of speaking of the affairs of the Holy Land. Next the king, whom he had invited to meet him, he retained almost as a captive. He thus by violence and fraud got procession of the kingdom.

After these achievements he passed over into Syria. Although in the beginning he promised to do marvels and although in the presence of the foolish he boasted loudly, he immediately sent to the Sultan of Babylon to demand peace. This conduct rendered him despicable in the eyes of the sultan and his subjects, especially after they discovered that he was not at the head of a numerous army which might have to some extent added weight to his words. Under the pretext of defending Joppa, he marched with the Christian army towards that city, in order to be nearer the sultan and in order to be able more easily to treat of peace or obtain a truce. What more shall I say? After long and mysterious conferences and without having consulted any one who lived in the country, he suddenly announced one day that he had made peace with the sultan. No one saw the text of the peace or truce when the emperor took the oath to observe the articles which were agreed upon. Moreover, you will be able to see clearly how great the malice was and how fraudulent the tenor of certain articles of the truce which we have decided to send to you. The emperor for giving credit to his word wished as a guarantee only the word of the sultan, which he obtained. For he said, among other things that the Holy City was surrendered to him.

He went thither with the Christian army on the eve of the Sunday when 'Oculi mei' is sung [third Sunday in Lent]. The Sunday following, without any fitting ceremony and although excommunicated, in the chapel of the sepulchre of our Lord, to the manifest prejudice of his honour and of the imperial dignity, he put the diadem upon his forehead, although the Saracens still held the temple of the Lord and Solomon's temple, and although they proclaimed publicly as before the law of Mohammed – to the great confusion and chagrin of the pilgrims.

This same prince, who had previously very often promised to fortify Jerusalem, departed in secrecy from the city at dawn on the following Monday. The Hospitallers and the Templars promised solemnly and earnestly to aid him with all their forces and their advice, if he wanted to fortify the city, as he had promised. But the emperor who did not care to set affairs right, and who saw that there was no certainty in what had been done, and that the city in the state in which it had been surrendered to him, could be neither defended nor fortified, was content with the name of surrender, and on the same day hastened with his family to Joppa. The pilgrims who had entered Jerusalem with the emperor, witnessing his departure, were unwilling to remain behind.

The following Sunday when 'Laetare Jerusalem' is sung [fourth Sunday in Lent], he arrived at Acre. There in order to seduce the people and to obtain their favour, he granted them a certain privilege. God knows the motive which made him act thus, and his subsequent conduct will make it known. As, moreover, the passage was near, and as all pilgrims, humble and great, after having visited the Holy Sepulchre, were preparing to withdraw, as if they had accomplished their pilgrimage, because no truce had been concluded with the Sultan of Damascus, we, seeing that the holy land was already deserted and abandoned by the pilgrims, in our council formed the plan of retaining soldiers, for the common good, by means of the alms given by the King of France, of holy memory.

When the emperor heard of this, he said to us that he was astonished at this, since he had concluded a truce with the Sultan of Babylon. We replied to him that the knife was still in the wound, since there was not a truce or peace with the Sultan of Damascus, nephew of the aforesaid sultan and opposed to him, adding that even if the Sultan of Babylon was unwilling, the former could still do us much harm. The emperor replied, saying, that no soldiers ought to be retained in his kingdom without his advice and consent, as he was now King of Jerusalem. We answered to that, that in the matter in question, as well as in all of a similar nature, we were very sorry not to be able, without endangering the salvation of our souls, to obey his wishes, because he was excommunicated. The emperor made no response to us, but on the following day he caused the pilgrims who inhabited the city to be assembled outside by the public crier, and by special messengers he also convoked the prelates and the monks.

Addressing them in person, he began to complain bitterly of us, by heaping up false accusations. Then turning his remarks to the venerable matter of the Templars, he publicly attempted to severely tarnish the reputation of the latter, by various vain speeches, seeking thus to throw upon others the responsibility for his own faults which were now manifest and adding at last, that we were maintaining troops with the purpose of injuring him. After that he ordered all foreign soldiers, if they valued their lives and property, not to remain in the land from that day on, and ordered count Thomas, whom he intended to leave as bailiff of the country, to punish with stripes any one who was found lingering, in order that the punishment of one might serve as an example to many. After doing all this he withdrew, and would listen to no excuses or answers to the charges which he had so shamefully made. He determined immediately to post some crossbowmen at the gates of the city, ordering them to allow the Templars to go out but not to return. Next he fortified with crossbows the churches and other elevated positions, and especially those which commanded the communications between the Templars and ourselves. And you may be sure that he never showed as much animosity and hatred against Saracens.

For our part, seeing his manifest wickedness, we assembled all the prelates and all the pilgrims, and menaced with excommunication all those who should aid the emperor with their advice or their services against the church, the Templars, the other monks of the holy land or the pilgrims.

The emperor realising that his wickedness could have no success, was unwilling to remain any longer in the country. And, as if he would have liked to ruin everything, he ordered the crossbows and engines of war, which for a long time had been kept at Acre for the defence of the Holy Land, to be secretly carried onto his vessels. He also sent away several of them to the Sultan of Babylon, as his dear friend. He sent a troop of soldiers to Cyprus to levy heavy contributions of money there and, what appeared to us more astonishing, he destroyed the galleys which he was not able to take with him. Having learned this, we resolved to reproach him with it, but shunning the remonstrance and the correction, he entered a galley secretly, by an obscure way, on the day of the Apostles, St. Philip and St. James, and hastened to reach the island of Cyprus, without saying adieu to any one, leaving Joppa destitute; and may he never return.

Very soon the bailiffs of the above-mentioned sultan shut off all departure from Jerusalem for the Christian poor and the Syrians, and many pilgrims died thus on the road. This is what the emperor did, to the detriment of the Holy Land and of his own soul, as well as many other things which are known and which we leave to others to relate. May the merciful God deign to soften the results! Farewell.

Ibn Wasil – The Handover of Jerusalem to the Franks[36]

The following account by the Arab historian Ibn Wasil gives the Muslim perspective of al-Kamil's negotiations with Frederick, the negative reaction by many Muslims to the surrender of Jerusalem and al-Kamil's defence of the treaty and his reasons for agreeing to it. He was a young man at the time of Frederick and al-Kamil's negotiations, but he composed his account much later in life when he had attained a position of stature (*Grand Qadi*) that would have allowed him access to important written and oral sources on the events of Frederick's crusade.

Then followed the negotiations between al-Malik al-Kamil and the emperor of which the object had been fixed earlier when al-Kamil and the emperor first met, before the death of al-Malik al-Mu'azzam. The Frankish King refused to return home except on the conditions laid down, which included the surrender of Jerusalem and of part of the area conquered by Saladin, whereas al-Malik al-Kamil was by no means prepared to yield him these territories. It was finally agreed that he should have Jerusalem on condition that he did not attempt to rebuild the walls, that nothing outside it should be held by the Franks, and that all the other villages within its province should be Muslim, with a Muslim governor resident at al-Bira, actually in the province of Jerusalem. The sacred precincts of the city, with the Dome of the Rock and the Masjid al-Aqsa were to remain in Muslim hands, and the Franks were simply to have the right to visit them, while their administration remained in the hands of those already employed in it, and Muslim worship was to continue there. The Franks excepted from the agreement certain small villages on the road from Acre to Jerusalem, which were to remain in their control unlike the rest of the province of Jerusalem.

The Sultan al-Malik al-Kamil maintained that if he broke with the emperor and failed to give him full satisfaction the result would be a war with the Franks in which the Muslims would suffer irreparably, and everything for which they were working would slip from their grasp. So he was in favour of satisfying the Franks with a disarmed Jerusalem and making a temporary truce with them. He would seize the concessions back from them later, when he chose to. The amir Fakhr ad-Din ibn ash-Shaikh conducted the negotiations for him, and many conversations and discussions took place between them, during which the emperor sent to al-Malik al-Kamil queries on difficult philosophic, geometric and mathematical points, to test the men of learning at his court. The sultan passed the mathematical questions on to Shaikh 'Alam ad-Din Qaisar, a master of that art, and the rest to a group of scholars, who answered them all. Then al-Malik al-Kamil and the emperor swore to observe the terms of the agreement and made a truce for a fixed term. In this way they arranged matters between themselves, and each side felt secure in its relations with the other. I was told that the emperor said to the amir Fakhr ad-Din: 'If I were not afraid that my prestige among the Franks would be destroyed if I should not have imposed these conditions on the sultan. I have no real ambition to hold Jerusalem, nor anything else; I simply want to safeguard my reputation with the Christians.'

After the truce the sultan sent out a proclamation that the Muslims were to leave Jerusalem and hand it over to the Franks. The Muslims left amid cries and groans and lamentations. The news spread swiftly throughout the Muslim world, which lamented the loss of Jerusalem and disapproved strongly of al-Malik al-Kamil's action as a most dishonourable deed, for the reconquest of that noble city and its recovery from the hand of the infidel had been one of al-Malik an-Nasir Saladin's most notable achievements — God sanctify his spirit! — But al-Malik al-Kamil of noble memory knew that the Muslims could not defend themselves in an unprotected Jerusalem, and that when he had achieved his aim and had the situation well in hand he could purify Jerusalem of the Franks and chase them out. 'We have only', he said, 'conceded to them some churches and some ruined houses. The sacred precincts, the venerated Rock and all the other sanctuaries to which we make our pilgrimages remain ours as they were; Muslim rites continue to flourish as they did before, and the Muslims have their own governor of the rural provinces and districts.'

After the agreement the emperor asked the sultan for permission to visit Jerusalem. This the sultan granted, and ordered the qadi of Nablus Shams ad-Din of blessed memory, who enjoyed great prestige and favour with the Ayyubid house, to be at the emperor's service during the time of his visit to Jerusalem and his return to Acre. The author Jamal ad-Din ibn Wasil says: 'The Qadi of Nablus Shams ad-Din of blessed memory told me: "I took my place beside him as the Sultan al-Malik al-Kamil had ordered me to and entered the Sacred Precinct with him, where he inspected the lesser sanctuaries. Then I went with him into al-Aqsa, whose construction he admired, as he did that of the Dome of the Rock. When we came to the mihrab he admired its beauty, and commended the pulpit, which he climbed to the top. When he descended he took my hand and we went out in the direction of al-Aqsa. There he found a priest with the Testament in his hand about to enter al-Aqsa. The emperor called out to him: 'What has brought you here? By God, if one of you comes here again without permission I shall have his eyes put out! We are the slaves and servants of al-Malik al-Kamil. He has handed over this church to me and you as a gracious gift. I do not want any of you exceeding your duties.' The priest made off, quaking with fear. Then the king went to the house that had been prepared for him and took up residence there." The Qadi Shams ad-Din said: "I recommend the muezzins not to give the call to prayer that night, out of respect for the King. In the morning I went to him, and he said: 'O qadi, why did the muezzins not give the call to prayer last night in the usual way?' 'This humble slave', I replied, 'prevented them, out of regard and respect for Your Majesty.' 'You did wrong to do that,' he said: ' My chief aim in passing the night in Jerusalem was to hear the call to prayer given by the muezzins, and their cries of praise to God during the night.'" Then he left and returned to Acre.'

When news of the loss of Jerusalem reached Damascus al-Malik an-Nasir began to abuse his uncle al-Malik al-Kamil for alienating the people's sympathies, and ordered the preacher, shaikh Shams ad-Din Yusuf, the nephew (sibt) of shaikh Jamal ad-Din ibn al-Juazi, who was in great public favour as a preacher, to preach a sermon in the Great Mosque in Damascus. He was to recall the history of Jerusalem, the holy traditions and legends associated with it, to make the people grieve for the loss of it, and to speak of the humiliation and disgrace that its loss brought upon the Muslims. By this means al-Malik an-Nasir Dawud proposed to alienate the people from al-Malik al-Kamil and to ensure their loyalty to himself in his contest with his uncle. So Shams ad-Din preached as he was told to, and the people came to hear him. It was a memorable day, one on which there rose up to heaven the cries, sobs and groans of the crowd. I myself was one of the crowd there, and among the matters to which I heard him refer was a qasida composed by him, rhyming in 't', into which he had inserted a few lines by the poet Di'bil al-Khuza, of which I recall the following:

In the sanctuary of the Ascent and of the Rock, which surpasses in glory every other rock in the world. There are Qur'anic schools now deprived of recitations of the sacred verses, and a seat of revelation in the now deserted courtyards. On that day one saw nothing but weeping men and women. Now that the truce between al-Malik al-Kamil and the emperor had been ratified the latter weighed anchor and returned home.

Sibt Ibn al-Jauzi – The Handover of Jerusalem to the Franks[37]

The following source from Sibt Ibn al-Jauzi also details the treaty between al-Kamil and Frederick II as well as Muslim concerns over the handover of Jerusalem. Yet al-Jauzi also provides insights into how Muslims viewed Frederick and his commitment to his professed Christian faith. As was Ibn Wasil, Sibt Ibn al-Jauzi was also a young man at the time of Frederick's crusade, but he probably wrote his later account using first-hand sources.

News of the loss of Jerusalem spread to Damascus, and disaster struck all the lands of Islam. It was so great a tragedy that public ceremonies of mourning were instituted: al-Malik an-Nasir Dawud invited me to preside over a meeting in the Great Mosque of Damascus and to speak of what had occurred in Jerusalem. I could not refuse him, considering obedience to his desire as one of my religious duties and part of my zeal for the cause of Islam. So I ascended (the pulpit) of the Great Mosque of Damascus, in the presence of al-Malik an-Nasir Dawud, at the gate of Mashhad 'Ali. It was a memorable day, for not one of the people of Damascus remained outside. In the course of my oration I said: 'The road to Jerusalem is closed to the companies of pious visitors! O desolation for those pious men who live there; how many times have they prostrated themselves there in prayer, how many tears have they shed there! By Allah, if their eyes were living springs they could not pay the whole of their debt of grief; if their hearts burst with grief they could not diminish their anguish! May God burnish the honour of the believers! O shame upon the Muslim rulers! At such an event tears fall, hearts break with sighs, grief rises up on the high...' and so on throughout a long discourse. The poets too composed many works on the same subject.

The emperor entered Jerusalem while Damascus was under siege. During his visit various curious incidents occurred: one was that when he went into the Dome of the Rock he saw a priest sitting near the imprint of the Holy Foot, and taking some pieces of paper from the Franks. The emperor went up to him as if he wanted to ask a benediction of him, and struck him a blow that knocked him to the ground. 'Swine!' he cried. 'The sultan has done us the honour of allowing us to visit this place, and you sit here behaving like this! If any of you comes in here again in this way I shall kill him!' The scene was described by one of the custodians of the Dome of the Rock. They said too that the emperor looked at the inscription that runs round the inside of the sanctuary, saying: 'Saladin purified this city of Jerusalem of the polytheists...' and asked: 'Who would these polytheists be?' He also asked the custodians: 'What are these nets at the doors of the sanctuary for?' 'They replied: "So that the little sparrows should not come in."' He said: 'God has brought the giants here instead!' When the time came for the midday prayer and the muezzins' cry rang out, all his pages and valets rose, as well as his tutor, a Sicilian with whom he was reading (Aristotle's) *Logic* in all its chapters, and offered the canonic prayer, for they were all Muslims. The emperor, as these same custodians recall, had a red skin, and was bald and short-sighted. Had he been a slave he would not have been worth two hundred dirham. It was clear from what he said that he was a materialist and that his Christianity was simply a game to him. Al-Kamil had ordered the Qadi of Nablus, Shams ad-Din, to tell the muezzins that during the emperor's stay in Jerusalem they were not to go up into their minarets and give the call to prayer in the sacred precinct. The qadi forgot to tell the muezzins, and so the muezzin 'Abd al-Karim mounted his minaret at dawn and began to recite the Qur'anic verses about the Christians, such as 'God has no son', referring to Jesus, son of Mary, and other such texts. In the morning the qadi called 'Abd al-Karim to him and said: 'What have you done? The sultan's command was thus and thus.' He replied: 'You did not tell me; I am sorry.' The second night he did not give the call. The next morning the emperor summoned the qadi, who had come to Jerusalem as his personal adviser and had been responsible for handing the city over to him, and said: 'O qadi, where is the man who yesterday climbed the minaret and spoke these words?' The qadi told him of the sultan's orders. 'You did wrong, qadi; would you alter your rites and law and faith for my sake? If you were staying in my country, would I order the bells to be silenced for your sake? By God, do not do this; this is the first time that we have found fault in you!' Then he distributed a sum of money among the custodians and muezzins and pious men in the sanctuary; ten dinar to each. He spent only two nights in Jerusalem and then returned to Jaffa, for fear of the Templars, who wanted to kill him.

CHAPTER TEN
THE CRUSADE OF LOUIS IX, 1248–1249

170
AL MAKRISI – THE CORRESPONDENCE OF ST. LOUIS
AND NEDJM EDDIN

171
LETTER OF GUY THE KNIGHT ON THE CAPTURE OF DAMIETTA

175
JEAN DE JOINVILLE – THE RETREAT FROM MANSOURA
AND THE CAPTURE OF KING LOUIS IX

177
JEAN DE JOINVILLE – LOUIS IN CAPTIVITY
AND NEGOTIATIONS FOR HIS RANSOM

179
JEAN DE JOINVILLE ON THE OATHS
OF LOUIS IX AND THE EMIRS

180
JEAN DE JOINVILLE ON THE EXECUTION OF THE TREATY
AND THE NEAR EXECUTION OF THE KING

182
AL MAKRISI – THE CRUSADERS' CAPTURE OF DAMIETTA

183
AL MAKRISI – THE DEATH OF THE SULTAN

185
AL MAKRISI – THE CRUSADERS
ATTACK MANSOURA

188
AL MAKRISI – THE DEFEAT OF THE CRUSADERS
AND THE CAPTURE OF KING LOUIS

190
AL MAKRISI – THE ASSASSINATION OF THE SULTAN

191
AL MAKRISI – THE KING'S RANSOM

192
AL MAKRISI – MUSLIM POETRY
ON THE HUMILIATION OF ST. LOUIS

Louis IX's crusade proved the best prepared, most lavishly funded and meticulously planned of all. It was also one of the most disastrous, its failure matching its ambition.
— Christopher Tyerman[1]

THE TROUBLING FAILURE OF A SAINT

The French King Louis IX seemed the perfect leader for a crusade. Unlike the excommunicated and impious Emperor Frederick II, Louis had a reputation for faithfulness and devotion. As a result, with great hope and enthusiasm, Louis began his first crusade in 1248. Yet his crusade led to a disaster that resulted not only in the defeat of Louis's army, but in the humiliating capture and imprisonment of the king himself. A worse result could not have been anticipated.

THE FIRST CRUSADE OF LOUIS IX

Crusaders were supposed to be repentant and strive for holiness to ensure God's favour during battle. Therefore, few seemed as ideal a candidate to lead a crusade as the French King Louis IX, who later became known as Saint Louis. Indeed, his devotion to crusading was evident from the beginning. Following news of the loss of Jerusalem in 1244, although seriously ill, Louis made a crusading vow. His domineering mother and former regent, Blanche of Castile, enlisted the Bishop of Paris in an effort to convince Louis that a vow taken during a time of illness was not valid and thus persuade him to abandon his plans for a crusade. Louis's response was to immediately retake his vow once he was well again.[2] Indeed, Louis's commitment to the crusade, both physically and financially, was absolute.[3]

Louis departed for Cyprus in August 1248, where he spent eight months mustering troops. As had been the plan for the Fourth and Fifth Crusades, the goal was the conquest of Egypt as a means of eventually securing the Holy Land. Louis and his crusaders had intended to target Alexandria, but a storm altered their plans and led their ships instead to the Nile River by Damietta in June 1249. The Muslim defenders of Damietta were stunned by the arrival of the Christian fleet, as they had already sent most of their soldiers to join a larger Muslim force awaiting the crusaders at Alexandria. As a result, they almost immediately abandoned the city, and the crusaders quickly occupied it as their operational base. The crusaders remained at Damietta for six months before finally beginning a major march to the Muslim stronghold of Mansoura. In February 1250, the crusaders engaged their opponents, and the battle settled, with Louis's troops holding the field while the Muslims held the city.

The crusaders, hampered by disease and exposed to constant harassment from their opponents, ultimately had little choice but to withdraw and try to reach Damietta. During the march, the crusaders were overcome by their Muslim opponents; having no other option, they were forced to surrender, and the king was taken prisoner.

Suffering the humiliation of captivity, Louis and others began negotiations for their ransom. During this time, Louis was threatened with torture and his captors even considered his execution.[4] Yet Louis's immense value as a prisoner probably made the idea of an enormous ransom far too appealing to resist. Indeed, an enormous ransom was paid and Damietta was surrendered to finalise the release of Louis and much of his captive army on 6 May.[5] While most of Louis's troops returned to France, the king went to Acre.[6] He wanted to ensure that all of his troops secured their freedom and assist in the defence of Latin settlements that might become victim to a new Muslim offensive in the wake of his failure.[7] Louis interpreted his misfortunes on the crusade as a punishment for his sins.[8] As a result, his religious devotion became more intense. He dedicated himself to alleviating the suffering of the poor and dressed and ate simply as he sought to atone for his failure through good kingship. Louis never gave up on crusading, regardless of his initial failure. Indeed, his death came sixteen years later while embarked on a second crusade to Tunis. On his death bed, the ill and dying king was heard to sigh, 'Jerusalem! Jerusalem!'[9]

BACKGROUND TO THE SOURCES

One of the most detailed Arab sources for Louis's first crusade is Al Makrisi's *The Road to Knowledge of the Return of Kings*. Although Makrisi's work was written in the mid-fifteenth century, he carefully composed his account based on the works of earlier writers and thus it is indispensable for understanding the Arab perspective of events in Ayyubid and Mamluk history from 1181 until 1436.[10] Included here are several selections from Makrisi's work on key events from Louis's first crusade. First is the fascinating correspondence that Makrisi claims took place between Louis and the Sultan of Egypt prior to the crusade. Makrisi provides the text of a letter sent by Louis to the Sultan Nedjm Eddin seeking his conversion and the Sultan's defiant reply.

The second source was a correspondence written in 1249 by a crusader at Damietta to a friend in Paris and is concerned about the affairs of the crusade. The author identifies himself only as Guy, a knight of the household of the viscount of Melun, and his letter provides valuable details about the capture of Damietta are not found in other sources. Of particular interest is Guy's account of Louis's speech to his men on their arrival at Damietta. It characteristically reflects his deep religiosity and supreme confidence in the divine inspiration of the crusaders' efforts.[11] Yet the rest of the work is devoted to the events of the capture of Damietta and reflects the jubilation Louis and other crusaders felt upon doing so. Guy details how the crusaders were helped by escaped slaves and 'faithful Orientals' who were baptised 'with true devotion'. Yet more than anything, it was the massive number of the crusaders that ultimately sent the defenders fleeing from the city and made possible its capture. Guy notes how the Muslims lacked weapons and troops and departed on the side of the city opposite the crusading army, taking with them their families and all that they could carry, but still leaving the city stocked full of supplies for the crusaders. Guy ends his account by noting how they are biding their time in Damietta while the leadership decides their next move. Guy would not have been aware that he was composing his letter at the high point of the crusade, with only disappointment to follow.

The remaining selections are taken from the eyewitness account of Jean de Joinville,[12] the most important and detailed Christian source for the crusade, and from the already referenced Arab source of Al Makrisi. Joinville provides useful information on a number of key moments of the crusade after the capture of Damietta, particularly the events leading to Louis's capture, which he claims were told to him directly by the king himself. He describes how, when the king was on the verge of negotiating a truce to end the fighting, a 'traitor' announced to the army that the king had commanded the army to yield when he had not. As a result, the soldiers stopped fighting and were taken prisoner, giving the Sultan no reason to negotiate a truce as he had already captured so many Christians. Indeed, with most of his army now captive to the Sultan, the king himself was taken prisoner. Joinville, also imprisoned with the king, reports on the conditions of Louis's captivity, noting that the king had been threatened with torture if he did not order the surrender of certain Christian strongholds. When Louis refused to be swayed by threats of torture, his captors instead asked for money, in addition to the surrender of Damietta, for the king's ransom. Thus began negotiations in which Louis ultimately agreed to a ransom in which money was paid for the release of his crusaders and Damietta was surrendered in exchange for the king's freedom.

Joinville also provides a fascinating report on the oaths taken by Louis and his captors concerning the king's ransom and release. He notes, for example, how Louis's concern over one aspect of the oath caused him to refrain from taking it. This resulted in the torture of the Patriarch of Jerusalem, who had travelled to visit Louis in captivity. A short time later, with Joinville unsure of how the matter was resolved, the king was able to take a satisfactory oath. Finally, Joinville's account of the handover of Damietta is also included here. Joinville accuses his former captors of bad faith on a number of issues. He notes, for example, that the Christian sick in Damietta were not evacuated as they were supposed to be cared for by the Muslims, but instead once Muslims took possession of the city they killed them all. Indeed, Joinville notes that his Muslim captors even considered at one point executing the king.

Of equal interest is Makrisi's Arab account of the crusade, in which he details the crusaders' capture of Damietta and the events leading up to the decisive Muslim victory at Mansoura. Makrisi's account agrees with the Christian account of Guy the Knight in ascribing the crusaders' victory at Damascus to the early withdrawal of Muslim forces in the face of the superior numbers of the crusaders. Makrisi also laments the distinction between the loss of Damietta during Louis's crusade, at a time when the city was well fortified and supplied, and the loss of the city during the Fifth Crusade, at a time when the city's Muslim defenders suffered from plague and famine yet were able to hold off the crusaders for sixteen months. Indeed, according to Makrisi, the Sultan ordered fifty of the principal officers of the garrison who had abandoned Damietta to be strangled for their cowardice.

Makrisi also provides details on the death of Nedjm Eddin in November 1249. Unsuccessful efforts were made to keep the news secret until the position of Sultan was filled by his son, Touran Chah. This change in authority came during the crucial period when the Muslim army was gathering its forces at Mansoura, the site where the crusaders suffered a stunning setback that led to the surrender of Louis's forces and the capture of King Louis. Makrisi describes the number of crusaders taken as slaves as 'so great, it was embarrassing', with most put to death. Louis, on the other hand, surrendered with the promise that his life would be spared, to which his value as a prisoner, without any doubt, contributed. The king was then bound with chains and, along with his brother, taken under guard. At this point, as Makrisi disparagingly notes, the new Sultan celebrated his victory by giving 'himself up to all sorts of debauchery'. Concerns over the Sultan's debaucheries and his excessive spending led to his assassination, which in turn led to the ascension of the Sultana Chegeret-Eddur, the surviving wife of Nedjm Eddin, as sovereign of Egypt. She then depended on the emirs to take care of the affairs of governance, including negotiations for the ransom of King Louis and other crusaders in exchange for money and the return of Damietta to Muslim control. Finally, this chapter also includes a selection of Arab poetry celebrating the humiliation of Louis, written by an Arab contemporary of the crusade, as reported by Makrisi.

THE SOURCES

Al Makrisi – The Correspondence of St. Louis and Nedjm Eddin[13]

Provided here is the correspondence that Makrisi claims took place between Louis and Nedjm Eddin immediately prior to the crusade. Louis declares that the only way the Sultan can avoid the crusade is through his conversion to Christianity. Nedjm Eddin, in response, defiantly reminds Louis of past Muslim military successes against Christian armies and declares his confidence in God's protection.

The King of France, before he commenced any hostilities, sent by a herald a letter to the Sultan Nedjm Eddin, conceived in the following words – 'You are not ignorant that I am the prince of those who follow the religion of Jesus Christ, as you are of those who obey the laws of Muhammad. Your power inspires me with no fear. How should it? I who make the Muslims in Spain tremble! I lead them as a shepherd does a flock of sheep. I have made the bravest among them perish, and loaded their women and children with chains. They endeavour by presents to appease me, and turn my arms to another quarter. The soldiers who march under my standards cover the plains, and my cavalry is not less redoubtable. You have but one method to avoid the tempest that threatens you. Receive priests, who will teach you the Christian religion, embrace it and adore the Cross; otherwise I will pursue you everywhere, and God shall decide whether you or I be master of Egypt.'

Nedjm Eddin, on reading this letter, could not restrain his tears. He caused the following answer to be written by the cadi Behaedin, his secretary:- 'In the name of the Omnipotent and All merciful God, salvation to our prophet Muhammad and his friends! I have received your letter, it is filled with menaces, and you make a boast of the great number of your soldiers. Are you ignorant that we know the use of arms, and that we inherit the valour of our ancestors? No one has ever attacked us without feeling our superiority. Recollect the conquests we have made from the Christians; we have driven them from the lands they possessed; their strongest towns have fallen under our blows.[14] Recall to your mind that passage of the Qu'ran, which says, "Those who make war unjustly shall perish...."'[15]

Letter of Guy the Knight on the Capture of Damietta[16]

The following source was written in 1249 by a crusader in Damietta to a friend in Paris. The letter provides a first-hand account on the progress of Louis's crusade up to this point and recounts how the crusaders came to take possession of Damietta, the high point of the crusade for Christians.

To his dear half brother and well beloved friend, Master B. of Chartres, student at Paris, Guy, a knight of the household of the viscount of Melun, greeting and a ready will to do his pleasure.

Because we know that you are uneasy about the state of the Holy Land and our lord, the King of France, and that you are interested in the general welfare of the church as well as the fate of many relatives and friends who are fighting for Christ under the king's orders, therefore, we think we ought to give you exact information as to the events of which a report has doubtless already reached you.

After a council held for that purpose, we departed from Cyprus for the East. The plan was to attack Alexandria, but after a few days a sudden tempest drove us over a wide expanse of the sea. Many of our vessels were driven apart and scattered. The Sultan of Cairo and other Saracen princes, informed by spies that we intended to attack Alexandria, had assembled an infinite multitude of armed men from Cairo, Babylon, Damietta and Alexandria, and awaited us in order to put us, while exhausted, to the sword. One night we were borne over the waves by a violent tempest. Toward morning the sky cleared, the storm abated, and our scattered vessels came together safely. An experienced pilot who knew all the coast in this part of the sea and many idioms, and who was a faithful guide, was sent to the masthead, in order that he might tell us if he saw land and knew where we were. After he had carefully and sorrowfully examined all the surrounding country, he cried out terrified, 'God help us, God help us, who alone is able; we are before Damietta.' Indeed all of us could see the land. Other pilots on other vessels had already made the same observation, and they began to approach each other. Our lord, the king, assured of our position, with undaunted spirit, endeavoured to reanimate and console his men.

'My friends and faithful soldiers', said he to them, 'we shall be invincible if we are inseparable in our love of one another. It is not without the divine permission that we have been brought here so quickly. I am neither the King of France nor the holy church, you are both. I am only a man whose life will end like other men's when it shall please God. Everything is in our favour, whatever may happen to us. If we are conquered, we shall be martyrs; if we triumph, the glory of God will be exalted thereby that of all France, yea, even of Christianity, will be exalted thereby. Certainly it would be foolish to believe that God, who foresees all, has incited me in vain. This is His cause, we shall conquer for Christ, He will triumph in us, He will give the glory, the honour and the blessing not unto us, but unto name.'

In the meantime our assembled vessels approached the land. The inhabitants of Damietta and of the neighbouring shores could view our fleet of 1500 vessels, without counting those still at a distance and which numbered 150. In our times no one, we believe, had ever seen such a numerous fleet of vessels. The inhabitants of Damietta, astonished and frightened beyond expression, sent four good galleys, with well-skilled sailors, to examine and ascertain who we were and what we wanted. The latter having approached near enough to distinguish our vessels, hesitated, stopped, and, as if certain of what they had to report, made ready to return to their own party; but our galleys with the fast boats got behind them and hemmed them in, so that they were compelled, in spite of their unwillingness, to approach our ships.

Our men, seeing the firmness of the king and his immovable resolution, prepared, according to his orders, for a naval combat. The king commanded to seize these mariners and all whom they met, and ordered us afterward to land and take possession of the country. We then, by means of our mangonels which hurled from a distance five or six stones at once, began to discharge at them fire darts, stones, and bottles filled with lime, made to be shot from a bow, or small sticks like arrows. The darts pierced the mariners and their vessels, the stones crushed them, the lime flying out of the broken bottles blinded them. Accordingly, three hostile galleys were soon sunk. We saved, however, a few enemies. The fourth galley got away very much damaged. By exquisite tortures we extracted the truth from the sailors who fell alive into our hands, and learned that the citizens of Damietta had left the city and awaited us at Alexandria. The enemies who succeeded in escaping and whose galley was put to flight, some mortally wounded, uttering frightful cries, went to tell the multitude of Saracens who were waiting on the shore, that the sea was covered with a fleet which was drawing near, that the King of France was coming in hostile guise with an infinite number of barons, that the Christians were 10,000 to one, and that they caused fire, stones and clouds of dust to rain down. 'However', they added 'while they are still fatigued from the labour of the sea, if your lives and your homes are dear to you, hasten to kill them, or at least to repulse them vigorously until our soldiers return. We alone have escaped with difficulty to warn you. We have recognised the ensigns of the enemy. See how furiously they rush upon us, equally ready to fight on land or sea.'

In consequence of this speech, fear and distrust seized the enemy. All of our men, assured of the truth, conceived the greatest hopes. In emulation of one another they leaped from their vessels into the barks; the water was too shallow along the shore, the barks and the small vessels could not reach the land. Several warriors, by the express order of the king, cast themselves into the sea. The water was up to their waists. Immediately began a very cruel combat. The first crusaders were promptly followed by others and the whole force of infidels was scattered. We lost only a single man by the enemy's fire. Two or three others, too eager for the combat, threw themselves into the water too quickly and owed their deaths to themselves rather than to others. The Saracens giving way, retired into their city, fleeing shamefully and with great loss. Great numbers of them were mutilated or mortally wounded.

We would have followed them closely, but our chiefs, fearing an ambush, held us back. While we were fighting some slaves and captives broke their chains, for the jailors had also gone out to fight us.[17] Only the women, children and the sick had remained in the city. These slaves and captives, full of joy rushed to meet us, applauding our king and his army, and crying 'Blessed is he Who cometh in the name of the Lord.' These events happened on Friday the day of our Lord's Passion; we drew from it a favourable augury. The king disembarked joyfully and safely, as well as the rest of the Christian army. We rested until the next day, When, with the aid and under the guidance of slaves who knew the country and the roads, we got possession of what remained to be captured of the land and shore. But during the night the Saracens, who had discovered that the captives had escaped, had killed those who remained. They thus made of them glorious martyrs in of Christ, to their own damnation.

In the darkness of the following night and on Sunday morning, as they lacked weapons and troops, the Saracens seeing the multitude of the Christians who were landing, their courage and firmness, and the sudden desolation of their own city, lacking leaders, superiors and persons to incite them, as well as destitute of strength and weapons for fighting, departed, taking their women and children and carrying off everything movable. They fled from the other side of the city by little gates which they had made long before. Some escaped by land, others by sea, abandoning their city filled with supplies of all kinds. That same day at nine o'clock, two captives who escaped by chance from the hands of the Saracens, came to tell us what had happened. The king, no longer fearing an ambush, entered the city before three o'clock without hindrance and without shedding blood. Of all who entered only Hugo Brun, earl of March, was severely wounded. He lost too much blood from his wounds to survive for he was careless of his life, because of the reproaches which had been inflicted upon him, and rashly rushed into the midst of the enemy. He had been stationed in the front rank, at his own request, because he knew that he was an object of suspicion.

I must not forget to say that the Saracens, after having determined to flee, hurled at us a great quantity of Greek fire,[18] which was very injurious to us, because it was carried by a wind which blew from the city. But this wind, suddenly changing, carried the fire back upon Damietta, where it burned several persons and fortresses. It would have consumed more property, if the slaves who had been left had not extinguished it by a process which they knew, and by the will of God, who did not wish that we should take possession of a city which had been burnt to the ground.

The king, having then entered the city in the midst of cries of joy, went immediately into the temple of the Saracens to pray and thank God, whom he regarded as the author of what had taken place. Before eating, all the Christians, weeping sweet and sacred tears of joy, and led by the legate, solemnly sang that hymn of the angels, the *Te Deum Laudamus*.[19] Then the mass of the blessed Virgin was celebrated in the place where the Christians in ancient times had been wont to celebrate mass and to ring the bells, and which they had now cleansed and sprinkled with holy water. In this place, four days before, as the captives told us, the foul Mohammed had been worshiped with abominable sacrifices, loud shouts and the noise of trumpets. We found in the city an infinite quantity of food, arms, engines, precious clothing, vases, golden and silver utensils and other things. In addition we had our provisions, of which we had plenty, and other dear and necessary objects brought from our vessels.

By the divine goodness, the Christian army, like a pond which is greatly swollen by the torrents pouring in, was added to each day by some soldiers from the lands of lord Villehardouin and some Templars and Hospitallers, besides pilgrims newly arrived, so that we were, by God's grace, largely reinforced. The Templars and Hospitallers did not want to believe in such a triumph. In fact, nothing that had happened was credible. All seemed miraculous, especially the Greek fire which the wind carried back onto the heads of those who hurled it against us. A similar miracle formerly took place at Antioch.[20] A few infidels were converted to Jesus Christ and up to the present time have remained with us.

We, instructed by the past, will in the future exercise much prudence and circumspection in our actions. We have with us faithful Orientals upon whom we can count. They know all the country and the dangers which it offers; they have been baptised with true devotion. While we write, our chiefs are considering what it is necessary to do. The question is whether to proceed to Alexandria or Babylon and Cairo. We do not know what will be decided. We shall inform you of the result, if our lives are spared. The Sultan of Babylon, having learned what has taken place, has proposed to us a general engagement for the morrow of St. John the Baptist's day, and in a place which the two armies shall choose, in order, as he says, that fortune may decide for the men of the East or the men of the West, that is between the Christians and themselves, and that the party to whom fate shall give the victory, may glory in it, and the conquered may humbly yield. The king replied that he did not fear the enemy of Christ one day more than another and that he offered no time for rest, but that he defied him tomorrow and every day of his life, until he should take pity on his own soul and should turn to the Lord who wishes the whole world to be saved, and who opens the bosom of His mercy to all those who turn to Him. We tell you these things in this letter through our kinsmen Guiscard. He seeks nothing else than that he may, at our expense prepare himself for a professorship and have a fit lodging for at least two years.

We have learned nothing certain worth reporting about the Tartars.[21] We can expect neither good faith from the perfidious, nor humanity from the inhuman, nor charity from dogs, unless God, to whom nothing is impossible, works this miracle. It is He who has purged the Holy Land from the wicked Charismians.[22] He has destroyed them and caused them to disappear entirely from under heaven. When we learn anything certain or remarkable of the Tartars, or others, we will send you word either by letter or by Roger de Montefagi, who is to return to France in the spring, to the lands of our lord the viscount, to collect money for us.

Jean de Joinville – The Retreat from Mansoura and the Capture of King Louis IX[23]

The following source is taken from the eyewitness account of Jean de Joinville, who accompanied Louis IX during his first crusade. This selection covers events that took place in April 1250 after the crusaders had left the safety of Damietta and sailed down the Nile to engage their Muslim opponents at Mansoura. After fighting to a stalemate and engaging in unsuccessful negotiations over the exchange of Jerusalem for Damietta, the demoralised Christian forces, racked by disease and dysentery, began their ill-fated retreat back to Damietta. During their retreat, the crusaders were overcome in battle and Louis was taken prisoner.

When the king saw that he could only remain there to die, he and his people, he ordered and arranged that they should strike their camp, late on Tuesday (5 April 1250), at night, after the octave of Easter, to return to Damietta. He caused his mariners who had galleys to be told that they should get together the sick, and take them thither. He also commanded Josselin of Cornaut, and his brothers, and the other engineers, to cut the ropes that held the bridge between us and the Saracens; but of this they did nothing.

We embarked on the Tuesday, after dinner, in the afternoon, I and two of my knights whom I had remaining, and the rest of my followers. When the night began to fall, I told my mariners to draw up their anchor, and let us go down the stream; but they said they dared not because the sultan's galleys, which were between us and Damietta, would surely put us to death. The mariners had made great fires to gather the sick into their galleys, and the sick had dragged themselves to the bank of the river. While I was exhorting the mariners to let us begone, the Saracens entered into the camp, and I saw, by the light of the fires, that they were slaughtering the sick on the bank.

While my mariners were raising their anchor, the mariners appointed to take away the sick cut the ropes of their anchors and of their galleys, and came alongside our little ship, and so surrounded us on one side and the other that they well-nigh ran us down. When we had escaped from this peril, and while we were going down with the stream, the king who had upon him the sickness of the host and a very evil dysentery, could easily have got away on the galleys, if he had been so minded; but he said that, please God, he would never abandon his people. That night he fainted several times; and because of the sore dysentery from which he suffered, it was necessary to cut away the lower part of his drawers, so frequent were his necessities.

They cried to us, who were floating on the water, that we should wait for the king; and when we would not wait, they shot at us with crossbows bolts; wherefore it behoved us to stop until such time as they gave us leave to fare forward.

Now I will leave off speaking of this matter, and tell you how the king was taken, as he himself related it to me. He told me how he had left his own division and placed himself, he and my lord Geoffry of Sargines, in the division that was under my Lord Gaucher of Chatillon, who commanded the rearguard.

And the king related to me that he was mounted on a little courser covered with a housing of silk; and he told me that of all his knights and sergeants there only remained behind with him my Lord Geoffry of Sargines, who brought the king to a little village, there where the king was taken; and as the king related to me, my Lord Geoffry of Sargines defended him from the Saracens as a good servitor defends his lord's drinking cup from flies; for every time that the Saracens approached, he took his spear, which he had placed between himself and the bow of his saddle, and put it to his shoulder, and ran upon them, and drove them away from the king.

And thus he brought the king to the little village; and they lifted him into a house, and laid him, almost as one dead, in the lap of a burgher-woman of Paris, and thought he would not last till night. Thither came my Lord Philip of Montfort, and said to the king that he saw the emir with whom he had treated of the truce, and, if the king so willed, he would go to him, and renew the negotiation for a truce in the manner that the Saracens desired. The king begged him to go, and said he was right willing. So my Lord Philip went to the Saracen; and the Saracen had taken off his turban from his head, and took off the ring from his finger in token that he would faithfully observe the truce.

Meanwhile a very great mischance happened to our people; for a traitor sergeant, whose name was Marcel, began to cry to our people: 'Yield, lord knights, for the king commands you, and do not cause the king to be slain!' All thought that the king had so commanded, and gave up their swords to the Saracens. The emir saw that the Saracens were bringing in our people prisoners, so he said to my Lord Phillip that it was not fitting that he should grant a truce to our people, for he saw very well that they were already prisoners.

Jean de Joinville – Louis in Captivity and Negotiations for His Ransom[24]

The following selection details Louis's time in captivity. Joinville describes how the king was threatened with torture and the negotiations for his ransom that followed.

The counsellors of the sultan had tried the king in the same manner that they had tried us, in order to see if the king would promise to deliver over to them any of the castles or the Temple of the Hospital, or any of the castles belonging to the barons of the land; and, as God so willed, the king had answered after the very same manner that we had answered. And they threatened him, and told him that as he would not do as they wished, they would cause him to be put in the bernicles. Now the bernicles are the most cruel torture that any one can suffer. They are made of two pieces of wood, pliable, and notched at the ends with teeth that enter the one into the other; and the pieces of wood are bound together at the end with strong straps of ox-hide; and when they want to set people therein, they lay them on their side, and put their legs between the teeth; and then they cause a man to sit on the pieces of wood. Hence it happens that, not half a foot of bone remains uncrushed. And to do the worst they can, at the end of three days, when the legs are swollen, they replace the swollen legs in the bernicles, and crush them all once more. To these threats the king replied that he was their prisoner, and that they could do with him according to their will.

When they saw that they could not prevail over the good king by threats, they came back to him and asked how much money he would give to the sultan, besides surrendering Damietta. And the king replied that if the sultan would accept a reasonable sum, he would advertise the queen to pay it for their deliverance. And they asked: 'How is it that you will not tell us definitely that these things shall be done?' And the king replied that he did not know if the queen would consent, seeing she was his lady and the mistress of her actions. Then the counsellors returned and spoke to the sultan, and afterwards brought back word to the king that if the queen would pay a million besants of gold, which are worth five hundred thousand livres, the sultan would release the king.

And the king asked them, on their oath, whether the sultan would release them, provided the queen consented. So they went back once more and spoke to the sultan, and on their return, made oath that the sultan would release the king on these conditions. And now that they had taken the oath, the king said and promised to the emirs, that he would willingly pay the five hundred thousand livres for the release of his people, and surrender Damietta for the release of his own person, seeing it was not fitting that such as he should barter himself for coin. When the sultan heard this he said: 'By my faith, this Frank is large-hearted not to have bargained over so great a sum! Now go and tell him,' said he, 'that I give him a hundred thousand livres towards the payment of the ransom'.

Jean de Joinville on the Oaths of Louis IX and the Emirs[25]

Here Joinville describes the complicated procedures involved in working out precise and acceptable language for the oaths both Louis and the emirs were to take to finalise their negotiations for the king's ransom.

The oaths which the emirs[26] were to swear to the king were devised and set forth in writing, and were to this effect: that if they did not observe this covenant with the king they should be as dishonoured as a man who, for his sin, goes on pilgrimage to Mahomet, at Mecca, with his head uncovered; and as dishonoured as a man who leaves his wife, and then takes her again (for in that case, according to the law of Mahomet, if a man leaves his wife, he can never have her again, save after seeing her in the arms of another man). The third oath was to this effect: that if they did not observe their covenant with the king, they should be as dishonoured as a Saracen who had eaten swine's flesh. The king was satisfied with the aforesaid oaths of the emirs, because Master Nicholas of Acre, who understood the Saracen tongue, said that, according to their law, they could devise no oaths stronger or more binding.

When the emirs had sworn they caused to be put in writing the oath they demanded of the king; and this oath was framed on the advice of the priests who had denied their faith and gone over to them, and the writing was to this effect: that if the king did not observe his covenants with the emirs, he should be as dishonoured as a Christian who denies God and His mother, and forfeits the fellowship of the twelve Companions of our Lord, and of all the saints. To this the king agreed right willingly. The last point in the oath was to this effect: that if the king did not observe his covenants with the emirs, he should be as dishonoured as a Christian who denies God and His law, and who, in despite of God, spits upon the cross and tramples upon it. When the king heard this he said that, please God, he would never take that oath!

The emirs sent Master Nicholas, who knew the Saracens tongue, to the king, and he spoke to the king in these words: 'Sire, the emirs are greatly incensed, forasmuch as they have sworn what your required of them, whereas you will not swear what they require of you; and be assured that if you do not swear this oath they will cause your head to be cut off, as well as the heads of all your people.' The king replied that they could act in this matter as it seemed best to them; but that he liked better to die as a good Christian rather than to live under the wrath of God and of His mother.

The patriarch of Jerusalem,[27] an old and reverend man of fourscore years, had obtained a safe conduct from the Saracens, and come to help the king to obtain his deliverance. Now it is the custom between the Christians and the Saracens that when the king or the sultan dies, those who are on an embassage, whether it be in a Christian or a pagan land, are made prisoners and slaves; and because the sultan, who had given the safe conduct to the patriarch, was now dead, the said patriarch was a prisoner like as we were. When the king had given his answer, one of the emirs said that it was given by the advise of the patriarch, and he said to the pagans: 'If you will believe me, I will make the king swear, for I will cause the head of the patriarch to fly into the king's lap.'

They would not listen to this; but they took the patriarch from the side of king, and tied him to the pole of the pavilion with his hands behind his back, and straitly bound that the said hands swelled to the size of his head, and that the blood started from between the nails. The patriarch cried to the king: 'Sire, for the love of God, swear without fear; for seeing that you intend to hold to your oath, I take upon my own soul whatsoever there may be of sin in the oath that you take!' I know not how this matter of the oath was settled; but in the end the emirs held themselves satisfied with the oath taken by the king, and by the other men of note there present.

Jean de Joinville on the Execution of the Treaty and the Near Execution of the King[28]

In the following selection, Joinville describes the Christian handover of Damietta to the Muslims in fulfilment of the ransom agreement. Joinville, however, accuses the Muslim side of bad faith for executing the Christian sick of Damietta and delaying the release of Louis and other Christian prisoners from captivity while debating their execution.

After the covenants between the king and the emirs had been settled and sworn to, it was agreed that they should release us on the day after Ascension Day; and that so soon as Damietta was delivered over to the emirs, they would release the person of the king and of the men of note who were with him, as has been already said. On the Thursday at night (5 May 1250) those who were in charge of our four galleys came to anchor in the midst of the river, before the bridge of Damietta, and caused a pavilion to be pitched before the bridge, there where the king should land.

At sun-rising my Lord Geoffry of Sargines went into the city, and caused the city to be given up to the emirs. The sultan's flags were hoisted on all the towers of the city. The Saracen knights got into the city, and began to drink the wines, and were soon all drunken; whereupon one of them came to our galley, and drew his sword all reeking with blood, and said that for his part he had killed six of our people.

Before Damietta was surrounded, the queen had been received into our ships, together with all our people who were in Damietta, save the sick only. These last the Saracens, by their oath, were bound to keep and guard; but they killed them all. The king's engines of war, which they were also bound to preserve, they knocked to pieces. And the salted meat, which they were bound to keep for us, inasmuch as they do not eat pork, they did not keep. They made a pile of the engines, and a pile of the bacon, and another of the dead people, and they set fire thereto; and the fire was so great that it lasted the Friday, the Saturday and the Sunday.

The king, and all we who were there, should have been set free at sunrise, but the Saracens kept us till sunset; and we had nothing to eat, nor the emirs either, and they were quarrelling the livelong day. And one of them spoke in this wise for those who belonged to his party: 'Lords, if you will listen to me, and to those who are of my party, you will kill the king and the men of note who are here; for then, for the space of forty years, we need fear nothing, seeing that their children are young, and that we hold Damietta; wherefore we can do this with the greater security.'

Another Saracen, whose name was Sebreci, and who was a native of Mauritania, spoke contrariwise, and said this: 'If we kill the king, after we have killed the sultan, it will be said that the Egyptians are the most evil people in the world and the most disloyal.' And those who desired that we should be killed rejoined: 'it is sooth that we have too wickedly rid ourselves of our sultan, whom we put to death; for we have therein gone counter to the commandments of Mahomet, in that he commanded us to guard our lord as the apple of our eye. And behold in this book, here is the commandment written. But listen', said he, 'to this other commandment of Mahomet, that comes after'. And with that he turned over the leaf of a book that held in his hand, and showed them another commandment, which was to this effect: 'For the assurance of the faith, slay the enemy of the law. Now have we disobeyed the commandments of Mahomet, in that we have killed our lord; but we shall do worse if we do not kill the king, whatever promise of safety has been given to him, seeing that he is the most powerful enemy of the pagan law.'

Our death was nearly agreed to; whence it happened that one of the
emirs, who was our adversary, thought we were all to be killed, and came
on the river, and began to cry, in the Saracen tongue, to those who had
the galleys in charge, and took his turban from his head, and made a sign
to them with his turban. And now they lifted anchor, and took us back
a full league up the stream towards Babylon. Then we gave ourselves
up for lost, and many were the tears shed.

As God, who does not forget His own, so willed, it was agreed, at about
the setting of the sun, that we should be released. So we were brought
back, and our four galleys drawn to the bank. We demanded to be let go.
They said they would not let us go until we had eaten, 'for it would be
a shame to our emirs if you left our prisons fasting.'

Al Makrisi – The Crusaders' Capture of Damietta[29]

In the following source, Makrisi confirms much of Guy the Knight's
account of the crusaders' capture of Damietta. He notes, for example,
how, at the sight of the enormous Christian army, the Muslim defenders
of the city fled, leaving Damietta and its resources in the hands of the
crusaders. Indeed, their actions resulted in charges of cowardice by the
Sultan and the execution of fifty officers. Although Makrisi wrote long
after the events he describes, he based his account on earlier works that
no longer survive, making his account indispensable for understanding
the Arab perspective of Louis's first crusade.

The French disembarked on the Saturday, on the same shore where
Fakreddin had made his encampment, and pitched a red tent for their
king. The Muslims made some movements to prevent their landing; and
the emirs Nedjm Eddin[30] and Sarimeddin were slain in these skirmishes.

At the beginning of the night the emir Fakreddin decamped with his
whole army, and crossed the bridge which leads to the eastern shore of
the Nile, whereon Damietta is situated. He took the road to Achmoum
Tanah, and by this march the French were left masters of the western
bank of that river.

It is impossible to paint the despair of the inhabitants of Damietta
when they saw the emir Fakreddin march away from their town, and
abandon them to the fury of the Christians.. They were afraid to wait
for the enemy, and quitted their town precipitately during the night.
This conduct of the Muslim general was so much the less excusable
as the garrison was composed of the bravest of the tribe of Beni-Kenane,

and as Damietta was in a better state of resistance than when it was besieged by the Franks during the reign of the Sultan al Kamil;[31] for, although plague and famine afflicted the town, the Franks could not conquer it until after sixteen months' siege.

On the Monday morning (6 June 1249), the French came before the town; but, astonished to see no one, they were afraid of a surprise. They were soon informed of the flight of its inhabitants, and, without striking a blow, took possession of this important place, and all the ammunition and provision they found there.

When the news of the capture of Damietta reached Cairo, the consternation was general. They considered how greatly this success would augment the courage and hopes of the French; for they had seen an army of Muslims timorously fly before them, and were in possession of an innumerable quantity of arms of all sorts, with plenty of ammunition and provision. The disorder of the sultan, which daily grew worse, and hindered him from acting in this critical state of affairs, overwhelmed the Egyptians with despair. No one now longer doubted but that the kingdom would be conquered by the Christians.

The sultan, indignant at the cowardice of the garrison, ordered fifty of the principal officers to be strangled. In vain did they allege in their defence the retreat of the emir Fakreddin: the sultan told them they deserved death, for having quitted Damietta without his orders. One of these officers, condemned to death with his son, requested to be executed first; but the sultan refused him this favour, and the father had the misery to see his son expire before his eyes. After this execution, the sultan, turning to the emir Fakreddin, asked with an enraged tone, 'What resistance have you made? What battles have you fought? You could not withstand the Franks one hour. You should have shown more courage and firmness'. The officers of the army, fearing for Fakreddin the rage of the sultan, made the emir understand by their gestures that they were ready to massacre their sovereign. Fakreddin refused his assent, and told them afterward that the sultan could not live more than a few days; and that, if the prince wished to trouble them, they were able at any time to get rid of him.

Al Makrisi – The Death of the Sultan[32]

In the following selection, Makrisi tells of the untimely death of the Sultan Nedjm Eddin and the unsuccessful efforts of the emirs and his wife to keep it secret until his son, Touran Chah, could replace him.

Makrisi suggests that it was the news of the Sultan's death and
the potential confusion this might have caused among the Muslim
leadership that inspired the crusaders to move into the interior
seeking an advantage.

Nedjm Eddin, notwithstanding his melancholy state, gave orders for his
departure for Mansoura. He entered his boat of war,[33] and arrived there
on Wednesday the 25th of the moon Sefer (9 June AD 1249). He put the
town in a posture of defence by employing his whole army on this service.
The boats ordered by the prince before his departure arrived laden with
soldiers, and all sorts of ammunition. Every one able to bear arms ranged
himself under his standards, and he was joined by the Arabs in great
numbers. While the sultan was making his preparations, the French were
adding new fortifications to Damietta, and placed there a considerable
garrison.

On Monday, the last day of the moon Rebiulewel (12 July ~ AD 1249)
thirty-six Christian prisoners were conducted to Cairo; they had belonged
to the guard of the camp against the inroads of the Arabs, among whom
were two knights. The 5th of the same moon, thirty-seven were sent
thither on the 7th, twenty-two; and on the 16th, forty-five other prisoners;
and among these last were three knights. Different Christian princes, who
held lands on the coast of Syria, had accompanied the French, by which
their places were weakened. The inhabitants of Damascus seized this
opportunity to besiege Sidon, which, after some resistance, was forced
to surrender. The news of this, when carried to Cairo, caused an excess
of joy, and seemed to compensate for the loss of Damietta. Prisoners
were made almost daily from the French, fifty of whom were sent to
Cairo the 18th of the moon Diemazilewel (29 August AD 1249).

The sultan continued daily to grow worse in health; and the physicians
despaired of his recovery, for he was attacked at the same time by a fistula
and an ulcer on his lungs. At length he expired, on the night of the 15th
of the moon Chaban (22 November), after having appointed as his
successor his son Touran Chah. Nedjm Eddin was forty-four years old
when he died, and had reigned ten years. It was he who instituted that
militia of slaves, or of Mamluk-Baharites, thus called from being quartered
in the castle which this prince had built in the island of Roudah, opposite
to old Cairo. This militia, in course of time, seized on the throne of Egypt.[34]

As soon as the sultan had expired, the Sultana Chegeret-Eddur, his
spouse, sent for the general Fakreddin and the eunuch Diemaleddin,
to inform them of the death of the sultan, and to request their assistance
in supporting the weight of government at such a critical period. All three

resolved to keep the sultan's death a secret, and to act in his name as if he were alive. His death was not to be made public until after the arrival of Touran Chah, to whom were sent messengers after messengers. Notwithstanding these precautions, the French were informed of his death. Their army instantly quitted the plains of Damietta, and encamped at Fariskour. Boats laden with provision and stores came up the Nile, and kept the army abundantly supplied.

The emir Fakreddin sent a letter to Cairo to inform the inhabitants of the approach of the French and to exhort them to sacrifice their lives and fortunes in the defence of the country. This letter was read in the pulpit of the great mosque, and the people answered only with sighs and groans. Every thing was in trouble and confusion; and the death of the sultan, which was suspected, added to the consternation. The most cowardly thought of quitting a town which they believed unable to withstand the French; but the more courageous, on the contrary, marched to Mansoura, to join the Muslim army.

On Tuesday, the 1st day of the moon Ramadan (7 December AD 1249), there were some trifling skirmishes between different corps of troops of each army. This, however, did not prevent the French army from encamping at Charmesah: the Monday following, being the 7th of the same moon, the army advanced to Bermoun.

Al Makrisi – The Crusaders Attack Mansoura[35]

The following source is Makrisi's account of the key battle of Mansoura that began when the crusaders arrived before the town in December 1249. Makrisi reports that it was in the months that followed, while the two sides were engaged in battle, that Touran Chah was made aware of the death of his father and replaced him as sultan. Makrisi credits the new sultan, who finally joined the battle at Mansoura in February 1250, with the unusual, but successful, tactic of building ships and then having them carried in pieces on camels to later be reassembled and launched on the Nile. These ships, seemingly appearing out of nowhere and stocked with soldiers, were able to cut off both the crusaders' resupply ships and their means of escape.

On Sunday, the 13th day of the same moon, the Christian army appeared before the town of Mansoura, the branch of the Achmoum was between it and the Egyptian camp. Nasir Daoud, Prince of Karak, was on the western bank of the Nile with some troops. The French traced out their camp, surrounding it with a deep ditch surmounted by a palisado, and erected machines to cast stones at the Egyptian army. Their fleet arrived at the same time; so that there were engagements on water and on land. On Wednesday, the 15th day of the same moon, six deserters passed over to the camp of the Muslims, and informed them that the French army was in want of provision.

The day of Bairam, a great lord, and relation to the King of France, was made prisoner. Not a day passed without skirmishes on both sides, and with alternate success. The Muslims were particularly anxious to make prisoners, to gain information as to the state of the enemy's army, and used all sorts of strategies for this purpose. A soldier from Cairo bethought himself of putting his head withinside of a watermelon, the interior of which he had scooped out, and of thus swimming toward the French camp; a Christian soldier, not suspecting a trick, leaped into the Nile to seize the melon; but the Egyptian was a stout swimmer, and catching hold of him, dragged him to his general.

On Wednesday, the 7th day of the moon Chewal (12 January 1250), the Muslims captured a large boat, in which were a hundred soldiers, commanded by an officer of distinction. On Thursday, the 15th of the same moon, the French marched out of their camp, and their cavalry began to move. The troops were ordered to file off, when a slight skirmish took place, and the French left on the field forty cavaliers with their horses. On the Friday, seventy prisoners were conducted to Cairo, among whom were three lords of rank. On the 22nd of the same moon, a large boat belonging to the French took fire, which was considered as a fortunate omen for the Muslims.

Some traitors having shown the ford over the canal of Achmoum to the French, fourteen hundred cavaliers crossed it, and fell unexpectedly on the camp of the Muslims, on a Tuesday, the 15th day of the moon Zilkalde (8 February), having at their head the brother of the King of France. The emir Fakreddin was at the time in the bath: he instantly quitted it with precipitation, and mounted a horse without saddle or bridle, followed only by some slaves. The enemy attacked him on all sides, but his slaves, like cowards, abandoned him when in the midst of the French, it was in vain he attempted to defend himself, he fell pierced with wounds. The French, after the death of Fakreddin, retreated to Djedile; but their whole cavalry advanced to Mansoura, and, having forced one of the gates, entered the town: the Muslims fled to the right and left. The King of France had already penetrated as far as the sultan's palace, and victory seemed ready to declare for him, when the Baharite slaves, led by Baibars,[36] advanced, and snatched it from his hands: their charge was so furious that the French were obliged to retreat. The French infantry, during this time, had advanced to cross the bridge; had they been able to join their cavalry, the defeat of the Egyptian army, and the loss of the town of Mansoura, would have been inevitable. Night separated the combatants, when the French retreated in disorder to Djedile, after leaving fifteen hundred of their men on the field. They surrounded their camp with a ditch and wall, but their army was divided into two corps: the least considerable body was encamped on the branch of the Achmoum, and the larger on the great branch of the Nile that runs to Damietta.

A pigeon had been let loose to fly to Cairo the instant the French had surprised the camp of Fakreddin, having a note under its wing, to inform the inhabitants of this misfortune. This melancholy event had created a general consternation in the town, which the runaways had augmented, and the gates of Cairo were kept open all the night to receive them. A second pigeon bearing the news of the victory over the French, had restored tranquillity to the capital. Joy succeeded sorrow; and each congratulated the other on this happy turn of affairs, and public rejoicings were made.

When Touran Chah heard of the death of his father, Nedjm Eddin, he set out from Huns Keifa. It was the 15th of the moon Ramadan when he departed, attended by only fifty horsemen, and he arrived at Damascus toward the end of that moon. After receiving the homage of all the governors of the towns in Syria, he set out on a Wednesday, the 27th day of the moon Chewal, and took the road to Egypt. The news of his arrival raised the courage of the Muslims. The death of Nedjm Eddin had not yet been publicly announced, the service of the sultan was performed as usual, his officers prepared his table as if he had been alive, and every order was given in his name. The sultana governed the kingdom, and found, in her own mind, resources for all. The moment she heard of Touran Chah's arrival, she waited on him, and laid aside the sovereign command, to invest him with it. This prince was anxious to appear at the head of his troops, and set out for Mansoura, where he arrived on the 5th of the moon Zilkade (8 February).

Boats sent from Damietta brought all sorts of provision to the French camp, and kept it abundantly supplied. The Nile was now at its greatest height. Touran Chah caused many boats to be built, which, when taken to pieces, he placed on the backs of camels, and had them thus carried to the canal of Mehale, when they were put together again, launched on the canal, and filled with troops for an ambuscade. As soon as the French fleet of boats appeared at the mouth of the canal of Mehale, the Muslims quitted their hiding-place, and attacked them. While the two fleets were engaged, other boats left Mansoura filled with soldiers, and fell on the rear of the French. It was in vain they sought to escape by flight: a thousand Christians were killed or made prisoners.

Al Makrisi – The Defeat of the Crusaders and the Capture of King Louis[37]

In the following selection, Makrisi describes the plight of the crusaders, cut off from supplies and suffering from starvation, and their attempt to reach Damietta by an overland march. Their efforts resulted in a military disaster at Fariskour, where Muslims routed the crusader army and took King Louis prisoner. Makrisi also notes the joy with which the new sultan exalted in triumph.

In this defeat, fifty-two of their boats laden with provision were taken, and their communication with Damietta by the navigation of the Nile was cut off, so that within a short time the whole army suffered the most terrible famine. The Muslims surrounded them on all sides, and they could neither advance nor retreat.

On the 1st of the moon Zilhige (7 March), the French surprised seven boats; but the troops on board had the good fortune to escape. In spite of the superiority of the Egyptians on the Nile, they attempted to bring up another convoy from Damietta, but they lost it: thirty-two of their boats were taken and carried to Mansoura, on the 9th of the same moon. This new loss filled the measure of their woes, and caused them to propose a truce and send ambassadors to treat of it with the sultan. The emir Zeineddin and the cadi Bedreddin were ordered to meet and confer with them, when the French offered to surrender Damietta, on condition that Jerusalem, and some other places in Syria, should be given in exchange for it. This proposal was rejected, and the conferences broken up.

On Friday, the 27th of the moon Zilhige (1 April), the French set fire to all their machines of war and timber for building, and rendered almost all their boats unfit for use. During the night of Tuesday, the 3rd day of the moon Mahasem (5 April), in the year of the Hegira 648, the whole of the French army decamped, and took the road to Damietta. Some boats which they had reserved fell down the Nile at the same time. The Muslims having, at break of day of the Wednesday, perceived the retreat of the French, pursued and attacked them.

The heat of the combat was at Fariskour. The French were defeated and put to flight: ten thousand of their men fell on the field of battle, some say thirty thousand. Upwards of one hundred thousand horsemen, infantry, trades-people and others, were made slaves. The booty was immense in horses, mules, tents and other riches. There were but one hundred slain on the side of the Muslims. The Baharite slaves, under the command of Baibars Elbondukdari, performed in this battle signal acts of valour. The King of France had retired, with a few of his lords, to a small hillock, and surrendered himself, under promise of his life being spared, to the eunuch Djemaddelin Mahsun Elsalihi: he was bound with a chain, and in this state conducted to Mansoura, where he was confined in the house of Ibrahim ben Lokman, secretary to the sultan, and under the guard of the eunuch Sahil. The king's brother was made prisoner at the same time, and carried to the same house. The sultan provided for their subsistence. The number of slaves was so great, it was embarrassing, and the sultan gave orders to Seifeddin Jousef ben tardi to put them to death. Every night this cruel minister of the vengeance of his master had from three to four hundred of the prisoners brought from their places of confinement, and, after he had caused them to be beheaded, their bodies were thrown into the Nile; in this manner perished one hundred thousand of the French.

The sultan departed from Mansoura, and went to Fariskour where he had pitched a most magnificent tent. He had also built a tower of wood over the Nile; and, being freed from a disagreeable war, he there gave himself up to all sorts of debauchery. The victory he had just gained was so brilliant that he was eager to make all who were subjected to him acquainted with it. He wrote with his own hand a letter in the following terms, to the emir Djemal Edden ben Jagmour, governor of Damascus:

'Thanks be given to the All-powerful, who has changed our grief to joy: it is to him alone we owe the victory. The favours he has condescended to shower upon us are innumerable, but this last is most precious. You will announce to the people of Damascus, or rather to all Muslims, that God has enabled us to gain a complete victory over the Christians, at the moment they had conspired our ruin. On Monday, the first day of this year, we opened our treasury, and distributed riches and arms to our faithful soldiers. We had called to our succour the Arabian tribes, and a numberless multitude of soldiers ranged themselves under our standards. On the nights between Tuesday and Wednesday, our enemies abandoned their camp with all their baggage, and marched towards Damietta: in spite of the obscurity of the night, we pursued them, and thirty thousand of them were left dead on the field, not including those who precipitated themselves into the Nile. We have beside slain our very numerous prisoners, and thrown their bodies into the same river. Their king had retreated to Minieh: he has implored our clemency, and we have granted him his life, and paid him all the honours due to his rank. We have regained Damietta.'

The sultan, with this letter, sent the king's cap, which had fallen in the combat: it was of scarlet, lined with a fine fur. The governor of Damascus put the king's cap on his own head when he read to the public the sultan's letter. A poet made these verses on the occasion: 'The cap of the French was whiter than paper: our sabres have dyed it with the blood of the enemy, and have changed its colour.'

Al Makrisi – The Assassination of the Sultan[38]

In the following selection, Makrisi comments on the assassination of the sultan resulting from his poor relations with the Mamluks, who along with many others were concerned over his debaucheries and wasteful spending. Touran Chan's execution marked the end of the Ayyubid dynasty in Egypt and signalled the rise of the Mamluk slave dynasty when Chegeret-Eddur (Shajar al-Durr), the slave wife of the former Sultan Nedjm Eddin, was declared sovereign of Egypt.[39]

The gloomy and retired life the sultan led had irritated the minds of his people. He had no confidence but in a certain number of favourites, whom he had brought with him from Huns Keifa, and whom he had invested with the principal offices of the state, in the room of the ancient ministers of his father. Above all, he showed a decided hatred to the Mamluks, although they had contributed so greatly to the last victory. His debaucheries exhausted his revenue; and, to supply the deficiencies, he forced the Sultana Chegeret-Eddur to render him an account of the riches of his father. The sultana, in alarm, implored the protection of the Mamluks, representing to them the services she had done the state in very difficult times, and the ingratitude of Touran-Chah, who was indebted to her for the crown he wore. These slaves, already irritated against Touran-Chah, did not hesitate to take the part of the sultana, and resolved to assassinate the prince. To execute this design, they fixed on the moment when he was at table; Baibars-Elbondukdari gave him the first blow with his sabre, and, though he parried it with his hand, he lost his fingers. He then fled to the tower which he had built on the banks of the Nile, and which was but a short distance from his tent. The conspirators followed him, and, finding he had closed the door, set fire to it. The whole army saw what was passing; but, as he was a prince universally detested, no one came forward in his defence.

It was in vain he cried from the top of the tower, that he would abdicate his throne, and return to Huns Keifa; the assassins were inflexible.

The flames at length gaining on the tower, he attempted to leap into the Nile; but his dress caught as he was falling, and he remained some time suspended in the air. In this state, he received many wounds from sabres, and then fell into the river, where he was drowned. Thus iron, fire, and water contributed to put an end to his life. His body continued three days on the bank of the Nile, without any one daring to give it sepulture. At length, the ambassador from the caliph of Baghdad obtained permission, and had it buried.

This cruel prince, when he ascended the throne, had his brother, Adil-Chah, strangled. Four Mamluk slaves had been ordered to execute this; but the fratricide did not long remain unpunished, and these same four slaves were the most bitter in putting him to death. With this prince was extinguished the dynasty of the Ayyubids, who had governed Egypt eighty years, under eight different kings.[40] After the massacre of Touran-Chah, the Sultana Chegeret-Eddur was declared sovereign of Egypt; she was the first slave who had reigned over this country. This princess was a Turk, but others said an Armenian. The Sultan Nedjm-Eddin had bought her, and loved her so desperately that he carried her with him to his wars, and never quitted her. She had a son by the sultan, called Khalil, but who died when very young. The emir Azeddin-Aibegh, of the Turcoman nation, was appointed general of the army; and the name of the sultana was imprinted on the coin.

Al Makrisi – The King's Ransom[41]

Fortunately for Louis and numerous other Christian prisoners in Egypt, the new sultana was willing to allow her emirs to continue negotiations for the ransom of the King and those who accompanied him. Unlike Joinville's account, Makrisi makes no mention of a delay in releasing Louis or the threats to his person while in captivity.

The emir Abou Ali was nominated to treat with the King of France for his ransom, and for the surrender of Damietta. After many conferences and disputes, it was agreed that the French should evacuate Damietta, and that the king, and all prisoners in Egypt, should be set at liberty, on condition of paying down one half of such ransom as should be fixed on. The King of France sent orders to the governor of Damietta to surrender that town: but he refused to obey, and new orders were necessary. At last it was given up to the Muslims, after having remained eleven months in the hands of the enemy. The king paid four hundred thousand pieces of gold, as well for his own ransom as for that of the queen, his brother and the other lords that had accompanied him.

All the Franks that had been made prisoners during the reigns of the Sultans al -Kamil, Salih Nedjm-Eddin and Touran-Chah, obtained their liberty: they amounted to twelve thousand one hundred men and ten women. The king, with all the French, crossed to the westward branch of the Nile, and embarked on a Saturday for Acre.

Al Makrisi – Muslim Poetry on the Humiliation of St. Louis[42]

The following selection is taken from the poetry of Essahib Giemal Edden Ben Matroub, as presented by Makrisi, and celebrates the defeat of Louis and his crusaders in Egypt. The poet gloats in the crusaders' misfortune as he reminds Louis that his former prison remains should he ever return.

The poet, Essahib Giemal Edden Ben Matroub made, on the departure of this prince, the following verses:

'Bear to the King of France, when you shall see him, these words, traced by a partisan of truth: The death of the servants of the Messiah has been the reward given to you by God.

'You have landed in Egypt, thinking to take possession of it. You have imagined that it was only peopled with cowards! You who are a drum filled with wind.

'You thought that the moment to destroy the Muslims was arrived; and this false idea has smoothed, in your eyes, every difficulty.

'By your excellent conduct, you have abandoned your soldiers on the plains of Egypt, and the tomb has gaped under their feet.

'What now remains of the seventy thousand who accompanied you? Dead, wounded, and prisoners!

'May God inspire you often with similar designs ! They will cause the ruin of all Christians, and Egypt will have no longer to dread any thing from their rage.

'Without doubt, your priests announced victories to you: their predictions were false.

'Refer yourselves to a more enlightened oracle.

'Should the desire of revenge urge you to return to Egypt, be assured the house of Lokman still remains, that the chain is ready prepared, and the eunuch awake.'[43]

CHAPTER ELEVEN
THE FALL OF ACRE, 1291

199
LUDOLPH OF SUCHEM – THE MUSLIM CONQUEST OF ACRE IN 1291

203
ABU L-FIDA – THE MUSLIM CONQUEST OF ACRE IN 1291

205
RAMON LULL – CALL FOR THE RECOVERY OF THE HOLY LAND

205
PHILIP V OF FRANCE – CALL FOR THE RECOVERY OF THE HOLY LAND

It was lost on no one that this was the crusaders' last stand.
— Thomas Madden[1]

THE DECLINE OF THE LATIN SETTLEMENTS

The failure of Louis IX's crusades and other less-spectacular expeditions in the late thirteenth century left the few remaining Latin Christian outposts in the Holy Land in a tough spot. Since the establishment of the crusader settlements in the first half of the twelfth century, Latin Christians witnessed a slow but steady decline in both influence and authority in the region. Many Christians were beginning to believe that the collective forces of Islam were becoming too powerful to resist much longer.[2] The main threat came from the Egyptian Mamluks, who, after defeating the Mongols in 1260, rose to power under their ruthless leader Baibars.[3] The Mamluks sought to completely remove any Christian presence in Palestine through the systematic destruction of Christian holy places and the slaughter or enslavement of Christians wherever they found them.[4] Even Muslim chroniclers were sometimes shocked at Baibar's treatment of Christian women and children, as when after his conquest of Antioch, he ordered the single largest slaughter of the entire crusading era without regard for age or sex.[5] In addition to Antioch, several smaller, although important, Christian places fell to Baibar's forces, including Caesarea, Arsuf, Jaffa and the Templar Fortress of Safad. Latin Christians desperately needed help from the West to have any chance of survival. A number of failed crusades, perhaps most significantly the second crusade of Louis IX,[6] sought to provide some relief, but ultimately proved to be of little help.

Baibars died in 1277, but Latin Christians found little solace in his replacement, Kalavun, who seized the sultanate in 1280. Kalavun, like Baibars, was committed to the eradication of Christians from the Holy Land, and early in his reign, he seized on Christian infighting and divisions to position his forces for several later victories.[7] Muslims captured the important port of Latakia in 1287 and the city of Tripoli in 1289. The Sultan then reaffirmed his truce with Acre, but few Christians were willing to trust him at this point. The leadership at Acre appealed for aid from the West, while the Templars, Hospitallers and Teutonic Knights summoned all available men from Europe to Acre, where they would be led by their grandmasters themselves. Pope Nicholas IV also raised a poorly trained army that rushed to the city's defence. This army caused more harm than good, as they slew Muslim merchants in the city and in doing so, gave Kalavun a justification to go on the offensive against Acre. The Christians arrested the perpetrators and sent an apology to the Sultan, but it was not enough.[8] Both sides prepared for war.

THE SIEGE AND CONQUEST OF ACRE

Although Kalavun died in 1290, his son al-Malik al-Ashraf, who adopted his father's policies of seeking the elimination of the crusader presence in the East, replaced him as Sultan. The new Sultan arrived at Acre with the single largest force ever assembled during the crusading era. He brought with him several siege engines to attack Acre's fortified walls and had no intention of leaving until the city was his. Although motivated, the Christian defenders were outnumbered seven to one.[9] The siege began on 6 April 1291, and after six ferocious weeks of attacking the walls with the siege engines and thousands of sappers, Muslim forces found a way into the city on 18 May and began slaughtering every Christian they came across.[10] The military orders fought hard, defending each street, while others fled to the harbour to escape by ship.

The lone defensive hold out was the Templars' house, which became the final place of refuge for Christians who could not escape.[11] The Templars fought bravely, and after a week, the Sultan offered them and the refugees a chance to leave Acre alive if they turned over their position. They agreed. But once Muslims soldiers entered the house, they began molesting Christian women and boys. The angry Templars expelled the Muslims and secured the house, but in the second round of fighting, the Muslims were able to undermine the building and collapse the outer wall, allowing their troops to rush in and begin gathering loot and refugees. A short time later, the entire building collapsed, killing the overly zealous Muslims and what remained of the Christian defenders of Acre.

Acre was the last Latin Christian stronghold in the Holy Land, and its fall meant disaster for the remaining Christian states. By August, the Christian cities of Tyre, Sidon and Beirut, as well as a number of important Christian castles and fortresses, surrendered to the Sultan. Any significant Latin Christian presence in the region was gone. While crusading continued in Spain, in the Baltic and elsewhere in Europe against later opponents such as the Hussites and Ottoman Turks, it was over in the Holy Land; never again was a crusade launched for the recovery of the Holy Land. There were repeated calls for its recovery and some efforts towards this goal, but none ever came to fruition.

BACKGROUND TO THE SOURCES

The first source presented in this chapter was written by the cleric Ludolph of Suchem.[12] Although Ludolph composed his work nearly sixty years after the fall of Acre, he had spent five years in the Holy Land, from 1336 to 1341, during which period he became well acquainted with its history and people. In 1350, he recorded what he had learned from eyewitnesses of the fall of Acre in 1291,[13] which he included in his work *Description of the Holy Land and of the Way Thither*.[14] Ludolph attributes Acre's capture to intra-Christian feuding, noting how various Christian parties had made varying truces with Muslims 'to the end that they might better fight against one another within the city'. He also describes how a force of 12,000 troops sent by the Pope to shore up Acre's defences had, through their behaviour, given cause to the Muslims to argue that any pre-existing truces between them and the Christians had become invalid. The Christian population of Acre was given a final opportunity to reinstate the treaty between Muslims and Christians through the payment of one Venetian penny for every citizen of Acre, but the residents of Acre would hear nothing of it, leading to a withering attack on the city by Muslim forces.

For several weeks, Muslim forces pounded the walls of Acre with frightening effect. Indeed, Ludolph highlights the intensity of the siege by citing the recollection of a knight who claimed that a lance, which he was about to hurl from one of the city's towers, 'was all notched with arrows before it left his hand'. Once the Muslims had breached the walls, the vastly outnumbered defenders of the city, especially the members of the military orders, fought bravely and covered the escape of many Christians to the port. Ludolph notes how Muslim forces, once they took the city, 'worked for many years' to destroy the defensive fortifications of the city, to guard against any possibility of Christians retaking the city and having a chance of holding it.

The scholar and Arab Emir Abu l-Fida has left us an eyewitness account of the fall of Acre in 1291. He was a young man in the service of the Emir during the fall of Acre and so was well positioned to record the events of the siege.[15] Like Ludolph, Abu also describes the fighting as intense. He notes how the Christians fought in front of their open gates and sent ships to batter Muslim forces that were entrenched along the shores of Acre. Abu even describes Christian soldiers making a sortie as far as the tents of the enemy camp, before being repulsed by Muslim soldiers. He notes that once the Muslims had taken control of the city, all those Christians who had surrendered and were taken alive were decapitated 'to the last man' outside the city's walls.

Considering the significance of the Muslim conquest of Acre, Abu recognises the event as signalling the end of the Christian crusading presence in the East. He points out that this victory struck 'despair into the hearts of the other Franks left in Palestine' and led to the surrender of several surrounding Christian cities, leaving 'the whole of Palestine in Muslim hands'. He also notes the Sultan's efforts to make sure all the fortifications of these cities were destroyed so that they would never again provide a stronghold for Christian armies. Abu praises the victorious Sultan, al-Malik al-Ashraf, as 'another Saladin',[16] yet he also suggests that al-Malik's deeds were greater, by pointing out how Acre was lost under Saladin's reign and won under al-Malik's reign.

The final two sources presented in this chapter are written by Latin Christians and are representative of those who called for a renewed military offensive to the East after the fall of Acre. The first selection is from the Franciscan intellectual Ramon Lull's 1305 treatise, *Liber de Fine*, which offers a broad commentary on crusading and specific advice for the recovery of the Holy land. Ramon notes that it is the principal responsibility of the pope and the cardinals to bring about the recovery of the Holy Land from 'unbelievers'. In doing so, Ramon argues, they should appoint a cardinal to oversee the efforts for Jerusalem's recovery, including the formation of a new military order with a warrior king to lead it. This king would be granted the Kingdom of Jerusalem and thus become more inspired to bring it under his control. The second source was written in September 1318 by Philip V, the Capetian King of France and Navarre. Like Ramon, Philip places great importance on finding the right Christian leader to win back the Holy Land. Philip places his confidence in his cousin, Louis of Clermont, whom he appoints as 'captain, leader and governor general' of a proposed force that will be gathered for the liberation of the Holy Land.

THE SOURCES

Ludolph of Suchem – The Muslim Conquest of Acre in 1291[17]

The following text, based on eyewitness testimony, is Ludolph of Suchem's account of the fall of Acre. Ludolph attributes the fall of Acre primarily to Christian infighting in the years prior to and even during the Muslim attack on the city. He also points out how vastly outnumbered the city's defenders were in comparison to the size of the Sultan's army.

After having told of the glories and beauties of Acre, I will now shortly tell you of its fall and ruin, and the cause of its loss, even as I heard the tale told by right truthful men, who well remembered it. While, then, the grand doings of which I have spoken were going on in Acre, at the instigation of the devil there arose a violent and hateful quarrel in Lombardy between the Guelfs and the Ghibellines,[18] which brought all evil upon the Christians. Those Lombards who dwelt at Acre took sides in this same quarrel, especially the Pisans and Genoese, both of whom had an exceedingly strong party in Acre. These men made treaties and truces with the Saracens, to the end that they might better fight against one another within the city.

When Pope Urban[19] heard of this, he grieved for Christendom and for the Holy Land, and sent twelve thousand mercenary troops across the sea to help the Holy Land and Christendom. When these men came across the sea to Acre they did no good, but abode by day and by night in taverns and places of ill repute, took and plundered merchants and pilgrims in the public street, broke the treaty and did much evil. Melot Sapheraph, Sultan of Babylon, an exceedingly wise man, most potent in arms and bold in action, when he heard of this, and knew of the hateful quarrels of the people of Acre, called together his counsellors and held a parliament in Babylon, wherein he complained that the truces had frequently been broken and violated, to the prejudice of himself and his people. After a debate had been held upon this matter, he gathered together a mighty host, and reached the city of Acre without any resistance, because of their quarrels with one another, cutting down and wasting all the vineyards and fruit trees and all the gardens and orchards, which are most lovely thereabout.

When the Master of the Templars,[20] a very wise and brave knight, saw this, he feared that the fall of the city was at hand, because of the quarrels of the citizens. He took counsel with his brethren about how peace could be restored, and then went out to meet the sultan, who was his own very especial friend, to ask him whether they could by any means repair the broken truce. He obtained these terms from the sultan, to wit, that because of his love for the sultan and the honour in which the sultan held him, the broken truce might be restored by every man in Acre paying one Venetian penny. So the Master of the Templars was glad, and, departing from the sultan, called together all the people and preached a sermon to them in the Church of St. Cross, setting forth how, by his prayers, he had prevailed upon the sultan to grant that the broken treaty might be restored by a payment of one Venetian penny by each man, that therewith everything might be settled and quieted. He advised them by all means so to do, declaring that the quarrels of the citizens might bring a worse evil upon the city than this – as indeed they did. But when the people heard this, they cried out with one voice that he was the betrayer of the city, and was guilty of death. The Master, when he heard this, left the church, hardly escaped alive from the hands of the people, and took back their answer to the sultan. When the sultan heard this, knowing that, owing to the quarrels of the people, none of them would make any resistance, he pitched his tents, set up sixty machines,[21] dug many mines beneath the city walls and for forty days and nights, without any respite, assailed the city with fire, stones and arrows, so that [the air] seemed to be stiff with arrows. I have heard a very honourable knight say that a lance which he was about to hurl from a tower among the Saracens was all notched with arrows before it left his hand.

There were at that time in the sultan's army six hundred thousand armed,[22] divided into three companies; so one hundred thousand continually besieged the city, and when they were weary another hundred thousand took their place before the same, two hundred thousand stood before the gates of the city ready for battle, and the duty of the remaining two hundred thousand was to supply them with everything that they needed. The gates were never closed, nor was there an hour of the day without some hard fight being fought against the Saracens by the Templars or other brethren dwelling therein. But the numbers of the Saracens grew so fast that after one hundred thousand of them had been slain two hundred thousand came back. Yet, even against all this host, they would not have lost the city had they but helped one another faithfully; but when they were fighting without the city, one party would run away and leave the other to be slain, while within the city one party would not defend the castle or palace belonging to the other, but purposely let the other party's castles, palaces and strong places be stormed and taken by the enemy, and each one knew and believed his own castle and place to be so strong that he cared not for any other's castle or strong place.

During this confusion the masters and brethren of the Orders alone defended themselves, and fought unceasingly against the Saracens, until they were nearly all slain; indeed, the Master and brethren of the house of the Teutonic Order, together with their followers and friends, all fell dead at one and the same time. As this went on with many battles and thousands slain on either side, at last the fulfilment of their sins and the time of the fall of the city drew near; when the fortieth day of its siege was come, in the year of our Lord one thousand two hundred and ninety-two, on the twelfth day of the month of May, the most noble and glorious city of Acre, the flower, chief and pride of all the cities of the East,[23] was taken. The people of the other cities, to wit, Jaffa, Tyre, Sidon and Ascalon, when they heard this, left all their property behind and fled to Cyprus.[24]

When first the Saracens took Acre they got in through a breach in the wall near the King of Jerusalem's castle, and when they were among the people of the city within, one party still would not help the other, but each defended his own castle and palace, and the Saracens had a much longer siege, and fought at much less advantage when they were within the city than when they were without, for it was wondrously fortified. Indeed, we read in the stories of the loss of Acre that because of the sins of the people thereof the four elements fought on the side of the Saracens. First the air became so thick, dark and cloudy that, while one castle, palace or strong place was being stormed or burned, men could hardly see in the other castles and palaces, until their castles and palaces were attacked, and then for the first time they would have willingly defended themselves, could they have come together. Fire fought against the city, for it consumed it. Earth fought against the city, for it drank up its blood. Water also fought against the city, for it being the month of May, wherein the sea is wont to be very calm, when the people of Acre plainly saw that because of their sins and the darkening of the air they could not see their enemies, they fled to the sea, desiring to sail to Cyprus, and whereas at first there was no wind at all at sea, of a sudden so great a storm arose that no other ship, either great or small, could come near the shore, and many who essayed to swim off to the ships were drowned. Howbeit, more than one hundred thousand men escaped to Cyprus.

I have heard from a most honourable Lord, and from other truthful men who were present, that more than five hundred most noble ladies and maidens, the daughters of kings and princes, came down to the seashore, when the city was about to fall, carrying with them all their jewels and ornaments of gold and precious stones, of priceless value, in their bosoms, and cried aloud, whether there were any sailor there who would take all their jewels and take whichever of them he chose to wife, if only he would take them, even naked, to some safe land or island. A sailor received them all into his ship, took them across to Cyprus, with all their goods, for nothing, and went his way. But who he was, whence he came, or whither he went, no man knows to this day. Very many other noble ladies and damsels were drowned or slain. It would take long to tell what grief and anguish was there.

While the Saracens were within the city, but before they had taken it, fighting from castle to castle, from one palace and strong place to another, so many men perished on either side that they walked over their corpses as it were over a bridge. When all the inner city was lost, all who still remained alive fled into the exceeding strong castle of the Templars, which was straightway invested on all sides by the Saracens; yet the Christians bravely defended it for two months, and before it almost all the nobles and chiefs of the Sultan's army fell dead. For when the city inside the walls was burned, yet the towers of the city, and the Templars' castle, which was in the city, remained, and with these the people of the city kept the Saracens within the city from getting out, as before they had hindered their coming in, until of all the Saracens who had entered the city not one remained alive, but all fell by fire or by the sword. When the Saracen nobles saw the others lying dead, and themselves unable to escape from the city, they fled for refuge into the mines which they had dug under the great tower, that they might make their way through the wall and so get out. But the Templars and others who were in the castle, seeing that they could not hurt the Saracens with stones and the like, because of the mines wherein they were, undermined the great tower of the castle, and flung it down upon the mines and the Saracens therein, and all perished alike.

When the other Saracens without the city saw that they had thus, as it were, failed utterly, they treacherously made a truce with the Templars and Christians on the condition that they should yield up the castle, taking all their goods with them, and should destroy it, but should rebuild the city on certain terms, and dwell therein in peace as heretofore. The Templars and Christians, believing this, gave up the castle and marched out of it, and came down from the city towers. When the Saracens had by this means got possession both of the castle and of the city towers, they slew all the Christians alike, and led away the captives to Babylon. Thus Acre has remained empty and deserted even to this day. In Acre and the other places nearly a hundred and six thousand men were slain or taken, and more than two hundred thousand escaped from thence. Of the Saracens more than three hundred thousand were slain, as is well known even to this day. The Saracens spent forty days over the siege of the city, fifty days within the city before it was taken, and two months over the siege of the Templars' castle. When the glorious city of Acre thus fell, all the Eastern people sung of its fall in hymns of lamentation, such as they are wont to sing over the tombs of their dead, bewailing the beauty, the grandeur, and the glory of Acre even to this day. Since that day all Christian women, whether gentle or simple, who dwell along the eastern shore [of the Mediterranean] dress in black garments of mourning and woe for the lost grandeur of Acre, even to this day.

After this the Saracens worked for many years endeavouring to utterly subvert and destroy down to their foundations all the walls, towers, castles and palaces, lest the Christians should rebuild them; yet in hardly any place have they been able to beat them down to the height of a man, but all the churches, walls and towers and very many castles and palaces, remain almost entire, and, if it pleased God, could with great care be restored throughout to their former state. At this day about sixty thousand Saracen mercenaries dwell in Acre as a garrison for the city and port, and make a living out of silk and birds, for there are so many partridges and pigeons to be found in Acre, that all the birds to be seen in this country are not to be compared to them. These mercenaries have an especial delight in Germans, whom they straightaway recognise by their appearance and walk, and drink wine deeply with them, albeit it is forbidden by their law. Thus have I told how the glorious city of Acre was lost by quarrels, and from that time forth all the glory of the Holy Land, of its kings, princes and other lords, has been carried over into Cyprus, as you have already heard.

Abu l-Fida – The Muslim Conquest of Acre in 1291[25]

The following eyewitness account of the fall of Acre was written by the scholar and Arab Emir Abu l-Fida. He describes the intense resistance of the Christian defenders, both during the siege and when Muslim soldiers had found their way into the city. He also recognises the Sultan's victory at Acre as signalling the end of any authoritative Latin Christian presence in the Holy Land.

The Muslim troops mustered at Acre in the first days of jumada I 690/beginning of May 1291, and the battle raged furiously. The Franks did not close most of the gates; in fact they left them wide open and fought in front of them in their defence. The Hamat army was in its

THE FALL OF ACRE, 1291

usual position on the extreme right wing. This meant that we were on the seashore, with the sea on our right when we faced Acre. We were attacked by troops landing from boats protected by wood faced frames covered with buffalo-hides, from which they shot at us with bows and ballistas. Thus we found ourselves fighting on two fronts, the city and the sea. A ship came up with a catapult mounted on it that battered us and our tents from the sea. We were severely hindered by it, but one night when a fierce wind blew up the ship was buffeted on the waves and the catapult broke up and was not rebuilt.

One night during the siege the Franks made a sortie, put the outposts to flight and reached the tents, where they became tangled up in the guy ropes. One knight fell into the latrine-trench of one of the amir's detachments and was killed. Our troops turned out in overwhelming numbers and the Franks turned tail and fled back to the city, leaving a number of dead accounted for by the Hamat army. The next morning al-Malik al-Muzzaffar, Lord of Hamat, had a number of Frankish heads attached to the necks of horses we had captured and presented them to the Sultan al-Malik al-Ashraf.

The blockade was continually reinforced, until God granted to the attackers victory over the city on Friday 10 jumada II/17 June 1291. As the Muslims stormed the city some of the citizens took to the sea in boats. Within the city was a number of well fortified towers, and some Franks shut themselves inside them and defended them. The Muslims killed vast numbers of people and gathered immense booty. The sultan forced all those in the towers to surrender, and they submitted to the last man, and to the last man were decapitated outside the city walls. At the sultan's command the city was razed to the ground.

An amazing coincidence occurred; the Franks seized Acre from Saladin at midday on 17 jumada II 587, and captured and then killed all the Muslims therein; and God in his prescience destined that this year it should be reconquered at the hand of another Saladin, the Sultan al-Malik al-Ashraf.

After the conquest of Acre God put despair into the hearts of the other Franks left in Palestine; they abandoned Sidon and Beirut, which (the amir) ash-Shuja'i took over at the end of rajab/end of July. The population of Tyre also abandoned the city and the sultan sent troops to occupy it. He received the surrender of Athlith on the first of sha'ban/30 July, and that of Tirtosa on 5 sha'ban of the same year. So this sultan had the good fortune, granted to none other, to conquer without effort and without striking a blow these great, well-fortified cities, all of which were at his command demolished.

With these conquests the whole of Palestine was now in Muslim hands, a result that no one would have dared to hope for or to desire. Thus the whole of Syria and the coastal zones were purified of the Franks, who had once been on the point of conquering Egypt and subduing Damascus and other cities. Praise be to God!

Ramon Lull – Call for the Recovery of the Holy Land[26]

In the following account written by Ramon Lull in 1305, the Franciscan calls for the recovery of the Holy Land through the establishment of a special crusading order under the leadership of a Christian warrior-king.

It is desirable that the Holy Land, and the other territories which the unbelievers keep from the Latins, should be recovered, through the angels who are in Paradise, through the saints and through the Latins themselves. It is the lord pope and cardinals who are principally charged with bringing about this great benefit, as well as honouring our Lord Jesus Christ and effecting the salvation of men. To this end they should choose a cardinal, most holy and devout, to whom may be entrusted everything which will be touched on in this section, just as was the case in the first section with the other cardinal.

The lord pope and the cardinals should select and establish a single noble [religious] order, to be called the order of knighthood (*ordo militiae*). The head of this order would be termed both master and warrior-king (*bellator rex*). 'Warrior', on the grounds that the subject matter of this section requires it; 'king' because of his magistracy of the knighthood. A kingdom should be granted to him; if at all possible, the Kingdom of Jerusalem should be assigned to him. This is just, since this king will have a more noble office than any other king of this world, and because the principal aim of this warrior-king must be to conquer Jerusalem.

Philip V of France – Call for the Recovery of the Holy Land[27]

In the following source written by the Capetian King Philip V in 1318, he appoints his cousin Louis of Clermont 'to exercise command, direction and authority' over a soon-to-be-created Christian army formed to recover the Holy Land.

Philip, by God's grace King of France and Navarre, greetings to each and all whom these letters reach. Our heart yearns to liberate the Holy Land, which is dedicated by the most precious blood of our Creator, Redeemer and Saviour, the Lord Jesus Christ. Our chief goal is to seize it from the hands of those who wickedly despise, blaspheme against and persecute His name. That name is above all else, and everybody on earth, in Heaven or in Hell, should perform obeisance to it, all tongues acknowledging that the same Lord Jesus Christ resides in the glory of God, the Father.

    We are giving our attention to both the general and specific measures necessary for the liberation of the Holy Land, and how to locate the persons who would be adequate and suitable to carry out these measures. Therefore, amongst the other nobles and magnates of our kingdoms who propose crossing over ahead of the general passage, we [are appointing] the illustrious Louis, count of Clermont and lord of Bourbon, our most dear kinsman, our knight, counsellor and familiar and chamberlain of France, to exercise command, direction and authority over the men-at-arms whom we intend to send to the [Holy] Land in advance of the general passage which we ourselves have undertaken, should we live, and with the assistance of divine grace.

    [We do this] not just because of Louis's distinguished family and kinship, in so far as he is descended through his father from the gracious confessor and blessed Louis [IX], our [great] grandfather and former King of France, who ended his days overseas in Christ's service, but also because of his special devotion for the Holy Land and the blessed Louis, in whose footsteps he is attempting to follow, and because he long since bound himself to it by a special vow, alongside a large number of barons, nobles and ordinary people who followed his lead. In addition, we consider him adequate and suitable by virtue of his strength, wisdom, prudence, prowess at arms and industriousness. We [therefore] declare that we are appointing and investing [Louis] as our captain, leader and governor general of all the men-at-arms whom we dispatch before the general passage by land or by sea for the assistance of the [Holy] Land, with effect from the day he sets out on the said *passagium*. We wish that everybody obeys, submits to and complies with him in everything relating to these matters or contingent upon them, in every way, just as they would if we were present. But if our dearly beloved uncles Charles, count of Valois and Louis, count of Evreux or our brother Charles, count of La Marche, should cross over ahead of the said general passage, in advance of the count of Clermont or in his company, then it is our intention that each or all of them take precedence over the count of Clermont on this business.

CHAPTER TWELVE
LIFE ON A CRUSADE, 1095–1270

211
COUNT STEPHEN TO HIS WIFE ADELE

211
GODFREY'S LETTER TO POPE PASCHAL II

212
GESTA FRANCORUM

213
DE EXPUGNATIONE

216
AMBROISE

216
OLD FRENCH CONTINUATION OF WILLIAM OF TYRE

217
BEHA-ED-DIN

219
IBN AL-ATHIR

221
JEAN DE JOINVILLE

230
IMAD AD-DIN

233
FULCHER OF CHARTRES

Rotrou of Perche…had left France [on the First Crusade] over three years before in the company of Robert of Normandy. He had shared the disorientation, the exhaustion and starvation, the disease and sickening cruelty, the loss of pack animals and horses and therefore of rank, the disintegration of morale and order, the stories of apparitions and ghostly armies, the penitential liturgies and hysterical religiosity, the discovery of relics and the euphoria of the final miraculous and bloody triumph at Jerusalem.
– Jonathan Riley-Smith[1]

PHYSICAL AND SPIRITUAL CONDITIONS

Life for crusaders, both men and women, was full of physical and spiritual dangers. Crusades began with long overland marches or lengthy journeys by ship in which hostile local populations, bad weather and the danger of shipwreck were often major concerns. Once engaged in a lengthy siege or battle, which might last several months, crusaders often found hunger and thirst as pressing a problem as did their Muslim foes. Indeed, both Muslim and Christian sources report instances of starving warriors driven to cannibalism. Perhaps of even greater concern, crusaders often had to worry about the possibility of capture, where in captivity they might be subject to rape, torture, enslavement and execution. One of the means by which the crusaders maintained their morale in the face of such hardships was through their spirituality. Their faith assured them that their hardships were the result of their sins, quite often involving women, and that their situation, no matter how hopeless, could be improved through repentance and proper devotion to God.

HUNGER AND THIRST

Logistics was a major issue throughout the crusading era.[2] Providing sufficient daily access to food and water for tens of thousands of crusaders was an enormous challenge for the crusading leadership. Individual crusaders did their best to equip themselves, often setting out on a crusade only after their families had sold or mortgaged properties to provide for the journey.[3] Yet even if crusaders could afford to purchase food during their journey, they still needed access to food stocks. To ensure availability of food and water, the leadership planned routes in which they could count on access to local markets or natural supplies. Sometimes, crusaders encountered villages along the route that would refuse or be unable to provide adequate supplies, resulting in foraging and near-starvation conditions. While supplies were sometimes sparse during the march, in no situation did hunger and thirst become as major an issue as during a lengthy battle or siege. In many cases, to avoid starvation, those under siege would surrender to the besieging army. On other occasions, the besiegers found themselves unable to sustain a lengthy attack for lack of food and access to water. The position on the battlefield was critical because an army cut off from water might, at best, fight effectively for a couple of days before extreme thirst led to desertion or surrender.

The first source included in this chapter, concerning problems of hunger and thirst, is a letter written by Stephen, Count of Blois and Chartres, to his wife, Adele. Stephen provides an eyewitness account of the hardships suffered by the crusaders during the lengthy siege of Antioch in 1098. He notes how many crusaders had exhausted their resources and, without his charity, would have died of starvation. The second source is a selection taken from Duke Godfrey of Bouillon's letter to Pope Paschal II. Godfrey's description of events begins when the crusaders had conquered nearly all of the city of Antioch, with the exception of a well-defended citadel, and then found themselves under siege by Muslim reinforcements that had arrived late and were now trying to retake the city. By the time the crusaders took the city, they had already besieged it for several months and it was poorly provisioned. Now, under near-starvation conditions, they found themselves under siege by the newly arrived Muslim army. Indeed, Godfrey notes that 'hunger so weakened us that some could scarcely refrain from eating human flesh'. The worst was yet to come. In Syria, the crusaders were driven by famine to eat 'the putrid bodies of the Saracens'. When the crusaders finally arrived at Jerusalem, they experienced similar hardships during their siege of the Holy City. The anonymous author of the *Gesta Francorum* describes the crusaders' concerns over food and water, noting that for ten days, they were not able to buy bread and that the nearest water was 6 miles away. This chapter also includes a selection from the *De Expugnatione Terrae Sanctae per Saladinum*, detailing the sufferings of the crusaders at the battle of Hattin in 1187. The anonymous author describes how the Christian army, already ravaged by thirst, made the mistake of setting up camp without access to water. Their Muslim opponents surrounded them and burned fires to their discomfort. The dire situation resulted in the surrender of the Christians and prompted the anonymous author to note poignantly how God had given them 'the bread of tears to eat and the wine of compunction to drink'.

THE SOURCES

Count Stephen to His Wife Adele on the Hunger of the Crusaders at Antioch in 1098[4]

Provided here is the partial text of a letter from Count Stephen of Blois to his wife, Adele. Stephen describes how many crusaders suffered from starvation at Antioch and would have died if he had not provided money to feed them.

We found the city of Antioch very extensive, fortified with incredible strength and almost impregnable. In addition, more than 5,000 bold Turkish soldiers had entered the city, not counting the Saracens, Publicans, Arabs, Tulitans, Syrians, Armenians and other different races of whom an infinite multitude had gathered together there. In fighting against these enemies of God and of our own we have, by God's grace, endured many sufferings and innumerable evils up to the present time. Many also have already exhausted all their resources in this very holy passion. Very many of our Franks, indeed, would have met a temporal death from starvation, if the clemency of God and our money had not saved them. Before the above-mentioned city of Antioch indeed, throughout the whole winter we suffered for our Lord Christ from excessive cold and enormous torrents of rain. What some say about the impossibility of bearing the heat of the sun throughout Syria is untrue, for the winter there is very similar to our winter in the west.

Godfrey's Letter to Pope Paschal II on Starvation and Cannibalism during the First Crusade[5]

Provided here is the partial text of a letter from Duke Godfrey of Bouillon, one of the most important leaders of the First Crusade and the first Latin Christian ruler of Jerusalem, to Pope Paschal II. Godfrey describes the sufferings of the crusaders from hunger in Antioch and Syria, noting that the starvation of the army was so great in Syria that they resorted to eating 'the putrid bodies of the Saracens'.

Inasmuch as we thought that these had been acquired by our own strength, and did not worthily magnify God who had done this, we were beset by so great a multitude of Turks that no one dared to venture forth at any point from the city. Moreover hunger so weakened us that some could scarcely refrain from eating human flesh. It would be tedious to narrate all the miseries which we suffered in that city. But God looked down upon his people, whom he had so long chastised, and mercifully consoled them. Therefore, he at first revealed to us, as a recompense for our tribulation and as a pledge of victory, his lance, which had lain hidden since the days of the apostles. Next he so fortified the hearts of the men that they who from sickness or hunger had been unable to walk, now were imbued with strength to seize their weapons and manfully to fight against the enemy.

After we had triumphed over the enemy, as our army was wasting away at Antioch from sickness and weariness and was especially hindered by the dissensions among the leaders, we proceeded into Syria, stormed Barra and Marra, cities of the Saracens, and captured the fortresses in that country. And while we were delaying there, there was so great a famine in the army that the Christian people now ate the putrid bodies of the Saracens. Finally, by the divine admonition, we entered into the interior of Hispania, and the most bountiful, merciful and victorious hand of the omnipotent Father was with us; for the cities and the fortresses of the country through which we were proceeding sent ambassadors to us with many gifts and offered to aid us and to surrender their walled places.

Gesta: The Lack of Water during the Siege of Jerusalem in 1099[6]

The following eyewitness account from the *Gesta* describes the sufferings of the crusaders from thirst during the siege of Jerusalem in 1099 and their desperate efforts to secure water.

For a period of ten days during the siege we were not able to buy bread at any price, until a messenger came announcing the arrival of our ships. We also suffered greatly for thirst. In fear and terror we were forced to water our horses and other animals at a distance of six miles from camp. The pool of Siloam, at the foot of Mount Zion, sustained us, but, nevertheless, water was sold among us very dearly…

…During this siege we were so distressed with thirst that we sewed up skins of oxen and buffalos and in these carried water for a distance of six miles. Between fetid water and barley bread we were daily in great want and suffering. Moreover, the Saracens hid in ambush at the watering places and either killed and wounded our animals or drove them away to caverns in the hills.

De Expugnatione: The Thirst of the Christians at the Battle of Hattin, 1187[7]

The following text from the *De Expugnatione* describes Christians' suffering from thirst at the Battle of Hattin during the Third Crusade. In spite of their being the most important Christian army in the Holy Land, their inability to secure water at Hattin was the cause of their destruction and made possible Saladin's later conquest of Jerusalem. The account is based on the testimony of Christian survivors who escaped to Jerusalem and made the events of the battle widely known.

They marched to Saffuriyah so that, as was said before, they could go on to Tiberias. Three miles from the city they came to a hamlet called Marescallia. At this place they were so constrained by enemy attacks and by thirst that they wished to go no further. They were going to pass through a confined, rocky area in order to reach the Sea of Galilee, which was a mile away. For this reason the count sent word to the king: 'We must hurry and pass through this area, so that we and our men may be safe near the water. Otherwise we will be in danger of making camp at a waterless spot.' The king replied: 'We will pass through at once.'

The Turks were meanwhile attacking the army's rear, so that the Templars and the others in the rear were barely able to struggle on. Suddenly the king (a punishment for sin) ordered the tents to be pitched. Thus were we betrayed to our death. The count, when he looked back and saw the tents pitched, exclaimed: 'Alas, Lord God, the battle is over! We have been betrayed unto death. The Kingdom is finished!'

And so, in sorrow and anguish, they camped on a dry site where, during the night, there flowed more blood than water The sons of Esau [the Muslim army] surrounded the people of God [Crusaders] and set fire to the desert [brush] round about them. Throughout the night the hungry and thirsty men were harassed further by arrows and by the fire's heat and flames.... That night God indeed gave them the bread of tears to eat and the wine of compunction to drink.

PRISONERS OF WAR

Perhaps the worst fate for many Christian and Muslim warriors was to be taken captive by the enemy. Most could expect to be enslaved or executed. Those having enough financial resources, or important political connections, could hope to be ransomed, but it was more common that if prisoners were spared, they would live in servitude and be compelled into religious conversion to their master's faith. Many captives were also executed because thousands of unruly prisoners needing food and water often presented too great a logistical challenge and security threat to the victors. Some elite fighters, such as members of the crusading orders, were given the choice of conversion or death to ensure that they would never again be a threat on the battlefield. The source selections dealing with these issues are presented in this chapter in two sections: the Christian treatment of Muslim prisoners and the Muslim treatment of Christian prisoners. Both sections provide commentary from Christian and Muslim authors on executions, enslavement and the ransoming of prisoners.

THE CHRISTIAN TREATMENT OF MUSLIM PRISONERS

The first set of sources examines Christian treatment of Muslim prisoners and begins with a selection from the *Gesta Francorum* on the crusaders' conquest of Jerusalem in 1099. The author highlights the danger of becoming a prisoner by noting that during a heated battle, euphoric crusaders infuriated the noble Tancred of Taranto when they indiscriminately slew his recently taken prisoners.[8] The second source in this section is attributed to Ambroise and describes a case in which Christian women set upon Muslim prisoners during a naval battle. The women ran to a captured Muslim galley as it was brought ashore and humiliated the prisoners by pulling their hair, cutting their throats and then decapitating them. Also included in this section are two sources on Richard the Lionheart's mass execution of Muslim prisoners at Acre during the Third Crusade. The first is taken from the *Old French Continuation of William of Tyre* and describes how Saladin had made an agreement for an exchange of prisoners following Richard's capture of Acre. Yet Saladin delayed the prisoner swap, until finally he abandoned the agreement altogether. In response Richard, perhaps influenced by the drain on his resources from maintaining thousands of Muslim prisoners, ordered their mass execution in full view of Saladin's army. The second source for Richard's slaughter of Muslim prisoners at Acre is taken from Beha ed-Din and provides a Muslim perspective on Richard's actions. Although acknowledging Saladin's delay in fulfilling his agreement with Richard, Beha ed-Din accuses Richard of treachery, pointing out that he had agreed to spare the prisoners' lives when they surrendered Acre to him. Another major discrepancy between the two accounts is the number of prisoners slain, as the *Continuation* records that 16,000 were executed, while Beha ed-Din mentions only 3,000.

THE SOURCES

Gesta: The Slaughter of Muslim Prisoners during the Conquest of Jerusalem in 1099[9]

The following eyewitness account from the *Gesta Francorum* describes the execution of Muslim prisoners on the roof of the Holy Sepulchre following the conquest of Jerusalem in 1099. The Muslims had recently been claimed as prisoners of the Christian noble Tancred of Taranto and their deaths at the hands of overzealous crusaders angered him.

The battle raged throughout the day, so that the Temple was covered with their blood. When the pagans had been overcome, our men seized great numbers, both men and women, either killing them or keeping them captive, as they wished. On the roof of the Temple a great number of pagans of both sexes had assembled, and these were taken under the protection of Tancred and Gaston of Beert. Afterward, the army scattered throughout the city and took possession of the gold and silver, the horses and mules and the houses filled with goods of all kinds.

Rejoicing and weeping for joy, our people came to the Sepulchre of Jesus our Saviour to worship and pay their debt [i.e. fulfil crusading vows by worshipping at the Sepulchre]. At dawn our men cautiously went up to the roof of the Temple and attacked Saracen men and women, beheading them with naked swords. Some of the Saracens, however, leaped from the Temple roof. Tancred, seeing this, was greatly angered.

Ambroise on the Humiliation and Execution of Muslim Prisoners by Christian Women during the Third Crusade[10]

The following source is taken from Ambroise's eyewitness account of the Third Crusade. The author describes a violent attack by Christian women against recently captured Muslim prisoners. Ambroise highlights the prolonged suffering of the Muslims on account of the women's 'physical weakness' and use of knives, rather than swords, to behead them.

The other side lost a galley in this naval engagement, and a galliot with its crew. Our people returned safe and sound, bearing a solemn triumph. The victors dragged the enemy galley back with them up on to dry land and left it on the shore to be plundered by our people of both sexes who came running to meet them. Our women pulled the Turks along by the hair, treated them dishonourably, humiliatingly cutting their throats; and finally beheaded them. The women's physical weakness prolonged the pain of death, because they cut their heads off with knives instead of swords.

Old French Continuation of William of Tyre: Richard's Execution of Muslim Prisoners at Acre in 1191[11]

The following source is taken from the *Old French Continuation of William of Tyre* and describes events that followed Richard the Lionheart's capture of Acre. Richard negotiated a prisoner-exchange agreement with Saladin that included the return of the 'true cross' to Christian control. After several delays by Saladin, Richard came to the conclusion that Saladin was bluffing or biding his time while the thousands of prisoners drained Richard's resources. As a result, Richard ordered the mass execution of thousands of Muslim prisoners in full view of Saladin's army. The author of the *Continuation* based his account on earlier sources.

When Acre was surrendered, Saladin, who was encamped at Saffran, had promised the kings of France and England that he would hand the Holy Cross back to the Christians and would release one Christian that he held in prison for every Saracen they had captured in the city. They agreed to this, for they were keen for the Christians to be released from Saracen captivity. Saladin fixed a day to fulfil the undertaking he had promised. It was said that he arranged for most of the prisoners that he had in his realm to be brought along together with the crosses that he had seized from the churches of the kingdom, and he was all set to hand over the Christians and receive the Saracens. But on the day that he had promised he did not come. He sent word requesting another day, saying that he had a good reason why he had been unable to come on the date he had promised. The kings had a great desire to recover the Holy Cross. They took counsel and agreed another day. That day came, and the kings and the knighthood of Christendom and all the men-at-arms were made ready in serried ranks. The priests and the clerks and the men of religion were vested, and they came forth from the city of Acre barefoot and in great devotion to the place that Saladin had specified. They had come expecting Saladin to bring them the Holy Cross, but he withdrew and reneged on the agreement and the promise that he had made. So the kings of France and England found themselves deceived, and there was great sorrow among the Christians; many tears were shed on that day, and all the men of the host were greatly troubled.

When King Richard saw the people weeping and lamenting because Saladin had deceived them, he had great pity and wanted to calm those who were in such great distress. He ordered that the Saracens whom he had captured in his sector be brought before him. He then had them taken between the Christian and Saracen hosts, near enough to the Saracens that they could see them well. The king boldly ordered that their heads should be immediately struck off. They took hold of them – there were 16,000 in all – and killed them there in the sight of the Saracens.

Beha ed-Din on Richard's Massacre of Muslim Prisoners at Acre in 1191[12]

The following source is taken from Beha ed-Din's account of Richard's massacre of Muslim prisoners at Acre in 1191. By this time, Beha ed-Din had entered service under Saladin and was accompanying him on his campaigns. As a result, Beha ed-Din might have witnessed the events at Acre in 1191 or, at least, had access to first-hand information. He estimates that 3,000 prisoners were slain as opposed to the 16,000 estimate given in the *Old French Continuation of William of Tyre*. Beha ed-Din also argues that Richard acted treacherously, as the Muslims had agreed to surrender Acre to him in exchange for the lives of the prisoners.

When the King of England saw that the sultan was making some delay in the fulfilment of the above-mentioned conditions, he acted treacherously with regard to the Moslem prisoners. He had promised to spare their lives if they surrendered the city, adding that if the sultan sent him what had been agreed upon, he would give them their liberty, with permission to take their wives and children with them and to carry away all their movable property; if the sultan did not fulfil the conditions, they were to become slaves. The king broke the solemn promises he had made them, openly showed the intentions he had hitherto concealed, and carried out what he had purposed to do as soon as he had received the money and the Frank prisoners. That is what the people of his nation said afterwards. About four o'clock in the afternoon of Tuesday, the 27th of Rejeb, he rode out with the whole of the Frankish army-infantry, cavalry and Turcopoles (that is, light-armed soldiers) – and advanced as far as the wells at the foot of Tell el-'A'yadiya, to which place he had already sent forward his tents. As soon as the Franks reached the middle of the plain between this tell and that of Kisan, which was occupied by the sultan's advanced guard, they brought out the Moslem prisoners, whom God had pre-ordained to martyrdom that day, to the number of more than three thousand, all tied together with ropes. The Franks rushed upon them all at once and slaughtered them in cold blood with sword and lance. The advanced guard had previously informed the sultan that the enemy had got to horse, and he sent them some reinforcements, but they did not arrive until the massacre had been accomplished. As soon as the Muslims saw what they were doing to the prisoners, they rushed down on the Franks, and a certain number were killed and wounded on both sides in the action that took place, and lasted until night separated the combatants. The following morning our people went out to see what had happened, and found all the Muslims who had been martyred for their faith stretched on the ground; they were able to recognise some of them. This was a terrible grief to them. The enemy had only spared the prisoners of note and such as were strong enough to labour. Various motives have been assigned for this massacre. According to some, the prisoners were killed to avenge the deaths of those slain previously by the Muslims; others say that the King of England, having made up his mind to try and take Ascalon, did not think it prudent to leave so many prisoners behind in Acre. God knows what his reason really was.

THE MUSLIM TREATMENT OF CHRISTIAN PRISONERS

The second set of sources in this section deals with the Muslim treatment of Christian prisoners. They are taken from the works of Joinville and the two Arab writers Ibn al-Athir and Beha ed-Din. Al-Athir's account describes the aftermath of Saladin's victory at Hattin and his efforts to execute as many survivors of the crusading orders as possible since 'they were the fiercest of all the Frankish warriors'. Yet so long as Christian captives did not represent a threat to Saladin's ambitions, he could show mercy. This is perhaps best demonstrated in Beha ed-Din's account of the Sultan's efforts to locate the kidnapped child of a Christian woman who had bravely travelled to his camp and threw herself at his mercy to help her find her child. Finally, a number of selections from Joinville's account of Louis's First Crusade give details on the experiences of the King and other crusaders during their time in captivity in Egypt. The four selections examine Joinville's treatment while in Muslim captivity, the Muslim treatment of sick Christian prisoners, the forced conversion of prisoners and the execution of those who refused, and finally the French Queen's fear of capture while in Damietta, resulting in the promise of an elderly knight to slay her before she could be taken.

THE SOURCES

Ibn al-Athir on Saladin's Execution of Captive Templars and Hospitallers in 1187[13]

The following account is taken from Ibn al-Athir's account of Saladin's execution of captive members of the Christian military orders after his victory at Hattin. He notes that Saladin had these particular men killed because they were the 'fiercest' of the Frankish warriors and because he did not want to face them again on the battlefield. Ibn al-Athir was an eyewitness of Saladin's career and might have been present at the battle of Hattin. If not, he certainly had access to first-hand information when composing his account.

When Saladin had brought about the downfall of the Franks he stayed at the site of the battle for the rest of the day, and on the Sunday returned to the siege of Tiberias. The Countess sent to request safe-conducts for

herself and her children, companions and possessions, and he granted her
this. She left the citadel with all her train, and Saladin kept his word to
her and let her escape unmolested. At the sultan's command the king and
a few of the most distinguished prisoners were sent to Damascus, while
the Templars and Hospitallers were rounded up to be killed. The sultan
realised that those that had taken them prisoner were not going to hand
them over, for they hoped to obtain ransoms for them, and so he offered
fifty Egyptians dinar for each prisoner in these two categories. Immediately
he got two hundred prisoners, who were decapitated at his command. He
had these particular men killed because they were the fiercest of all the
Frankish warriors, and in this way he rid the Muslim people of them. He
sent orders to his commander in Damascus to kill all of those found in his
territory, whoever they belonged to, and this was done.

A year later I crossed the battlefield, and saw the land all covered with
their bones, which could be seen even from a distance, lying in heaps or
scattered around. These were what was left after all the rest had been
carried away by storms or by the wild beasts of these hills and valleys.

Beha ed-Din on Saladin's Kindness to a Distraught Christian Mother during the Third Crusade[14]

The following source from Beha ed-Din describes the plight of
a Christian woman whose child had been kidnapped by Muslims.
To find her child, she boldly went to Saladin's camp, pleading for his
help. Saladin took pity on the woman and helped her find her child
and allowed her to return to the Christian camp unharmed.

The Muslims kept a number of thieves whose business it was to carry off
people from the enemy's camp. On one of their nightly expeditions they
seized a little nursling of three months, and brought it to the sultan's tent,
the rule being that they should bring all they had taken to the prince, who
gave it back at once into their hands. When the child's mother found that
her child had disappeared, she spent the whole night in weeping and
lamentations, and in seeking assistance. When the princes of the Franks
heard what had happened, they said to the woman: 'The sultan is very
compassionate; we will give you permission to leave the camp and repair
to him, to ask for your child; he is certain to give it back to you.' She
thereupon left the camp and went up to the (Moslem) advanced guard,
to whom she told her story. They brought her to the sultan, who was on

horseback and attended by his suite, of whom I was one. She threw herself on her face upon the ground and began weeping and lamenting. When the sultan heard the cause of her grief he was affected even to tears, and commanded the child to be brought. When he was told that it had been sold in the market, he commanded that the purchaser should be reimbursed the price he had paid, and the child taken away from him. He remained where he was until the child was brought, and then gave it back to the poor mother, who pressed it to her breast whilst the tears ran down her cheeks. It was such an affecting sight that all who witnessed it were moved to tears. Then, by the sultan's command, she and her child were put on a mare and taken back to the enemy's camp.

Jean de Joinville on His Capture and Treatment while in Captivity[15]

The following source is taken from Jean de Joinville's eyewitness account of Louis IX's crusade to Egypt. Here Joinville describes his capture and the favourable treatment he received by misleading his captors into believing he was the cousin of the King and a valuable prisoner.

When I saw that we must be taken, I took my casket and my jewels, and threw them into the river, and my relics also. Then said one of my mariners to me: 'Lord, if you do not suffer me to say you are the king's cousin, they will kill you all, and us also.' And I told him I was quite willing he should say what he pleased. When the people on the first galley that came towards us to strike us amidships heard this, they threw down their anchors near to our boat. Then did God send me a Saracen belonging to the emperor's land.[16] He had on drawers of unbleached linen, and came swimming across the stream to our vessel, and threw his arms about my waist, and said: 'Lord if you do not take good heed, you are but lost; for it behoves you to leap from your vessel on to the beak that rises from the keel of that galley; and if you leap, these people will not mind you, for they are thinking only of the booty to be found in your vessel.' They threw me a rope from the galley, and I leapt on to the beak, so as God willed. And you must know that I tottered so that if the Saracen had not leapt after me, and held me up, I should have fallen into the water.

They set me in the galley, where there were full fourteen score men of their people, and he held me always in his arms. Then they threw me to the ground, and jumped upon my body to cut my throat, for any one would have thought it an honour to kill me. But the Saracen held me constantly in his arms, and cried: 'Cousin to the king!' In this manner they bore me down to the ground twice, and once upon my knees, and then I felt the knife at my throat. In this extremity God saved my life by the help of the Saracen, who took me to the castle of the ship, where the Saracen knights were assembled. When I came among them they took off my hauberk; and for the pity they had upon me, they threw over me a scarlet coverlet lined with miniver, which my lady mother had given me erewhile; and one of them brought me a white belt, and I girt myself over the coverlet; and in the coverlet I had made a hole, donning it as a garment. And another brought me a hood which I put upon my head. And then, because of the fear in which I was, I began to tremble very much, and also because of the sickness. Then I asked for drink and they brought me some water in a jar; and as soon as I set the water to my mouth to drink it down, it spurted out through my nostrils.

When I saw this, I sent for my people, and told them I was a dead man, seeing I had the tumour in my throat; and they asked how I knew it; and I showed them; and as soon as they saw the water spurting from my throat and from my nostrils, they took to weeping. When the Saracen knights who were there saw my people weeping, they asked the Saracens who had rescued us why they were weeping; and he replied that he understood I had the tumour in the throat, so that I could not recover. Then one of the Saracen knights told him to bid us be of good comfort, for he would give me somewhat to drink whereby I should be cured within two days; and this he did.

My Lord Raoul of Wanou, who was one of my following, had been hamstrung in the great battle on Shrove Tuesday, and could not stand upon his feet; and you must know that an old Saracen knight, who was in the galley, would carry him, hanging from his neck, whenever the sick man's necessities so required.

The chief emir of the galleys sent for me and asked me if I were cousin to the king; and I said, 'No', and told him how and why the mariner had said I was the king's cousin. And he said I had acted wisely, for otherwise we should all have been put to death. And he asked me if I was in any manner of the lineage of the Emperor Fredric of Germany, who was then living. I replied that I thought my lady mother was the emperor's cousin-german [sic]. And he said that he loved me the more for it.

While we were at meat, he caused a citizen of Paris to be brought before us. When the citizen came in, he said to me: 'Lord, what are you doing?' 'Why, what am I doing?' said I. 'In God's name', said he, 'you are eating flesh on a Friday!' When I heard that, I put my bowl behind me. And the emir asked my Saracen why I had done so, and he told him. And the emir replied that God would not take what I had done amiss, seeing I did it unwittingly. And you must know that this same reply was given to me by the Legate after we were out of prison; and yet, notwithstanding, I did not afterwards forbear to fast on bread and water, every Friday in Lent; wherefore the legate was very wroth with me, seeing that I was the only man of substance that had remained with the king.

Jean de Joinville on the Muslim Treatment of Sick Christian Prisoners in Egypt[17]

Here Joinville describes an incident in which his Muslim captors systematically inspected Christian prisoners to weed out the sick or injured for execution. Joinville notes, quite interestingly, that he made an effort to get them to stop by citing the example of Saladin, but they were unimpressed with his efforts and responded that they were only destroying men too ill to be of any use.

On the Sunday after, the emir caused me, and all the other prisoners taken on the water, to be landed on the bank of the river. While they were taking my Lord John, my good priest, out of the hold of the galley, he fainted, and they killed him and threw him into the river. His clerk fainted also, by reason of the sickness of the host that was upon him, and they threw a mortar on his head, so that he died, and they threw him into the river. While the other sick people were being disembarked from the galleys in which they had been kept prisoner, there were Saracens standing by, with naked swords, who killed those that fell, and cast them all into the river. I caused them to be told , through my Saracen, that is seemed to me this was not well done; for it was against the teachings of Saladin, who said you ought never to kill a man after he had partaken of your bread and of your salt. And the emir answered that the men in question were of no account, seeing they were helpless because of the sickness they had upon them.

Jean de Joinville on the Forced Conversion of Christian Prisoners[18]

Here Joinville provides an eyewitness account of how his Muslim captors systematically demanded the conversion of several Christian prisoners and beheaded those who refused.

We had not been there long before they caused one of the chief men that were there to rise, and took us to another pavilion. Many of the knights and the other people were kept by the Saracens in a court enclosed by mud walls. From this enclosed place they caused them to be taken, one after the other, and asked them, 'Wilt thou abjure they faith?' Those who would not abjure were set to one side, and their heads were cut off; and those who abjured were set on the other side.

Jean de Joinville on the Queen's Fear of Capture at Damietta[19]

Here Joinville describes the Queen's fear while at Damietta over the turn of events that had resulted in her husband's (Louis IX's) capture and imprisonment. Joinville relays a story he heard in which the Queen sought the protection of an elderly knight to watch over her while she slept. At one point the Queen asked the knight to kill her if it seemed she was about to fall into enemy hands. The knight responded that he had already planned to do so long before her request.

Now you have heard, in what has gone before, of the great tribulations which the king and all of us endured. From such tribulations the queen did not escape, as you shall presently be told. For, three days before she was brought to bed, came the news that the king was taken; with which news she was so affrighted that, as oft as she slept in her bed, it seemed to her that the chamber was full of Saracens, and she cried out, 'Help! Help!' And so that the child she bore in her body should not perish, she caused an ancient knight, of eighty years, to lie near her bed, and hold her by the hand; and every time she so cried out, he said: 'lady, have no fear, for I am here.' Before she was brought to bed she caused everyone to leave her chamber, save this knight only, and knelt before him, and besought him to do her a service; and the knight consented, and gave her his oath. And she said: 'I ask of you, by the troth you have now pledged me, that if the Saracens take this city, you will cut off my head before I fall into their hands.' And the knight replied: 'Be assured that I shall do so willingly; for I was already fully minded to kill you or ever you should be taken.'

SPIRITUALITY

Christians and Muslims alike turned to their faiths for motivation and encouragement during their hardships. Both Christian and Muslim authors regularly ascribed their misfortunes to God's will, often as a type of punishment for their sins. Hence many reasoned that the proper way to restore God's favour was through proper repentance and religious observance. Without doubt, such thinking was comforting to those seeking to understand the failures of an expedition they believed had been sanctioned by God. Spirituality provided hope in times of despair, that by God's favour anything could be accomplished no matter how dire the situation.

The first two selections in this section are taken from the *Gesta*. The first deals with the discovery of the Holy Lance at Antioch during the First Crusade. The author describes how its discovery was interpreted and promoted by the clergy as a sign of God's favour to motivate the crusaders during the otherwise lengthy and demoralising siege. The second selection from the *Gesta* describes the spiritual preparations of the newly inspired crusaders before engaging in battle. These preparations included making confessions and receiving communion, which were common for Christians about to engage in battle throughout the crusading era. The *Gesta* sources are followed by a selection from Godfrey's letter to Pope Paschal in which he credits the crusaders' victory at Antioch to their efforts to appease God's anger by marching barefoot through the city. This is followed by a short selection by Ibn al-Athir, which describes how the capture of the 'True Cross' at Hattin by Saladin's forces during the Third Crusade was one of the 'heaviest blows' against the Christian army and how its demoralising effect 'made their death and destruction certain'. The final selection presented in this section provides Joinville's description of his daily spiritual regimen, while accompanying Louis IX in the East, following their release from captivity in Egypt. He notes how each morning he had two chaplains to say his hours and chant mass to him before he began his day in service to the King.

THE SOURCES

Gesta: The Discovery of the Holy Lance at Antioch in 1098[20]

The following selection from the *Gesta* describes the discovery of a lance at Antioch that was believed to be the one that pierced Christ's body on his side. Its location was reportedly revealed to the crusaders by the Apostle Andrew at a time when they were desperately in need of a morale boost. Although its authenticity was doubted by many contemporaries, the sources claim the discovery proved useful in restoring the spirits of the crusaders.

'Seignors, if you do not believe that this is true, let me climb up into this tower, and I will throw myself down, and if I am unharmed, believe that this is true. If, however, I shall have suffered any hurt, behead me, or cast me into the fire.' Then the Bishop of Puy ordered that the Gospel and the Cross be brought, so that be might take oath that this was true.

All our leaders were counselled at that time to take oath that not one of them would flee, either for life or death, as long as they were alive. Bohemund is said to have been the first to take the oath, then the Count of St. Gilles, Robert of Normandy, Duke Godfrey and the Count of Flanders. Tancred, indeed, swore and promised in this manner: that as long as he had forty knights with him he would not only not withdraw from that battle, but, likewise, not from the march to Jerusalem. Moreover, the Christian assemblage exulted greatly upon hearing this oath.

There was a certain pilgrim of our army, whose name was Peter, to whom before we entered the city St. Andrew, the apostle, appeared and said: 'What art thou doing, good man?' Peter answered, 'Who art thou?' The apostle said to him: 'I am St. Andrew, the apostle. Know, my son, that when thou shalt enter the town, go to the church of St. Peter. There thou wilt find the Lance of our Saviour, Jesus Christ, with which He was wounded as He hung on the arm of the cross.' Having said all this, the apostle straightway withdrew.

But Peter, afraid to reveal the advice of the apostle, was unwilling to make it known to the pilgrims. However, he thought that he had seen a vision, and said: 'Lord, who would believe this?' But at that hour St. Andrew took him and carried him to the place where the Lance was hidden in the ground. When we were a second time situated in such (straits) as we have stated above, St. Andrew came again, saying to him: 'Wherefore hast thou not yet taken the Lance from the earth as I commanded thee? Know verily, that whoever shall bear this lance in battle shall never "be overcome by an enemy".' Peter, indeed, straightway made known to our men the mystery of the apostle.

The people, however, did not believe (it), but refused, saying: 'How can we believe this?' For they were utterly terrified and thought that they were to die forthwith. Thereupon, this man came forth and swore that it was all most true, since St. Andrew had twice appeared to him in a vision and had said to him: 'Rise go and tell the people of God not to fear, but to trust firmly with whole heart in the one true God and they will be everywhere victorious. Within five days the Lord will send them such a token that they will remain happy and joyful, and if they wish to fight, let them go out immediately to battle, all together, and all their enemies will be conquered, and no one will stand against them.' Thereupon, when they heard that their enemies were to be overcome by them, they began straightway to revive and to encourage one another, saying: 'Bestir yourselves, and be everywhere brave and alert, since the Lord will come to our aid in the next battle and will be the greatest refuge to His people whom He beholds lingering in sorrow.'

Accordingly, upon hearing the statements of that man who reported to us the revelation of Christ through the words of the apostle, we went in haste immediately to the place in the church of St. Peter which he had pointed out. Thirteen men dug there from morning until vespers. And so that man found the Lance, just as he had indicated. They received it with great gladness and fear, and a joy beyond measure arose in the whole city.

Gesta: The Crusaders Make Themselves Holy Before Battle at Antioch in 1098[21]

The following account from the *Gesta* describes the spiritual preparations of the crusaders as they made themselves holy for battle against Kerbogha's forces at Antioch in 1098. Such preparations, including confession and the celebration of the mass, were common for Christian armies before battle throughout the crusading era.

At length, when the three days fast had been fulfilled, and a procession had been held from one church to another, they confessed their sins, were absolved and faithfully took the communion of the body and blood of Christ; and when alms had been give they celebrated mass. Then six battle lines were formed from the forces within the city.

Godfrey's Letter to Pope Paschal II on How Repentance Led to Victory at Antioch in 1098[22]

In the following selection from Godfrey's letter to Pope Paschal II, the Duke reports on how he and the other leaders of the suffering Christian army at Antioch determined that to win God's favour, a barefoot procession through the city was necessary. Godfrey believed that God was indeed 'appeased by this humility' and soon 'delivered the city' to the crusaders.

And after the army had suffered greatly in the siege, especially on account of the lack of water, a council was held, and the bishops and princes ordered that all should march around the walls of the city with bare feet, in order that he who entered it humbly in our behalf might be moved by our humility to open it to us and to exercise judgment upon his enemies. God was appeased by this humility, and on the eighth day after the humiliation he delivered the city and his enemies to us.

Ibn al-Athir on the Muslim Capture of the True Cross at Hattin in 1187[23]

In the following selection taken from Ibn al-Athir's account of the Battle of Hattin in 1187, the author describes the capture of the 'true cross' and the demoralising effect it had on Christian forces.

The surviving Franks made for a hill near Hittin [Hattin], where they hoped to pitch their tents and defend themselves. They were vigorously attacked from all sides and prevented from pitching more than one tent, that of the king. The Muslims captured the 'True Cross', in which they say is a piece of the wood upon which, according to them, the Messiah was crucified. This was one of the heaviest blows that could be inflicted on them and made their death and destruction certain. Large numbers of their cavalry and infantry were killed or captured.

Jean de Joinville's Daily Spirituality during Louis's Crusade[24]

Here Joinville provides a brief description of his daily spiritual regimen in the years that he accompanied Louis in the Holy Land after their release from captivity in Egypt.

Hereinafter will I tell you how I planned and arranged my affairs during the first four years that I remained in the land overseas, after the king's brothers had departed. I had two chaplains, who said my hours to me. The one chanted my mass as soon as the dawn of day appeared; the other waited till my knights belonging to my division, had risen. When I had heard my mass, I went to the king.

WOMEN ON A CRUSADE

One challenge to the proper spirituality of the crusaders, so clerical sources argue, was the presence of women. If crusaders were to avoid sin, many felt that they should avoid women as otherwise they might face too great a temptation to sexual immorality. Such attitudes, of course, resulted in numerous difficulties for women on a crusade. In the wake of defeat, when demoralised crusaders sought the source of their failure, the finger was often pointed at women and the assumed immorality that took place as a result of their presence.[25] Regardless of such difficulties, women were present on crusades throughout the crusading era as laundresses, cooks, prostitutes or as wives accompanying their husbands.

The first two source selections presented on this topic are taken from the Arab historian Imad ad-Din's account of events leading to the Third Crusade. The first selection provides his unlikely claim that Christian women participated effectively as knights in offensive combat during the crusades. He notes, for example, how Christian women 'rode into battle' dressed like men and fought like knights. Modern scholars are sceptical of such claims, as Latin Christian society was overwhelmingly intolerant of the idea. Moreover, it is probable that Arab authors may have been motivated to make this claim because it would cast shame on their Christian enemies, as Arab culture found the idea of women as combatants equally undesirable.[26] The second source by Imad ad-Din describes the abuse and humiliation of Christian women by Muslim forces after Saladin's capture of Jerusalem in 1187. The author notes approvingly, but perhaps with some hyperbole, how Christian women were 'dishonoured…deflowered…tamed' and taken as 'concubines' by Muslim soldiers. Certainly the threat of rape or of becoming a concubine of the enemy was nearly constant for both Christian and Muslim women during the crusading era. Indeed, even in Robert the Monk's account of Urban II's calling of the First Crusade in 1095, the Pope cited the rape of Christian women by Muslims as a means of stirring his listeners to action.[27]

The remaining sources provided in this section are all by Christian authors. They include two seemingly contradictory selections from the *Gesta* in which women are praised for their aid to the crusaders during the battle at Dorylaeum and then later condemned as a source of sin and failure at Antioch. In the first case, women are praised for comforting and bringing water to thirsty troops during intensive fighting at the siege of Dorylaeum in 1097. Since the author of the *Gesta* was probably a knight, who participated in the fighting at Dorylaeum, he may have personally benefited from such efforts. Yet in the second selection, from the same work, the author describes how the clergy cited women as the source of the crusaders' problems during the siege of Antioch in 1098. Specifically, the clergy attributed the crusaders' problems to God's displeasure with them on account of sexual immorality in the camps. Indeed, the account of Fulcher of Chartres confirms the crusaders' concerns over the presence of women as a source of sin at Antioch. Fulcher describes how the crusaders, desperate for a remedy to their problems, made the decision to expel the women from their camps, hoping to eliminate any opportunities for sin. The two final Christian selections in this section are taken from Joinville's account of Louis IX's crusade and reflect the continued concerns of crusaders over the presence of women more than a century and a half after the events at Antioch. In the first selection, Joinville describes the harsh punishment given by Louis IX to a knight who had visited a brothel. The pious King was no doubt worried about the effects of sexual immorality on his crusade, as had been a common concern throughout the crusading era.[28] As punishment, the knight was given a choice: either he could give up his horse and weapons and leave the crusade or he could be tied up with a rope and led around the camp by a prostitute. The second selection by Joinville is brief but provides fascinating insights into the tense environment of Louis's crusade with regard to women. Indeed, the fear of the presence of women during the crusade and the threat of their sexuality to its success prompted Joinville to make careful arrangements in his sleeping quarters in the pavilion, positioning himself in such a way that he could be seen by all who entered and thus prevent any 'ill suspicion as concerning women'.

THE SOURCES

Imad ad-Din on Christian Women as Combatants During the Third Crusade[29]

The following source is taken from Imad ad-Din's contemporary account of the Third Crusade. Here he makes the controversial claim that Christian women rode into combat dressed as men and fought as knights. Because such claims would have served to shame his Christian opponents, who traditionally rejected any notion of the suitability of women for combat, modern scholars have viewed his claims with caution.

Among the Franks there were indeed women who rode into battle with cuirasses and helmets, dressed in men's clothes; who rode out into the thick of the fray and acted like brave men although they were but tender women, maintaining that all this was an act of piety, thinking to gain heavenly rewards by it, and making it their way of life. Praise be to him who led them into such error and out of the paths of wisdom! On the day of battle more than one woman rode out with them like a knight and showed (masculine) endurance in spite of the weakness (of her sex); clothed only in a coat of mail they were not recognised as women until they had been stripped of their arms. Some of them were discovered and sold as slaves; and everywhere was full of old women. These were sometimes a support and sometimes a source of weakness. They exhorted and incited men to summon their pride, saying that the Cross imposed on them the obligation to resist to the bitter end, and that the combatants would win eternal life only by sacrificing their lives, and that their God's sepulchre was in enemy hands. Observe how men and women led them into error; the latter in their religious zeal tired of feminine delicacy, and to save themselves from the terror of dismay (on the day of judgment) became the close companions of perplexity, and having succumbed to the lust for vengeance, became hardened, and stupid and foolish because of the harm they had suffered.

Imad ad-Din on the Abuse of Christian Women After Saladin's Capture of Jerusalem in 1187[30]

Here Imad ad-Din revels in the abusive treatment of Christian women after Saladin's victory at Jerusalem in 1187. Although most Christian inhabitants of the city had been allowed to leave through the payment of a modest ransom, thousands were unable to afford the ransom and were left behind to the mercy of their new Muslim masters.

Women and children together came to 8,000 and were quickly divided up among us, bringing a smile to Muslim faces at their lamentations. How many well guarded women were profaned, how many queens were ruled, and nubile girls married, and noble women given away, and miserly women forced to yield themselves, and women who had been kept hidden stripped of their modesty, and serious women made ridiculous, and women kept in private now set in public, and free women occupied, and precious ones used for hard work, and pretty things put to the test, and virgins dishonoured and proud women deflowered, and lovely women's red lips kissed, and dark women prostrated, and untamed ones tamed and happy ones made to weep. How many noblemen took them as concubines, how many ardent men blazed for one of them, and celibates were satisfied by them, and thirsty men sated by them and turbulent men able to give vent to their passion. How many lovely women were the exclusive property of one man, how many great ladies were sold at low prices, and close ones set at a distance, and lofty ones abased, and savage ones captured and those accustomed to thrones dragged down!

Gesta: Women as a Blessing to the Crusading Army at Dorylaeum in 1097[31]

On rare occasions, women received praise for their efforts during a crusade. Such was the case with the author of the *Gesta* who briefly praised women for their actions during one of the earliest victories of the First Crusade at Dorylaeum in 1097. As a Christian knight present at the battle for Dorylaeum, the author of the *Gesta* may have personally benefited from the efforts of these women.

By the time all this had been done, the Turks had already surrounded us on all sides. They attacked us, slashing, hurling, and shooting arrows far and wide, in a manner strange to behold. Although we could scarcely hold them back or even bear up under the weight of such a host, nevertheless we all managed to hold our ranks. Our women were a great blessing to us that day, for they carried drinking water zip to our fighting men and comforted the fighters and defenders.

Gesta: Women as a Source of Sin and the Cause of Failure at Antioch in 1098[32]

Praise for women during the First Crusade was short-lived as by the time the crusaders engaged their opponents at Antioch and experienced a number of military setbacks, clerical leaders pointed to the presence of women as the cause of their misfortunes. In the following selection, the author of the *Gesta* records an incident in which a priest claimed that Jesus had appeared to him and told him that the cause of the crusaders' hardships were the result of their evil pleasures with both 'Christian and depraved pagan women'.

But one day as our leaders, sad and disconsolate, were standing back before the fortress, a certain priest came to them and said: 'Seignorss, if it please you, listen to a certain matter which I saw in a vision. When one night I was lying in the church St. Mary, Mother of God, our Lord Jesus Christ, the Saviour of the world, appeared to me with His mother and St. Peter, Prince of the apostles, and stood before me and said, "Knowest thou me?" I answered, "No." At these words, lo, a whole cross on His head. A second time, therefore, the Lord asked me "Knowest thou, me?" To Him I replied: "I do not know Thee except that I see a cross on thy head like that of Our Saviour." He answered, "I am He."'

'Immediately I fell at His feet, humbly beseeching that He help us in the oppression which was upon us. The Lord responded: "I have helped you in goodly manner and I will now help you. I permitted you to have the city of Nicaea, and to win all battles and I conducted you hither to this point, and I have grieved at the misery which you have suffered in the siege of Antioch. Behold with timely aid I sent you safe and unharmed into the city, and lo! (you are) working much evil pleasure with Christian and depraved pagan women, whereof a stench beyond measure arises unto heaven."'

Fulcher of Chartres on the Expulsion of Christian Women from Antioch in 1098[33]

In the following selection, taken from an eyewitness account of the First Crusade written by Fulcher of Chartres, the author describes how the crusading leadership at Antioch was advised by the clergy that their problems were the result of their sins. Consequently, the leadership decided to 'drive out' both married and unmarried women from their camps.

They had no supplies on which they could live. It was with great fear that they sought food far away, in going distances of forty or fifty miles from the siege, that is, in the mountains, where they were often killed by the Turks lying in ambush. We believed that these misfortunes befell the Franks, and that they were not able for so long a time to take the city because of their sins. Not only dissipation, but also avarice or pride or rapaciousness corrupted them. After holding council, they drove out the women from the army, both married and unmarried, lest they, stained by the defilement of dissipation, displease the Lord. These women then found places to live in the neighbouring camps.

Jean de Joinville on Louis IX's Harsh Treatment of a Knight Who Visited a Brothel[34]

Here Jean de Joinville reports an instance in which a knight was discovered in a brothel. Such an act was considered a serious threat to the well-being of the crusade because it was believed that such immorality could bring God's wrath on the crusaders. Louis provided the knight with a choice of punishments: he could relinquish his horse and weapons to the king and leave the army or be bound and led around the camp by a prostitute.

Hereinafter you shall hear tell of the justice and judgments that I saw rendered at Caesarea while the king was sojourning there. First we will tell of a knight who was taken in a brothel, and to whom a certain choice was left, according to the customs of the country. And the choice was this: that either the wanton woman should lead him through the camp, in his shirt, and shamefully bound with a rope, or that he should lose his horse and arms and be driven from the host. The knight gave up his horse to the king, and his arms, and left the host.

Jean de Joinville's Efforts to Avoid Suspicion with Regard to Women During Louis's Crusade[35]

Here Jean de Joinville briefly describes the curious precautions he took concerning his sleeping arrangements (during Louis's First Crusade) to ensure that nobody would be suspicious of him with regard to women. It gives a sense of the concern that the crusading leadership had over the detrimental effects of sexual immorality, for which they primarily blamed women, on the outcome of a crusade.

My bed was laid in my pavilion after such a manner that none could enter in without seeing me as I lay in my bed; and this I did so that there should be no ill suspicion as concerning women.

CHAPTER THIRTEEN
LIFE IN THE CRUSADER STATES, 1098–1291

239
WILLIAM OF TYRE – ELECTION OF GODFREY IN JERUSALEM

241
FULCHER OF CHARTRES – CONDITIONS IN THE HOLY LAND IN THE EARLY YEARS

242
WILLIAM – THE REPOPULATION OF THE KINGDOM OF JERUSALEM UNDER BALDWIN I

243
JACQUES DE VITRY – THE FOUNDING OF THE KNIGHTS TEMPLAR

245
USAMAH IBN MUNQIDH – BALDWIN EXEMPTS HIS UNCLE FROM AN INDEMNITY

246
FULCHER – GOING NATIVE IN THE HOLY LAND

247
USAMAH – A FRANK GOING NATIVE IN THE HOLY LAND

248
USAMAH – THE FRIENDLY FRANK

249
USAMAH – MUSLIM AND CHRISTIAN MEDICINE

251
USAMAH – POSITIVE REFLECTIONS OF CHRISTIAN AND MUSLIM PIETY

252
BURCHARD OF MOUNT SION – DESCRIPTION OF MUSLIMS AND SYRIAN AND GREEK CHRISTIANS

253
USAMAH – FRANKS DEVOID OF JEALOUSY

255
IMAD AD-DIN – ON FRANKISH PROSTITUTES

257
JACQUES ON THE IMMORAL PULANI

Even though the crusader-colonists brought with them various feudal worldviews of how states and societies should be organised, they did not occupy an empty land. The rich multicultural traditions of lands that had been settled and organised since the dawn of agriculture influenced the types of governments and societies carved out by the Franks in the Levant.

– Alfred J. Andrea[1]

COHABITATION AND COOPERATION

The era of crusading in the East did not represent non-stop hostilities between Christians and Muslims. To the contrary, the majority of the nearly two centuries of the crusaders' presence in the Holy Land was spent in relatively peaceful cohabitation and much-needed economic cooperation between Christians, Muslims and Jews.[2] Certainly Muslims and Christians held a number of prejudices towards one another and their rulers were almost always seeking the upper hand, but they also became dependent on each other and there were occasions of admiration and even friendship.

The major crusader states in the Levant, all founded during or soon after the First Crusade, consisted of the County of Edessa (founded in 1098), the Principality of Antioch (1098), the Kingdom of Jerusalem (1099) and the County of Tripoli (1104). There were also important vassals of the Kingdom of Jerusalem, including the Principality of Galilee and the County of Jaffa and Ascalon. The Kingdom of Jerusalem was the most prominent and influential of all the crusader states and, as a result, provides the largest amount of source materials. For these reasons, this chapter focuses extensively, but not exclusively, on events in the Latin Kingdom of Jerusalem.

GOVERNMENT AND ADMINISTRATION

Early efforts to establish proper government in the crusader states were paramount. Indeed, within days of the conquest of Jerusalem, leading members of the First Crusade met in council to determine a ruler. The members of the council ultimately chose the highly regarded Duke of Lower Lorraine, Godfrey of Bouillon, to serve as ruler of the nascent Kingdom of Jerusalem.[3] Yet their deliberations were not uneventful, as seen in William of Tyre's account of the election, provided in this chapter. William describes, for example, how the secular lords clashed with the clergy, who had their own agenda during the deliberations. More importantly, William provides a detailed account of the process by which the electors weighed up the prospective candidates. He notes how the servants of each candidate were interviewed in an effort to better understand the true character of their Lords. According to William, Godfrey's servants cited his devotion to religious matters as their biggest complaint – for example, waiting for him to leave a church one day resulted in a cold meal. Unsurprisingly, such pious devotion won over the electors who praised Godfrey's fault as a virtue.

Godfrey and the rulers who came after him inherited a number of concerns upon their ascension. Conditions in the Holy Land were tough for the new rulers, who could barely sustain a sizeable populace to do the work necessary to build up and secure the new settlements. Security for Latin Christians in the region was minimal in the years following the establishment of the crusader states, as Muslims, hostile to their presence, continued their attacks on Christians in the outlying areas. Indeed, the cleric Fulcher of Chartres notes how, during the reign of Godfrey's successor Baldwin I, for whom Fulcher served as a chaplain, the land route to the crusader states was completely obstructed, which forced European Christians to travel to the Holy Land by ship. Yet even when travelling by ship, pilgrims faced the threat of hostile pirates. This situation was a major cause of the small population of the Kingdom of Jerusalem and led to efforts by Baldwin, as recorded by William, to convince native Christians in the region, living under non-Christian rule, to relocate and populate the crusader states, with the assurance of improved conditions. Yet even though Baldwin's policies met with some success, security for both native Christians living in the crusader states and pilgrims travelling to these states remained a problem. One of the means by which security concerns were addressed was the founding of the Order of the Knights Templar.[4] In the selection provided here, Jacques de Vitry, who shortly before his death in 1240 had been named Patriarch of Jerusalem, describes how the founding of the Templars was primarily inspired by the goal of protecting pilgrims and pilgrimage routes. Finally, this chapter presents a short selection from Arab historian and diplomat Usamah ibn Munqidh, who interacted extensively with Latin Christians throughout the second half of the twelfth century.[5] Usamah points out that, although Muslims were a constant concern for the crusading states, Christian rulers, under certain circumstances, were benevolent towards Muslims. Usamah notes that this was the case when Baldwin II exempted his uncle from an indemnity required by other Muslims because of the kind treatment Baldwin had received as a captive of the uncle.

THE SOURCES

William of Tyre – Election of Godfrey in Jerusalem[6]

The following source from William of Tyre tells the story of Godfrey of Bouillon's election as the first Latin Christian ruler of Jerusalem in 1099. He describes in detail the careful deliberations of the electors and their efforts to gather information about the candidates before making their final decision. William composed his account of Godfrey's election using earlier sources and documents that he could access by virtue of his position as Archbishop of Tyre.

Seven days glided by in much rejoicing, tempered, indeed, by the fear of the Lord and spiritual gladness. On the eighth day the leaders assembled for consultation. It was their purpose, after invoking the grace of the Holy Spirit, to choose someone from among their own number to rule over the region and to bear the royal responsibility for that province.

But while they were deliberating over the matter, some of the clergy, puffed up with the spirit of pride and intent on their own interests rather than on those of Jesus Christ, also gathered. They sent a message to the chiefs saying that they had certain private matters which they wished to bring before those who were now sitting in council. On being admitted, they said, 'It has been reported to the clergy that you have met for the purpose of choosing one of your number as king. This purpose of yours seems to us holy and well advised and, if it were reached in its proper order, worthy of being carried out with all care. It is undoubtedly true that spiritual matters are of higher importance than temporal and ought therefore to be considered first. In our opinion, the order should be reversed, and, before election to a secular office is thought of, some person of religious life, pleasing to God, ought to be chosen who will be capable of presiding over the church of God for its advancement and benefit. If it pleases you to proceed in this order, it will be most agreeable to us, and we are with you in body and spirit. But if not, we shall pronounce whatever you decree without our approval invalid and without force.'

Although this proposition of the clergy seemed on the surface to be reasonable and honourable…in reality there was underlying it much malevolence, as results will show. The prime leader of this faction was a certain bishop of Calabria, from Martirano [Matera]. An intimate friend of that Arnulf of whom quite enough has already been said in the foregoing pages. The bishop was scheming to place in the patriarchal chair this very Arnulf, a man who, though in holy orders, was notorious for his loose conduct and who was, moreover, the son of a priest. During the entire expedition his reputation had been the subject of common talk among the people, and the wanton singers of the chorus had made him the butt of their lascivious songs. Such was the man whom the bishop, contrary to the sacred canons and against the will of all honourable men, was endeavouring to raise to the office of patriarch. The bishop himself was a man of perverse mind, who had no regard for honour. Hence he could easily reach an agreement with Arnulf, for, as says the ancient proverb, 'As is the true nature of a man, so does he delight in the companionship of those of the same mind, for like to like is easily joined.'

This same man had seized upon the church of Bethlehem, for he had made a bargain with Arnulf that, if the latter through the bishop's exertions should be raised to the patriarchate, the said church without question or difficulty should belong to the bishop in perpetuity. Death, however, soon put an end to all these schemes of his, as will be related in the following pages.

Among the clergy pure religion and all sense of honour had fallen from its high estate. Everywhere decadent, it had been flowing at hazard through forbidden channels from the time when Adhemar, bishop of Puy, the legate of the apostolic see, of pious memory in the Lord, had succumbed to death. After the passing of this holy man, William, bishop of Orange, a religious and God fearing man, assumed the responsibility of that charge and, as long as he lived, faithfully administered it. Only a short time elapsed, however, before he too rested in the Lord at Maara. After the death of these two holy men, it happened as says the prophet: 'Like people, like priest.' Only the bishop of Albara and a few others who had the fear of the Lord before their eyes continued in the straight way.

The princes regarded the objections of the clergy stated in the preceding chapter as frivolous and of no importance. Though intent on carrying out their plan, yet they took the proposal under consideration. Some accounts say that, in order that the election might be conducted in accordance with the will of God and that the merits of the candidates receive due consideration, individuals from the households of those proposed for the honour were secretly interviewed. Each man was forced to take an oath that, when questioned concerning the life and character of his lord, he would speak the truth without deviating from the facts. This course was adopted so that the electors might obtain full and accurate information as to the worth of the several candidates. When later these people were asked searching questions by the electors, they were bound by the oath which they had taken to acknowledge under seal of secrecy many faults as well as virtues in their masters. By this means it was hoped that an unbiased judgment of the character and personality of each candidate might be formed. When, among others, members of Godfrey's staff were examined they declared that of all the doings of the lord duke, the following seemed to them the most trying: namely, that when he once entered a church he could not be induced to leave, even after the celebration of the divine office was concluded. He continued to question the priests and others cognizant of such matters as to the meaning of each image and picture until his companions, whose interests were different, were excessively bored. Moreover, because of this habit of his, the viands which has been prepared for a fixed and suitable hour were, when finally eaten, overdone and tasteless as the result of the long delay.

On hearing this complaint, the electors exclaimed, 'Happy the man who possesses these characteristics, to whom that is ascribed as the fault which others would boast of as a virtue!' After carefully considering all aspects of the matter, the electors unanimously agreed upon the duke as their choice. Godfrey was elected and escorted with great devotion to the Sepulchre of the Lord, attended by the singing of chants and hymns. It is said, however, that the majority of the electors had agreed upon Raymond, count of Toulouse, as their choice. They knew, however, that if he did not obtain the kingdom he intended to return home at once. Hence, drawn by an intense longing for the soil of their beloved native land, they had invented many reasons, even against the dictates of conscience, why the count should be considered unfit for the office.

Fulcher of Chartres – Conditions in the Holy Land in the Early Years[7]

The following selection by Fulcher of Chartres describes the challenges faced by Latin Christians in the Kingdom of Jerusalem during the reign of Baldwin I (r.1100–1118). The major concern reported here by Fulcher, who served as a chaplain to Baldwin I, was the issue of maintaining a sizable enough population to provide security for the Kingdom, its citizens and Christian pilgrims.

In the beginning of his reign, Baldwin [Baldwin I] was the possessor of very few cities and people; yet, through that same winter he protected his kingdom well against enemies on all sides. And because they found out that he was a very courageous fighter, although he had few men, they did not dare to attack him. If he had had more soldiers, he would have met the enemy gladly. The land route was still completely obstructed to our pilgrims – Franks, Angles, Italians and Venetians – who with from one to four ships came timidly by sea to Joppa, the Lord leading them as they sailed through the midst of hostile pirates and past the cities of the Saracens. At first Joppa was our only port. When we saw that they had come from our western lands, immediately and joyfully we advanced to meet them as if they were saints. Each of us inquired anxiously from them concerning his own home and his loved ones. The newcomers told us all that they knew. When we heard good news, we rejoiced; when they told of misfortune, we were saddened. They came on to Jerusalem; they visited the Holy of Holies, for which purpose they had come. Then some remained here in the Holy Land; but others returned to their native country. For this reason Jerusalem was depopulated and there were not enough people to defend the city from the Saracens, if [they] only dared to attack us…

William – The Repopulation of the Kingdom of Jerusalem under Baldwin I[8]

The following selection from William of Tyre describes King Baldwin's efforts to address the problem of depopulation in the Latin Kingdom of Jerusalem. According to William, Baldwin addressed the issue by actively recruiting native Christians living under Muslim rule to come as settlers to the newly formed crusader states.

At this time, the king [Baldwin I] realised with great concern that the Holy City, beloved of God, was almost destitute of inhabitants. There were not enough people to carry on the necessary undertakings of the realm. Indeed there were scarcely enough to protect the entrances to the city and defend the walls and towers against sudden hostile attacks. Accordingly, he gave much anxious thought to the problem, turning the question over in his own mind and talking with others concerning plans for filling it with faithful people, worshippers of the true God. The gentiles who where living there at the time the city was taken by force had perished by the sword, almost to a man; and if any had by chance escaped they were not permitted to remain in the city. For to allow any one not belonging to the Christian faith to live in so venerated a place seemed like sacrilege to the chiefs in their devotion to God. The people of our country were so few in number and so needy that they scarcely filled one street, while the Syrians who had originally been citizens of the city had been so reduced through the many tribulations and trials endured in the time of hostilities that their number was as nothing. From the time that the Latins came into Syria, and particularly when the army began to march toward Jerusalem after the capture of Antioch, their infidel fellow citizens began to abuse these servants of God greatly. Many were slain for the most trivial remarks, and neither age nor condition was spared. The Gentiles distrusted them intensely, for they believed that it was these people who, through their messengers and letters, had summoned the princes of the West, who, it was said, were coming to destroy the infidels.

The king felt that the responsibility for relieving the desolation of the city rested upon him. Accordingly, he made careful investigations in regard to some source whence he might obtain citizens. Finally he learned that beyond the Jordan in Arabia there were many Christians living in villages under hard conditions of servitude and forced tribute. He sent for these people and promised them improved conditions. Within a short time he had the satisfaction of receiving them with their wives and children, flocks and herds and all their households. They were attracted thither not only by reverence for the place but also by affection for our people and the love of liberty. Many, even without being invited, cast off the harsh yoke of servitude and came that they might dwell in the city worthy of God. To these the king granted those sections of the city which seemed to need this assistance most and filled the houses with them.

Jacques de Vitry – The Founding of the Knights Templar [9]

The following selection by Jacques de Vitry, which he based on earlier sources and records, describes the founding of the Knights Templar, the most famous and powerful of the crusading orders. Jacques describes their humble origins and how they were formed primarily for the defence of Christian pilgrims in the Holy Land.

Now, after this, seeing that as time went on people from all parts of the world, both rich and poor, young men and maidens, old men and children, went to Jerusalem to visit the holy places, certain thieves, footpads and highway robbers used to lay ambushes for careless pilgrims, plundered many of them and slew some of them. Now, certain devout Knights, beloved by God, out of their fervent charity renounced the world, made themselves bondslaves of Christ, and by a solemn profession and vow bound themselves to defend pilgrims from the aforesaid robbers, and keep guard over the public roads, living, like Canons Regular, in poverty, chastity and obedience, as soldiers of the King of Kings. Their chiefs were those venerable men, beloved by God, Hugh de Payens and Geoffrey de St. Omer. Only nine at first undertook this holy project. They did service for nine years, wearing secular habits, such as the faithful gave them out of charity; but the king and his Knights, having compassion on the aforesaid noblemen, who had given up all for Christ's sake, and together with the Lord Patriarch, supported them out of their own private means, and afterwards bestowed upon them gifts and grants for the benefit of their souls; and, since they had not as yet any church of their own, or any fixed abode, our Lord the king allowed them to lodge for a time in a part of his palace near the Lord's Temple. The Abbot and Canons of the Lord's Temple gave them an open space which they had near the king's palace to use for offices. As they dwelt near the Lord's Temple, they were afterwards called brethren of the Knights Templar.

Now after they had passed nine years in this profession and holy poverty, living their lives in common in holy poverty, and had dwelt in concord and of one mind in the house, in the year of grace 1128, by the mandate of our Lord Pope Honorius and of the Lord Stephen, Patriarch of Jerusalem, they were given a rule and a white habit, without any cross. This was done in a General Council held at Troyes in Champagne, under the presidency of the Lord Bishop of Alba, the Legate of the Holy See, in the presence of the Archbishops of Rheims and Sens, the Abbots of the Cistercian Order and many other prelates of churches. After this, in the time of our Lord Pope Eugenius, they attached red crosses to the outside of their garments, while they wore white as a symbol of innocency; by the red crosses they alluded to martyrdom, because, according to the terms of their rule, they were bound to shed their own blood in defence of the Holy Land, and manfully overthrow the enemies of the Cross of Christ, and drive them away from the borders of Christendom. At their leader's command they were to join battle, not rashly or disorderly, but wisely and with all caution, being the first to attack and the last to retreat. They were not allowed to turn their backs and flee, nor to retreat without orders. Wherefore, seeing that they were stout and brave soldiers of Christ, like a second race of Maccabees, who did not presume upon their own strength but whose whole hope was in the power of God, and all their trust in the Cross of Jesus Christ, they exposed to death for Christ's sake their bodies, which were right dear in the sight of the Lord; and the Lord fought with them and fought for them. Thus they became so terrible to the enemies of Christ's faith that one of them used to chase a thousand and two of them ten thousand; when they were called to arms, they did not ask how many of the enemy their were, but where they were. They were lions in war, and gentile as lambs at home; in the field they were fierce soldiers. In church they were like hermits or monks; they were harsh and savage to the enemies of Christ, but kindly and gracious to Christians…

They showed due obedience and humble reverence to the Lord Patriarch of Jerusalem; to whom they owed the establishment of their Order and their subsistence in things temporal, rendering tithes and other things that are God's unto God, and unto Caesar the things that are Caesar's.

Usamah ibn Munqidh – Baldwin Exempts His Uncle from an Indemnity[10]

The following short selection from Usamah ibn Munqidh describes an incident in which Baldwin II extended a courtesy to Usamah's uncle by allowing him to forgo the payment of an indemnity imposed on other Muslims. Baldwin did this, according to Usamah, because Baldwin had once been held captive under the charge of Usamah's uncle and was treated kindly.

Baldwin, the prince, took possession of Antioch. My father and uncle (may Allah's mercy rest upon their souls!) had him under great obligation to them because Nur al-Din Balak (may Allah's mercy rest upon his soul!) had taken him captive and after the death of Balak he passed into the possession of Husam al-Din Timurtash ibn Ilghazi, who brought Baldwin to us in Shayzar so that my father and my uncle (may Allah's mercy rest upon their souls!) might act as an intermediary in determining the price of his ransom. Both of them treated him with benevolence. Now when he became king and we owed indemnity to Antioch, Baldwin exempted us from its payment. After that, we became very influential in the affairs of Antioch.

CULTURAL AND SOCIAL INTERACTION IN THE HOLY LAND

Perhaps the most fascinating aspect of life in the crusader states was the relation between Latin Christians and the native peoples, particularly Muslims. Latin Christians adopted many native customs and manners. Fulcher describes this phenomenon and notes how those who were Occidentals (Westerners) 'now have been made Orientals'. Usamah addresses the same phenomenon in citing the specific case of a Frank who had adopted Muslim dietary practices. Indeed, Usamah made a number of interesting social and cultural observations of Latin Christians. He notes, for example, how Franks could be quite friendly with Muslims, especially those Franks who had spent a lot of time in the Holy Land as against those recently arrived, who were more militant and less friendly. Usamah also makes some fascinating observations of Frankish medicine and Christian piety. Equally, the later-thirteenth-century German Dominican monk and chronicler Burchard of Mount Sion provides a fascinating view of Muslim and Syrian and Greek Christian religious devotion and practices.

THE SOURCES

Fulcher – Going Native in the Holy Land[11]

The following selection by Fulcher is perhaps one of the most fascinating descriptions of cultural interactions during the crusades. Here Fulcher provides his observations on how Western Christians in the Levant during the early twelfth century were adopting local customs and habits to the extent that he could claim Westerners 'have been made Orientals'.

Consider, I pray, and reflect how in our time God has transferred the West into the East, for we who were Occidentals now have been made Orientals. He who was a Roman or a Frank is now a Galilaean, or an inhabitant of Palestine. One who was a citizen of Rheims or of Chartres now has been made a citizen of Tyre or of Antioch. We have already forgotten the places of our birth; already they have become unknown to many of us, or, at least, are unmentioned. Some already possess here homes and servants which they have received through inheritance. Some have taken wives not merely of their own people, but Syrians, or Armenians or even Saracens who have received the grace of baptism. Some have with them father-in-law, or daughter-in-law, or son-in-law, or stepson or step-father. There are here, too, grandchildren and great-grandchildren. One cultivates vines, another the fields. The one and the other use mutually the speech and the idioms of the different languages. Different languages, now made common, become known to both races, and faith unites those whose forefathers were strangers. As it is written, 'The lion and the ox shall eat straw together.' Those who were strangers are now natives; and he who was a sojourner now has become a resident. Our parents and relatives from day to day come to join us, abandoning, even though reluctantly, all that they possess. For those who were poor there, here God makes rich. Those who had few coins, here possess countless besants; and those who had not had a villa, here, by the gift of God, already possess a city. Therefore why should one who has found the East so favourable return to the West? God does not wish those to suffer want who, carrying their crosses, have vowed to follow Him, nay even unto the end. You see, therefore, that this is a great miracle, and one which must greatly astonish the whole world. Who has ever heard anything like it? Therefore, God wishes to enrich us all and to draw us to Himself as His most dear friends. And because He wishes it, we also freely desire the same; and what is pleasing to Him we do with a loving and submissive heart, that with Him we may reign happily throughout eternity.

Usamah – A Frank Going Native in the Holy Land[12]

The following selection by Usamah confirms the earlier observations of Fulcher concerning the adoption of native customs by Latin Christians. Here Usamah describes the case of a retired Christian knight who had adopted Muslim dietary laws and protected one of Usamah's men from hostile Christians.

Among the Franks are those who have become acclimatised and have associated long with the Muslims. These are much better than the recent comers from the Frankish lands. But they constitute the exception and cannot be treated as a rule.

Here is an illustration. I dispatched one of my men to Antioch on business. There was in Antioch at that time al-Ra'is Theodoros Sophianos, to whom I was bound by mutual ties of amity. His influence in Antioch was supreme. One day he said to my man, 'I am invited by a friend of mine who is a Frank. Thou shouldst come with me so that thou mayest see with their fashions.' My man related the story in the following words:

I went along with him and we came to the home of a knight who belonged to the old category of knights who came with the early expeditions of the Franks. He had been by that time stricken off the register and exempted from service, and possessed in Antioch an estate on the income of which he lived. The knight presented an excellent table, with food extraordinarily clean and delicious. Seeing me abstaining from food, he said 'Eat, be of good cheer! I never eat Frankish dishes, but I have Egyptian women cooks and never eat except their cooking. Besides, pork never enters my home.' I ate, but guardedly, and after we departed.

As I was passing in the market place, a Frankish woman all of a sudden hung to my clothes and began to mutter words in their language, and I could not understand what she was saying. This made me immediately the centre of a big crowd of Franks. I was convinced that death was at hand. But all of a sudden that same knight approached. On seeing me, he came and said to that woman, 'What is the matter between thee and this Moslem?' She replied, 'This is he who has killed my brother Hurso.' This Hurso was a knight in Afamiyah who was killed by someone of the army of Hamah. The Christian knight shouted at her, saying, 'This is a bourgeois [i.e. a merchant] who neither fights nor attends a fight.' He also yelled at the people who had assembled, and they all dispersed. Then he took my by the hand and went away. Thus the effect of that meal was my deliverance from certain death.

Usamah – The Friendly Frank[13]

In the following selection, Usamah describes his personal friendship with a Christian knight. He notes that he kept constant company with the knight and that the two men even developed an 'intimate fellowship'. Indeed, the knight even offered to take Usamah's son back to Western Europe with him to provide for his training as a knight.

Mysterious are the works of the Creator, the author of all things! When one comes to recount cases regarding the Franks, he cannot but glorify Allah (exalted is he!) and sanctify him, for he sees them as animals possessing the virtues of courage and fighting, but nothing else; just as animals have only the virtues of strength and carrying loads. I shall now give some instances of their doings and their curious mentality.

In the army of King Fulk, son of Fulk, was a Frankish reverend knight who had just arrived from their land in order to make the holy pilgrimage and then return home. He was of my intimate fellowship and kept such constant company with me that he began to call me 'my brother'. Between us were mutual bonds of amity and friendship. When he resolved to return by sea to his homeland, he said to me:

My brother, I am leaving for my country and I want you to send with me thy son (my son, who was then fourteen years old, was at that time in my company) to our country, where he can see the knights and learn wisdom and chivalry. When he returns, he will be like a wise man. Thus there fell upon my ears words which would never come out of the head of a sensible man; for even if my son were to be taken captive his captivity could not bring him a worse misfortune than carrying him into the lands of the Franks. However, I said to the man:

By thy life, this has exactly been my idea. But the only thing that prevented me from carrying it out was the fact that his grandmother, my mother, is so fond of him and did not this time let him come out with me until she exacted an oath from me to the effect that I would return him to her. Thereupon he asked, 'Is thy mother still alive?' 'Yes', I replied. 'Well', said he, 'disobey her not'.

Usamah – Muslim and Christian Medicine[14]

In the following source, Usamah provides his observations of Western medical treatment in the Levant. To begin with, he disdainfully, and graphically, describes two operations by an arrogant Western physician on a knight and a woman that resulted in their deaths. Yet Usamah also describes the curative abilities of Western medicines for a knight and for a Muslim child.

The lord of al-Munaytirah wrote to my uncle asking him to dispatch a physician to treat certain sick persons among his people. My uncle sent him a Christian physician named Thabit. Thabit was absent but ten days when he returned. So we said to him, 'How quickly hast thou healed thy patients!' He said:

'They brought before me a knight in whose leg an abscess had grown; and a woman afflicted with imbecility. To the knight I applied a small poultice until the abscess opened and became well; and the woman

I put on a diet and made her humour wet. Then a Frankish physician came to them and said, "This man knows nothing about treating them." He then said to the knight, "Which wouldst thou prefer, living with one leg or dying with two?" The latter replied, "Living with one leg." The physician said, "Bring me a strong knight and a sharp axe." A knight came with the axe. And I was standing by. Then the physician laid the leg of the patient on a block of wood and bade the knight strike his leg with the axe and chop it off at one blow. Accordingly he struck it – while I was looking on – one blow, but the leg was not severed. He dealt another blow, upon which the marrow of the leg flowed out and the patient died on the spot. He then examined the woman and said, "This is a woman in whose head there is a devil which has possessed her. Shave off her hair." Accordingly they shaved it off and the woman began once more to eat their ordinary diet – garlic and mustard. Her imbecility took a turn for the worse. The physician then said, "The devil has penetrated through her head." He therefore took a razor, made a deep cruciform incision on it, peeled off the skin at the middle of the incision until the bone of the skull was exposed and rubbed it with salt. The woman also expired instantly. Thereupon I asked them whether my services were needed any longer, and when they replied in the negative I returned home, having learned of their medicine what I knew not before.'

I have, however, witnessed a case of their medicine which was quite different from that. The King of the Franks had for a treasurer a knight named Bernard [Barnad], who (may Allah's curse be upon him!) was one of the most accursed and wicked among the Franks. A horse kicked him in the leg, which was subsequently infected and which opened in fourteen different places. Every time one of these cuts would close in one place, another would open in another place. All this happened while I was praying for his perdition. Then came to him a Frankish physician and removed from the leg all the ointments which were on it and began to wash it with very strong vinegar. By this treatment all the cuts were healed and the man became well again. He was up again like a devil.

Another case illustrating their curious medicine is the following: In Shayzar we had an artisan named Abu-al-Fath, who has a boy whose neck was afflicted with scrofula. Every time a part of it would close, another part would open. This man happened to go to Antioch on business of his, accompanied by his son. A Frank noticed the boy and asked his father about him. Abu-al-Fath replied, 'This is my son'. The Frank said to him, 'Wilt thou swear by thy religion that if I prescribe to thee a medicine which will cure the boy, thou wilt charge nobody fees for prescribing it thyself? In that case, I shall prescribe to thee a medicine which will cure the boy.' The man took the oath and the Frank said:

Take uncrushed leaves of glasswort, burn them, then soak the ashes
in olive oil and sharp vinegar. Treat the scrofula with them until the spot
on which it is growing is eaten up. Then take burnt lead, soak it in ghee
butter [samn] and treat him with it. That will cure him. The father treated
the boy accordingly, and the boy was cured. The sores closed and the boy
returned to his normal condition of health. I have myself treated with this
medicine many who were afflicted with such a disease, and the treatment
was successful in removing the cause of the complaint.

Usamah – Positive Reflections of Christian and Muslim Piety[15]

In the following source, Usamah offers a fascinating comparison
of Christian and Muslim piety. Impressed by the devotion of some
elderly Christian priests whom he had once encountered in a church,
Usamah becomes distraught that he had never seen Muslims worship
with such devotion. Yet he later encountered, to his relief, Sufis whom
he considered even more zealous than the pious Christian priests who
had been the cause of his concern.

I paid a visit to the tomb of John the son of Zechariah – God's blessing on
both of them! – in the village of Sebastea in the province of Mablus. After
saying my prayers, I came out into the square that was bounded
on one side by the Holy Precinct. I found a half-closed gate, opened
it and entered a church. Inside were about ten old men, their bare
heads as white as combed cotton. They were facing east, and wore
(embroidered?) on their breasts staves ending in crossbars turned
up like the rear of a saddle. They took their oath on this sign, and gave
hospitality to those who needed it. The sight of their piety touched
my heart, but at the same time it displeased and saddened me, for I
had never seen such zeal and devotion among the Muslims. For some
time I brooded on this experience, until one day, as Mu'in ad-Din and I
were passing the Peacock House he said to me: 'I want to dismount
here and visit the Old Men [the ascetics].' 'Certainly', I replied, and we
dismounted and went into a long building set at an angle to the road.
For the moment I thought there was no one there. Then I saw about
a hundred prayer mats, and on the each a sufi, his face expressing
peaceful serenity, and his body humble devotion. This was a reassuring
sight, and I gave thanks to Almighty God that there were among the
Muslims men of even more zealous devotion than those Christian priests.

Before this I had never seen sufis in their monastery, and was ignorant of the way they lived.

Burchard of Mount Sion – Description of Muslims and Syrian and Greek Christians[16]

The following source is by the late-thirteenth-century Christian chronicler Burchard of Mount Sion. Here Burchard provides brief observations of the religious beliefs and practices of various native peoples of the East, including Muslims, Syrian Christians and Greek Christians.

Besides the Latins there are many other races there; for example, the Saracens, who preach Mahomet and keep his law. They call our Lord Jesus the greatest of the prophets, and confess that he was conceived of the Holy Ghost and born of the Virgin Mary. But they deny that he suffered and was buried, but choose to say that He ascended into heaven and sitteth upon the right hand of the Father, because they admit him to be the Son of God. But they declare that Mahomet sits on His left hand. They are very unclean, [and] have as many wives as they can feed; yet, nevertheless, they practice unnatural sins, and have *ephebiae* in every city. Yet they are very hospitable, courteous and kindly.

Besides these there are the Syrians. The whole land is full of these. They are Christians, but keep no faith with the Latins. They are clothed most wretchedly, and are stingy, giving no alms. They dwell among the Saracens, and for the most part are their servants. In dress they are like the Saracens, except that they are distinguished from them by a woollen girdle.

The Greeks in like manner are Christians, but schismatics, save that a great part of them returned to obedience to the Church at a General Council [Lyons in 1274] held by our Lord Gregory X. In the Greek Church all the prelates are monks, and are men of exceeding austerity of life and wondrous virtue. The Greeks are exceedingly devout, and for the most part greatly honour and revere their Prelates.

COMPETING VIEWS OF MORALITY IN THE HOLY LAND

Latin Christian and Muslim authors also made a number of interesting observations about one another's morality. Usamah, for example, provides two instances of Frankish immodesty concerning their wives. The first example concerns a Frank's relatively restrained reaction upon finding his wife in bed with another man; the second example concerns the bizarre request of a Frank to a Muslim bathkeeper to shave his and his wife's genital areas. The Arab chronicler Imad ad-Din, who elsewhere writes of the abuse of Western women under Muslim rule,[17] also wrote of Frankish morality with regard to their women as he describes the arrival of a ship full of 'lovely Frankish women' and goes on at length about their sinful and scandalous intentions and behaviour. The final source selection provided in this chapter is from Jacques de Vitry, who, indeed, confirms much of the immoral behaviour among Latin Christians as reported by Arab sources. Jacques's focus is on the so-called Pulani, the descendants of the earliest Latin Christians to arrive in the Holy Land and often their native wives. According to Jacques, the Pulani were, in contrast to the earlier Christian settlers, slothful and negligent of their Christian duties, preferring to engage in various immoral behaviours.

THE SOURCES

Usamah – Franks Devoid of Jealousy[18]

Here Usamah provides some rather odd observations on the morality of Western Christians in the Holy Land. He argues that they are 'void of all zeal and jealousy' and to support this claim, he provides the example of a Frank who found his wife in bed with another man and reacted with relatively little emotion. Even more so, he describes a bizarre incident in which a Frankish knight, uninhibited by modesty, requests that a Muslim bath attendant shave his and his wife's pubic areas.

The Franks are void of all zeal and jealousy. One of them may be walking along with his wife. He meets another man who takes the wife by the hand and steps aside to converse with her while the husband is standing on one side waiting for his wife to conclude the conversation. If she lingers too long for him, he leaves her alone with the conversant and goes away.

Here is an illustration which I myself witnessed: When I used to visit Nablus, I always took lodging with a man named Mu'izz, whose home was a lodging house for the Muslims. The house had windows which opened to the road, and there stood opposite to it on the other side of the road a house belonging to a Frank who sold wine for the merchants. He would take some wine in a bottle and go around announcing it by shouting, 'So and so, the merchant, has just opened a cask full of this wine. He who wants to buy some of it will find it in such and such a place.' The Frank's pay for the announcement made would be the wine in that bottle. One day this Frank went home and found a man with his wife in the same bed. He asked him, 'What could have made thee enter into my wife's room?' The man replied, 'I was tired, so I went into rest.' 'But how', asked he, 'didst thou get into my bed?' The other replied, 'I found a bed that was spread, so I slept in it.' 'But', said he, 'my wife was sleeping together with thee!' The other replied, 'Well, the bed is hers. How could I therefore have prevented her from using her own bed?' 'By the truth of my religion', said the husband, 'if thou shouldst do it again, thou and I would have a quarrel'. Such was for the Frank the entire expression of his disapproval and the limit of his jealousy.

Another illustration: We had with us a bath-keeper named Salim, originally an inhabitant of al-Ma'arrah, who had charge of the bath of my father (may Allah's mercy rest upon his soul!). This man related the following story.

I once opened a bath in al-Ma'arrah in order to earn my living. To this bath there came a Frankish knight. The Franks disapprove of girdling a cover around one's waist while in the bath. So this Frank stretched out his arm and pulled off my cover from my waist and threw it away. He looked and saw that I had recently shaved off my pubes. So he shouted, 'Salim!' As I drew near him he stretched his hand over my pubes and said, 'Salim, good! By the truth of my religion, do the same for me.' Saying this, he lay on his back and I found that in that place the hair was like his beard. So I shaved it off. Then he passed his hand over the place and, finding it smooth, he said, 'Salim, by the truth of my religion, do the same to madame (al-dama)' (al-dama in their language means the lady), referring to his wife. He then said to a servant of his, 'Tell madame to come here.' Accordingly the servant went and brought her and made enter the bath. She also lay on her back. The knight repeated, 'Do what thou hast done to me.' So I shaved all that hair while he husband was sitting looking at me. At last he thanked me and handed me the pay for my service.

Consider now this great contradiction! They have neither jealousy nor zeal but they have great courage, although courage is nothing but the product of zeal and of ambition to be above ill repute.

Imad ad-Din – On Frankish Prostitutes[19]

In the following source, the Arab chronicler Imad ad-Din describes the arrival by ship of three hundred 'lovely' Frankish prostitutes. Imad writes with colourful rhetorical flourish in describing the women's sinful acts and notes how their charms led even Muslims, prompted by the 'fierce goad of lust', to seek out their services.

There arrived by ship three hundred lovely Frankish women, full of youth and beauty, assembled from beyond the sea and offering themselves for sin. They were expatriates come to help expatriates, ready to cheer the fallen and sustained in turn to give support and assistance, and they glowed with ardour for carnal intercourse. They were all licentious harlots, proud and scornful, who took and gave, foul fleshed and sinful, singers and coquettes, appearing proudly in public, ardent and inflamed, tinted and painted, desirable and appetising, exquisite and graceful, who ripped open and patched up, lacerated and mended, erred and ogled, urged and seduced, consoled and solicited, seductive and languid, desired and desiring, amused and amusing, versatile and cunning, like tipsy adolescents, making love and selling themselves for gold, bold and ardent, loving and passionate, pink faced and unblushing, black-eyed and bullying, callipygian and graceful, with nasal voices and fleshy thighs, blue-eyed and grey-eyed, broken down little fools. Each one trailed the train of her robe behind her and bewitched the beholder with her effulgence. She swayed like a sapling, revealed herself like a strong castle, quivered like a small branch, walked proudly with a cross on her breast, sold her graces for gratitude and longed to lose her robe and her honour. They arrived after consecrating their persons as if to works of piety, and offered and prostituted the most chaste and precious among them. They said that they set out with the intention of consecrating their charms, that they did not intend to refuse themselves to bachelors, and they maintained that they could make themselves acceptable to God by no better sacrifice than this. So they set themselves up each in a pavilion or tent erected for her use, together with other lovely young girls of their age, and opened the gates of pleasure.

They dedicated as a holy offering what they kept between their thighs; they were openly licentious and devoted themselves to relaxation; they removed every obstacle to making of themselves free offerings. They plied a brisk trade in dissoluteness, adorned the patched-up fissures, poured themselves into the springs of libertinage, shut themselves up in private under the amorous transports of men, offered their wares for enjoyment, invited the shameless into their embrace, mounted breasts on backs, bestowed their wares on the poor, brought their silver anklets up to touch their golden ear-rings, and were willingly spread out on the carpet of amorous sport. They made themselves targets for men's darts, they were permitted territory for forbidden acts, they offered themselves to the lances' blows and humiliated themselves to their lovers. They put up the tent and loosed the girdle after agreement had been reached. They were the places where tent-pegs are driven in, they invited swords to enter their sheaths, they razed their terrain for planting, they made javelins rise towards shields, excited the plough to plough, gave the birds a place to peck with their beaks, allowed heads to enter their antechambers and raced under whoever bestrode them at the spur's blow. They took the parched man's sinews to the well, fitted arrows to the bow's handle, cut off sword-belts, engraved coins, welcomed birds into the nest of their thighs, caught in their nets the horns of butting rams, removed the interdict from what is protected, withdrew the veil from what is hidden. They interwove leg with leg, slaked their lover's thirsts, caught lizard after lizard in their holes, disregarded the wickedness of their intimacies, guided pens to inkwells, torrents to the valley bottom, streams to pools, swords to scabbards, gold ingots to crucibles, infidel girdles to women's zones, firewood to the stove, guilty men to low dungeons, money-changers to dinar, necks to bellies, motes to eyes. They contested for tree-trunks, wandered far and wide to collect fruit, and maintained that this was an act of piety without equal, especially to those who were far from home and wives. They mixed wine, and with the eye of sin they begged for its hire. The men of our army heard tell of them, and were at a loss to know how such women could perform acts of piety by abandoning all decency and shame. However, a few foolish mamluks and ignorant wretches slipped away, under the fierce goad of lust, and followed the people of error. And there were those who allowed themselves to buy pleasure with degradation, and those who repented of their sin and found devious ways of retracing their steps, for the hand of any man who shrinks from (absolute) apostasy dares not stretch out, and it is the nature of him who arrives there to steal away from them, suspecting that what is serious, is serious, and the door of pleasure closes in his face. Now among the Franks a woman who gives herself to a celibate man commits no sin, and her justification is even greater in the case of a priest, if chaste men in dire need find relief in enjoying her.

Jacques de Vitry on the Immoral Pulani[20]

Concerns about Latin Christian immorality were not held only by Muslim writers as seen in the following selection from Jacques de Vitry. Here, he describes the immoral behaviour of the so-called Pulani, those Latin Christians who had been born in the Holy Land and were the descendants of earlier crusaders and usually their native wives. Jacques laments that they have abandoned serious military efforts against Muslims and notes how they had become 'more used to baths than battles'.

It was an evil and perverse generation, wicked and degenerate sons, corrupt men, Who proceeded from the aforesaid pilgrims, religious men, acceptable to God and full of grace, even as lees from wine, dregs from olives, tares from wheat, and rust from silver, they successed to their father's property, but not to their good morals; they squandered the worldly wealth which their fathers had won by the shedding of their own blood, fighting manfully against the infidels for the honour of God. Their children, who are called Pullani, were brought up in luxury, soft and effeminate, more used to baths than battles, addicted to unclean and riotous living, clad like women in soft robes, and ornamented even as the polished corners of the Temple; how slow and slothful, how timid and cowardly they proved themselves against the enemies of Christ, is doubted by no one who knows how greatly they are despised by the Saracens.

A multitude of Saracens would flee from before their fathers, even though they were few; at the voice of their thunder they hasted away; but they feared their cowardly descendants no more than so many women, unless they had some French or other Westerns with them. They make treaties with the Saracens, and are glad to be at peace with Christ's enemies; they are quick to quarrel with one another and skirmish and levy civil war against one another; they often call upon the enemies of the faith to help them against Christians, and are not ashamed to waste the forces and treasure which they ought to use against the infidels to God's glory, in fighting against one another to the injury of Christendom. They have so learned to disguise their meaning in cunning speeches, covered and bedecked with leaves, but no fruit, like barren willow trees. That those who do not by experience know them thoroughly can scarce understand their reservations and tricks of speech or avoid being deceived by them.

They are suspicious and jealous of their wives, whom they lock up in close prison, and guard in such strict and careful custody that even their brethren and nearest relatives can scarce come at them; while they forbid them so utterly to attend churches, processions, the wholesome preaching of God's Word and other matters appertaining to their salvation, that they scarce suffer them to go to church once a year; howbeit some husbands allow their wives to go out to the bath three times a week under strict guard. The richest and most powerful of them, to show that they are Christians, and to somewhat excuse their conduct, cause altars to be set up to near their wives beds, and get Masses performed by…half fledged priests. But the more strictly the Pullani lock up their wives, the more do they by a thousand arts and endless contrivances struggle and try to find their way out. They are wondrously and beyond belief learned in witchcraft and wickedness innumerable, which they are taught by the Syrian women. Now, the pilgrims who come, with very great toil and at ruinous expense, from far away, out of devotion and to help them, offering themselves and all that they have to the Lord, are not only treated with ingratitude by these Pullani, but they make themselves offensive to them in diverse ways; for they would rather indulge their sloth and gratify their carnal desires than fight the Saracens when the truce is broken or run out. When by their outrageous charges for lodging, their trafficking and money changing, and many other kinds of trading, they have cheated and plundered pilgrims, and so have gained great wealth, they then pour contempt upon those warriors and exiles for Christ's sake, insulting them and calling them idiots, as though they were fools and half-witted, and reproaching those who are about to fight on their own behalf…So great, and much worse than this, in the perverse wickedness and wicked perversity of those men who rejoice to do evil, and delight in the forwardness of the wicked, for whom is reserved the blackness of darkness for ever. They indeed pass their days in all good things, but in a moment they shall go down to the depths of hell.

CHAPTER FOURTEEN
CRUSADES AND THE CANON LAW

268
CAUSA XXIII – INTRODUCTION,
THE STATEMENT OF THE ISSUE

269
DECRETALES, 5.6.12, *QUOD OLIM*

269
DECRETALES, 4.17.15, *GAUDEMUS*

270
DECRETALES, 4.19.7, *QUANTO TE*

270
DECRETALES, 4.19.8, *GAUDEMUS*

271
DECRETALES, 3.34.8, *QUOD SUPER HIS*

272
INNOCENT IV, COMMENTARY ON 3.34.8,
QUOD SUPER HIS

273
HOSTIENSIS, COMMENTARY ON 3.34.8,
QUOD SUPER HIS

History in her solemn page informs us, that the Crusaders were but ignorant and savage men, that their motives were those of bigotry unmitigated, and that their pathway was one of blood and tears.

– Charles Mackay[1]

THE RATIONALITY OF THE CRUSADES

The popular vision of the crusades is of masses of violent Latin Christians rushing off to battle with the peoples of the Near East. A popular nineteenth-century writer described the crusades as a form of 'Popular Delusion and the Madness of Crowds', a movement as irrational as alchemy, fortune-telling and witchcraft.[2] While mass movements such as the Children's Crusade and the crusade led by Peter the Hermit certainly share the characteristics associated with irrational mass movements, the crusading movement as a whole did not. One may, of course, debate vigorously whether the strategy of the crusaders was a suitable one given the circumstances involved; one may ask whether they failed to change their tactics to address conditions on the ground in the Near East; whether they should have been more diplomatically astute in their dealings with the Byzantines and the Christian inhabitants of the Near East; and whether they could have more pragmatic in their dealings with the Muslims. Nevertheless the professional warriors who took up the cross were, generally speaking, neither deluded nor mad, although they were often mistaken. Indeed, they were quite rational and organised in what they sought to do, even if the actual working out of their rational planning often failed due to a lack of control on the ground, conflicts among the leaders of the crusades and so on. The conflicts among the leaders of the crusades and with the Byzantines were alone sufficient to prevent the success of the crusading movement.

The rationality of the crusades appears in several ways. Geoffrey de Villehardouin's description of the negotiations between the crusaders and the Venetians in order to mount the Fourth Crusade provides a good example of the careful planning that went into crusading, even though the consequences – the crusader seizure of Constantinople and the establishment of the Latin Empire – were clearly not intended. Rather than rushing to attack the Muslims in disorganised fashion, the leaders of the crusaders met to organise the proposed crusade, and in spite of fears that there might not be enough volunteers to staff the crusading army, they did send a team of negotiators to Venice because it was there that 'they might expect to find a greater number of vessels than in any other port'. The result was a contract for transporting thousands of crusaders and their horses to the Holy Land in the following year.[3] The fear that there would not be enough crusaders turned out to be true. In addition, many of those who did arrive at Venice to join the crusade were unable to pay the cost of their voyage. So, the Venetians re-negotiated the agreement to their own advantage, leading to the use of the crusading army against fellow Christians and finally to the conquest of Constantinople and the establishment of the Latin Empire in 1204. This crusade is a striking example of rational calculations leading to completely unforeseen irrational consequences.

A second rational element of the crusading movement was the legal framework within which the crusaders operated. Crusading marked an important change in the Church's approach to the use of violence, a change linked to the Gregorian Reform movement of the eleventh and twelfth centuries that sought to create a Christian moral order for the direction of Europe.[4] One of the goals of the reform movement was to bring the seemingly endemic in European society under control by containing it within a framework of law. Until the Gregorian Reform movement, churchmen saw violence as a necessary but evil aspect of the social order so that those who killed even in self-defence had to confess and atone for their sin.[5] During the reform movement, however, some thinkers gradually developed the argument that under proper circumstances, violence could be used for positive ends and did not require atonement, thus contributing to the theory of the just war. As the leading student of the theory of the just war pointed out, 'The most crucial issue in any just war theory is the locus of authority capable of waging war.'[6] Legitimate Christian rulers – above all, the pope – were the loci of such authority. This legitimacy-of-force theory was being developed as the crusades were beginning. Urban II was one of the most forceful exponents of the Gregorian reform with its emphasis on the role of the pope as the leader of Christian society. His famous sermon at Clermont called on European warriors to stop fighting among themselves and instead channel their violence to a positive goal, regaining the Holy Land from the Muslims, was characteristic of the reforming movement's desire to place the pope actively at the head of Christian society.[7]

The development of a body of ecclesiastical law, the canon law, was an important element in creating the universal ecclesiastical administrative structure headed by the pope, a fundamental goal of the Gregorian reform movement. About 1140, a monk named Gratian in Bologna produced the *Decretum*, a collection of fundamental texts dealing with particular aspects of Church law and administration that would be applicable throughout the entire Christian world.[8] The principles contained in these legal texts were implemented in a system of canon law courts that existed throughout Latin Christendom. At the apex of this system was the papal court in which the pope regularly sat to hear cases and render decisions.[9] During much of the thirteenth century in particular, the concept of the pope as the *iudex omnium*, the judge of all men everywhere, was not a metaphor but a formal statement of the law.[10] The appointment of a papal legate, Adhémar of Le Puy, to lead the First Crusade was another sign of the leadership role that the papacy was asserting during the Investiture Controversy.[11]

Gratian's *Decretum* dealt with issues relating to the crusades individually, not as a unified body of law. In one section – *Causa XXIII*, 'Concerning War and Military Affairs' – Gratian raised the question of whether Christians could legitimately call upon the secular power to defend them against the heretics who attacked them and offered a number of excerpts from the writings of the Church fathers, especially St. Augustine (d.430), on the use of violence to protect Christians against their enemies.[12] The canon lawyers seem, however, to have been uncomfortable with justifying the use of violence in Christian society and never produced a full-scale treatise on crusading.[13] For the most part, the lawyers justified war in terms of defence, as a legitimate use of force to protect the Christian community when threatened with violence. To be just, a war had to be defensive in nature.[14]

Urban II's call for a crusade in 1095 reflected the canonists' notion of a just war. He stressed the need to defend Christendom from the attacks by the hordes of infidels that threatened them and to liberate the Christians of the East from Muslim domination. The horrors of the conquest of the Christian East that he attributed to the Muslims justified waging war against them. As long as the crusaders fought with the right intention and not simply as aggressors seeking to acquire the lands of others, they were engaged in a righteous activity. Throughout the crusading era, the theme of the defence of Christians and Christendom was the dominant justification employed.

In addition to justifying the crusades, the lawyers provided a protected legal status for the crusaders. Drawing on the existing legal protections authorised for pilgrims designed to protect them while engaged in the pious act of visiting religious sites, the canonists developed a body of privileges designed to protect the lives and property of crusaders, because they were, in legal terms, armed pilgrims.[15] A true crusade was a war authorised by the pope to achieve a religious goal. An individual who publicly engaged to go on crusade by taking a vow to do so received a plenary indulgence, relieving him of the punishment due to his sins and a series of temporal benefits as well. These included protection of his person and property so that anyone who attacked a crusader or stole from him was subject to excommunication. Such a protection was eventually extended to members of a crusader's family as well.[16] To retain the privileges attached to pilgrim status, the crusaders had to operate within the rules of the legal system and adhere to the terms of the applicable law.[17]

Once in motion, the crusades generated a number of practical legal problems that came before Church courts. For example, what should an individual do if he finds himself unable to fulfil his crusading vow? Urban II and other responsible leaders saw the crusades in operational terms. What were needed were trained soldiers prepared for serious combat, not masses of well-intentioned but untrained men and women who expected that, by going to Jerusalem, they would be participating in the great eschatological battle that would pit Christians against the Antichrist.[18] An individual who was in ill-health or in poor physical condition or who had obligations that required his immediate attention would be a poor soldier. It would be far better for such an individual to pay the expenses of a qualified soldier who was too poor to pay his own. As the negotiations of the crusaders with the Venetians at the outset of the Fourth Crusade demonstrated, there were many trained soldiers who were potential crusaders but who required financial assistance if they were to go. A financial settlement that allowed an unsuitable crusader to pay the cost of a qualified but poor warrior in place of actually going on crusade was a reasonable solution to two problems.[19]

Other cases involved relations with Muslims. For example, was it permissible to engage in trade with Muslims or must Christians avoid such commerce? Obviously this was a serious issue for the Italian merchants who dominated European trade with the East. The canonists had no objection to trade with the Muslims in principle, although reasonably enough they condemned the sale of materials useful in warfare to the Muslims when at war with them.[20]

Another set of problems arose from the fact that one of the consequences of the crusading movement was the conversion of some Muslims to Christianity. Difficulties arose from the imposition of Christian behavioural standards on the converts. The difference between Christian and Muslim marriage practices was one such source of problems. If a polygamous Muslim man accepted baptism, what would be the effect on his wives? Were polygamous marriages legitimate? There was after all the example of the Hebrew patriarchs who had been polygamous. Should polygamy be tolerated for those already so married but forbidden to later generations? What would happen to the women who were the second or third wives of their husbands? What would happen if they all wished to be baptised and remain married? What would they do if the Church declared that they were not validly married to their husbands? What were, so to speak, the social consequences of the imposition of Christian marriage law on a non-Christian society in the process of converting to Christianity?

The marriage issue was of great importance because of its implications not only for the position of women but also for the legal status of the children of such marriages. If a marriage was invalid, then the children born out of that marriage were illegitimate and subject to various limitations in both secular and canon law. Illegitimate children had no inheritance rights and could be prevented from entering the priesthood or a religious order.[21]

One of the long-term consequences of the discussion of legal issues that arose in connection to the crusades was the development of some rudimentary principles of what was to become international law. Were relations between Christian and non-Christian societies always to be understood in terms of conflict, or would it be possible for Christians and non-Christians to live at peace with one another? The canonists' discussion of trade with Muslims suggests that peaceful relations were possible. Were then the crusades an aberration, an exception to a general rule of peaceful relations between Christians and non-Christians, or were they a special case? The question of the possibility of peaceful relations between Christian and non-Christian societies was answered in a curious way. As we have seen, the canon lawyers never directly addressed the question of the legitimacy of the crusades in a coherent fashion, although we might expect that they had done so because of the intrinsic importance of the issue. It was not until the leading canon lawyer of the thirteenth century, Sinibaldo Fieschi, better known as Pope Innocent IV (1243–1254), wrote a commentary on a letter of his predecessor, Innocent III, that dealt with the crusader's vow, did any canonist wrestle with the question of by what right the crusaders could seek to claim possession of the Holy Land and other lands that the Muslims ruled. Were the crusades based on a Christian claim to universal jurisdiction? Could Christians legitimately claim the right to seize any and all lands throughout the world?

Innocent IV's answer to this question was to provide the basis for discussions of Christian relations with non-Christians for the next three centuries at least. He argued that all mankind had the right to *dominium*, that is the right to own property and to self-government. Christians had no right to claim the lands of non-believers simply because the latter were non-believers. Christians could legitimately take the Holy Land from the Muslims, because in a presumably unjust war the Muslims took it from Christians who had legitimately possessed it, but Christians had no claim to other lands that the Muslims held. Innocent IV may have been encouraged to think this way because as pope he was involved in some very preliminary negotiations with the Mongol Khan that might have led to a Christian–Mongol alliance against the Muslims.[22]

The views of Innocent IV on the rights of non-Christians were not unchallenged. The leading canon lawyer of the next generation, Henry of Segusio (d. 1270), better known as Hostiensis, argued that with the coming of Christ, only those who were in the state of grace could legitimately possess land and secular power, thus in effect claiming that Christians had a right to rule the world.[23] This would justify dispossessing Muslims and all other non-believers.

The competing views of Innocent IV and Hostiensis remained the basis for the canonists' discussion of relations with non-Christian societies for the next several centuries, long after the fall of the last crusader fortress in the Holy Land, Acre, in 1291. At the Council of Constance (1414–1417), these legal arguments were the core of the debate between the Teutonic Knights and the King of Poland over possession of Lithuania. Could the Knights claim Lithuania on the basis of conquering it in the course of a crusade against the infidel Lithuanians?[24] Subsequently, these claims received their fullest expression in the great debate about the legitimacy of the conquest of the Americas in the sixteenth century that roiled the Spanish intellectual world and contributed to the formation of modern international law.[25]

BACKGROUND TO THE SOURCES[26]

The basic materials of the canon law appear in two volumes, Gratian's *Decretum* (1140) and the *Decretales* (1234), the latter being a collection of about 2,000 papal decretals, judgments that popes had issued in cases brought before them. In addition, there were commentaries on these texts. For each volume, there was a *glossa ordinaria*, a basic commentary that explained obscure points, linked cases with one another, and developed the principles contained in the decretal. In addition, there were other commentaries written by prominent lawyers to explain and develop the law. These commentaries tended to grow longer and longer, so that by the late fifteenth century when they were first printed, a commentary on the *Decretales* might run to several volumes and the commentaries on particular decretal letters might run to several pages, virtual legal and political treatises in themselves.

THE SOURCES

Causa XXIII – Introduction, The Statement of the Issue

The first source here is the introduction to *Causa XXIII* of the *Decretum*, the title of which is 'Concerning War and Military Affairs'. The introduction sets up the case that provided the basis for Gratian's discussion of the use of force and illustrates the scholastic method of breaking a problem up into its constituent elements, dealing with each in a logical way by citing texts on each side of the questions and eventually drawing a conclusion.

A certain bishop along with those entrusted to his care having fallen into heresy began to threaten and torment neighbouring Catholics in order to force them to become heretics. The pope asked the Catholic bishops of the adjacent regions who were under the civil jurisdiction of the emperor to defend the Catholics from the heretics and to employ any means possible to compel them, the heretics, to return to the true faith. The bishops, having received this mandate of the pope, gathered soldiers and began to fight against the heretics openly and by means of stratagems. Finally, some of the heretics having been handed over to death, others having been deprived of their ecclesiastical positions, others sent to the workhouse or to prison, under pressure they returned at last to the unity of the Catholic faith.

1. The first question to ask is whether it is a sin to wage war.
2. The second question concerns what constitutes a just war and how just wars were waged by the children of Israel.
3. The third question is whether injuries can be warded off by the armed assistance of allies.
4. The fourth question is whether it is legitimate to get revenge.
5. The fifth question is whether it is a sin for a judge or an official to kill criminals.
6. The sixth question is whether the wicked can be forced to be good.
7. The seventh question is whether goods can be seized from the heretics and from their church and who can possess such goods and whether someone who possesses goods taken from the heretics is said to possess the goods [belonging] to someone else.

8. The eighth question is whether it is licit for bishops or any clerics on their own authority or that of the pope or by the order of the emperor to bear arms.

Decretales, 5.6.12, *Quod olim*

The second source is from the *Decretales*, a letter of Pope Clement III (1187–1191) that forbade trading with the Muslims in time of war.

…Indeed rightly the [Third] Lateran Council (1179) strongly forbade [trading with Saracens]. We however place under excommunication all those who up until now engaged in trade with the Saracens either directly or through the use of the ships of others or in any other clever fashion provide them with assistance of any sort while we were at war with them. We leave to your discretion the carrying out of this charge so that neither directly nor through the use of your ships or by any other means or device shall any merchandise, advice or any other kind of assistance be provided to them. If there are some so hardened in their evil ways that they presume to do these things, not only do they fall under that excommunication by the law, they also incur the wrath of the living God.

Decretales, 4.17.15, *Gaudemus*

The third group of sources deals with issues of marriage law and its consequences. Christian marriage law forbade marriages between persons related in the first four degrees of consanguinity, the so-called forbidden degrees, although it was possible to obtain a dispensation from the law under some circumstances. Muslim society, however, did not have such rules, so that many marriages took place between individuals related in the second, third and fourth degrees. Innocent III (1198–1216) ruled that converts whose marriage fell into one of these degrees would be recognised as valid even though no dispensation had been obtained and therefore the children of such marriages would be considered legitimate.

….For the sake of public utility, we wish that a certain child born of a marriage between infidels who have received the faith be reckoned as legitimate [even though] they were related in the second, third or more distant degree according to their custom.

Decretales, 4.19.7, Quanto te

A second issue that arose concerned the effect upon a marriage between infidels if one partner became a Christian but the other did not. Innocent III demarcated what one should do under these circumstances.

Sensibly...you made known to us that one [spouse] having deserted the marriage bond [becoming] a heretic, the one who remained desired to enter in a second marriage. [You asked] what we could advise in this matter in the letters you sent: can he do this?...For if one spouse of the marriage of infidels is converted to the Catholic faith and the other spouse being unwilling to remain without blaspheming the divine name or in order to bring the other into a state of mortal sin , the spouse who has been left, ignoring his vows, [may] if he wishes [marry] a second wife....[The reason is that] insult to the creator dissolves the law of marriage with regard to the one who has been left behind. For even if true marriage exists among infidels, it is not, however, it is not [canonically] valid

Decretales, 4.19.8, Gaudemus

The third issue of marriage law that arose for Innocent III's consideration concerned multiple wives.

We rejoice in the Lord. You asked us to instruct you from the apostolic writings whether pagans having married wives related to them in the second, third or other degrees, if, having been converted ought to remain together after their conversion or be separated from one another. Concerning this we answer that since the sacrament of marriage exists among believers and non-believers as the Apostle (Paul) says: if a brother has an infidel wife and she agrees to remain with him, he should not send her away and in the marriages by infidels within the aforementioned grades of relationship licit marriages may be contracted because they were not bound by the established canons

Decretales, 3.34.8, Quod Super His

Another issue that the canonists addressed concerned the vow that a crusader took. What if he could not fulfil it? One section of the *Decretales*, section 3.34, contained nine texts dealing with 'The vow and the commutation of a vow'. What is especially interesting is that it was at this point that a canonist raised the question of the legitimacy of the crusades and therefore the legitimacy of the crusader's vow in connection with a decretal of Innocent III.

About these matters you ask about those who having taken the sign of the cross in order to come to the aid of the Holy Land [find themselves] unable to fulfil the vow in a useful fashion because of physical infirmity, poverty or for some other reason, you ask this because you understood our command in an undiscriminating manner so that you ordered those who rejected the sign of the cross they had taken [i.e. failed to fulfil the vow] to take it up again and fulfill their vow. We however responding to your request respond thus. The weak and the poor slow rather than advance the crusade since they are unable to fight and they are forced to beg unless as it happens that there are nobles and magnates who provide for the expenses of the soldiers who accompany them. There are not many mechanics and farmers who from their labours are able to obtain the necessities and to provide support for the [Holy] Land because of their limited nature of their possessions and the scarcity there of inhabitants suitable for the task. We believe therefore that you ought to distinguish between those who are temporarily prevented from fulfilling their vows and those who are believed to have some permanent obstacle to its fulfilment. A delay is to be granted to the first category [the weak and the poor], but for the second category, some form of redemption of the vow is required based on what they are able to pay or what they would have expended [if they had gone on crusade], besides compensating for the labour of those individuals whom they send to the assistance of the Holy Land, accomplishing through these individuals that which they could not do themselves. Again, we ought to distinguish between those who made a vow to go to the defence of the Holy Land and those upon whom a pilgrimage was imposed in order to atone for their crime. It should be noted that those of the first category [provided] more assistance for the Holy Land and those of the second category do it more for the burden of the journey according to whether they made a vow or did it as punishment. Whence if anyone of the latter who made a vow in this fashion is useless as a soldier however suitable otherwise he is for it is better that he redeem the vow than waste the expenses involved.... Concerning wives, however, we believe that it should be observed that those who do not wish to remain behind accompany their husbands. Others however unless they happen to be rich women who bear the expenses of the soldiers who accompany them should redeem the vow that they made.

Innocent IV, Commentary on 3.34.8, *Quod Super His*

The debate about the right of non-Christians to possess dominium began with Innocent IV's lengthy commentary on the *Decretales*, 3.34.8. In his commentary, he dealt briefly with the problem of the man who vowed to go on crusade only to be unable to do so, but then he moved quickly from the narrow technical question about commuting the vow to the fundamental question of why there were crusades in the first place.

There is no doubt that it is proper for the pope to encourage the faithful to defend the Holy Land and the faithful who live there and to grant them indulgences (for this purpose).... But is it licit to invade a land that infidels possess or which belongs to them? And we respond that in truth the earth is the Lord's and His power is over the entire world and all who live in it, for He is the creator of everything, He made everything.... Men can select rulers for themselves as [the Israelites] selected Saul and many others.... Sovereignty, possessions and jurisdiction can exist licitly, without sin, among infidels, as well as among the faithful, because they hold them without sin, but we believe rightly, however, that the pope who is the vicar of Jesus Christ has power not only over Christians also over all infidels, for Christ had power over all men.... Thus to Peter and his successors He gave the keys to the kingdom of heaven.... Elsewhere He said, 'Feed My Sheep'. Both infidels and the faithful belong to Christ's flock by virtue of the creation, although the infidels do not belong to the sheepfold of the Church, and so it seems from the aforementioned, that the pope has jurisdiction over all men and power over them in law but not in fact, so that through this power which the pope possesses I believe that if a gentile, who has no law except the law of nature [to guide him], does something contrary to the law of nature, the pope can lawfully punish him, as for example in Genesis 19 where we see that the inhabitants of Sodom who sinned against the law of nature were punished by God. Since, however, the judgments of God are examples for us, I do not see why the pope, who is the vicar of Christ, cannot do the same and he ought to do so as long as he has the means to do so. And so some say that if they worship idols [the pope can judge and punish them] for it is natural for man to worship the one and only God, not creatures. Also the pope can judge the Jews if they violate the law of the Gospel in moral matters if their leaders do not punish them. However, the pope can grant indulgences to those who invade the Holy Land for the purpose of recapturing it although the Saracens possess it...[but] they possess it illegally...and against those infidels who now hold the Holy Land where Christian princes once ruled, the pope can lawfully order and command that [infidel rulers] not molest unjustly the Christians who are their subjects.... Indeed, if they treat Christians badly the pope can deprive them of the jurisdiction and sovereignty they possess over Christians by judicial sentence.... Infidels should not be forced to become Christians, because all should be left to their free will in this matter.... The pope can order infidels to admit preachers of the Gospel in the lands that they administer, because every rational creature is made for the worship of God.... If infidels prohibit preachers from preaching, they sin and so they ought to be punished. In all the aforementioned cases and in all others where it is licit for the pope to command those things, if the infidels do not obey, they ought to be compelled by the secular arm and war may be declared against them by the pope and not by anyone else.

Hostiensis, Commentary on 3.34.8, *Quod Super His*

It seems to me that with the coming of Christ every public office and every government and all sovereignty and jurisdiction, both by law and from just cause, was taken from infidels and given over to the faithful through Him who has the highest power and cannot err.... And we assert that by law infidels ought to be subject to the faithful and not the reverse.... We concede, however, that infidels who recognise the sovereignty of the Church ought to be tolerated by the Church, because they should not be forced to accept the faith.

ENDMATTER

277
CRUSADES TIMELINE

281
MAPS

285
**SOURCES AND
COPYRIGHT HOLDERS**

291
BIBLIOGRAPHY

297
NOTES

327
INDEX

CRUSADES TIMELINE

- 610–632 Rise of Islam
- 622–750 Arab Conquests
    - 638 Islamic conquest of Jerusalem
    - 642 Islamic conquest of Egypt
    - 652 Short-lived Islamic invasion of Sicily
    - 677 Islamic siege of Constantinople
    - 711 Initial Muslim invasion of Iberian Peninsula
    - 716 Second Islamic siege of Constantinople
    - 722 Battle of Covadonga
    - 732 Battle of Tours
    - 736 Islamic conquest of Avignon
    - 737 Franks under Charles Martel retake Avignon
    - 756 Umayyad State founded in Iberian Peninsula
    - 831 City of Palermo (Sicily) conquered by Islamic forces
    - 842 Rome sacked by Muslims
    - 909 Cluny Monastery founded
    - 965 All of Sicily falls under Muslim control
    - 989 Peace of God
    - 1009 Destruction of Church of the Holy Sepulchre by al-Hakim
    - 1031 Collapse of the Cordoba Caliphate
    - 1037 Rise of the Seljuk Turkish Dynasty
    - 1041 Truce of God
- 1064–1065 Great German Pilgrimage to Jerusalem
    - 1071 Battle of Mantzikert
    - 1074 Pope Gregory VII proposes a crusade to aid Byzantium
    - 1075 Seljuk Turks capture Nicaea
    - 1084 Seljuk Turks capture Antioch
    - 1091 Normans conquer Muslim Sicily
    - 1095 Councils of Piacenza and Clermont
- 1095–1099 First Crusade
    - 1096 Crusader attacks on Rhineland Jews
        Beginning of Princes' Crusade
    - 1097 Crusader victory at Nicaea
    - 1098 Crusader victory at Antioch
    - 1099 Crusader victory at Jerusalem
        Founding of the Kingdom of Jerusalem
- 1118–1119 Founding of the Knights Templar
    - 1140 Gratian's *Decretum*
    - 1144 Zengi captures Edessa

1145–1148 Second Crusade
    1146 Death of Zengi, accession of Nur ad-Din
    1147 Crusade against the Wends
    1148 Failure of the Second Crusade at Damascus
    1169 Saladin conquers Egypt
    1171 Saladin founds the Ayyubid dynasty in Egypt
    1182 Massacre of Latin inhabitants of Constantinople
    1185 Death of the Leper King (Baldwin IV)
    1187 Battle of Hattin
        Saladin's conquest of Jerusalem
1188–1192 Third Crusade
    1190 Founding of the Teutonic Order
    1191 Battle of Arsuf
    1192 Richard and Saladin negotiate a treaty allowing pilgrims access to Jerusalem
    1193 First Baltic Crusade Proclaimed by Pope Celestine III
    1198 Ascension of Pope Innocent III
1201–1204 Fourth Crusade
        Crusaders begin to assemble in Venice
    1202 Crusader conquest of Zara
    1204 Crusader sack of Constantinople
    1208 Murder of papal legate Pierre de Castelnau
1209–1229 Albigensian Crusade
    1212 Battle of Las Navas de Tolosa
        Children's Crusade
    1215 Fourth Lateran Council
1217–1221 Fifth Crusade
    1226 Coronation of Louis IX
    1227 Emperor Frederick II excommunicated by Pope Gregory IX
1228–1229 Crusade of Frederick II
        Frederick II negotiates for nominal Christian control of Jerusalem
    1234 Publication of the *Decretales*
1243–1260 Mongol attacks on Near Eastern Muslim powers
    1244 Muslims retake Jerusalem
1248–1254 Louis IX's First Crusade
    1250 Louis IX taken captive in Egypt
    1254 Louis IX abandons the crusade
    1260 Rise of the Mamluks in Egypt, Baibars becomes the Mamluk Sultan
    1270 Louis XI's Second Crusade. Louis dies while on crusade
1271–1272 Ninth Crusade
    1291 The Fall of Acre
    1297 Canonization of Louis IX
    1309 Knights Hospitallers occupy Rhodes

1312	Dissolution of the Templars
1396	Crusade of Nicopolis
1420–1434	Hussite Crusades
1444	Crusade of Varna
1453	Turkish conquest of Constantinople – effective end of the Byzantine Empire
1453–1503	Ottoman Wars with Venice
1492	Christian conquest of Grenada – all of Iberian Peninsula now under Christian control
1523	Ottoman capture of Rhodes
1526–1699	Ottoman Wars in Europe

THE CRUSADER STATES c.1100

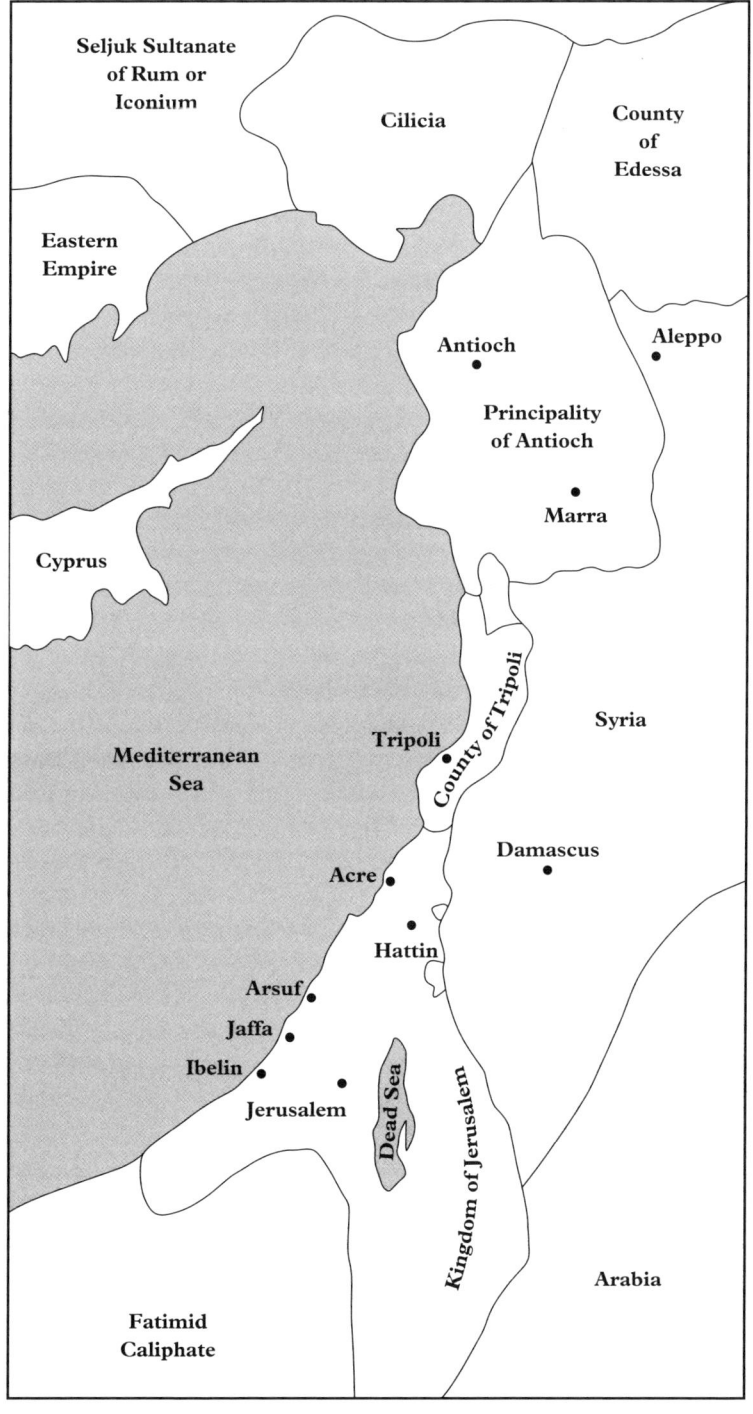

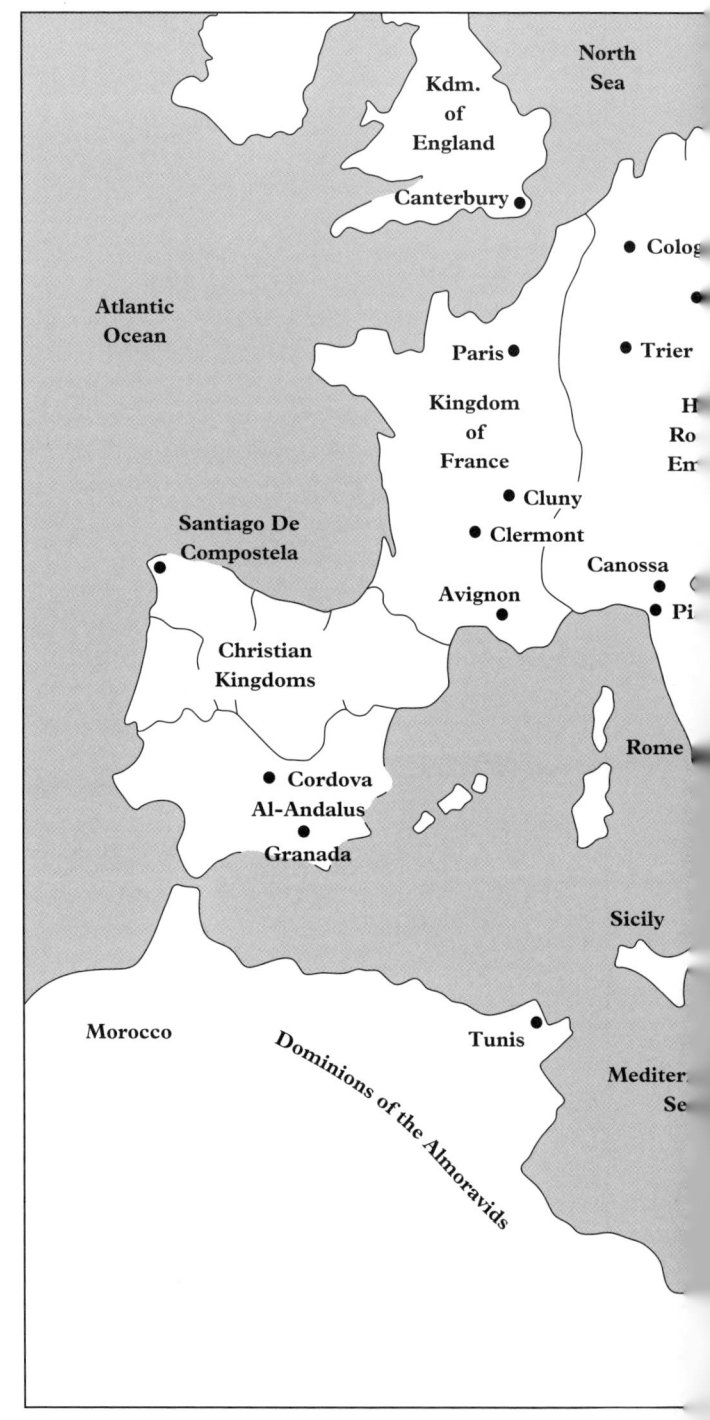

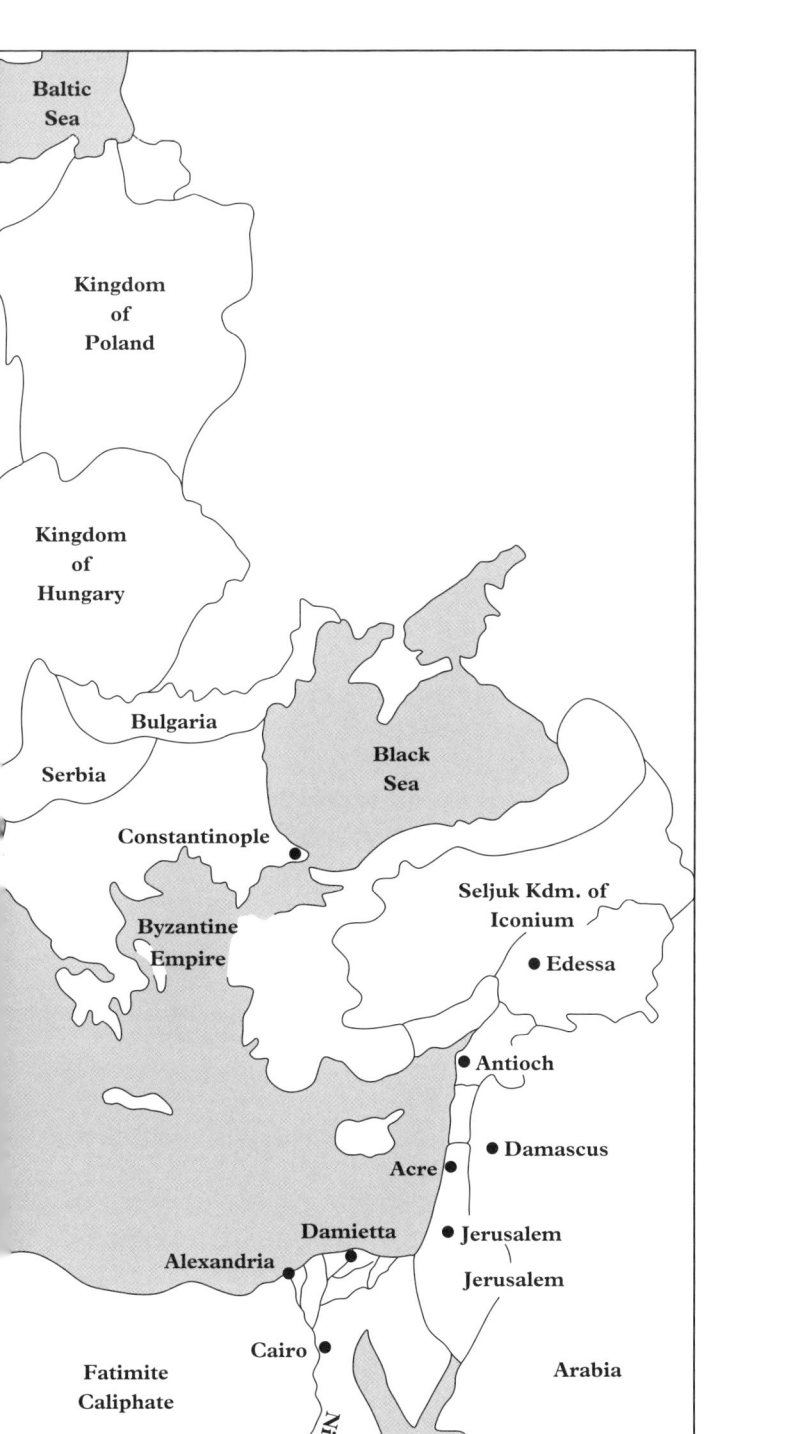

SOURCES AND COPYRIGHT HOLDERS

Every effort has been made to contact copyright holders of material reproduced in this book. Any omissions will be rectified in subsequent printings if notice is given to the publishers.

Chapter One: Pope Urban II's Calling of the First Crusade, 1095

1. **Letter of Alexius to Count Robert of Flanders, c.1088–1099.** Einar Joranson, 'The Problem of the Spurious Letter of Emperor Alexius to the Court of Flanders', *The American Historical Review* (1950), 813–815.

Chapter Two: Attacks on the Jews During the First Crusade, 1096

1. **Solomon bar Samson on the Slaughter of the Rhineland Jews, 1096.** Extracts from 'The Crusaders in Mayence, May 27, 1096' from Jacob R. Marcus, *The Jew in the Medieval World: A Sourcebook 315–1791* (New York: JPS, 1938), 115–120. Reprinted with the kind permission of Hebrew Union College Press.
2. **Bernard of Clairvaux's Preaching against Rudolph according to Otto of Freising, 1146.** Extract from Edward A. Synan, *The Popes and the Jews in the Middle Ages: An Intense Exploration of Judaeo-Christian Relationships in the Medieval World* (New York: MacMillan, 1965), 74–75. © Edward A. Synan 1965. Reprinted with the permission of Scribner, an imprint of Simon & Schuster Adult Publishing Group. All rights reserved.
3. **Bernard of Clairvaux: Defense of the Jews recorded by Ephraim bar Jacob, 1146.** Extract from Edward A. Synan, *The Popes and the Jews in the Middle Ages: An Intense Exploration of Judaeo-Christian Relationships in the Medieval World* (New York: MacMillan, 1965), 75. © Edward A. Synan 1965. Reprinted with the permission of Scribner, an imprint of Simon & Schuster Adult Publishing Group. All rights reserved.

Chapter Three: Crusader Massacre of the Inhabitants of Jerusalem, 1099

1. **Ibn al-Qalanisi on the Crusaders' Capture of Jerusalem in 1099.** Extracts from Ibn al-Qalanisi, *The Damascus Chronicle of the Crusades: Exacted and Translated from the Chronicle of Ibn al-Qalanisi*, trans. H. A. R. Gibb (London: Luzac, 1967), 47–48. Reprinted with permission of Dover Publications.
2. **Ibn al-Althir on the Crusaders' Conquest of Jerusalem in 1099.** All extracts by from Francesco Gabrieli (ed.), *Arab Historians of the Crusades*, trans. E. J. Costello (Berkeley and Los Angeles: University of California Press, 1969), 10–11. Reprinted with permission of Taylor & Francis and Giulio Einaudi editore, Italy.

Chapter Four: The Siege of Damascus During the Second Crusade, 1148

1. **William of Tyre – The Fiasco at Damascus in 1148.** Extracts from James A. Brundage, *The Crusades: A Documentary Survey* (Milwaukee: Marquette University Press, 1962), 115–121. Reprinted with the kind permission of the author.
2. **Ibn al-Qalanisi – The Muslim Defeat of the Crusaders at Damascus in 1148.** Extracts from Ibn al-Qalanisi, *The Damascus Chronicle of the Crusades: Exacted and Translated from the Chronicle of Ibn al-Qalanisi*, trans. H. A. R. Gibb (London: Luzac, 1967), 282–287. Reprinted with permission of Dover Publications.

Chapter Five: The Failure of the Second Crusade

1. **Odo of Deuil on the Problem of Non-Combatants during the Second Crusade.** Odo of Deuil, *De Profectione Ludovici VII in Orientem* [The Journey of Louis VII to the East], trans. Virginia Gingerick Berry (New York: W. W. Norton, 1948), 95. Extracts from Odo of Deuil, *The Journey of Louis VII to the East: De Profectione Ludovici VII*, trans. Virginia G. Berry (New York: Columbia University Press, 2001). Reprinted with permission of Columbia University Press.
2. **The Anonymous Annalist of Wurzburg on the impious motivations of opportunists, the indebted and the poor during the Second Crusade.** Extracts from James A. Brundage (ed.), *The Crusades: A Documentary Survey* (Milwaukee: Marquette University Press, 1962), 121–122. Reprinted with the kind permission of the author.
3. **Odo of Deuil on the Treachery of Manuel I Comnenus during the Second Crusade.** Odo of Deuil, *De Profectione Ludovici VII in Orientem: The Journey of Louis VII to the East*, trans. Virginia Gingerick Berry (New York: W. W. Norton, 1948), 81–83. Extracts from Odo of Deuil, *The Journey of Louis VII to the East: De Profectione Ludovici VII*, trans. Virginia G. Berry (New York: Columbia University Press, 2001). Reprinted with permission of Columbia University Press.
4. **Odo of Deuil of the betrayal of the Byzantines during the Second Crusade.** Odo of Deuil, *De profectione Ludovici VII in orientem*, trans. Virginia Gingerick Berry (New York: W. W. Norton, 1948), 137. Extracts from Odo of Deuil, *The Journey of Louis VII to the East: De Profectione Ludovici VII*, trans. Virginia G. Berry (New York: Columbia University Press, 2001). Reprinted with permission of Columbia University Press.
5. **Criticism of the Clerical Advocates of the Second Crusade by the Anonymous Annalist of Wurzburg.** Extracts from James A. Brundage (ed.), *The Crusades: A Documentary Survey* (Milwaukee: Marquette University Press, 1962), 121–122. Reprinted with the kind permission of the author.
6. **Bernard of Clairvaux's Apologia for the Second Crusade.** Extracts from James A. Brundage (ed.), *The Crusades: A Documentary Survey* (Milwaukee: Marquette University Press, 1962), 122–124. Reprinted with the kind permission of the author.

Chapter Six: The Battle of Hattin, 1187

1. ***De Expugatione*: Saladin's Victory at Hattin in 1187.** Extracts from James A. Brundage (ed.), *The Crusades: A Documentary Survey* (Milwaukee: Marquette University Press, 1962), 153–159. Reprinted with the kind permission of the author.
2. **Letter to Archumbald on Hattin, 1187.** Short extracts from Peter Edbury (ed.), *The Conquest of Jerusalem and the Third Crusade: Sources in Translation* (Aldershot: Ashgate, 1998), 160–161. Reprinted with permission of Ashgate Publishing Limited.

3. **Letter of Patriarch Eraclius of Jerusalem to Pope Urban III on Hattin, 1187.** Short extracts from Peter Edbury (ed.), *The Conquest of Jerusalem and the Third Crusade: Sources in Translation* (Aldershot: Ashgate, 1998), 162–163. Reprinted with permission of Ashgate Publishing Limited.
4. **Ibn al-Athir – How the suffering Franks ended up at Hattin in 1187.** All extracts by Francesco Gabrieli (ed.), *Arab Historians of the Crusades*, trans. E. J. Costello (Berkeley and Los Angeles: University of California Press, 1969), 120–122. Reprinted with permission of Taylor & Francis and Giulio Einaudi editore, Italy.

Chapter Seven: Saladin's Conquest of Jerusalem, 1187

1. ***De Expugatione*: Saladin's Siege of Jerusalem in 1187.** Extracts from James A. Brundage (ed.), *The Crusades: A Documentary Survey* (Milwaukee: Marquette University Press, 1962), 159–163. Reprinted with the kind permission of the author.
2. **Ibn al-Athir – Negotiations for the Surrender of Jerusalem, September 1187.** All extracts by Francesco Gabrieli (ed.), *Arab Historians of the Crusades*, trans. E. J. Costello (Berkeley and Los Angeles: University of California Press, 1969), 141–142. Reprinted with permission of Taylor & Francis and Giulio Einaudi editore, Italy.

Chapter Eight: The Sack of Constantinople, 1204

1. **William of Tyre – The massacre of Latins living in Constantinople in 1182.** Extracts from William of Tyre, *A History of Deeds Done beyond the Sea*, 2nd edn., ed. and trans. E. Babcock and A. C. Krey (New York: Columbia University Press, 1943), 464–465. Reprinted with permission of Columbia University Press.
2. **Nicholas Mesarites – The Sack of Constantinople.** Extract from Nicholas Mesarites, 'Crusaders Run Wild in Constantinople', in Deno John Geanakoplos (ed.), *Byzantium: Church, Society, and Civilization Seen through Contemporary Eyes* (Chicago: The University of Chicago Press, 1984), 369. Reprinted with permission of The University of Chicago Press.
3. **Pope Innocent III – Reprimand of a Papal Legate.** Pope Innocent III, Extracts from Pope Innocent III, 'Pope Innocent III Reprimands a Papal Legate', in *The Crusades: A Documentary Survey*, ed. James A. Brundage (Milwaukee: The Marquette University Press, 1962), 208–209. Reprinted with the kind permission of the author.
4. **Philip de Novare – The Crusade of Frederick II.** Extracts from James A. Brundage (ed.), *The Crusades: A Documentary Survey* (Milwaukee: Marquette University Press, 1962), 227–232. Reprinted with the kind permission of the author.

Chapter Nine: The Crusade of Frederick II, 1228–1229

1. **Ibn Wasil – The Handover of Jerusalem to the Franks.** All extracts by Francesco Gabrieli (ed.), *Arab Historians of the Crusades*, trans. E. J. Costello (Berkeley and Los Angeles: University of California Press, 1984), 269–273. Reprinted with permission of Taylor & Francis and Giulio Einaudi editore, Italy.
2. **Sibt Ibn al-Jauzi – The Handover of Jerusalem to the Franks.** All extracts by Francesco Gabrieli (ed.), *Arab Historians of the Crusades*, trans. E. J. Costello (Berkeley and Los Angeles: University of California Press, 1984), 273–275. Reprinted with permission of Taylor & Francis and Giulio Einaudi editore, Italy.

Chapter Eleven: The Fall of Acre, 1291

1. **Abu L-Fida – The Muslim Conquest of Acre in 1291.** All extracts by Francesco Gabrieli (ed.), *Arab Historians of the Crusades*, trans. E. J. Costello (Berkeley and Los Angeles: University of California Press, 1984), 345–346. Reprinted with permission of Taylor & Francis and Giulio Einaudi editore, Italy.
2. **Ramon Lull – Call for the Recovery of the Holy Land.** Extracts from Norman Housley (ed.), *Documents on the Later Crusades, 1274–1580* (New York: St. Martin's, 1996), 36–37. Reprinted with permission of Palgrave Macmillan.
3. **Philip V of France – Call for the Recovery of the Holy Land.** Extracts from Norman Housley (ed.), *Documents on the Later Crusades, 1274–1580* (New York: St. Martin's, 1996), 51–52. Reprinted with permission of Palgrave Macmillan.

Chapter Twelve: Life on a Crusade, 1095–1270

1. ***De Expugnatione*: The Thirst of the Christians at the Battle of Hattin, 1187.** Extracts from James A. Brundage (ed.) *The Crusades: A Documentary Survey* (Milwaukee: Marquette University Press, 1962), 156–157. Reprinted with the kind permission of the author.
2. ***Old French Continuation of William of Tyre*: Richard's Execution of Muslim Prisoners at Acre in 1191.** Short extracts from Peter Edbury (ed.), *The Conquest of Jerusalem and the Third Crusade: Sources in Translation* (Aldershot: Ashgate, 1998), 107–108. Reprinted with permission of Ashgate Publishing Limited.
3. **Ibn al-Athir on Saladin's Execution of Captive Templar and Hospitallers in 1187.** All extracts by Francesco Gabrieli (ed.), *Arab Historians of the Crusades*, trans. E. J. Costello (Berkeley and Los Angeles: University of California Press, 1969), 124–125. Reprinted with permission of Taylor & Francis and Giulio Einaudi editore, Italy.
4. **Ibn al-Athir on the Muslim Capture of the True Cross at Hattin in 1187.** All extracts by Francesco Gabrieli (ed.), *Arab Historians of the Crusades*, trans. E. J. Costello (Berkeley and Los Angeles: University of California Press, 1969), 122. Reprinted with permission of Taylor & Francis and Giulio Einaudi editore, Italy.
5. **Imad ad-Din on Christian Women as Combatants during the Third Crusade.** All extracts by Francesco Gabrieli (ed.), *Arab Historians of the Crusades*, trans. E. J. Costello (Berkeley and Los Angeles: University of California Press, 1969), 207. Reprinted with permission of Taylor & Francis and Giulio Einaudi editore, Italy.
6. **Imad ad-Din on the abuse of Christian women after Saladin's capture of Jerusalem in 1187.** All extracts by Francesco Gabrieli (ed.), *Arab Historians of the Crusades*, trans. E. J. Costello (Berkeley and Los Angeles: University of California Press, 1969), 163. Reprinted with permission of Taylor & Francis and Giulio Einaudi editore, Italy.
7. **Fulcher of Chartres on the Expulsion of Christian Women from Antioch in 1098.** Extract from Edward Peters (ed.), *The First Crusade: The Chronicle of Fulcher of Chartres and Other Source Material*, trans. Martha E. McGinty (Philadelphia: University of Pennsylvania Press, 1971), 54. Reprinted with permission of the University of Pennsylvania Press.

Chapter Thirteen: Life in the Crusader States, 1098–1291

1. **William of Tyre – Election of Godfrey in Jerusalem.** Extracts from William of Tyre, *A History of Deeds Done beyond the Sea*, 2nd edn., ed. and trans. E. Babcock and A. C. Krey (New York: Columbia University Press, 1943), 379–383. Reprinted with permission of Columbia University Press.

2. **William of Tyre – The Repopulation of the Kingdom of Jerusalem Under Baldwin I.** Extracts from William of Tyre, *A History of Deeds Done beyond the Sea*, 2nd edn., ed. and trans. E. Babcock and A. C. Krey (New York: Columbia University Press, 1943), 507–508. Reprinted with permission of Columbia University Press.
3. **Usamah Ibn Munqidh – Baldwin Exempts his Uncle From an Indemnity.** Extracts from Usamah ibn Munqidh, *An Arab-Syrian Gentleman & Warrior in the Period of the Crusades*, trans. Philip K. Hitti (New York: Columbia University Press, 2000), 150. Reprinted with permission of Columbia University Press.
4. **Usamah Ibn Munqidh – A Frank Going Native in Holy Land.** Extracts from Usamah ibn Munqidh, *An Arab-Syrian Gentleman & Warrior in the Period of the Crusades*, trans. Philip K. Hitti (New York: Columbia University Press, 2000), 169–170. Reprinted with permission of Columbia University Press.
5. **Usamah Ibn Munqidh – The Friendly Frank.** Extracts from Usamah ibn Munqidh, *An Arab-Syrian Gentleman & Warrior in the Period of the Crusades*, trans. Philip K. Hitti (New York: Columbia University Press, 2000), 161. Reprinted with permission of Columbia University Press.
6. **Usamah Ibn Munqidh – Muslim and Christian Medicine.** Extracts from Usamah ibn Munqidh, *An Arab-Syrian Gentleman & Warrior in the Period of the Crusades*, trans. Philip K. Hitti (New York: Columbia University Press, 2000), 162–163. Reprinted with permission of Columbia University Press.
7. **Usamah Ibn Munqidh – Positive Reflections of Christian and Muslim Piety.** All extracts by Francesco Gabrieli (ed.), *Arab Historians of the Crusades*, trans. E. J. Costello (Berkeley and Los Angeles: University of California Press, 1984), 83–84. © Columbia University Press 1929. Reprinted with permission of Taylor & Francis and Giulio Einaudi editore, Italy.
8. **Usamah Ibn Munqidh – Franks Devoid of Jealousy.** Extracts from Usamah ibn Munqidh, *An Arab-Syrian Gentleman & Warrior in the Period of the Crusades*, trans. Philip K. Hitti (New York: Columbia University Press, 2000), 164–166. Reprinted with permission of Columbia University Press.
9. **Imad ad-Din – On Frankish Prostitutes.** All extracts by Francesco Gabrieli (ed.), *Arab Historians of the Crusades*, trans. E. J. Costello (Berkeley and Los Angeles: University of California Press, 1984), 204–206. Reprinted with permission of Taylor & Francis and Giulio Einaudi editore, Italy.

BIBLIOGRAPHY

Abulafia, David. 1988. *Frederick II: A Medieval Emperor*. New York: Oxford University Press.
Edgington, Susan (ed.). 2007. *Albert of Aachen:* Historia Ierosolimitana [History of the Journey to Jerusalem]. Oxford: Clarendon Press.
Ali, Tariq. 2002. *The Clash of Fundamentalisms: Crusades, Jihads and Modernity*. London: Verso.
Anderssohn, J. C. 1947. *The Ancestry and Life of Godfrey of Bouillon*. Bloomington: University of Indiana Press.
Andrea, Alfred J. 1997. 'Essay on Primary Sources'. Pp. 299–344 in *The Fourth Crusade: The Conquest of Constantinople*. Edited by Donald E. Queller and Thomas F. Madden. Philadelphia: University of Pennsylvania Press.
———. 1997. *The Medieval Record: Sources of Medieval History*. Boston: Houghton.
———. 2003. *Encyclopedia of the Crusades*. Westport, CT: Greenwood.
Asbridge, Thomas. 2004. *The First Crusade: A New History*. Oxford: Oxford University Press.
Aube, Pierre. 1985. *Godefroy de Bouillon*. Paris: Fayard.
Barber, Malcolm. 1994. *The New Knighthood: A History of the Order of the Temple*. Cambridge: Cambridge University Press.
Baron, Salo. 1957. *A Social and Religious History of the Jews: High Middle Ages, 500–1200*, vol. 4, Meeting of East and West. New York: Columbia University Press.
Beha ed-Din. 1897. 'Life of Saladin'. *The Library of the Palestine Pilgrims Text Society*. 8. Translated by C. W. Wilson. London: 24 Hanover Square, W.
Bernard of Clairvaux. 1977. *In Praise of the New Knighthood*. Translated by Conrad Greenia. Kalamazoo, MI.: Cictercian.
Berry, Virginia Gingerick. 1948. 'Introduction'. Pp. 13–44 in *De Profectione Ludovici VII in Orientem*. Translated by Virginia Gingerick Berry. New York: W. W. Norton.
Blumenthal, Uta-Renate. 1988. *The Investiture Controversy: Church and Monarchy from the Ninth to the Twelfth Century*. Philadelpia: University of Philadelphia Press.
Brown, Peter. 2003. *The Rise of Western Christendom: Triumph and Diversity, AD 200–1000*. 2nd edn. Oxford: Blackwell.
Brundage, James A. 1962. *The Crusades: A Documentary History*. Milwaukee: Marquette University Press.
———. 1969. *Medieval Canon Law and the Crusader*. Madison: University of Wisconsin Press.
———. 1985. 'Prostitution, Miscegenation and Sexual Purity in the First Crusade'. Pp. 57–65 in *Crusade and Settlement: Papers Read at the First Conference of the Society for the Study of the Crusades and the Latin East and Presented to R. C. Smail*. Edited by Peter Edbury. Cardiff: University College Cardiff Press.
———. 1987. *Law, Sex, and Christian Society in Medieval Europe*. Chicago: University of Chicago Press.
Bull, Marcus. 1993. *Knightly Piety and the Lay Response to the First Crusade: The Limousin and Gascony, c.970–c.1130*. Oxford: Clarendon.
———. 1993. 'The Roots of Lay Enthusiasm for the First Crusade'. *History*. 78: 353–372.
Burchard of Mount Sion. 1896. 'A Description of the Holy Land by Burchard of Mount Sion'. *Palestine Pilgrims Text Society*, 12. Translated by Aubrey Stewart. London: 24 Hanover Square, W.
Carroll, Warren. 1993. *The Glory of Christendom*. Front Royal, VA: Christendom Press.
Chazan, Robert. 1987. *European Jewry and the First Crusade*. Berkeley and Los Angeles: University of California Press.
———. 1996. *In the Year 1096: The First Crusade and the Jews*. Philadelphia: The Jewish Publication Society.
Chevedden, Paul E. 2000. 'The Invention of the Counterweight Trebuchet: A Study in Cultural Diffusion'. *Dumberton Oaks Papers*. 54: 71–116.

Chodorow, Stanley. 1972. *Christian Political Theory and Church Politics in the Mid-Twelfth Century*. Berkeley and Los Angeles: University of California Press.

Choniates, Niketas. 1984. *O City of Byzantium, Annals of Niketas Choniates*. Translated by Harry J. Magoulias. Detroit: Wayne State University Press.

Clinton, Bill. 2001. 'Speech at Georgetown University'. Available online at the Salon.com Web site. http://archive.salon.com/news/feature/2001/11/10/speech/ (cited 10 April 2008).

Cohn, Norman. 1970. *The Pursuit of the Millennium*. Revised edition. New York: Oxford University Press.

Constable, Giles. 2001. 'The Historiography of the Crusades'. Pp.1–22 in *The Crusades from the Perspective of Byzantium and the Muslim World*. Edited by Angeliki E. Laiou and Roy Parviz Mottahedeh. Washington DC: Dumbarton Oaks.

Cowdrey, H. E. J. 1970. 'The Peace and the Truce of God in the Eleventh Century'. *Past and Present*. 46: 42–67.

———. 1970. 'Pope Urban II's Preaching of the First Crusade'. *History*. 55: 177–188.

Curry, Andrew. 2002. 'The First Holy War'. U.S. News and World Report. http://www.usnews.com/usnews/culture/articles/020408/archive_020533.htm (cited 3 September 2007).

Dershowitz, Alan. 1999. 'My Crusade against Crusading'. *Jewish World Review*. http://www.jewishworldreview.com/0899/crusades1.asp (cited 3 September 2006).

Duncalf, Frederic. 1969–1989. 'The Councils of Piacenza and Clermont'. Pp.220–254 in *A History of the Crusades* (Kenneth Meyer Setton, Editor-in-Chief), vol. 1, *The First Hundred Years*. Edited by Marshall W. Baldwin, Madison: University of Wisconsin Press.

Edbury, Peter (ed.). 1998. *The Conquest of Jerusalem and the Third Crusade: Sources in Translation*. Aldershot: Ashgate.

Edgington, Susan B. 2001. 'Albert of Aachen, St. Bernard and the Second Crusade'. Pp.54–70 in *The Second Crusade: Scope and Consequences*. Edited by Jonathan Phillips and Martin Hoch. Manchester: Manchester University Press.

Edgington, Susan, and Sarah Lambert (eds.). 2001. *Gendering the Crusades*. Cardiff: University of Wales Press.

El-Cheikh, Nadia Maria. 2001. 'Byzantium through the Islamic Prism from the Twelfth to the Thirteenth Century'. Pp.53–69 in *The Crusades from the Perspective of Byzantium and the Muslim World*. Edited by Angeliki E. Laiou and Roy Parviz Mottahedeh. Washington DC: Dumberton Oaks.

Erdmann, Carl. 1977. *The Origins of the Idea of the Crusade*. Translated by M. W. Baldwin and Walter Goffart. Princeton: Princeton University Press. (Originally published in German in 1935.)

Finley, M. I. 1976. 'Colonies – An Attempt at a Typology'. *Transactions of the Royal Historical Society*. 5th series. 26: 167–188.

Finucane, Ronald C. 1983. *Soldiers of the Faith: Crusaders and Moslems at War*. New York: St. Martin's Press.

Fletcher, R. A. 1987. 'Reconquest and Crusade in Spain, c.1050–1150'. *Transactions of the Royal Historical Society*. 5th series. 37: 31–47.

France, John. 1994. *Victory in the East: A Military History of the First Crusade*. Cambridge: Cambridge University Press.

———. 1997. 'Patronage and the Appeal of the First Crusade'. Pp.5–20 in *The First Crusade*. Edited by J. Phillips, Manchester: Manchester University Press.

———. 1999. *Western Warfare in the Age of the Crusades: 1000–1300*. Ithaca, NY: Cornell University Press.

Fulcher of Chartres. 1971. 'Deeds of the Franks on Their Pilgrimage to Jerusalem'. Pp.23–90 in *The First Crusade: The Chronicle of Fulcher of Chartres and Other Source Materials*. Edited by Edward Peters and translated by Martha E. McGinty. Philadelphia: University of Pennsylvania Press.

Gabrieli, Francesco. 1969. *Arab Historians of the Crusades*. Translated by E. J. Costello. Berkeley and Los Angeles: University of California Press.
Geanakoplos, Deno John (ed.). 1984. *Byzantium: Church, Society, and Civilization Seen through Contemporary Eyes*. Chicago: The University of Chicago Press.
Gibbon, Edward, and D. M. Low. 1960. *The Decline and Fall of the Roman Empire*. New York: Harcourt Brace.
Giles, J. A. et al. 1848. *Chronicles of the Crusades: Being Contemporary Narratives of the Crusade of Richard Coeur De Lion*. London: H. G. Bohn.
Gledhill, Ruth. 2004. 'The Last Crusade of the Templars'. *The Times*. http://www.timesonline.co.uk/article/0, 2-1379629,00.html (cited 3 September 2007).
Glick, Leonard B. 1999. *Abraham's Heirs: Jews and Christians in Medieval Europe*. Syracuse, NY: Syracuse University Press.
Grabar, Oleg. 1996. *The Shape of the Holy: Early Islamic Jerusalem*. Princeton: Princeton University Press.
'Greek Fury over Pope Visit'. 2001. BBC News. http://news.bbc.co.uk/2/hi/europe/1310347.stm (cited 12 June 2007).
Guibert of Nogent. 1997. *The Deeds of God through the Franks: Gesta Dei Per Francos*. Translated by Robert Levine, Suffolk: Boydell.
Gunther of Pairis. 1997. *The Capture of Constantinople: The 'Hystoria Constantinopolitana' of Gunther of Pairis*. Edited and translated by Alfred J. Andrea, Philadelphia: University of Pennsylvania Press.
Hanke, Lewis. 1949. *The Spanish Struggle for Justice in the Conquest of America*. Philadelphia: University of Pennsylvania Press.
Head, Thomas, and Richard Landes (eds.). 1995. *The Peace of God: Social Violence and Religious Response in France around Year 1000*. Ithaca, NY: Cornell University Press.
Henderson, Ernest F. 1910. *Select Historical Documents of the Middle Ages*. London: George Bell and Sons.
Hill, John Hugh. 1951. 'Raymond of Saint Gilles in Urban's Plan of Greek and Latin Friendship'. *Speculum*. 26.2: 265–276.
Hoch, Martin. 2001. 'The Price of Failure: The Second Crusade as a Turning Point in the History of the Latin East'. Pp.180–200 in *The Second Crusade: Scope and Consequences*. Edited by Jonathan Phillips and Martin Hoch. Manchester: Manchester University Press.
Housley, Norman. 1992. *The Later Crusades: From Lyon's to Alcazar, 1274–1580*. Oxford: Oxford University Press.
——— (ed.). 1996. *Documents on the Later Crusades, 1274–1580*. New York: St. Martin's.
———. 2006. *Contesting the Crusades*. Oxford: Blackwell.
Ibn al-Qalanisi. 1967. *The Damascus Chronicle of the Crusades: Extracted and Translated from the Chronicle of Ibn Al-Qalanisi*. Translated by H. A. R. Gibb. London: Luzac.
Jacques de Vitry. 1896. 'The History of Jerusalem'. *Palestine Pilgrims Text Society*. 11: 1–119. Translated by Aubrey Stewart. London: 24 Hanover Square, W.
Johnson, James Turner. 1981. *Just War Tradition and the Restraint of War*. Princeton: Princeton University Press.
Joranson, Einor. 1949–1950. 'The Problem of the Spurious Letter of Emperor Alexius to the Court of Flanders'. *American Historical Review*. 55: 811–832.
Jordan, William Chester. 1979. *Louis IX and the Challenge of the Crusade: A Study in Rulership*. Princeton: Princeton University Press.
Jotischky, Andrew. 2004. *Crusading and the Crusader States*. New York: Pearson Longman.
Jurgens, William A (ed.). 1970. *The Faith of the Early Fathers*. 2. Collegeville, MN: The Liturgical Press.
Kedar, Benjamin Z., Hans Eberhard Mayer, and R. C. Smail. 1982. *Outremer: Studies in the History of the Crusading Kingdom of Jerusalem Presented to Joshua Prawer*. Jerusalem: Yad Izhak Ben-Zvi Institute.

Krey, August C. 1921. *The First Crusade: The Accounts of Eyewitnessess and Participants*. Princeton: Princeton University Press.

Ludolph von Suchem. 1896. 'Description of the Holy Land and of the Way Thither'. Pp.1–136 in *The Library of the Palestine Pilgrims Text Society*. 12. Translated by Aubrey Stewart. London: 24 Hanover Square, W.

Madden, Thomas. 1999. *A Concise History of the Crusades*. Lanham, MD: Rowman & Littlefield.

———. 2001. 'Crusade Propaganda: The Abuse of Christianity's Holy Wars'. *National Review Online*. http://article.nationalreview.com/?q=MzhhODMiMDhkYWMx NTRiYm RjMzg2NmY2YjM3ZTRiZDQ= (cited 21 May 2007).

———. 2002. 'Crusade Myths'. *Catholic Dossier*. http://www.catholic.net/rcc/Periodicals/Dossier/2002-02/toc.html (cited 3 September 2006).

MacKinney, Loren C. 1930. 'The People and Public Opinion in the Eleventh-Century Peace Movement'. *Speculum*. 5.2: 181–206.

Mackay, Charles. 1841. *Extraordinary Popular Delusions and the Madness of Crowds*. London: Richard Bentley.

Marcus, Jacob. 1938. *The Jew in the Medieval World: A Sourcebook*. Pp.315–1791. New York: JPS.

Marzials, Frank T (ed.). 1908. *Memoirs of the Crusades*. London: J. M. Dent (repr. E. P. Dutton, 1958)

Mastnak, Tomaz. 2002. *Crusading Peace: Christendom, the Muslim World, and Western Political Order*. Berkeley and Los Angeles: University of California Press.

Mayer, Hans Eberhard. 1972. *The Crusades*. Translated by John Gillingham. Oxford: Oxford University Press. (First published in German in 1965.)

Metcalf, D. M. 1983. *Coinage of the Crusades and the Latin East in the Ashmolean Museum*. Oxford. London: Royal Numismatic Society and Society for the Study of the Crusades and the Latin East.

Michaud, Joseph Francois. 1881. *The History of the Crusades*. 3. Translated by W. Robson, New York: A. C. Armstrong & Son.

Morocco Times. 2005. 'Al-Azhar – The Vatican Official Apologies Demanded'. http://www.amren.com/mtnews/archives/2005/03/alazharathe_vat.php (cited 9 March 2006).

Muldoon, James. 1979. *Popes, Lawyers, and Infidels: The Church and the Non-Christian World 1250–1550*. Philadelphia: University of Pennsylvania Press.

Munro, Dana Carleton (ed.). 1894. *Letters of the Crusaders: Translations and Reprints from the Original Sources of European History*. 1.4. Philadelphia: The Department of History of the University of Pennsylvania.

———. 1895. *Urban and the Crusaders: Translations and Reprints from the Original Sources of European History*. 1.2. Philadelphia: The Department of History of the University of Pennsylvania.

———. 1901. *The Fourth Crusade: Translations and Reprints from the Original Sources of European History*. Revised edition. 3.1. Philadelphia: The Department of History of the University of Pennsylvania.

———. 1906. 'The Speech of Pope Urban II, At Clermont, 1095'. *The American Historical Review*. 11.2: 231–242.

Nicholson, Helen, and David Nicolle, 2005. *God's Warriors: Crusaders, Saracens and the Battle for Jerusalem*. Oxford: Osprey.

Nicholson, Helen (ed.). 1997. *The Chronicle of the Third Crusade:* The Itinerarium Peregrinorum et Gesta Regis Ricardi. Aldershot: Ashgate.

———. 1997. 'Women on the Third Crusade'. *Journal of Medieval History*. 23: 335–349.

Odo of Deuil. 1948. *De Profectione Ludovici VII in Orientem*. Translated by Virginia Gingerick Berry, New York: W. W. Norton.

Otto of Freising. 1994. *The Deeds of Frederick Barbarossa*. Translated by Charles Christopher Mierow, Toronto: University of Toronto Press.

Parry, J. H. 1940. *The Spanish Theory of Empire in the Sixteenth Century*. Cambridge: Cambridge University Press.
Peter Tudebode, 1974. *Historia de Hierosolymitano Itinere*. Translated by John Hugh Hill and Laurita L. Hill, Philadelphia: The American Philosophical Society.
Peters, Edward (ed.). 1971. *The First Crusade: The Chronicle of Fulcher of Chartres and Other Source Material*. Philadelphia: University of Pennsylvania Press.
Philip de Novare. 1936. *The Wars of Frederick II Against the Ibelins in Syria and Cyprus*. Translated by John L. La Monte, with verse translation of the poems by Merton Jerome Hubert, New York: Columbia University Press.
Phillips, Jonathan. 2004. *The Fourth Crusade and the Sack of Constantinople*. New York: Penguin.
'Pope's Visit Opens Old Wounds'. 2001. BBC. http://news.bbc.co.uk/2/hi/europe/1312306.stm (cited 2 September 2006).
Powell, James. M. 1986. *Anatomy of a Crusade: 1213–1221*. Philadelphia: University of Pennsylvania Press.
Prawer, Joshua. 1972. *The Crusaders' Kingdom: European Colonialism in the Middle Ages*. New York: Praeger.
———. 1980. *Crusader Institutions*. Oxford: Clarendon Press; New York: Oxford University Press.
Pryor, John H. (ed.). 2006. *Logistics of Warfare in the Age of the Crusades*. Aldershot: Ashgate.
Queller, Donald E., and Thomas F. Madden. 1997. *The Fourth Crusade: The Conquest of Constantinople*. Philadelphia: University of Pennsylvania Press.
Richard, J. 1979. *The Latin Kingdom of Jerusalem*. 2 vols. Amsterdam; New York: North-Holland.
Riley-Smith, Jonathan. 1977. *What Were the Crusades?* London: Macmillan.
———. 1980. 'Crusading as an Act of Love'. *History*. 65: 177–192.
———. 1986. *The First Crusade and the Idea of Crusading*. Philadelphia: University of Pennsylvania Press.
———. 1987. *The Crusades: A Short History*. New Haven: Yale University Press.
———. 1997. *The First Crusaders: 1095–1131*. Cambridge: Cambridge University Press.
———. 1999. 'The Crusading Movement and Historians'. Pp.1–15 in *The Oxford History of the Crusades*. Edited by Jonathan Riley-Smith, Oxford: Oxford University Press.
———. 2000. 'Rethinking the Crusades'. *First Things: The Journal of Religion, Culture, and Public Life*. 101: 20–23.
Robert of Clari. 1936. *The Conquest of Constantinople*. Translated by Edgar Holmes McNeal, New York: Columbia University Press.
Robinson, James Harvey. 1904. *Readings in European History*. 1. Boston: Ginn and Company.
Roger of Hoveden. 1853. *The Annals, Comprising the History of England and of Other Countries of Europe from AD 732 to AD 1201*. 2 vols. Translated by Henry T. Riley, London: H. G. Bohn (repr. New York: AMS, 1968).
Russell, Frederick. 1975. *The Just War in the Middle Ages*. Cambridge: Cambridge University Press.
———. 1980. 'Paulus Vladimiri's Attack on the Just War: A Case Study in Legal Polemics'. Pp.237–254 in *Authority and Power: Studies on Medieval Law and Government*. Edited by Brian Tierney and Peter Linehan. Cambridge: Cambridge University Press.
Siberry, Elizabeth. 1985. *Criticism of Crusading, 1095–1274*. Oxford: Clarendon Press.
Sweetenham, Carol. 2005. 'The Textual History of the *Historia Iherosolimitana*'. Pp.1–11 in *Robert the Monk's History of the First Crusade:* Historia Iherosolimitana. Aldershot: Ashgate.
Synan, Edward A. 1965. *The Popes and the Jews in the Middle Ages: An Intense Exploration of Judaeo-Christian Relationships in the Medieval World*. New York: MacMillan.

Thatcher, Oliver J., and Edgar Holmes McNeal (eds.). 1905. *A Source Book for Medieval History*. New York: Scribners.
Tierney, Brian. 1962. '"*Tria Quippe Distinguit Iudicia...*" A Note on Innocent III's *Decretal Per Venerabilem*'. *Speculum*. 37: 48–59.
Tolan, John V. 2002. *Saracens: Islam in the Medieval European Imagination*. New York: Columbia University Press.
Tyerman, Christopher. 2004. *Fighting for Christendom: Holy War and the Crusades*. Oxford: Oxford University Press.
———. 2006. *God's War: A New History of the Crusades*. London: Penguin.
Usamah ibn Munqidh. 2000. *An Arab-Syrian Gentleman & Warrior in the Period of the Crusades*. Translated by Philip K. Hitti, New York: Columbia University Press.
Vasiliev, Alexander A. 1938. 'Mesarites as a Source'. *Speculum*. 13.2: 180–182.
De Villehardouin, Geoffrey, and Jean de Joinville. 1963. *Chronicles of the Crusades*. Translated by M. R. B. Shaw, London: Penguin.
Ware, Kallistos. 1980. *The Orthodox Church*. New York: Penguin.
William of Tyre. 1943. *A History of Deeds Done beyond the Sea*. 2 vols. Translated by E. Babcock and A. C. Krey, New York: Columbia University Press.
Winroth, Anders. 2000. *The Making of Gratian's* Decretum. Cambridge: Cambridge University Press.

NOTES

Introduction

1. Christopher Tyerman, *God's War: A New History of the Crusades* (London: Penguin, 2006), xiii.
2. For modern Muslims demanding an apology for the crusades, see 'Al-Azhar – The Vatican Official Apologies Demanded', *Morocco Times*, 17 March 2005, http://www.amren.com/mtnews/archives/2005/03/alazharathe_vat.php (cited 3 September 2006); for the modern Templars, see Ruth Gledhill, 'The Last Crusade of the Templars', *U.K. Times*, 29 November 2004, http://www.timesonline.co.uk/tol/news/uk/article396786.ece (cited 3 September 2007); and for Eastern Christians, see the BBC article, 'Pope's Visit Opens Old Wounds', *BBC News*, 4 May 2001, http://news.bbc.co.uk/2/hi/europe/1312306.stm (cited 2 September 2006).
3. Alan Dershowitz, 'My Crusade against Crusading', *Jewish World Review*, August 1999, http://www.jewishworldreview.com/0899/crusades1.asp (cited 3 September 2006).
4. Tariq Ali, *The Clash of Fundamentalisms: Crusades, Jihads and Modernity* (London: Verso, 2002), 40.
5. Andrew Curry, 'The First Holy War', *U.S. News and World Report*, 8 April 2002, http://www.usnews.com/usnews/culture/articles/020408/archive_020533.htm (cited 3 September 2007).
6. For an extended examination of the issues concerning the traditionalists and pluralists debates, see Jonathan Riley-Smith, 'The Crusading Movement and Historians', in Jonathan Riley-Smith (ed.), *The Oxford History of the Crusades* (Oxford: Oxford University Press, 1999), 1–15, and Giles Constable, 'The Historiography of the Crusades', in Angeliki E. Laiou and Roy Parviz Mottahedeh (eds), *The Crusades from the Perspective of Byzantium and the Muslim World* (Washington DC: Dumbarton Oaks, 2001), 1–22.
7. Among the most notable of the traditionalists is the German historian Hans Eberhard Mayer. In *The Crusades* (London: Oxford University Press, 1972), first published in German in 1965, Mayer defined a crusade as having Christian domination over the Holy Sepulchre as its goal.
8. Jonathan Riley-Smith, *What Were the Crusades?* (London: Macmillan, 1977), 12.
9. John France, 'Patronage and the Appeal of the First Crusade', in Jonathan Phillips (ed.), *The First Crusade: Origins and Impact* (Manchester: Manchester University Press, 1997), 5–20.
10. Jonathan Riley-Smith, 'Crusading as an Act of Love', *History*, 65 (1980), 177–192.
11. Jonathan Riley-Smith, 'Rethinking the Crusades', *First Things: The Journal of Religion, Culture, and Public Life*, 101 (March 2000), 20–23.
12. Thomas Madden, 'Crusade Propaganda: The Abuse of Christianity's Holy Wars', *National Review Online*, 2 November 2001, http://www.nationalreview.com/comment/comment-madden110201.shtml (cited 3 September 2006).
13. A number of crusades historians, including Jonathan Riley-Smith, Thomas Madden and Helen Nicholson, have commented negatively on the value and motivations for modern apologies for the crusades.
14. St. Basil the Great, for example, in his *First Canonical Letter* to Amphilochius (c.374) notes, 'Our Fathers [Israelites] did not reckon killings in war as murders, but granted pardon, as it seems to me, to those who were fighting in defence of virtue and piety,' see William A. Jurgens (ed.), *The Faith of the Early Fathers*, 2 (Collegeville, Minnesota: The Liturgical Press, 1970), 7.

15. Jonathan Riley-Smith, *The Crusades: A Short History* (New Haven: Yale University Press, 1987), 5. For example, Riley-Smith notes that crusades preachers turned 'to scholars for justification of Christian violence and Gregory VII had found in Anselm of Lucca a partisan who, through a careful reading of the Fathers, above all St. Augustine of Hippo, would build a convincing case for Christian violence as something which could be commanded by God, was at the disposal of the Church and would, when properly used, be an expression of Christian love'.
16. For a discussion of the newfound benefits some religious minorities found under Islamic rule, see Peter Brown, *The Rise of Western Christendom: Triumph and Diversity, AD 200–1000*, 2nd edn. (Oxford: Blackwell, 2003), 305–309.
17. Antioch and Tarsus, for example.
18. Riley-Smith, *The Crusades*, 2.
19. See, for example, Edward Gibbon, *Decline and Fall of the Roman Empire*, Book LII.
20. The Christians conquered lands that had been under Muslim control, in some cases, for eight centuries, and their efforts would not end until the capture of Grenada in 1492.
21. For more on the Investiture Controversy, see Uta-Renate Blumenthal, *The Investiture Controversy: Church and Monarchy from the Ninth to the Twelfth Century* (Philadelpia: University of Philadelphia Press, 1988).
22. See, for example, H. E. J. Cowdrey, 'Pope Urban II's Preaching of the First Crusade', *History*, 55 (1970): 177–188.
23. The argument that the Church effectively sought to sanctify warfare in the eleventh and twelfth centuries was first made in the 1930s by Loren C. MacKinney, 'The People and Public Opinion in the Eleventh-Century Peace Movement', *Speculum* 3:2 (1930), 181–206, at 201 and Carl Erdmann, *The Origin of the Idea of the Crusade*, trans. M. W. Baldwin and Walter Goffart (Princeton: Princeton University Press, 1977), originally published in German in 1935. A more recent treatment of the issue is found in Tomaz Mastnak, *Crusading Peace: Christendom, the Muslim World, and Western Political Order* (Berkeley and Los Angeles: University of California Press, 2002).
24. See H. E. J. Cowdrey, 'The Peace and the Truce of God in the Eleventh Century', *Past and Present*, 46 (1970), 42–67 and Thomas Head and Richard Landes (eds.), *The Peace of God: Social Violence and Religious Response in France Around the Year 1000* (Ithaca, NY: Cornell University Press, 1992).
25. Marcus Bull, 'The Roots of Lay Enthusiasm for the First Crusade', *History*, 78:254 (1993): 353–372.
26. Ibid.
27. The reinvigorated effort to wrest Iberia from Muslim control during the eleventh century, for example, was a reflection of the Church's support for specific wars with particular goals. In this case, the Church viewed the so-called reconquest of Muslim-controlled Iberia as a positive good that was pleasing to God and that offered greater security for the Christian West. I should also note that while dated historical works (e.g. Carl Erdmann's *The Origin of the idea of Crusading*) tend to view the *Reconquista* movement in Iberia as a precursor to the crusades, more recent historiography has argued that it was instead Gregorian Reform-era popes that reinspired, changed and subsumed military efforts against Muslims in Iberia as part of the new crusading movement. See R. A. Fletcher, 'Reconquest and Crusade in Spain, *c*.1050–1150', *Transactions of the Royal Historical Society*, 5th series, 37 (1987): 31–47.
28. Some historians have described ecclesiastical attempts to redirect Christian violence towards non-Christians, particularly Muslims in the Holy Land, as amounting to an 'export of violence', as the violence of Christian warriors was directed to the East. Such a view was held by Carl Erdmann, for example, in his seminal work *The Origin of the Idea of Crusading* and more recently has been argued by Tomaz Mastnak in his 2002

work *Crusading Peace*. Yet the bulk of more recent crusades scholarship has challenged the usefulness of such a framework for understanding the motivations of the crusades. Indeed, scholars such as H. E. J. Cowdrey, Marcus Bull and Jonathan Riley-Smith have in various works challenged the notion that the true goal of the crusades leadership, or especially the crusaders, was simply to export their problem with violence to the East. Instead, such scholars have argued that a genuine concern about the Church in the East, both its people and its holy places, was the prime motivator of the crusading movement. This, of course, does not challenge the notion that the reform clergy of the late eleventh century saw the crusade as a suitable outlet for the violent energies of its warrior class, but only that such an issue was the root cause of the crusading movement. It was instead, for the clerical leadership, an agreeable by-product of the crusades.

29. For more on the Council of Piacenza, see Frederic Duncalf, 'The Councils of Piacenza and Clermont', in *A History of the Crusades* (Editor in Chief, Kenneth Meyer Setton) Vol. I, *The First Hundred Years*, ed. Marshall W. Baldwin (Madison: University of Wisconsin Press, 1969-89), 220-254.
30. See James A. Brundage, *Medieval Canon Law and the Crusader* (Madison: University of Wisconsin Press, 1969) for an examination of the evolution of crusading and crusading vows as distinct from pilgrimage and pilgrimage vows.
31. Guibert of Nogent, *The Deeds of God through the Franks: Gesta Dei Per Francos*, trans. Robert Levine (Suffolk: Boydell, 1997), 43.
32. Ibid. 43. See also Fulcher of Chartres' account of Urban's speech.

Chapter One: Pope Urban II's Calling of the First Crusade, 1095

1. Ronald C. Finucane, *Soldiers of the Faith: Crusaders and Muslims at War* (New York: St. Martin's Press, 1983), 20.
2. Thomas Madden, *A Concise History of the Crusades* (Lanham, MD: Rowman & Littlefield, 1999), 9.
3. Because the crusades developed in the context of an armed pilgrimage, the earliest crusading vows were essentially pilgrimage vows. It was not until around the year 1200 that church lawyers began to make clear distinctions between crusading vows and pilgrimage vows. For a further examination of the evolution of the crusading vow, see James A. Brundage, *Medieval Canon Law and the Crusader* (Madison: University of Wisconsin Press, 1969).
4. For estimates of the total number of participants of the First Crusade, see Christopher Tyerman, *Fighting for Christendom: Holy War and the Crusades* (Oxford: Oxford University Press, 2004), 39; and Jonathan Riley-Smith, *The Crusades: A Short History* (New Haven: Yale University Press, 1987), 11.
5. Riley-Smith, *The Crusades*, 13.
6. Thomas Asbridge, *The First Crusade: A New History* (Oxford: Oxford University Press, 2004), 69.
7. On the issue of crusading as an act of charity (resulting from the crusaders' willingness to risk their life to go to the aid of Eastern Christians), see Jonathan Riley-Smith, 'Crusading as an Act of Love', *History*, 65 (1980), 177-192. On the issue of economic gain (or even greed) as a motivator, see John France, 'Patronage and the Appeal of the First Crusade', in Jonathan Phillips (ed.), *The First Crusade: Origins and Impact* (Manchester: Manchester University Press, 1997), 5-10.
8. Asbridge, *The First Crusade*, 68. He notes, 'But perhaps the most significant insight into the medieval mentality offered by the First Crusade is the unequivocal demonstration that authentic Christian devotion and a heartfelt desire for material wealth were not mutually exclusive impulses in the eleventh century.'

9. Historians have debated a number of potential motivations for the papacy. In 1935 crusades scholar Carl Erdmann published his important work, *Die Entstehung des Kreuzzugsgedankens*, published in English as *The Origins of the Idea of the Crusade*, trans. M. W. Baldwin and Walter Goffart (Princeton: Princeton University Press, 1977), which argued that the crusades were a means of redirecting violence from the West to the East. In this scenario, the liberation of Jerusalem was not the goal of the crusade, but only a means to inspire enthusiasm for it. The true goal was to redirect the destructive energies of warriors away from each other and, to what was considered the more noble cause, of aiding Eastern Christians against their Islamic foes. Other scholars have rejected, or substantially modified, the so-called Erdmann thesis, and the accounts of Urban's speech have been central to their research. Most notable among them is H. E. J. Cowdrey, who in a 1970 article ('Pope Urban II's Preaching of the First Crusade', *History*, 55 (1970), 177–188) argued that Urban's concern for the status of Jerusalem under Turkish rule was in fact central to his motivations.
10. Dana Carleton Munro, 'The Speech of Pope Urban II, At Clermont, 1095', *The American Historical Review*, 11:2 (1906), 231.
11. Riley-Smith, *The Crusades*, 4.
12. H. E. J. Cowdrey, 'Pope Urban II's Preaching of the First Crusade', 177.
13. Alfred Andrea, *The Medieval Record: Sources of Medieval History* (Boston: Houghton, 1997), 342.
14. Munro, 'The Speech of Pope Urban II, At Clermont, 1095', 234–235.
15. August C. Krey, *The First Crusade: The Accounts of Eyewitnesses and Participants* (Princeton: Princeton University Press, 1921), 9.
16. There are several references to the Holy Sepulchre throughout crusading literature, including the versions of the Pope Urban's speech examined here. The Church of the Holy Sepulchre held enormous significance for the crusaders as a holy site as it was the chief Christian church of Jerusalem and was (and still is) believed to cover the sites where Christ was crucified, buried and resurrected.
17. Andrea, *Medieval Record*, 344.
18. The Peace and Truce of God movements originated in local French councils in late tenth and eleventh centuries and were efforts by the Church to pacify the militant culture of the West and end intra-Christian warfare. Clerical leaders sought to do this by proscribing attacks on certain social groups (clergy, women, children etc.) and on several days of religious significance. Anyone who violated these terms was subject to excommunication. See H. E. J. Cowdrey, 'The Peace and the Truce of God in the Eleventh Century', *Past and Present*, 46 (1970), 42–67; and Thomas Head and Richard Landes (eds.), *The Peace of God: Social Violence and Religious Response in France Around the Year 1000* (Ithaca, NY: Cornell University Press, 1995).
19. The export of violence theory was covered extensively in Carl Erdmann's *The Origins of the Idea of Crusade* (see n. 9 for additional information on Erdmann's treatment of the topic). A more recent examination is found in Tomaz Mastnak, *Crusading Peace: Christendom, the Muslim World, and Western Political Order* (Berkeley and Los Angeles: University of California Press, 2002). Marcus Bull effectively challenges essential aspects of the Erdmann thesis in his *Knightly Piety and the Lay Response to the First Crusade: The Limousin and Gascony, c.970–c.1130* (Oxford: Clarendon, 1993).
20. Carol Sweetenham, 'The Textual History of the *Historia Iherosolimitana*', in *Robert the Monk's History of the First Crusade:* Historia Iherosolimitana (Aldershot: Ashgate, 2005), 7. This work provides an excellent full-text translation of the *Historia Iherosolimitana*.
21. The best edition of the *Gesta Francorum* is Rosalind Hill, *Gesta Francorum et Aliorum Hierosolimitanorum: The Deeds of the Franks and the Other Pilgrims to Jerusalem*, ed. and trans. Rosalind Hill (London: Thomas Nelson, 1962). It provides the text in both the Latin original and in English translation.

22. Krey, *The First Crusade*, 7. Krey notes, 'His somewhat secular point of view in regard to events, occasional impersonal remarks upon the clergy or participation in battle, have led modern critics to the belief that he was a knight, though his lack of intimacy with the leaders would indicate that he was a lesser knight.' However, the more recent account of the First Crusade by Thomas Asbridge holds out the possibility that the author of the *Gesta Francorum* was a cleric. See Asbridge, *The First Crusade*, 95.
23. This language is identical to the 'Letter of Alexius to Count Robert of Flanders', suggesting either Robert's familiarity with the letter or that the letter was a forgery partially based on Robert's account. See Einor Joranson, 'The Problem of the Spurious Letter of Emperor Alexius to the Court of Flanders', *The American Historical Review*, 55:4 (1949–1950), 811–832. Alexius tells Robert, 'For they circumcise the boys and youths of the Christians over the Christian baptismal fonts, and in contempt of Christ they pour the blood from the circumcision into the said baptismal fonts....'
24. On the issue of the crusades as an early form of colonialism, see the now-classic work by Joshua Prawer, *The Crusaders' Kingdom: European Colonialism in the Middle Ages* (New York: Praeger, 1972). It may be that the Pope saw the potential for colonization while later generations of crusaders determined that there was no future for most of them in the Holy Land. If one sees the crusades as draining from Europe a violent segment of the population, it might have seemed logical initially to encourage them to settle out there permanently to protect the new Latin Christian settlements.
25. Thomas Madden, for example, has rejected the assertion that the crusades represented an early form of colonialism. He notes, 'Despite modern laments about medieval colonialism, the crusades' real purpose was to turn back Muslim conquests and restore formerly Christian lands to Christian control.... During the peak of European colonialism, historians began extolling the medieval crusades as Europe's first colonial venture. By the twentieth century, when imperialism was discredited, so too were the crusades....The truth is that the crusades had nothing to do with colonialism or unprovoked aggression. They were a desperate and largely unsuccessful attempt to defend against a powerful enemy.' Thomas Madden, 'Crusade Propaganda: The Abuse of Christianity's Holy Wars', *National Review Online*, 2 November 2001, http://article.nationalreview.com/?q=MzhhODM1MDhkYWMxNTRiYmRjMzg2NmY2YjM3ZTRiZDQ= (cited 21 May 2007). See also the interesting article by M. I. Finley, 'Colonies – An Attempt at a Typology', *Transactions of the Royal Historical Society*, 5th ser., 26 (1976), 167–188. Finley, an ancient-history scholar, objects to using the terms *colonial*, *colonisation* and so on, with regard to the crusades because in his opinion they do not fit the classical model. For more on the issue of maintaining populations in the crusader states, see Chapter 14.
26. Sweetenham, 'The Textual History of the *Historia Iherosolimitana*', 8–9.
27. Psalm 45.3.
28. The reference to Moses is from Exodus 17.8–13, which tells the story of how the Israelites were only successful in battle against the Amalekites so long as Moses kept his arms lifted to heaven. When Moses dropped his arms, the Amalekites began to win the battle, so he had to keep them raised until the end of the battle to ensure an Israelite victory. This language is also similar to the language used by Charlemagne in his correspondence with Pope Leo III in 796. Charlemagne also made a clear distinction between his forces and the role of the clergy in a time of war: 'Your task, holy father [Pope Leo III], is to raise your hands to God like Moses to ensure the victory of our arms. Helped thus by your prayers to God, ruler and giver of all, the *populus christianus* may always and everywhere have the victory over the enemies of his holy name, and the name of Our Lord Jesus Christ resound throughout the world.' See Charlemagne to Leo III, AD 796 (Alcuin *Epistolae* no. 93, p.37–138).
29. The Maccabees were Jewish rebels who fought against the rule of Antiochus IV of the Hellenistic Seleucid Dynasty. The war began around AD 167 after Antiochus attempted

to forbid Jewish religious practice in Judea. The war lasted about three years and ended with a Jewish victory. For more information, see Maccabees books 1–4, especially books 1 and 2, which are included in both the Catholic and Orthodox canons of the Bible.
30. Additional accounts include those by the English monk and historian William of Malmesbury, the German historian and Benedictine monk Ekkehard of Aura, the Norman monk and chronicler Ordericus Vitalis, the Archbishop and historian William of Tyre and English chronicler and Benedictine monk Roger of Wendover.
31. Munro, 'The Speech of Pope Urban II, at Clermont, 1095', 234.
32. This source selection is taken from Einor Joranson, 'The Problem of the Spurious Letter of Emperor Alexius to the Court of Flanders', *American Historical Review*, 55:4 (1949–1950), 811–832. According to Joranson, thirty-nine manuscript copies of the letter have survived, of which twenty-seven were written after the year 1200, with the oldest extant copies dating to the early years of the twelfth century.
33. The language about circumcision is very similar to language attributed by Robert the Monk to Pope Urban II during his speech at Clermont (included in this chapter). According to Robert, Urban claimed that Muslims in the East 'circumcise the Christians, and the blood of the circumcision they either spread upon the altars or pour into the vases of the baptismal font'.
34. Hagia Sophia became perhaps the most impressive church in the medieval Christian world after it was rebuilt on a grand scale by the Byzantine Emperor Justinian I in the sixth century.
35. This source selection is taken from Oliver J. Thatcher and Edgar Holmes McNeal (eds.), *A Source Book for Medieval History* (New York: Scribners, 1905), 513–517.
36. Luke 16.19–24.
37. See n.25.
38. The seven battles Urban refers to are not certain, but likely included those of Mantzikert (1071), Nicaea (1075) and Antioch (1084). Nicaea, along with many other cities, would be returned to Byzantine control as a result of the First Crusade, while Antioch became one of the earliest and most important of the so-called crusader states.
39. This source selection is taken from Dana C. Munro, 'Urban and the Crusaders', in *The Fourth Crusade: Translations and Reprints from the Original Sources of European History*, 1:2 (Philadelphia: University of Pennsylvania, 1895), 5–8.
40. Similar language about circumcision is found in the so-called Letter of Alexius to Count Robert of Flanders (included in this chapter). The Emperor Alexius notes, 'For they circumcise the boys and youths of the Christians over the Christian baptismal fonts, and in contempt of Christ they pour the blood from the circumcision into the said baptismal fonts....'
41. It is probable that Urban meant to remind his French listeners of the once-special relationship of the Franks with the Church dating back to Pope Leo III's coronation of Charlemagne as Holy Roman Emperor on Christmas day in the year 800.
42. Matthew 19.29.
43. Numbers 13.27.
44. Jerusalem was literally the centre of the world to medieval Christians in the West, as even their maps were oriented towards the city.
45. This source selection is taken from Krey, *The First Crusade*, 33–36.
46. St. Mary in the Valley of Josaphat, or the Tomb of the Blessed Virgin, is an ancient underground church over a tomb believed to be that of the Blessed Mother (prior to her bodily assumption into Heaven).
47. See n.14.
48. Psalms 79.1–3.
49. Psalm 45.3.
50. See n.25.

51. See n.45.
52. This source selection is taken from Krey, *The First Crusade*, 36–40.
53. Isaiah 2.3.
54. Daniel 11.45.
55. Jerome, *Commentarii in Danielem*, in F. Glorie (ed.), CCSL 75A (Turnhout, 1964), 933–935. This is referring to the influential late-fourth-century church father and translator of the bible, St. Jerome, one of the most prominent biblical scholars of his time.
56. The Mount of Olives is a mountain ridge located to the east of Jerusalem and is the site of many important biblical events. Jerome, and (according to Guibert) Pope Urban as well, took this reference to mean that much of the Antichrist's career, including his demise, was to be associated with this site. As such it would have special significance for the crusaders whom Urban implies will help bring about the demise of the Antichrist (who in this case is associated with Muslims in the Holy Land).
57. This is a reference to the Apostle Paul's Second Letter to the Thessalonians 2.3–4. 'Let no one in any way deceive you, for it will not come unless the apostasy comes first, and the man of lawlessness is revealed, the son of destruction, who opposes and exalts himself above every so-called god or object of worship, so that he takes his seat in the temple of God, displaying himself as being God.' For the man of perdition, or the Antichrist, to sit in the Temple and fulfil the biblical prophecy, Christians knew that the Temple would first have to be rebuilt. Perhaps Urban (or at least Guibert) is implying that a strong Christian presence in the Holy Land might enable the rebuilding of the Temple to allow the fulfilment of this prophecy.
58. This reference may reflect Guibert's awareness of the Islamic conquests of these formerly Christian lands (see Chapter 2).
59. Luke 21.24.
60. John 7.6.
61. Luke 21.24. 'and they will fall by the edge of the sword, and will be led captive into all the nations; and Jerusalem will be trampled under foot by the Gentiles until the times of the Gentiles are fulfilled'.
62. 1 Timothy 4.1, see also Matthew 24.12.
63. Urban may be referring to the Great German Pilgrimage of 1064–1065, during which pilgrims headed to the Holy Land reportedly suffered considerable hardships at the hands of local Muslims. In the eleventh and twelfth century, the Holy Land was often referred to as 'Outremer', which in Old French means 'across the sea'.

Chapter Two: Attacks on the Jews during the First Crusade, 1096

1. Jonathan Riley-Smith, 'Rethinking the Crusades', *First Things: The Journal of Religion, Culture, and Public Life*, 101 (March 2000), 20–23.
2. Jonathan Riley-Smith, *The First Crusaders: 1095–1131* (Cambridge: Cambridge University Press, 1997), 12.
3. Salo Baron, *Meeting of East and West: A Social and Religious History of the Jews – High Middle Ages, 500–1200*, 4 (New York: Columbia University Press, 1957), 133. The great Jewish historian Salo Baron described the situation as follows: 'From the hoped for mass killings of cruel Muslims to similar unrestrained extermination of the near by Jewish "infidels" was an easy transition'. For a more recent analysis, see Robert Chazan's, *European Jewry and the First Crusade* (Berkeley and Los Angeles: University of California Press, 1987), 76.
4. Concerning the economic motives of the crusaders (which only partially explains their actions), see Jonathan Riley-Smith, *The First Crusade and the Idea of Crusading* (Philadelphia: University of Pennsylvania Press, 1986), 52–53. He notes, 'An obsession

with cash, in fact, showed itself in their [crusaders'] treatment of the Jews before they left western Europe.... One near contemporary [Albert of Aachen] was in no doubt that the pogroms were inspired by greed.'
5. Robert Chazan, *In the Year 1096: The First Crusade and the Jews* (Philadelphia: The Jewish Publication Society, 1996), 129. Salo Baron put the number slain possibly as high as 5,000. See Baron, *Meeting of East and West*, 105.
6. Leonard B. Glick, *Abraham's Heirs: Jews and Christians in Medieval Europe* (Syracuse, NY: Syracuse University Press, 1999), 104. The army of Folkmar attacked Jews in Prague while Gottschalk's army attacked Jews in Regensburg.
7. Chazan, *In the Year 1096*, 48. Chazan notes that the attention brought to the crusaders' attacks on Jews in 1096 'must not, however, be allowed to distort the broader picture. The fate of these three great Jewish communities was anomalous; they were not the norm.' See also the commentary of Salo Baron, who notes, 'The few facts standing out in all these reports indicate that, although religious fanaticism was the main propelling force behind the Crusaders' attacks on Jews, the Church as such cannot be held responsible for the bloodshed.' See Baron, *Meeting of East and West*, 97.
8. Susan B. Edgington, 'Introduction', in Albert of Aachen, *Historia Ierosolimitana* [History of the Journey to Jerusalem], ed. and trans. Susan Edgington (Oxford: Clarendon Press, 2007), 35.
9. Chazan, *European Jewry*, 38–39.
10. Ibid. 39.
11. The only complete English translation of Albert's work is Susan Edgington's recently released, Albert of Aachen, *Historia Ierosolimitana* [History of the Journey to Jerusalem], trans. Susan Edgington (Oxford: Clarendon Press, 2007).
12. Chazan, *European Jewry*, 39.
13. Edgington, *Historia Ierosolimitana*, xxiii.
14. See James Brundage, 'Prostitution, Miscegenation and Sexual Purity in the First Crusade', *Crusade and Settlement: Papers Read at the First Conference of the Society for the Study of the Crusades and the Latin East and Presented to R.C. Smail*, ed. Peter Edbury (Cardiff: University College Cardiff Press, 1985), 57–65.
15. Chazan, *European Jewry*, 38–42.
16. Chazan, *In the Year 1096*, 108. Chazan notes that it is possible that some portions were written earlier.
17. Chazan, *European Jewry*, 43–45. Chazan notes how none of the Hebrew authors could have composed their accounts without access to other sources and specifically cites Solomon's self-professed dependence on the oral testimony of the elders of Mainz for his account.
18. Archbishop Ruthard of Mainz may have been bribed by the Jews to prevent the violence, although this is not certain. See Chazan, *European Jewry*, 90.
19. This was a common theme among medieval Christian writers as well, who regularly explained the defeat of medieval Christian armies with similar reasoning. See Chapter 6.
20. This source selection is taken from August C. Krey, *The First Crusade: The Accounts of Eyewitnesses and Participants* (Princeton: Princeton University Press, 1921), 54–56.
21. The Kingdom of Lorraine should not be confused with the modern-day French administrative region of Lorraine. The Kingdom of Lorraine was established in the ninth century, and its boundaries extended to the Rhine.
22. Neuss is a German city located on the west bank of the Rhine.
23. Rothard was archbishop of Mainz at the time of the persecutions in 1096. Concerning Rothard's efforts to protect the Mainz Jewry, historian Robert Chazan had noted that there is 'little room to doubt the sincerity of Archbishop Ruthard [sic]. Even after the massive failure in Mainz, he remained committed to saving the remnant of Mainz Jewry.' See Chazan, *European Jewry*, 93.

24. When Emicho's crusaders arrived at the borders of Hungary, their reputation for trouble followed them and the King of Hungary refused to allow them entrance. Fighting broke out, and the Hungarians eventually routed them resulting in the dissolution of Emicho's army. Emicho fled back to Germany and never made it to the Holy Land. See Ashbridge, *The First Crusade: A New History* (Oxford: Oxford University Press, 2004), 88.
25. This source selection is taken from Krey, *The First Crusade*, 53–54.
26. This source selection is taken from Jacob Marcus, *The Jew in the Medieval World, A Sourcebook: 315–1791* (New York: JPS, 1938), 115–120.
27. Tuesday, 27 May.
28. The 'hanged one' has been used since the first century by Jews to refer to Jesus. Christians would not likely have used the term 'hanged one' as Solomon claims.
29. Edomites were among the main enemies of the biblical Jews as recorded in the Hebrew Scriptures. See, for example, Psalms 137.7–9, Isaiah 34.5–8 and Jeremiah 49.7–22.
30. In Jewish law. the four death penalties were stoning, burning, beheading and strangulation.
31. The Romans martyred Akiba during the Bar Kokba revolt, about CE 135.
32. A nick in the knife would make it unfit for ritual slaughter.
33. Esther 9.5.
34. Daniel 3.21.
35. Isaiah 14.19.
36. Isaiah 33.7.
37. Jeremiah 4.28.
38. Deuteronomy 18.13.
39. Hosea 10.14.
40. Lamentations 1.11.
41. This source selection is taken from James Harvey Robinson, *Readings in European History*, 1 (Boston: Ginn, 1904), 330–333.
42. 1 John 4.1.
43. Psalm 59.12. Cited twice – in this letter and in the account of Bernard's preaching by Ephraim bar Jacob of Bonn. See the final selection in this chapter.
44. This is a reference to the Christian argument that the Jews were to be allowed to exist within Christian society to serve as a historical witness to the Bible.
45. Psalm 59.12.
46. Romans 11.26.
47. This source selection is taken from Edward A. Synan, *The Popes and the Jews in the Middle Ages: An Intense Exploration of Judaeo-Christian Relationships in the Medieval World* (New York: MacMillan, 1965), 74–75.
48. Perhaps a reference to Bernard's oft-cited Psalm 59.12: 'Slay them not, lest my people forget.' See also nn.44, 46 and 53.
49. This source selection is taken from Synan, *The Popes and the Jews in the Middle Ages*, 75.
50. Baron, *Meeting of East and West*, 119.
51. The term *Ishmaelite* was used commonly to refer to Muslims in the Middle Ages. It was believed that they were descended from the biblical Hagar and her son Ishmael.
52. Psalm 59.12. See also 'Bernard of Clairvaux's Letter Promoting the Second Crusade' in this chapter.

Chapter Three: Crusader Massacre of the Inhabitants of Jerusalem, 1099

1. Former U.S. President Bill Clinton in a speech given at Georgetown University on 7 November 2001. Available online at the Georgetown University Web site, http://www.georgetown.edu/admin/publicaffairs/protocol_events/events/clinton_glf110701.htm.

Equating the crusades with modern Islamic terrorism was a common theme in the former president's speeches after the terrorist bombing on 11 September 2001. In another speech given at Yale University on 6 October 2001, Clinton remarked that if we 'look through history honestly', then terrorism could be found in 'uncomfortable places'. He then said that during the conquest of Jerusalem in 1099, 'they [crusaders] burned a mosque, slaughtered 300 Jews and killed every mother and child on the Temple Mount who was a Muslim'.
2. Thomas Madden, 'Crusade Myths', *Catholic Dossier*, 8:1, January/February 2002, http://www.catholic.net/rcc/Periodicals/Dossier/2002-02/toc.html (cited 3 September 2006). Thomas Madden is Professor of History at St. Louis University.
3. See Chapter 2, n.10 for Pope Urban II's speech at Clermont.
4. Jonathan Riley-Smith, *The Crusades: A Short History* (New Haven: Yale University Press, 1987), 34.
5. These five nobles were among the chief leaders of the First Crusade as no kings or emperors took part. Godfrey of Bouillon and Robert of Normandy were both Dukes, while Robert of Flanders and Raymond of St. Gilles were Counts. Tancred of Taranto would eventually prove himself as one of the ablest rulers of the crusader states. See Riley-Smith, *The Crusades*, 22, 25–28.
6. A number of works celebrating the deeds of the First Crusaders were composed in the period between the capture of Jerusalem and the Second Crusade. See, for example, the *Gesta Tancredi* of Ralph of Caen, which primarily celebrated the deeds of Tancred, or the *Gesta Francorum*, which celebrates the deeds of the Norman Prince Bohemond. The crusaders' capture of Jerusalem was also celebrated in later epic poems such as the *Chanson de Jerusalem*.
7. See Chapter 1 for biographical information about the author of the *Gesta Francorum* and for additional background information on the text.
8. Raymond served as a chaplain to Raymond de Saint Gilles, who was the Count of Toulouse and a leader of French forces during the First Crusade.
9. See the primary source accounts included in this chapter.
10. See, for example, Jonathan Riley-Smith, 'Rethinking the Crusades', *First Things: The Journal of Religion, Culture, and Public Life*, 101 (March 2000), 20–23. 'We also know that the figure for the Muslim dead, which used to range from 10,000 to 70,000 on the basis of accounts written long after the event, ought to be revised downwards. A recently discovered contemporary Muslim source puts the number at three thousand.'
11. Thomas Madden, 'Crusade Myths'.
12. Certainly there is no claim by any Christian chronicler to have wandered through the city making an accurate count of the dead. Nor would they have had the time to make such a tally, as tens of thousands of corpses would have been a public health hazard requiring their disposal as soon as possible. In this case, exaggerated numbers, such as 30,000, are not meant to be understood as exact but instead were meant only to signify a large number. Certainly the 'massacre' of a few thousand people in Jerusalem would also qualify as a large number and to inflate such numbers to claims of 30,000 would have fallen within the accepted literary licence of the day.
13. During the Third Crusade, for example, Saladin himself was reportedly inspired to retake Jerusalem and initially planned to do to the Christians what he understood had been done to Muslims during the conquest of Jerusalem in the First Crusade. See both Chapter 8 of this book and Helen Nicholson and David Nicolle, *God's Warriors: Crusaders, Saracens and the Battle for Jerusalem* (Oxford: Osprey, 2005), 79. John France has addressed this issue as follows: 'The shock expressed by Ibn al-Athir, for example, and his statement that 70,000 were killed, owes something to the later spirit of Jihad and the thirst for vengeance which it engendered.' See John France, *Victory*

in the East: A Military History of the First Crusade (Cambridge: Cambridge University Press, 1994), 355.
14. France, *Victory in the East*, 355. France notes that regardless of the scale of the massacre at Jerusalem, the reported treatment of the population was not uncommon during the Middle Ages for any place that resisted an ultimately successful conquest. Thomas Madden also notes that the crusaders' actions adhered to the 'accepted moral standard in all pre-modern European and Asian civilizations'. See Madden, 'Crusade Myths'.
15. Madden, 'Crusade Myths'.
16. This source selection is taken from August C. Krey, *The First Crusade: The Accounts of Eyewitnesses and Participants* (Princeton: Princeton University Press, 1921), 256–257.
17. Although scholars in general assume the *Gesta Francorum* as the earliest and most valuable source of the First Crusade, John and Laurita Hill have challenged this notion, arguing that the accounts of Peter Tudebode and of the *Gesta* were based on an earlier unknown text and the authors of both the accounts added their unique insights based on their experiences during the crusade. Hence they are essentially of equal value. See the introduction in Peter Tudebode, *Historia de Hierosolymitano Itinere*, trans. John Hugh Hill and Laurita L. Hill (Philadelphia: The American Philosophical Society, 1974), 4–10.
18. Medieval armies employed various types of siege engines of which the most popular was the trebuchet (in its various forms). The trebuchet employed a sling action that was driven by a counterweight – either a human counterweight or heavy stones. Its superior power allowed for hurling larger projectiles against or over city walls from great distances. In recent experiments, a trebuchet having a 200 kilogram counterweight threw a 15 kilogram ball to a distance of 180 metres and a 47 kilogram ball to a distance of 100 metres, all within a target area of only six square metres. Because of their enormous size, trebuchets were usually built at the siege site using local materials. Defensive weapons such as mobile siege towers allowed attackers to move into position to bridge high walls and fight from an elevated position, while mantlets served as large shields that protected advancing forces from enemy arrows and other types of missiles. For more information, see Paul E. Chevedden, 'The Invention of the Counterweight Trebuchet: A Study in Cultural Diffusion', *Dumbarton Oaks Papers*, 54 (2000), 71–116; and John France, *Western Warfare in the Age of the Crusades: 1000–1300* (New York: Cornell University Press, 1999).
19. The denarius was a coin, ideally with some silver content, that was relatively common in medieval Europe. The denarius originated in ancient Rome, with its name taken from the fact that at that time it was meant to signify the equivalent of ten asses in value. It was of varying value during the Middle Ages. For more information, see D. M. Metcalf, *Coinage of the Crusades and the Latin East in the Ashmolean Museum, Oxford* (London: Royal Numismatic Society and Society for the Study of the Crusades and the Latin East, 1983).
20. The Citadel, or Tower, of David was the most impressive of Jerusalem's defensive fortifications and was located on the western side of the city.
21. Because the crusaders entered Jerusalem from the west by the Tower of David, they would have had to traverse the entire width of the city during the daylong battle to reach the Temple area as it was adjacent to the eastern walls.
22. By right, the prisoners would have become Tancred's property, to do with as he pleased. Therefore, Tancred perhaps viewed the assault upon the Muslim captives just as he would an assault on any other of his property. See n.14 and Madden, 'Crusade Myths'.
23. This source selection is taken from Krey, *The First Crusade*, 257–262.
24. Ronald C. Finucane, *Soldiers of the Faith: Crusaders and Moslims at War* (London: Dent, 1983), 100.

25. See n.15 for information on mantlets and towers.
26. The Valley of Josaphat is just east of the city of Jerusalem.
27. Mount Zion is a mountain near Jerusalem, which over time came to refer to the entire city of Jerusalem and the Land of Israel. It is often commonly referred to as just 'Zion'.
28. Many medieval Europeans mistakenly believed that Muslims worshipped Muhammad, rather than Allah. See John V. Tolan, *Saracens: Islam in the Medieval European Imagination* (New York: Columbia University Press, 2002), 113, 116, 119–120.
29. There are few references to women taking part in the battles of the crusades, so the claim of Muslim women acting as witches to affect the outcome of the battle is particularly interesting.
30. Revelation 14.20.
31. Raymond's comment here is reflective of the common Latin Christian belief that God favoured those armies who were most pleasing to him through the avoidance of sin. Consequently, according to Raymond's reasoning, it follows that the destruction of the Muslims in this case was because they were 'unbelievers' and 'blasphemers'.
32. The 'pilgrims' in this case are the crusaders, who at the time understood themselves as pilgrims, rather than as crusaders, a term that would only be used much later. See Chapter 2.
33. 15 July.
34. This source selection is taken from Ibn al-Qalanisi, *The Damascus Chronicle of the Crusades: Extracted and Translated from the Chronicle of Ibn Al-Qalanisi*, trans. H. A. R. Gibb (London: Luzac, 1967), 47–48.
35. See the introduction by H. A. R. Gibb in Ibn al-Qalanisi, *The Damascus Chronicle of the Crusades*, 8.
36. Whether this incident happened in any form or not is uncertain, and if so it is not certain that the crusaders were targeting Jews. Jonathan Riley-Smith has noted, 'Recent work on the sack of Jerusalem in July 1099, one of the most notorious incidents and the one commemorated by those repentant modern Christians, is leading some historians to look at the evidence again. We know it to be a myth that the crusaders targeted the Jewish community in Jerusalem.' See Jonathan Riley-Smith, 'Rethinking the Crusades', 20–23.
37. This source selection is taken from Francesco Gabrieli, *Arab Historians of the Crusades* (Berkeley and Los Angeles: University of California Press, 1969), 10–11.
38. See n.11.
39. Located on the Bay of Haifa in northern Palestine, Acre became the chief port of the Latin Kingdom of Jerusalem after its capture by the crusaders in 1104. Muslim forces under Saladin recaptured Acre in 1187, but then lost it again to the forces of the Third Crusade in 1191. For the next one hundred years, with the exception of about two months, the city remained in Christian hands until the Mamluks recaptured it in 1291, a date traditionally associated with the end of the crusaders' presence in the Holy Land. See Chapter 12 for additional reading on the fall of Acre in 1291. For more reading on Acre during the crusading era, see Alfred J. Andrea [sole author and editor], *Encyclopedia of the Crusades* (Westport, CT: Greenwood, 2003), 1–3.
40. Ascalon was an important port city on the Palestinian coast that was not captured by the crusaders until 1153. After 1153 the city alternated under Christian or Islamic control until Ayyubid forces from Egypt captured it in 1247. From then on, it remained under Muslim control. For more reading on Ascalon during the crusading era, see Andrea, *Encyclopedia*, 26–27.
41. The Dome of the Rock is an Islamic shrine built in the late seventh century in the Temple Mount in Jerusalem. The site on which the Dome of the Rock was built is believed by Muslims to be the spot from which the prophet Muhammad ascended to heaven. For further reading, see Oleg Grabar, *The Shape of the Holy: Early Islamic Jerusalem* (Princeton: Princeton University Press, 1996).

42. Ramadan is the ninth month of the Islamic calendar and covers the period from late September to late October. It was established in the year 638 and is perhaps the most important religious observance of the Islamic year as prayers, fasting and charity are emphasised throughout the month.
43. The fast of Ramadan is extreme, lasting from sunrise to sundown for a month.
44. This source selection is taken from Krey, *The First Crusade*, 264–265.
45. The cities of Reims and Arras are both located in what is today northern France.
46. Pope Paschal II was the successor to Pope Urban II, who died on 29 July 1099.
47. Godfrey of Bouillon (1058–1100) actually declined the title of King of Jerusalem, even if he ultimately held an equal authority, in favour of the title of Defender of the Holy Sepulchre. Upon Godfrey's death, he was succeeded by his brother Baldwin, who, unlike Godfrey, was willing to accept the title of King of Jerusalem. For additional reading, see J. C. Anderssohn, *The Ancestry and Life of Godfrey of Bouillon* (Bloomington, IN: University of Indiana Press, 1947).
48. A large number of people who had taken the cross had not yet journeyed to the East by the time Jerusalem was captured in 1099. Others had abandoned the crusade before reaching Jerusalem. Consequently, the joy expressed in Europe over the conquest of the Holy City in 1099 resulted in notoriety for procrastinators and deserters. As Riley-Smith notes, 'His [Pope Urban II's] successor Paschal II, threatened, as Urban had done, to excommunicate those who had not yet fulfilled their vows to crusade and this was taken up by bishops. Paschal also threatened to excommunicate deserters. Hugh of Vermandois and Stephen of Blois were among many in this humiliating condition who decided to retrace their steps to the East....' See Riley-Smith, *The Crusades*, 35.
49. It was not uncommon for Christian clerical leaders during the crusades to refer to those who died on crusade as 'martyrs'. See, for example, the account by the cleric Fulcher of Chartres, who in his account of the First Crusade noted, 'Oh how many thousands met a martyr's blessed death on this expedition!' See Fulcher of Chartres, 'Deeds of the Franks on Their Pilgrimage to Jerusalem', in Edward Peters (ed.), *The First Crusade: The Chronicle of Fulcher of Chartres and Other Source Materials*, trans. Martha E. McGinty. (Philadelphia: University of Pennsylvania Press, 1971), 25.

Chapter Four: The Siege of Damascus during the Second Crusade, 1148

1. Christopher Tyerman, *Fighting for Christendom: Holy War and the Crusades* (Oxford: Oxford University Press, 2004), 49.
2. See, for example, Thomas Madden, *A Concise History of the Crusades* (Lanham, MD: Rowman & Littlefield, 1999), 53. 'News of the fall of Edessa had a profound effect on Christians and Muslims alike. It was the first loss of territory the Christians had suffered since their arrival more than four decades earlier. Their aura of invincibility was shattered.'
3. Jonathan Riley-Smith, *The Crusades: A Short History* (New Haven, CT: Yale University Press, 1987), 94. Eugenius's crusading encyclical was not the first, as has been claimed. See, for example, the papal letters of the Spanish 'Reconquest' and the letters of Pope Calixtus II written in the 1120s.
4. Their hardships and the lack of Byzantine support was the cause of later speculation that Manuel I had schemed for their demise. See Riley-Smith, *The Crusades*, 101.
5. Martin Hoch, 'The Price of Failure: The Second Crusade as a Turning Point in the History of the Latin East?', in Jonathan Phillips and Martin Hoch (eds.), *The Second Crusade: Scope and Consequences* (Manchester: Manchester University Press, 2001), 181–182. Recent poor relations between Damascus and Jerusalem posed a serious threat to the security of the Latin Kingdom.
6. Riley-Smith, *The Crusades*, 102.

7. Phillips and Hoch, *The Second Crusade*, 182–183.
8. Riley-Smith, *The Crusades*, 102.
9. Ibid. 94.
10. Virginia Gingerick Berry, 'Introduction', Odo of Deuil, *De Profectione Ludovici VII in Orientem: The Journey of Louis VII to the East*, trans. Virginia Gingerick Berry (New York: W. W. Norton, 1948), 14.
11. Odo of Deuil was a personal chaplain to King Louis VII during the Second Crusade; thus he was well positioned to write an account of the expedition. See Odo of Deuil, *De Profectione Ludovici VII in Orientem*, 15.
12. Odo of Deuil, *De Profectione Ludovici VII in Orientem*, 119. The sole surviving reference to the siege of Damascus in Odo's work is a comment he made following a terrible battle with the Turks: 'The flowers of France withered before they could bear fruit in Damascus.'
13. Ibid. 13.
14. Otto of Freising, *The Deeds of Frederick Barbarossa*, trans. Charles Christopher Mierow (Toronto: University of Toronto Press, 1994), 103. Otto wrote his account of the Second Crusade no more than nine years after its conclusion, for he died in 1158. See page 3 of the same work for Charles Mierow's introduction to Otto and his work.
15. Ibid. 103.
16. William was born in Jerusalem around 1130, making him a teenager during the time of the Second Crusade. See Emily A. Babcock and A. C. Krey, 'Introduction', *A History of Deeds Done beyond the Sea*, 1, ed. and trans. Emily A. Babcock and A.C. Krey (New York: Columbia University Press, 1943), 6.
17. Babcock and Krey, *A History of Deeds Done Beyond the Sea*, 8.
18. Phillips and Hoch, *The Second Crusade*, 182–183.
19. See biographical information for Ibn al-Qalanisi in Chapter 4.
20. Ernest F. Henderson, *Select Historical Documents of the Middle Ages* (London: George Bell and Sons, 1910), 333–336.
21. Pope Urban II.
22. The army of the First Crusade.
23. Jerusalem.
24. The Pope's concerns about clothing are similar to Bernard of Clairvaux's concerns about knightly fashion in *Liber ad milites Templi de laude novae militiae*. A full-text English translation by Conrad Greenia is available in Bernard of Clairvaux, *In Praise of the New Knighthood* (Kalamazoo, MI: Cictercian, 1977).
25. The need for confession was essential to the crusaders' ability to spiritually benefit from the crusade. The crusading indulgence only covered the penance of previously confessed sins. It was not an unconditional grant of forgiveness for sins, but, as is the case in modern Catholic theology, an indulgence only mediated the penance for previously forgiven sin. This is a fine, but important, distinction.
26. James Brundage, *The Crusades: A Documentary History* (Milwaukee: Marquette University Press, 1962), 115–121.
27. Isaiah 7.8.
28. Baldwin III was King of Jerusalem from 1143 to 1162.
29. This is a reference to King Conrad III, who was not technically an emperor. In fact, Conrad was the first German king in 200 years who had not received the imperial crown from the pope. Susan B. Edgington, 'Albert of Aachen, St. Bernard and the Second Crusade', in Jonathan Phillips and Martin Hoch (eds.), *The Second Crusade: Scope and Consequences* (Manchester: Manchester University Press, 2001), 57.
30. The ballista was a powerful torsion-driven crossbow that fired heavy darts or stone projectiles. It was declining in use at this time in favour of either the more powerful siege weapons such as the trebuchet or the less powerful, although more accurate,

common crossbow. The greater range of the longbow also contributed to the ballista's decline.
31. Psalm 9.4.
32. This may be a reference to an aborted attack on Ascalon that was planned for shortly after the failed siege of Damascus, but never came to pass. See Conrad III's Second Letter to Wibald in Chapter 6 in which he complains of waiting eight days after the agreed date for the local leadership to take part in the venture, but when they did not show up he noted how the crusaders '[d]eceived a second time…turned to our own affairs'. At this point, with no confidence in the local leadership, the crusaders returned home.
33. See Conrad III's Letter to Wibald in Chapter 6, in which he attributes the failure of the crusade to the local leadership in the Holy Land.
34. Ibn al-Qalanisi, The Damascus Chronicle of the Crusades: Extracted and Translated from the Chronicle of Ibn al-Qalanisi, trans. H. A. R. Gibb (London: Luzac, 1967), 282–287.

Chapter Five: The Failure of the Second Crusade

1. Hans Eberhard Meyer, *The Crusades*, trans. John Gillingham (Oxford: Oxford University Press, 1972), 108.
2. Jonathan Riley-Smith, *The First Crusade and the Idea of Crusading* (Philadelphia: University of Pennsylvania Press, 1986), 35.
3. Elizabeth Siberry, *Criticism of Crusading, 1095–1274* (Oxford: Clarendon, 1985), 26–27.
4. This source selection is taken from Odo of Deuil, *De profectione Ludovici VII in Orientem*, ed. and trans. Virginia Gingerick Berry (New York: W. W. Norton, 1948), 95. See Chapter 4 for more information on Odo of Deuil.
5. This source selection is taken from James Brundage, *The Crusades: A Documentary History* (Milwaukee, WI: Marquette University Press, 1962), 121–122.
6. 'Baal' was a common medieval reference to a powerful demon if not the Devil himself.
7. The term 'Holy of Holies' is used in reference to the Temple in Jerusalem.
8. A number of instances during the First Crusade, sometimes resulting in outright hostilities, were cited by Latin Christian writers as a cause for mistrust of the Byzantine Empire. Not only did skirmishes take place between Byzantine and crusader forces as they made their way to Constantinople, but on the crusaders' arrival at the capital city, the Emperor demanded oaths of loyalty from the crusade leadership, a problem for Western nobility already sworn in allegiance to other Western rulers and a major source of controversy during the crusade. For more information on criticism of crusading (throughout the crusading era), see Elizabeth Siberry, *Criticism of Crusading, 1095–1274*.
9. Odo of Deuil, *De Profectione Ludovici VII in Orientem*, 91.
10. This source selection is taken from Odo of Deuil, *De profectione Ludovici VII in Orientem*, 81–83.
11. This source selection is taken from Odo of Deuil, *De profectione Ludovici VII in Orientem*, 137.
12. Siberry, *Criticism of Crusading, 1095–1274*, 200.
13. See Conrad's *Second Letter to Wibald* written in 1148 and included in this chapter.
14. See Chapter 4 for biographical information on William of Tyre and a source selection highlighting William's criticisms of the Second Crusade leadership.
15. This source selection is taken from Dana Carleton Munro (ed.), 'Letters of the Crusaders', in *The Fourth Crusade: Translations and Reprints from the Original Sources of European History* (Philadelphia: Department of History, University of Pennsylvania, 1894) 1:4, 14.

16. This source selection is taken from James Brundage, *The Crusades*, 121–122.
17. This source selection is taken from James Harvey Robinson, *Readings in European History*, 1 (Boston: Ginn, 1904), 334–335.
18. See James Brundage, 'Prostitution, Miscegenation and Sexual Purity in the First Crusade', *Crusade and Settlement: Papers Read at the First Conference of the Society for the Study of the Crusades and the Latin East and Presented to R.C. Smail*, ed. Peter Edbury (Cardiff: University College Cardiff Press, 1985), 57–65.
19. This source selection is taken from Brundage, *The Crusades*, 122–124.
20. Bernard is referring to his promise to the Pope to complete this very work, the treatise *De Consideratione*.
21. 1 Corinthians 4.5.
22. 2 Corinthians 1.17.
23. 1 Corinthians 9.26.
24. Psalm 32.7.
25. Mark 16.20.
26. Exodus 32.9.
27. Isaiah 5.20.
28. Martin Hoch, 'The Price of Failure: The Second Crusade as a Turning Point in the History of the Latin East?', in Jonathan Phillips and Martin Hoch (eds.), *The Second Crusade: Scope and Consequences* (Manchester: Manchester University Press, 2001), 184.
29. Crusading encyclicals were issued in 1157, 1165, 1166, 1169, 1173, 1181 and 1184. These efforts did have some effect in raising money to send to the East to provide for its defence, and several small expeditions did make it to the East, but they were nothing of the scale of the First and Second Crusades. See Jonathan Riley-Smith, *The Crusades: A Short History* (New Haven: Yale University Press, 1987), 104.

Chapter Six: The Battle of Hattin, 1187

1. Thomas Madden, *A Concise History of the Crusades* (Lanham: Rowman & Littlefield, 1999), 79.
2. Saladin took control of Jerusalem on 2 October 1187. See Chapter 7 for more details.
3. Helen Nicholson and David Nicolle, *God's Warriors: Crusaders, Saracens, and the Battle for Jerusalem* (Oxford: Osprey, 2005), 9.
4. Crusaders felt that the Byzantines had acted treasonably on several occasions during the era of the First and Second Crusades. Byzantine Christians were equally suspicious of Latin Christians, resulting in major attacks on Latin Christians in Constantinople in the 1170s and 1180s (see also the chapters on Criticism of Crusading the Sack of Constantinople).
5. Nicholson and Nicolle, *God's Warriors*, 12–13.
6. Madden, *A Concise History of the Crusades*, 80. 'Saladin had planned to avenge the First Crusade massacre of Muslims in 1099 by killing the Christians of Jerusalem in 1187.'
7. Nicholson and Nicolle, *God's Warriors*, 71. This was a genuine symbol of generosity by Saladin, as 'according to Arab custom a man who had taken food or drink from his captor was thereafter safe from harm'.
8. Ibid. 72.
9. Madden, *A Concise History of the Crusades*, 79. Madden notes, 'He [Saladin] ordered the mass execution of all captured Hospitallers and Templars....Thousands of common foot soldiers who could not purchase their freedom were sold on the slave markets.'
10. Peter Edbury (ed.), *The Conquest of Jerusalem and the Third Crusade: Sources in Translation* (Aldershot: Ashgate, 1998), 158.

11. Ibid.
12. Ibid.
13. See Chapter 5 for additional biographical data on Ibn al-Athir.
14. This source selection is taken from James Brundage, *The Crusades: A Documentary History* (Milwaukee, WI: Marquette University Press, 1962), 153–159.
15. Saladin.
16. Guy de Lusignan.
17. Raymond III of Tripoli.
18. Reginald de Chatillon.
19. Balian d'Ibelin.
20. Reginald Garnier.
21. Walter Garnier.
22. According to Brundage, 'King Henry II of England had previously donated money for the defence of the Holy Land. His treasury, which had been placed at the disposal of the military order, was now broken open and used to hire mercenaries to help throw back Saladin's attack.' See Brundage, *The Crusades*, 153–159.
23. Turcopoles (literally 'sons of Turks') were native mercenary troops frequently employed by the crusader states and military orders.
24. Presumably a piece of the 'true cross' on which Christ was crucified that was discovered in 1099 following the crusaders capture of Jerusalem in the First Crusade.
25. Countess Eschiva, the wife of Raymond III of Tripoli.
26. Ecclesiastes 10.6.
27. This source selection is taken from Edbury, *The Conquest of Jerusalem and the Third Crusade*, 160–161.
28. Ibid. 162–163.
29. This source selection is taken from Francesco Gabrieli (ed.), *Arab Historians of the Crusades* (Berkeley and Los Angeles: University of California Press, 1969), 120–122.
30. This source selection is taken from Beha ed-Din, 'Life of Saladin', *The Library of the Palestine Pilgrims Text Society*, 8, trans. C.W. Wilson (London: 24 Hanover Square, W., 1897), 110–115.
31. Beha ed-Din mistakenly refers to King Guy of Lusignan, the King of Jerusalem, as 'Geoffrey'. Here we use 'Guy' to avoid confusion for the reader.
32. Beha ed-Din actually refers to Raynald de Chatillon as 'Prince Arnat'. We have changed the name to avoid confusion for the reader.
33. Honfroi de Toron.
34. Raymond of Tripoli.
35. 'God is most great!'
36. 'There is no other god but God!'

Chapter Seven: Saladin's Conquest of Jerusalem, 1187

1. Jonathan Riley-Smith, *The Crusades: A Short History* (New Haven: Yale University Press, 1987), 109.
2. Helen Nicholson and David Nicolle, *God's Warriors: Crusaders, Saracens, and the Battle for Jerusalem* (Oxford: Osprey, 2005), 73.
3. Ibid.
4. Ibid.
5. Hans Eberhard Meyer, *The Crusades*, trans. John Gillingham (Oxford: Oxford University Press, 1972), 132. Between the battle of Hattin and the siege of Jerusalem, Saladin's forces cut a swath through Palestine and Syria, capturing many towns and fortresses.

6. Balian was reportedly torn over his decision to take command of the defence as he had been under oath not to take up arms against Saladin, who had allowed him safe passage to Jerusalem to collect his family. The Patriarch absolved him from his promise to Saladin, after which Balian wrote a letter to Saladin explaining his decision. Saladin, in what was perhaps a reflection of the respect the two men had for each other, seemed to have accepted Balian's reasoning without great concern over his broken pledge. For an excellent summary of these events, see Nicholson and Nicolle, *God's Warriors*, 74–75.
7. Meyer, *The Crusades*, 132.
8. Nicholson and Nicolle, *God's Warriors*, 75.
9. Ibid. 79. 'Whether this showed that the fanaticism of the First Crusade was still alive in Jerusalem, or whether it was a last desperate gamble, no one knows.'
10. Ibid.
11. Christopher Tyerman, *Fighting for Christendom: Holy War and the Crusades* (Oxford: Oxford University Press, 2004), 50.
12. See Chapter 6 for more information about this source and its author.
13. See Chapter 6 for additional biographical information on Ibn al-Athir.
14. This source selection is taken from Roger of Hoveden, *The Annals, Comprising the History of England and of Other Countries of Europe from AD 732 to AD 1201*, trans. Henry T. Riley, 2 vols. (London: H. G. Bohn, 1853; repr. New York: AMS, 1968), 68–70.
15. This source selection is taken from James Brundage (ed.), *The Crusades: A Documentary Survey* (Milwaukee: Marquette University Press, 1962), 159–163.
16. 26 September.
17. See the selection by Ibn al-Athir, provided in this chapter, for a detailed account of the negotiations leading up to the treaty.
18. *fakihs* and *kadis* were judges.
19. 'God is great!'
20. Latin Christians had controlled Jerusalem since its conquest during the First Crusade in 1099. See Chapter 3.
21. This source selection is taken from Beha eh-Din, 'The Life of Saladin', *The Library of the Palestine Pilgrims Text Society*, trans. C. W. Wilson (London: 24 Hanover Square W. 1897), 118–120.
22. A text of the sermon is provided in Joseph Francois Michaud, *The History of the Crusades*, 3, trans. W. Robson (New York: A. C. Armstrong & Son, 1881), 376–379.
23. This source selection is taken from Francesco Gabrieli (ed.), *Arab Historians of the Crusades*, trans. E. J. Costello (Berkeley and Los Angeles: University of California Press, 1969), 141–142.
24. Another even more graphic account of Balian's threats to Saladin during their negotiation is provided by Imad al-Din in Gabrieli, *Arab Historians of the Crusades*, 156–157.

Chapter Eight: The Sack of Constantinople, 1204

1. Jonathan Phillips, *The Fourth Crusade and the Sack of Constantinople* (New York: Penguin, 2004), xv.
2. For an overview of this issue, see John Hugh Hill, 'Raymond of Saint Gilles in Urban's Plan of Greek and Latin Friendship', *Speculum*, 26:2 (April 1951): 265–276.
3. See Chapter 5 for Latin Christian concerns over Byzantine treachery during the crusades.
4. See the source selection and introduction on William of Tyre provided in this chapter.
5. Donald E. Queller and Thomas F. Madden, *The Fourth Crusade: The Conquest of Constantinople* (Philadelphia: University of Pennsylvania Press, 1997), 145–147, 152–153.
6. Phillips, *The Fourth Crusade and the Sack of Constantinople*, 67–72.

7. Ibid. 102–104. Many crusaders made alternative plans to depart from other ports. As a result, the collective contributions of the crusaders in Venice were insufficient to pay the Venetians.
8. Ibid. 110.
9. Ibid. 120.
10. Queller and Madden, *The Fourth Crusade*, 82–83. Some of the crusade leadership had been aware of Alexius IV's offer much earlier, but they were waiting for an opportune time to present it to the army.
11. Phillips, *The Fourth Crusade and the Sack of Constantinople*, 127–134.
12. Ibid. 200.
13. Ibid. 190, 223–227. As emperor, Alexius Ducas Murtzuphlus took the name Alexius V. Among his first acts, he imprisoned the sickly and elderly Isaac II, who died a short time later.
14. In a 2001 visit by the former Pope John Paul II to the Orthodox nation of Greece, angry Orthodox clerics cited the Fourth Crusade in protest of his visit. BBC News, 'Greek Fury over Pope Visit', 4 May 2001 [Online] http://news.bbc.co.uk/2/hi/europe/1310347.stm, last accessed 6 December 2007.
15. See Chapter 4 for biographical information on William of Tyre.
16. Other violence against Western Christians took place in 1179 and 1185, for example, as well as during the Fourth Crusade when Greeks attacked the Latin Quarter of Constantinople, sending its residents fleeing to the camps of the crusaders. See Queller and Madden, *The Fourth Crusade*, 144–145.
17. Indeed, Deno John Geanakoplos, Professor Emeritus of History at Yale University, in his highly regarded sourcebook on Byzantium has grouped sources reflecting such hostilities before 1204 with those accounts of the sacking of Constantinople as a reflection of the generally poor state of Latin–Greek relations during the period. See Deno John Geanakoplos (ed.), *Byzantium: Church, Society, and Civilization Seen Through Contemporary Eyes* (Chicago: The University of Chicago Press, 1984), 362–372. Catholic scholar Dr Warren Carroll has also connected the events of 1182 with those of 1204, noting, 'Horrible and utterly indefensible as the sack was, it should in justice be remembered that it was not totally unprovoked; more than once (as in the massacre of 1182) the Greeks of Constantinople had treated the Latins there as they were now being treated....' See Warren Carroll, *The Glory of Christendom* (Front Royal, VA: Christendom Press, 1993), 131, 157. Finally, the highly respected Orthodox Bishop Kallistos Ware, while addressing the historical legacy of mistrust between Catholic and Orthodox Christians, has noted, 'Orthodox, for example, must blame themselves for the pride and contempt with which during the Byzantine period they regarded the west; they must blame themselves for incidents such as the riot of 1182, when many Latin residents at Constantinople were massacred by the Byzantine populace.' See Kallistos Ware, *The Orthodox Church* (New York: Penguin, 1980), 70.
18. Much of William's account is confirmed by other contemporary sources. Indeed, the Byzantine historian Nicetas Choniates, examined later in this chapter, notes that during 1182, 'Those apprehended were condemned to death, and all lost their properties and possessions.' See Niketas Choniates, *O City of Byzantium, Annals of Niketas Choniates*, trans. Harry J. Magoulias (Detroit: Wayne State University Press, 1984), 140–141. The Arab chronicler Ibn Jubayr also recorded a confused and inaccurate version of the events of 1182, in which Muslims carried out the rampage in their sacking of the Constantinople. He connects the events of 1182 and 1204 as the two momentous events in the history of the city. See Nadia Maria El-Cheikh, 'Byzantium through the Islamic Prism from the Twelfth to the Thirteenth Century', in Angeliki E. Laiou and Roy Parviz Mottahedeh (eds.), *The Crusades from the Perspective of Byzantium and the Muslim World* (Washington, D.C.: Dumberton Oaks Research Library and Collection, 2001), 60.

19. Queller and Madden, *The Fourth Crusade*, 144.
20. A full-text English translation is in Geoffrey de Villehardouin and Jean de Joinville, *Chronicles of the Crusades*, trans. M. R. B. Shaw (London: Penguin, 1963), 29–165.
21. Alfred J. Andrea, 'Essay on Primary Sources', in Donald E. Queller and Thomas F. Madden (eds.), *The Fourth Crusade: The Conquest of Constantinople*, 2nd edn. (Philadelphia: University of Pennsylvania Press, 1997), 301. Andrea notes, '…he also, at times, failed to report certain disquieting facts that could place the crusades, and especially the leaders, in a bad light. These unreported events include…the sacking of Constantinople's churches in April of 1204.'
22. Ibid. 299.
23. For a full-text English translation see Robert of Clari, *The Conquest of Constantinople*, trans. Edgar Holmes McNeal (New York: Columbia University Press, 1936).
24. Andrea, 'Essay on Primary Sources', 302.
25. The reference to 'evil women' and their dismissal from the crusaders' camp fits into a larger theme in crusading thought that feared the presence of women on a crusade as sources of temptation to sin. Sexual purity was believed to be a necessity for God's approval of the crusaders and their success in battle. See James Brundage, 'Prostitution, Miscegenation, and Sexual Purity in the First Crusade', in *Crusade and Settlement: Papers Read at the First Conference for the Society for the Study of the Crusades and the Latin East and Presented to R. C. Smail*, ed. Peter Edbury (Cardiff: University College Cardiff Press, 1985), 57–64.
26. Andrea, 'Essay on Primary Sources', 310. For a full-text English translation of Nicetas's *History* that covers the Byzantine period from 1118 to 1207, see Niketas Choniates, *O City of Byzantium*.
27. For a full-text English translation, see Gunther of Pairis, *The Capture of Constantinople: The 'Hystoria Constantinopolitana' of Gunther of Pairis*, ed. and trans. Alfred J. Andrea (Philadelphia: University of Pennsylvania Press, 1997).
28. Phillips, *The Fourth Crusade and the Sack of Constantinople*, 94.
29. William of Tyre, *A History of Deeds Done beyond the Sea*, 2nd edn., ed. and trans. E. Babcock and A. C. Krey (New York: Columbia University Press, 1943), 464–465.
30. Matthew 23.33.
31. Geoffrey de Villehardouin, 'The Compact of Division', in *The Fourth Crusade: Translations and Reprints from the Original Sources of European History*, ed. and trans. Dana Carleton Munro (Philadelphia: The Department of History of the University of Pennsylvania, 1901), 14–15.
32. M. R. B Shaw, 'Introduction', in Joinville and Villehardouin, *Chronicles of the Crusades*, 14.
33. Robert de Clari, 'The Sack of Constantinople', in *The Fourth Crusade: Translations and Reprints from the Original Sources of European History*, ed. and trans. Dana Carleton Munro (Philadelphia: The Department of History of the University of Pennsylvania, 1901), 13–14.
34. Edgar Holmes McNeal, 'Introduction', in Robert of Clari, *The Conquest of Constantinople*, 7.
35. This is probably a reference to the historic schism between the Eastern and Western churches. The formal excommunication of 1054 is often cited as a significant break, but its impact was diminished as less than twenty years later, Pope Gregory VII was in negotiations with Byzantine authorities to personally lead a crusade of 50,000 men to Byzantium's aid against the Turks. See Jonathan Riley-Smith, *The Crusades: A Short History* (New Haven: Yale University Press, 1987), 2.
36. 11 April 1204.
37. Halberstadt.
38. Nicetas Choniates, 'The Sack of Constantinople', in *The Fourth Crusade: Translations and Reprints from the Original Sources of European History*, ed. and trans. Dana Carleton

Munro (Philadelphia: The Department of History of the University of Pennsylvania, 1901), 15–16.
39. A reference to the consecrated bread and wine distributed during the Divine Liturgy for Orthodox Christians and the Mass for Latin Christians.
40. Nicholas Mesarites, 'Crusaders Run Wild in Constantinople', in Deno John Geanakoplos (ed.), *Byzantium: Church, Society, and Civilization Seen Through Contemporary Eyes* (Chicago: The University of Chicago Press, 1984), 369.
41. For more information on Mesarites, see Alexander A. Vasiliev, 'Mesarites as a Source', *Speculum*, 13:2 (1938): 180–182.
42. Both are figures in Greek mythology associated with Hades. Cerberus was the ferocious and monstrous three-headed dog that guarded the gate to Hades while Charon was the ferryman of Hades.
43. Gunther von Pairis, 'List of Relics Stolen by Abbot Martin', in *The Fourth Crusade: Translations and Reprints from the Original Sources of European History*, ed. and trans. Dana Carleton Munro (Philadelphia: The Department of History of the University of Pennsylvania, 1901), 18–19.
44. Alfred J. Andrea, 'Introduction', in Gunther of Pairis, *The Capture of Constantinople: The 'Hystoria Constantinopolitana' of Gunther of Pairis*, ed. and trans. Alfred J. Andrea (Philadelphia: University of Pennsylvania Press, 1997), 11.
45. Located in the Alsace region of France.
46. Pope Innocent III, 'Pope Innocent III Reprimands a Papal Legate', in *The Crusades: A Documentary Survey*, trans. James A. Brundage (Milwaukee: Marquette University Press, 1962), 208–209.
47. Pope Innocent III, 'Crusaders to Stay at Constantinople', in *The Fourth Crusade: Translations and Reprints from the Original Sources of European History*, ed. and trans. Dana Carleton Munro (Philadelphia: The Department of History of the University of Pennsylvania, 1901), 20.
48. The name Romania was regularly given to the Latin Empire of Constantinople by contemporaries.

Chapter Nine: The Crusade of Frederick II, 1228–1229

1. James A. Brundage (ed.), *The Crusades: A Documentary Survey* (Milwaukee: Marquette University Press, 1962), 230.
2. David Abulafia, *Frederick II: A Medieval Emperor* (New York: Oxford University Press, 1988), 148. Preoccupations with the Muslims of Sicily made it difficult for Frederick to pay much attention to the Muslims of the East.
3. The best account of the Fifth Crusade is James. M. Powell, *Anatomy of a Crusade: 1213–1221* (Philadelphia: University of Pennsylvania Press, 1986).
4. Thomas Madden, *A Concise History of the Crusades* (Lanham, MD: Rowman & Littlefield, 1999), 155–156. Madden notes, 'Returning soldiers accused Frederick of reckless disregard for the crusade. He had strung them along, insisting that he and his vast armies were just beyond the horizon, thus keeping the enterprise in a limbo that ultimately proved fatal.'
5. Ibid. 156.
6. Abulafia, *Frederick II*, 151.
7. Ibid. 152; and Madden, *A Concise History of the Crusades*, 158.
8. Madden, *A Concise History of the Crusades*, 146.
9. Christopher Tyerman, *God's War: A New History of the Crusades* (Cambridge: The Belknap Press of Harvard University Press, 2006), 745–746.
10. See, for example, the account of Philip of Novare included in this chapter for an example of Frederick's efforts to wrest control of Beirut from John d'Ibelin at the beginning of the crusade.

11. Tyerman, *God's War*, 746; and Madden, *A Concise History of the Crusades*, 160–161.
12. Madden, *A Concise History of the Crusades*, 161–162.
13. See the source selection by Ibn Wasil in this chapter.
14. Ibid. 164.
15. See the account of Philip of Novare provided in this chapter.
16. A full-text English translation is Philip de Novare, *The Wars of Frederick II Against the Ibelins in Syria and Cyprus*, trans. John L. LaMonte, with verse translation of the poems by Merton Jerome Hubert (New York: Columbia University Press, 1936).
17. James Brundage, for example, notes, 'Instead of using his army against the Moslems, it was Frederick's intention to negotiate with the Egyptian sultan for a peaceful territorial settlement in the Holy Land. Frederick proposed to use his army principally against the Latins in the East, to try to force them to acknowledge his position as regent and de facto ruler of the Latin states in the East.' See James Brundage, *The Crusades: A Documentary Survey* (Milwaukee, WI: Marquette University Press, 1962), 230.
18. These source selections were translated by James Brundage, in James Brundage, *The Crusades: A Documentary Survey*, 227–232.
19. Philip is mistaken. Frederick actually left on 28 June 1228.
20. Gregory IX had already excommunicated Frederick before he left.
21. 21 July 1228.
22. John d'Ibelin, Lord of Beirut during 1197–1226.
23. Henry the Fat, King of Cyprus.
24. Gautier III, Count of Caesarea and brother-in-law of John d'Ibelin.
25. Demetrius of Monterrat, titular King of Salonica.
26. Manfred II, Marquis of Lancia and vicar-general of Lombardy.
27. Brundage notes, 'John was Constable of Jerusalem, 1194–1200, and traded this post for Beirut, as stated. Beirut had been conquered by Saladin in 1187 and was restored to Christian hands in 1197.' Brundage, *The Crusades, A Documentary Survey*, 252.
28. The correct year is 1228.
29. The infant Conrad IV, titular King of Jerusalem.
30. Al-Kamal was Sultan of Egypt, and not at this time ruling in Damascus, which was under his nephew, an-Nasir Dawud (referenced in both Arab sources included in this chapter).
31. Actually the following year, 1229.
32. Troops from Southern Italy.
33. This source selection is taken from Dana Carleton Munro (ed.), 'Letters of the Crusaders', in *The Fourth Crusade: Translations and Reprints from the Original Sources of European History*, ed. and trans. Dana Carleton Munro (Philadelphia: The Department of History of the University of Pennsylvania, 1898–1912), 24–27.
34. Here Frederick is referring to the events of the Fifth Crusade.
35. This source selection is taken from Dana Carleton Munro (ed.), *Letters of the Crusaders*, 27–31.
36. This source selection is taken from Francesco Gabrieli (ed.), *Arab Historians of the Crusades*, trans. E. J. Costello (Berkeley and Los Angeles: University of California Press, 1984), 269–273.
37. This source selection is taken from Francesco Gabrieli (ed.), *Arab Historians of the Crusades*, 273–275.

Chapter Ten: The Crusade of Louis IX, 1248–1249

1. Christopher Tyerman, *Fighting for Christendom: Holy War and the Crusades* (Oxford: Oxford University Press, 2004), 62.

2. Jonathan Riley-Smith, *The Crusades: A Short History* (New Haven: Yale University Press, 1987), 157.
3. Louis IX made exceptional financial contributions to the crusade, underwriting contingents raised by the ancillary leaders of the crusade. See William Chester Jordan, *Louis IX and the Challenge of the Crusade: A Study in Rulership* (Princeton: Princeton University Press, 1979), 69–71, 79–104.
4. See the selection by Jean de Joinville provided in this chapter.
5. Jordan, *Louis IX and the Challenge of the Crusade*, 77–78.
6. Louis did not return home to France until 1254.
7. Riley-Smith, *The Crusades*, 161. Louis led an effort for a massive refortification of the cities of Acre, Caesarea, Jaffa and Sidon.
8. Jordan, *Louis IX and the Challenge of the Crusade*, 127.
9. Riley-Smith, *The Crusades*, 175.
10. Francesco Gabrieli (ed.), *Arab Historians of the Crusades*, trans. E. J. Costello (Berkeley and Los Angeles: University of California Press, 1969), *xxxiv*.
11. Dana C. Munro (ed.), 'Letters of the Crusaders', in *The Fourth Crusade: Translations and Reprints from the Original Sources of European History*, 1:4 (Philadelphia: The Department of History for the University of Pennsylvania, 1896), 34.
12. Jean Sire de Joinville was born in 1224 and accompanied Louis IX during his first crusade and his extended stay in the Holy Land that followed (from 1248 to 1254). He died in 1317.
13. The following source selection is taken from Makrisi, '*Essoulouk li Mariset il Muluk*' [The Road to Knowledge of the Return of Kings], in *Chronicles of the Crusades*, ed. Henry G. Bohn (London: Henry G. Bohn, 1848: reissued New York: AMS Press, 1969), 542–543.
14. Perhaps two-thirds of the known Christian world had been conquered by Islamic armies prior to the calling of the First Crusade, including much of the Byzantine Empire, the Levant, North Africa and much of Iberia and parts of Italy.
15. This is likely a paraphrased reference to Koran 5:33.
16. Munro, 'Letters of the Crusaders', 34–40.
17. The 'slaves and captives' were Christians who, according to Makrisi, were in some cases crusaders captured during the Fifth Crusade.
18. *Greek fire*, believed to have originated with the Byzantine Greeks, was a type of burning liquid usually used in sea battles.
19. A Christian hymn of praise.
20. This appears to be a reference to the siege of Antioch in 1098 during the First Crusade.
21. Tartars, more commonly known as Tatars, were Turkic people of Eastern Europe and Central Asia. They were an enormous threat to Muslim and some Christian populations during the thirteenth century. They are perhaps best known from this period for the deeds of the Mongol ruler Genghis Khan.
22. The Charismians were an eastern tribe who had been driven from their lands by Genghis Khan and had relocated to a new home on the Euphrates from where they launched attacks on the Holy Land in the first half of the thirteenth century.
23. This selection is taken from Geoffrey de Villehardouin and Jean de Joinville, 'Joinville's Chronicle of the Crusade of St. Lewis', *Memoirs of the Crusades*, trans. Frank T. Marzials (London: J. M. Dent, 1908), 210–212.
24. This selection is taken from Villehardouin and Joinville, 'Joinville's Chronicle of the Crusade of St. Lewis', 219–220.
25. This selection is taken from Villehardouin and Joinville, 'Joinville's Chronicle of the Crusade of St. Lewis', 224–226.
26. Makrisi notes that it was the Emir Abou Ali who chiefly negotiated with the King of France for the latter's ransom and for the surrender of Damietta.

27. Robert of Nantes was the Patriarch of Jerusalem at the time of Louis's captivity in Egypt.
28. This selection is taken from Villehardouin and Joinville, 'Joinville's Chronicle of the Crusade of St. Lewis', 226–228.
29. This source selection is taken from Makrisi, '*Essulouk li Mariset il Muluk*', 543–555. In many cases the spelling has been modernised. For example, *soldan*, in the original, has been changed to *sultan*. In other cases, spellings have been modified so that they are the same in both Latin and Arabic source translations. El Mansura in Joinville's account, for example, had been replaced by Mansoura as used in Makrisi's account.
30. Not to be confused with the sultan of the same name.
31. Here Makrisi is referencing the events of the failed Fifth Crusade.
32. This source selection is taken from Makrisi, '*Essulouk li Mariset il Muluk*', 544–547.
33. The Arabic word properly signifies 'firework boat'. Such were probably made use of to carry the Greek fire and the machines to throw it. Makrisi, in the history of the first siege of Damietta, speaks much of these fire ships, saying that the Muslims made use of them to set fire to the vessels of the Christians. [Adapted from the notes provided in the translation, see page 544.]
34. The Mamluk-Baharites were Turkish slaves who had earned the highest level of trust of the sultan and contributed greatly to the last victory of the Egyptians over St. Louis. Shortly after they assassinated Touran Chah, the last prince of the Ayyubid dynasty, they seized the throne for themselves and reigned in Egypt and Syria for 136 years and had 27 Sultans. See notes on pages 545–546 of Bohn's *Chronicles of the Crusades*.
35. This source selection is taken from Makrisi, '*Essulouk li Mariset il Muluk*', 547–550.
36. Also known as Baybars, he went on to become the future Mamluk Sultan of Egypt in 1260. Muslim forces under his leadership devastated the crusader states in the Levant until his death in 1277. Additional information is provided in Chapter 11.
37. This source selection is taken from Makrisi, '*Essulouk li Mariset il Muluk*', 550–552.
38. This source selection is taken from Makrisi, '*Essulouk li Mariset il Muluk*', 552–553.
39. Political pressure for a male leader made the sultana marry the Mamluk commander Aybak, who was later assassinated, and in the power struggle that followed, the vice-regent Qutuz took over and formally founded the first Mamluk Sultanate. In 1260, Baibars murdered Qutuz and took the sultanate for himself.
40. The Ayyubid dynasty was a Muslim dynasty founded by Saladin that ruled Syria, Egypt and other areas in the Middle East during the twelfth and thirteenth centuries. Egypt had been conquered by Saladin's forces in 1169.
41. This source selection is taken from Makrisi, '*Essulouk li Mariset il Muluk*', 553–554.
42. Ibid. 554.
43. This is a reference to the prison of St. Louis and the eunuchs who guarded him during his captivity. Makrisi notes earlier that Louis was imprisoned in 'the house of Ibrahim ben Lokman, secretary to the sultan, and [placed] under the guard of the eunuch Sahil'. See the source selection included in this chapter under 'The Defeat of the Crusaders and the Capture of King Louis'.

Chapter Eleven: The Fall of Acre, 1291

1. Thomas Madden, *A Concise History of the Crusades* (Lanham, MD: Rowman & Littlefield, 1999), 188.
2. Ibid. 186.
3. Norman Housley, *The Later Crusades: From Lyon's to Alcazar, 1274–1580* (Oxford: Oxford University Press, 1992), 9–10. For additional background on Baibars as a military commander, see Chapter 10.
4. Christopher Tyerman, *God's War: A New History of the Crusades* (London: Penguin, 2006), 722. See also Madden, *A Concise History of the Crusades*, 181.

5. Madden, *A Concise History of the Crusades*, 181.
6. Louis began his second crusade to Tunis in 1270. He died in the same year.
7. Housley, *The Later Crusades*, 16.
8. Madden, *A Concise History of the Crusades*, 188.
9. Ibid.
10. Tyerman, *God's War*, 821. Sappers were engineers who dug tunnels under the city walls in an effort to destroy their foundation.
11. Madden, *A Concise History of the Crusades*, 189. The Templars' house was partially protected by the harbour.
12. See Ludolph von Suchem, 'Description of the Holy Land and of the Way Thither', *The Library of the Palestine Pilgrims Text Society*, 12, trans. Aubrey Stewart (London: 24 Hanover Square, W. 1896), 1–136.
13. Von Suchem, 'Description of the Holy Land and of the Way Thither', 54. Ludolph notes, 'I heard the tale [of the fall of Acre in 1291] told by right truthful men, who well remembered it.'
14. Ibid. 1. Ludolph notes that he composed the work for Baldwin von Steinfurt, the Bishop of Paderborn.
15. Francesco Gabrieli (ed.), *Arab Historians of the Crusades*, trans. E. J. Costello (Berkeley and Los Angeles: University of California Press, 1969), 35.
16. For more on Saladin, see Chapters 6 and 7.
17. Von Suchem, 'Description of the Holy Land and of the Way Thither', 54–61.
18. The Guelfs (or Guelphs) and Ghibellines were Christian factions that originated during the twelfth and thirteenth centuries in northern and central Italy and were divided in their support for the papacy and the Holy Roman Empire.
19. Here Ludolph is confused, as it was Nicholas IV who reigned as Pope from 1288 to 1292. Pope Urban IV reigned from 1261 to 1264.
20. The Master of the Templars was William of Beaujeu. He was elected Master in 1273 and died fighting in the defence of Acre in 1291.
21. One of them was a massive mangonel brought from the fortress of Crac des Chevaliers that had been captured by Baibars in 1271. It was transported in 100 carts and took a month to haul to Acre. See Tyerman, *God's War*, 820.
22. Tyerman puts the actual numbers of the Muslim army at 30,000 to 40,000. See Tyerman, *God's War*, 820.
23. Normally such praise was reserved for Jerusalem, but it had been under Muslim control for over a century by the time of Ludolph's writing. Also, here Ludolph notes that Acre fell in 1292, but he is mistaken, as nearly all modern scholarship dates the fall of the city to 1291.
24. During the Third Crusade, Richard I of England conquered Cyprus, on his way to the Holy Land. It was later given to the displaced King of Jerusalem Guy of Lusignan in 1192 and became an important crusader outpost in later crusades.
25. This source selection is taken from Gabrieli, *Arab Historians of the Crusades*, 345–346.
26. This source selection is taken from Norman Housley (ed.), *Documents on the Later Crusades, 1274–1580* (New York: St. Martin's 1996), 36–37.
27. Ibid. 51–52.

Chapter Twelve: Life on a Crusade, 1095–1270

1. Jonathan Riley-Smith, *The First Crusaders: 1095–1131* (Cambridge: Cambridge University Press, 1997), 144.
2. The best and most recent work to examine logistics during the crusades is the collection of essays edited by John H. Pryor: John H. Pryor (ed.), *Logistics of Warfare in the Age of the Crusades* (Aldershot: Ashgate, 2006).

3. Riley-Smith provides an excellent chapter on the careful financial planning and sacrifices necessary to prepare for a crusade. See Riley-Smith, *The First Crusaders*, 106–143.
4. This selection is taken from Dana Carleton Munro (ed.), 'Letters of the Crusaders', *The Fourth Crusade: Translations and Reprints from the Original Sources of European History*, 6 vols. (Philadelphia: The University of Pennsylvania History Department, 1898–1912) 6–7. The original booklet released by the University of Pennsylvania nowhere contains the date of publication, so the series dates are included in its place.
5. This selection is taken from James Harvey Robinson (ed.), *Readings in European History*, 1 (Boston: Ginn, 1904), 326–327.
6. This selection is taken from August C. Krey, *The First Crusade: The Accounts of Eyewitnesses and Participants* (Princeton: Princeton University Press, 1921), 249–250.
7. This selection is taken from James A. Brundage (ed.), *The Crusades: A Documentary Survey* (Milwaukee: Marquette University Press, 1962), 156–157.
8. Although no record exists of Tancred's intentions for his prisoners, he almost certainly hoped to either ransom them or use them as slaves.
9. This selection is taken from Krey, *The First Crusade*, 256–257.
10. This selection is taken from Helen J. Nicholson (ed.), *Chronicle of the Third Crusade: A Translation of the Itinerarium Peregrinorum et Gesta Regis Ricardi with Introduction and Notes* (Aldershot: Ashgate, 1997), 89
11. This selection is taken from Peter W. Edbury (ed.), *The Conquest of Jerusalem and the Third Crusade: Sources in Translation* (Aldershot: Ashgate, 1998), 107–108.
12. This source is taken from Beha ed-Din, 'Life of Saladin', in *The Library of the Palestine Pilgrims Text Society*, 13, trans. C. W. Wilson (London: 24 Hanover Square, W. 1897), 272–274.
13. This source selection is taken from Francesco Gabrieli (ed.), *Arab Historians of the Crusades*, trans. E. J. Costello (Berkeley and Los Angeles: University of California Press, 1969), 124–125.
14. This source is taken from Beha ed-Din, 'Life of Saladin', 244–245.
15. This selection is taken from Geoffrey de Villehardouin and Jean de Joinville, 'Joinville's Chronicle of the Crusade of St. Lewis', *Memoirs of the Crusades*, trans. Frank T. Marzials (London: J. M. Dent, 1908), 214–216.
16. This is a reference to Frederick II of Germany, who at this time held some possessions in the East.
17. This selection is taken from Villehardouin and Joinville, 'Joinville's Chronicle of the Crusade of St. Lewis', 216–217.
18. Ibid. 217–218.
19. Ibid. 234.
20. This selection is taken from Krey, *The First Crusade*, 174–176.
21. Ibid. 183.
22. This selection is taken from James Harvey Robinson (ed.), *Readings in European History*, 1 (Boston: Ginn, 1904), 327.
23. This source selection is taken from Francesco Gabrieli (ed.) *Arab Historians of the Crusades*, trans. E. J. Costello (Berkeley and Los Angeles: University of California Press, 1969), 122.
24. This selection is taken from Villehardouin and Joinville, 'Joinville's Chronicle of the Crusade of St. Lewis', 261.
25. The seminal work on the issue of clerical concerns over feminine sexuality, and thereby women, as a threat to the success of a crusade is that of James Brundage, 'Prostitution, Miscegenation and Sexual Purity in the First Crusade', in *Crusade and Settlement: Papers Read at the First Conference of the Society for the Study of the Crusades and the Latin*

East and Presented to R.C. Smail, ed. Peter Edbury (Cardiff: University College Cardiff Press, 1985), 57–65.
26. Both the Christian and Muslim ethos on war during the Crusades would not have sanctioned a strictly combat role for women. Some Muslim accounts, including that of Imad ad-Din presented in this chapter, claim that Christian women sometimes went into combat as soldiers during the crusades in the Holy Land, but these accounts are highly suspect as such an attribution would have shamed their enemies. Also, no Christian account of the time makes the specific claim of Christian women taking part in offensive combat. For example, while Guibert of Nogent (*Gesta Dei*) recorded that a 'troop of Amazons' accompanied Emperor Conrad to Syria, there is no account of their exploits on the battlefield. If such combat did occur, it is likely to have gone unrecorded in the light of the potential shame for crusader armies. For additional reading, see Susan Edgington and Sarah Lambert (eds.), *Gendering the Crusades* (University of Wales Press, 2001); and Helen Nicholson, 'Women on the Third Crusade', in *Journal of Medieval History*, 23 (1997): 335–49.
27. See Robert the Monk's account of Pope Urban II's speech at Clermont provided in Chapter 2.
28. See Brundage, 'Prostitution, Miscegenation and Sexual Purity in the First Crusade', for the foundational development of the clerical view of women as a threat to the spiritual purity of the crusaders during the First Crusade. Such concerns clearly carried over into later crusades during the twelfth and thirteenth centuries as demonstrated by numerous references in the major sources of the later crusades.
29. This source selection is taken from Gabrieli, *Arab Historians of the Crusades*, 207.
30. Ibid. 163.
31. This source is taken from Brundage, *The Crusades*, 49.
32. This source is taken from Krey, *The First Crusade*, 174.
33. This source is taken from Edward Peters (ed.), *The First Crusade: The Chronicle of Fulcher of Chartres and Other Source Material* (Philadelphia: University of Pennsylvania Press, 1971), 54.
34. This selection is taken from Villehardouin and Joinville, 'Joinville's Chronicle of the Crusade of St. Lewis', 262.
35. Ibid. 261.

Chapter Thirteen: Life in the Crusader States, 1098–1291

1. Alfred J. Andrea, 'Crusader States', *Encyclopedia of the Crusades* (Westport, CT: Greenwood, 2003), 88.
2. For more information on the crusader states and institutions in the Holy Land, see J. Richard, *The Latin Kingdom of Jerusalem*, 2 vols. (Amsterdam, NY: North-Holland Publishing, 1979); J. Prawer, *Crusader Institutions* (Oxford: Clarendon Press, 1980; New York: Oxford University Press, 1980); B. Z. Kedar et al. (eds.), *Outremer* (Jerusalem: Yad Izhak Ben-Zvi Institute, 1982); P. W. Edbury (ed.), *Crusade and Settlement* (Cardiff: University College Cardiff Press, 1985); and A. Jotischky, *Crusading and the Crusader States* (New York: Pearson Longman, 2004).
3. Perhaps the best biography of Godfrey of Bouillon is Pierre Aube, *Godefroy de Bouillon* (Paris: Fayard, 1985).
4. Perhaps the best scholarly work on the Templars is by Malcolm Barber, *The New Knighthood: A History of the Order of the Temple* (Cambridge: Cambridge University Press, 1994).
5. Philip K. Hitti, 'Introduction', in Usamah ibn Munqidh, *An Arab Syrian Gentleman & Warrior in the Period of the Crusades*, trans. Philip K. Hitti (New York: Columbia University Press, 2000), 16–17.

6. This source selection is taken from William of Tyre, *A History of Deeds Done Beyond the Sea*, 1, trans. Emily A. Babcock and August C. Krey (New York: Columbia University Press, 1943), 379–383.
7. This source selection is taken from August C. Krey, *The First Crusade: The Accounts of Eyewitnesses and Participants* (Princeton: Princeton University Press, 1921), 280.
8. This source selection is taken from William of Tyre, *A History of Deeds Done Beyond the Sea*, 507–508.
9. This source selection is taken from Jacques de Vitry, 'The History of Jerusalem', *The Library of the Palestine Pilgrims Text Society*, 11, trans. Aubrey Stewart (London: 24 Hanover Square, W. 1896), 51–53.
10. Usamah ibn Munqidh, *An Arab-Syrian Gentleman & Warrior in the Period of the Crusades*, 150.
11. This source selection is taken from Krey, *The First Crusade*, 280–281.
12. Usamah ibn Munqidh, *An Arab-Syrian Gentleman & Warrior in the Period of the Crusades*, 169–170.
13. Ibid. 161.
14. Ibid. 162–163.
15. This source selection is taken from Francesco Gabrieli (ed.), *Arab Historians of the Crusades*, trans. E. J. Costello (Berkeley and Los Angeles: University of California Press, 1984), 83–84.
16. Burchard of Mount Sion, 'A Description of the Holy Land by Burchard of Mount Sion', *The Library of the Palestine Pilgrims Text Society*, 12, trans. Aubrey Stewart (London: 24 Hanover Square, W. 1896), 103–104.
17. See Imad ad-Din's selection 'The Abuse of Christian Women after Saladin's Capture of Jerusalem in 1187' in Chapter 12.
18. Usamah ibn Munqidh, *An Arab-Syrian Gentleman & Warrior in the Period of the Crusades*, 164–166.
19. This source selection is taken from Gabrieli, *Arab Historians of the Crusades*, 204–206.
20. This source selection is taken from Jacques de Vitry, 'The History of Jerusalem', 64–66.

Chapter Fourteen: Crusades and the Canon Law

1. Charles Mackay, *Extraordinary Popular Delusions and the Madness of Crowds* (London: Richard Bentley, 1841; reprint New York: Farrar, Straus and Giroux, n.d.), 354.
2. Mackay, *Extraordinary Popular Delusions and the Madness of Crowds*, 354.
3. Geoffrey de Villehardouin and Jean de Joinville, *Memoirs of the Crusades*, ed. Frank T. Marzials (New York: E. P. Dutton, 1958), 4–16.
4. On the reform movement and the development of canon law, see Stanley Chodorow, *Christian Political Theory and Church Politics in the Mid-Twelfth Century* (Berkeley and Los Angeles: University of California Press, 1972).
5. On the importance of the Gregorian reform movement, see Uta-Renata Blumenthal, *The Investiture Controversy: Church and Monarchy from the Ninth to the Twelfth Century* (Philadelphia: University of Pennsylvania Press, 1988).
6. Frederick Russell, *The Just War in the Middle Ages* (Cambridge: Cambridge University Press, 1975), 68.
7. Ibid. 35–36.
8. For a convenient introduction to the canon law, see James A. Brundage, *Medieval Canon Law* (London: Longman, 1995). Since Brundage wrote, there has been a great deal of discussion about the origins of the *Decretum* as it presently exists; see Anders Winroth, *The Making of Gratian's Decretum* (Cambridge: Cambridge University Press, 2000).
9. Brundage, *Medieval Canon Law*, 123–126.

10. On the pope as universal judge, see Brian Tierney, '"*Tria quipped distnguit iudicia...*" A Note on Innocent III's *Decretal Per Venerabilem*', *Speculum*, 37 (1962): 48–59.
11. The importance of the role of the papal legate leading to the First Crusade has been much debated; see Norman Housley, *Contesting the Crusades* (Oxford: Blackwell, 2006), 30–36.
12. The basic book on the canonists and the just war is Frederick Russell, *The Just War in the Middle Ages* (Cambridge: Cambridge University Press, 1975). Pages 55–86 provide a discussion of *Causa XXIII*.
13. Russell, *The Just War in the Middle Ages*, 295–299; James A. Brundage, *Medieval Canon Law and the Crusader* (Madison: University of Wisconsin Press, 1969), 189–190.
14. On the just war in general, see James Turner Johnson, *Just War Tradition and the Restraint of War* (Princeton: Princeton University Press, 1981).
15. Brundage, *Canon Law and the Crusader*, 3–18. The use of the pilgrim model may reflect the canonists' discomfort with legitimizing violence.
16. Ibid. 115–190.
17. Ibid. *xv*.
18. See Norman Cohn, *The Pursuit of the Millennium*, rev. ed. (New York: Oxford University Press, 1970).
19. Villehardouin and Joinville, *Memoirs of the Crusades*, 15–16.
20. James Muldoon, *Popes, Lawyers, and Infidels: The Church and the Non-Christian World, 1250–1550* (Philadelphia: University of Pennsylvania Press, 1979), 101–102.
21. James A. Brundage, *Law, Sex, and Christian Society in Medieval Europe* (Chicago: University of Chicago Press, 1987), 102, 300.
22. Muldoon, *Popes, Lawyers, and Infidels*, 5–6, 41–45.
23. Ibid. 15–19.
24. Frederick H. Russell, 'Paulus Vladimiri's Attack on the Just War: A Case Study in Legal Polemics', in *Authority and Power: Studies on Medieval Law and Government*, ed. Brian Tierney and Peter Linehan (Cambridge: Cambridge University Press, 1980), 237–254.
25. Lewis Hanke, *The Spanish Struggle for Justice in the Conquest of America* (Philadelphia: University of Pennsylvania Press, 1949); see also J. H. Parry, *The Spanish Theory of Empire in the Sixteenth Century* (Cambridge: Cambridge University Press, 1940).
26. The texts from the *Decretum* and the *Decretales* are taken from the *Corpus Iuris Canonici* (Lyons, 1614). The excerpt from Innocent IV is Innocent IV, *Commentaria Doctissima in Quinque Libros Decretalium* (Turin: apud haeredes Nicolai, 1581). The excerpt from Hostiensis is Hostsiensis, *Lectura quinque decretalium*, 2 vols. (Paris, 1512). All the translations are by James Muldoon.

INDEX

Abu l-Fida, Arab Emir 197
   Muslim conquest of Acre
     in 1291 203–5
Acre
   decline of Latin settlements 197
   Muslim conquest of 199–205
   Richard's execution of Muslim
     prisoners 216–18
   siege and conquest of 196
Adhémar of Le Puy 263
   adultery 9, 137
Albert of Aachen, slaughter of Rhineland
   Jews 26, 29–31
Alexius I Comnenus, Byzantine
   Emperor 4–5
   Pope Urban II's calling of First
     Crusade 9–12
Alexius III 123–5
Alexius IV 123, 124
Ali, Tariq xiv
Alp Arslan, Sultan xix
Amalekites 273
Ambroise, execution of Muslim prisoners
   by Christian women 214, 216
Annales Herbipolenses 76, 77, 82
Anonymous Annalist of Wurzburg,
   criticisms of (Second Crusade) 76
   on clerical advocates 82
   on impious motivations of crusaders 77
   See also Second Crusade, failure of
Antioch xx
   discovery of the Holy Lance 225–7
   expulsion of Christian women 233–4
   Godfrey's letter on repentance leading
     to victory 227–8
   hunger and starvation of crusaders
     210, 211
   spiritual preparation of crusaders
     in 1098 225, 227
   women as source of sin and cause
     of failure 232–3
Apologia 84–6
Archumbald, letter to (battle
   of Hattin) 97–9
Arnulf, Lord 240
Avidus 10

Baibars 195
Baldric of Dol, Pope Urban II's calling
   of First Crusade 7, 16–19

Baldwin I, King of Jerusalem
   problem of depopulation in Kingdom
     of Jerusalem 241–2
   repopulation of Kingdom
     of Jerusalem 242–3
Baldwin II's exemption of Usamah's uncle
   from indemnity 245
Balian of Ibelin 109–10, 112
   negotiations for surrender
     of Jerusalem 119–20
Bartholomew I, Ecumenical Patriarch xiv
Beha ed-Din 92, 111–12, 215, 219
   battle of Hattin 102–5
   Richard's massacre of Muslim prisoners
     at Acre 217–18
   Saladin's kindness to a distraught
     Christian mother 220–1
   Saladin's siege of Jerusalem
     in 1187 117–19
Bernard of Clairvaux 26, 28, 57, 81, 82–4
   Apologia 84–6
   defence of the Jews 37
   letter promoting Second Crusade 35–6
   preaching against Rudolph 36–7
   See also Geoffrey of Clairvaux; Second
     Crusade, failure of
Burchard of Mount Sion, religious beliefs
   and practices of peoples of East 252
Byzantine Empire xvii–xx, 5, 15, 77–8, 123,
   125, 128
Byzantines 77, 123, 261

canon law, crusades and 261–73
Causa XXIII (Concerning War and
   Military Affairs) 263, 268–9
Charles Martel xx
Chegeret-Eddur, wife of Sultan Nedjm
   Eddin 169, 190
Children's Crusade 261
Christian prisoners
   forced conversion of 223–4
   Muslim treatment of sick 223
   Saladin's execution of captive
     Christians 219–20
   Saladin's kindness to distraught
     Christian mother 220–1
Christians
   expulsion of women at Antioch 233–4
   marriage law and consequences 265–6,
     269–70

See also Christian prisoners; Christian treatment of Muslim prisoners
Christian treatment of Muslim prisoners 214–18
  execution by Christian women 216
  Richard's execution at Acre in 1191 216–18
  slaughter during conquest of Jerusalem 215
Clement III, Pope 269
clerical advocates 82
Clermont, Council of 6, 7, 25, 26
Conrad III, King of Germany 57, 75
  failures of crusaders' siege of Damascus 58, 80, 81
Constantinople
  bad relations between East and West 125
  events leading to sack of 123–4
  massacre of Latins living in 129–30
  plan for division of 131
  Pope Innocent III's command for crusaders to stay at 137–8
  sack of 124–5, 132–4
  sermons before attack on 131–2
crusaders 25, 41, 59, 80–1, 89, 137–8, 185, 227
  capture of Damietta 182–3
  capture of Jerusalem 44–53
  failure to attack Damascus, reasons for 63–8
  hunger and thirst of 209–10, 212
  morality during Second Crusade 84–6
  motivation of 3, 77
  Muslim defeat of crusaders at Damascus 68–71
  physical and spiritual conditions 209
  reduced enthusiasm 86
  spiritual preparation of 225, 227
crusader states, life in
  cohabitation and cooperation 237
  competing views of morality in Holy Land 252–8
  cultural and social interaction in Holy Land 246–52
  government and administration 237–45
crusade(s), 27
  and canon law 261–73
  criticisms of preachers 81–4
  definition of xv
  expenses of 3
  scholarly perspectives of xiv–xvi
  women on 229–34

Damascus
  attack on 58
  reasons for crusaders' failure to attack 63–8
  and Second Crusade 57–8
Damascus Chronicle 50
Damietta 165, 166
  crusaders' capture of 182–3
  Louis's capture of 167, 171–5
  Queen's fear of capture 224
De Consideration 84
Decretales, 3.34.8, Quod super his 271–2
Decretales, 4.17.15, *Gaudemus* 269–70
Decretales, 4.19.7, Quanto te 270
Decretales, 4.19.8, Gaudemus 270
Decretales, 5.6.12, Quod olim 269
Decretum 262, 263
The Deeds of Frederick Barbarossa 36, 59
De Expugatione Terrae Sanctae per Saladinum 91, 111
Saladin's siege of Jerusalem in 1187 114–17
Saladin's victory at Hattin 93–7
thirst of Christians at battle of Hattin 213
Dershowitz, Allen xiv
Description of the Holy Land and of the Way Thither 197
Devil, Satan 199, 250
dominium 266, 272
Dorylaeum 229, 230, 232

Ekkehard of Aura, slaughter of Rhineland Jews 26, 27, 31
Emicho of Flonheim 25
Ephraim bar Jacob of Bonn 28, 37
Eraclius (Latin Patriarch of Jerusalem) on Hattin 91–2, 99–100
Essahib Giemal Edden Ben Matroub (poet) 192
Eugenius III, Pope 57, 58, 75, 86
  calling of Second Crusade 61–3

First Council of Nicaea xx
First Crusade 4, 8, 25
  crusaders' victory at Jerusalem 44–52
  People's Crusade, attack on Jews by 25
  Peasants' Crusade, attack on Jews by 25
  slaughter of Rhineland Jews 29–35
  starvation and cannibalism of crusaders 211–12
Fourth Crusade 123, 124, 126, 127, 131–2
Frankish prostitutes 255–6

Frank(s)
    adopting Muslim dietary laws 247–8
    devoid of jealousy 253–4
    friendly relationship with
        Usamah 248–9
    sufferings ended-up at Hattin 92,
        100–2
Frederick II, King of Norman Sicily
    crusade of 141–3
    excommunication of 141, 142
    Gerold, Patriarch's criticism 144,
        153–6
    letter to King Henry III 143, 150–3
    negotiations with al-Kamil 141, 142
    and tensions with papacy 141
Fulcher of Chartres
    adoption of local customs by Western
        Christians 246–7
    Baldwin's efforts to maintain sizable
        population 241–2
    expulsion of Christian women 233–4
    Pope Urban II's calling of First
        Crusade 5–6, 12–14

Geoffrey of Clairvaux 81
    defence of Bernard of Clairvaux 82–4
    See also Second Crusade, failure of
Gerold, Patriarch's criticism on
    Frederick II 142, 143, 144, 153–6
Gesta Dei per Francos (The Deeds of God
    through the Franks) 7, 8
*Gesta Francorum et Aliorum
    Hierosolimitanorum* (The Deeds of the
    Franks and the Other Pilgrims
    to Jerusalem) 6, 42
crusaders' victory at Jerusalem 44–5
    discovery of Holy Lance at Antioch
        in 1098 225–7
    execution of Muslim prisoners 214,
        215
    spiritual preparation of crusaders
        at Antioch 227
    thirst of crusaders during siege
        of Jerusalem 210, 212–13
    women as blessing to crusading
        army 232
    women as source of sin and cause
        of failure 232–3
glossa ordinaria 267
Godfrey of Bouillon
    election of 239–241
    repentance leading to victory
        at Antioch 227–8

starvation and cannibalism during
    First Crusade 210, 211–12
Gratian in Bologna 262, 263
Greek Fire 116, 174
Gregorian Reform movement 262
Gregory VII, Pope xix
Gregory IX, Pope 141, 142
Guibert of Nogent 7–8, 19–22
Gunther von Pairis, catalogue of relics
    stolen by abbot Martin 127, 134–5
Guy the knight on capture of
    Damietta 167, 171–5
Guy de Lusignan, King of
    Jerusalem 89, 90

Hattin, battle of (1187) 89–90
    Eraclius' letter to Pope Urban III
        on 91–2, 99, 100
    letter to Archumbald on 91, 97–8
    Muslim capture of 'true cross', 228
    Muslims tactics to defeat Christian
        army 92, 102–5
    Saladin's victory at Hattin 91, 93–7
    sufferings of Franks 92, 100–2
    thirst of Christians during Third
        Crusade 213
Henry III, King of England 143, 150–3
Henry of Segusio. *See* Hostiensis
Historia Francorum qui Ceperunt Iherusalem
    (The History of the Franks who
    Captured Jerusalem) 42
Historia Iherosolimitana (History of the
    Journey to Jerusalem) 5, 6, 7, 12, 14, 29
*Historia rerum in partibus transmarinis
    gestarum* (History of Deeds Done
    beyond the Sea) 59, 63, 129
A History of the Expedition to Jerusalem 5
Holy cross (True cross), 93, 98, 102,
    114 217
    Muslim capture of 'true cross'
        at Hattin 228
Holy Land 8, 19, 57, 60
    and battle of Hattin 89
    call for recovery of 205
    competing views of morality 252–8
    criticisms of crusading
        leadership 79–81
    cultural and social interactions 246–52
    Eugenius III, Pope's call 75
    Pope Urban's calling of the First
        Crusade 3
Holy Sepulchre 16, 41, 44, 49, 152,
    155, 215

329

Honorius III, Pope 141
Horns of Hattin 90
Hostiensis 266
   commentary on *Decretales* 3.34.8, *Quod super his* 273
Hussites 196

Ibn al-Athir 42
   crusaders' capture of Jerusalem in 1099 51–2
   Muslim capture of 'true cross' at Hattin 228
   negotiations for surrender of Jerusalem 119–20
   Saladin's execution of captive Christians in 1187 219–20
   sufferings of Franks ended-up at Hattin 92, 100–2
Ibn al-Qalanisi
   crusaders' capture of Jerusalem in 1099 50–1
   Muslim account of crusaders' defeat at Damascus 60, 68–71
Ibn Wasil, handover of Jerusalem to Franks 144, 156–9
Iconoclasm Controversy xx
Imad ad-Din 57, 229
   abuse of Christian women 231–2
   Christian women as combatants during Third Crusade 230–1
   Frankish prostitutes 255–6
Innocent III, Pope 124, 128, 141, 265, 269
   Christian marriage law and consequences 265–6, 269–70
   command for crusaders to stay at Constantinople 137–8
   conversion of single partner 270
   on multiple wives 270
   reprimand of papal legate 136–7
Innocent IV, Pope
   commentary on *Decretales* 3.34.8, *Quod super his* 272–3
   on non-Christians 265–6
Investiture Controversy xxii, 263
Isaac II, Byzantine Emperor 123–4
Islam before crusades
   and Eastern Christianity xvii–xx
   and Western Christianity xx–xxii
iudex omnium 263

Jacques de Vitry
   founding of Knights Templar 243–5
   immoral behaviour of Pulani 257–8

Jerusalem
   battle for 41–2
   execution of Muslim prisoners 215
   importance to crusaders 41
   siege and conquest of 109–10
   thirst of crusaders during siege of 212–13
Jesus Christ 41, 95, 135, 151, 161, 206, 226, 232
Jews, attack on 37
   forced conversion 27
   by Peasants' Crusade 25
   by People's Crusade 25
   slaughter of Rhineland Jews 29–35
jihad 43, 51, 89
John VIII, Pope xxi
John Paul II, Pope xiii
Joinville, Jean de 167–8, 219, 230
   capture and treatment in captivity 221–3
   capture of King Louis IX 175–7
   daily spirituality regimen of 228
   efforts to avoid suspicion with regard to women 234
   execution of treaty and near execution of King Louis 168, 180–2
   forced conversion of Christian prisoners 223–4
   Louis IX's harsh treatment of a knight 234
   Louis in captivity and negotiations for ransom 177–8
   Muslim treatment of sick Christian prisoners 223
   oaths of Louis IX and emirs 168, 179–80
   Queen's fear of capture at Damietta 224
The Journey of Louis VII to the East 59

Kalavun 195
al-Kamil's negotiation with Frederick II, King of Norman Sicily 141, 142
Knights Hospitallers 89
Knights Templar 89, 238, 243–5

Lambert, Bishop of Arras 52
Leo IV, Pope xxi
Liber de Fine 198
The Life of Saladin 111–12
Louis VII, King of France 57

Louis IX, King of France
  capture of 167, 168, 175–7, 188–90
  capture of Damietta 167, 171–5
  and correspondence of Nedjm
    Eddin 166, 170
  First Crusade and 165–6
  Muslim poetry on humiliation of 169,
    192
Ludolph of Suchem, Muslim conquest
  of Acre in 1291 197, 199–203

Maccabees 8
Madden, Thomas xvi
Mainz, attack against Jews in 25
al Makrisi 166
  assassination of Sultan Touran
    Chah 169, 190–1
  battle of Mansoura 168, 185–8
  capture of King Louis 168, 188–90
  correspondence of St. Louis and Sultan
    Nedjm Eddin 166, 170
  crusaders' capture of Damietta 168,
    182–3
  death of Nedjm Eddin, Sultan 168,
    183–5
  Muslim poetry on humiliation
    of St. Louis 169, 192
  ransom of King Louis 169, 191–2
al-Malik al-Ashraf 196, 198
Manasses, Archbishop of Reims 52–3
Mansoura, battle of 168, 185–8
Manuel I Comnenus, Byzantine
  emperor attitude towards Second
    Crusade 78–9
marriage law
  and consequences 265–6, 269–70
  and conversion of single partner 270
  and multiple wives 270
Martin of Pairis 127, 134–5
Mary, Mother of Jesus 17, 161, 233
Michael VII Dukas, Byzantine
  Emperor xix
militant Christianity and Islam xvi–xvii
Murtzuphlus, Alexius Ducas 126
Muslim prisoners
  execution by Christian women 214, 216
  Richard's execution of 216–18
Muslims
  capture of 'true cross' at Hattin 228
  conquest of Acre in 1291 199–205
  defeat of crusaders at Damascus 68–71
  tactics to defeat Christian army 92,
    102–5
See also Muslim prisoners; Muslim
  treatment of Christian prisoners; Turks
Muslim treatment of Christian
  prisoners 219–24
  forced conversion 223–4
  Joinville's capture and treatment
    in captivity 221–3
  Queen's fear of capture
    at Damietta 224
  Saladin's execution of captive
    Christians 219–20
  Saladin's kindness to distraught
    Christian mother 220–1
  treatment of sick Christian prisoners
    in Egypt 223

Nedjm Eddin, Sultan
  correspondence with St. Louis 166, 170
  death of 168, 183–5
Nicene Creed xx
Nicetas Choniates, sack of
  Constantinople 127, 132–4
Nicholas IV, Pope 195
Nicholas Mesarites, sack of
  Constantinople 127, 134

Odo of Deuil, criticisms of (Second
    Crusade) 59, 77
  on betrayal of Byzantines 79
  on non-combatants 76
  on treachery of Manuel I
    Comnenus 78–9
See also Second Crusade, failure of
Old French Continuation of William
  of Tyre 214
  Richard's execution of Muslim
    prisoners at Acre 216–17
Ottoman Turks 196
Otto of Freising 36–7, 59

pagans, Muslims as 62, 215
Paschal II, Pope 52
  Godfrey's letter on repentance leading
    to victory 227–8
  Godfrey's letter on starvation and
    cannibalism 211–12
Patzinaks 9, 11, 12
Peace of God xxiii, 5, 7
Peasants' Crusade 25
People's Crusade 25
Philip V, King of France 198
  on call for recovery of Holy
    Land 205–6

Philip de Novare, Frederick II's
    crusade 143, 146–50
Piacenza, Council of xxiii
pilgrimage 3, 41, 271
pilgrims 3, 241, 243, 363–4
'Popular Delusion and the Madness
    of Crowds', 261
prisoners of wars
    Christian treatment of Muslim
        prisoners 214–18
    Muslim treatment of Christian
        prisoners 219–24
Propontis 10
Pulani 257–8

Quantum Praedecessores 57, 58–9, 61, 86
Quia Maior 141

Ramon Lull, call for recovery of Holy
    Land 198, 205
rape 6, 15, 209, 229
*The Rare and Excellent History
    of Saladin* 92
Raymond d'Aguiliers, crusaders' capture
    of Jerusalem 42, 46–50
Raynald of Chatillon 89
    execution by Saladin 90, 104
Reconciliation Walk movement xiii
Ricau, William 46
Richard's execution of Muslim prisoners
    at Acre 214–15, 216–18
Riley-Smith, Jonathan xv
*The Road to Knowledge of the Return
    of Kings* 166
Robert of Clari, sermons before the attack
    on Constantinople 127, 131–2
Robert of Flanders
    letter from Alexius, Byzantine
        Emperor 9–12
    See also Urban II, Pope's calling of First
        Crusade, views on
Robert of Rheims, Pope Urban II's calling
    of First Crusade 6, 14–16
Romanus IV Diogenes, Emperor xix
Rudolph, German monk 28, 36–7

St. Bernard of Clairvaux 25
Saladin (Sultan Salah al-Din Yusuf) 89
    kindness to a distraught Christian
        mother 220–1
    negotiations for surrender
        of Jerusalem 119–20
    Raynald's execution 90, 104

siege and conquest
    of Jerusalem 109–10, 113
tactics used to defeat Christian
    army 102–5
victory at Hattin 93–7
Second Nicean Council xx
Second Crusade 28, 59, 84
    Bernard of Clairvaux's letter
        promoting 35–6
    consequences of 57
    Eugenius III's call for 61–3
    events of, until siege of Damascus 57–8
Second Crusade, failure of
    Byzantine treachery 77–9
    crusade preachers 81–4
    morality of crusaders 84–6
    poor leadership 80
    problem of non-combatants 75–7
    reduced enthusiasm for crusading 86
Sibt Ibn al-Jauzi, handover of Jerusalem
    to Franks 145, 159–61
Sinibaldo Fieschi. *See* Innocent IV, Pope
sodomy 10
Solomon bar Samson, slaughter
    of Rhineland Jews 27, 31–5
Speyer, attack against Jews in 25
spirituality of crusaders 224–8
    discovery of Holy Lance
        at Antioch 225–7
    Godfrey's letter to Pope Paschal II
        on 227–8
    Joinville's daily spirituality regimen 228
    Muslim capture of 'true cross'
        at Hattin 228
    spiritual preparation of crusaders
        at Antioch 227
Stephen (Count of Blois and Chartres)
    on hunger of crusaders 211

Tancred of Taranto 214, 215
Temple of Solomon 42, 44
Terricius (Master of the Temple)
    on capture of Jerusalem 113–14
Third Crusade 94, 110, 213, 214
    Christian women as combatants 230–1
    execution of Muslim prisoners
        by Christian women 214, 216
    thirst of Christians at battle
        of Hattin 213
Touran Chah 168, 183, 185
    assassination of 168, 190–1
Truce of God xxiii, 5, 7, 12
Turks 9, 11, 12

and Christians' suffering from thirst
at Hattin 213
and crusade of Conrad III 57
execution by Christian women 216
desecration of holy places 3, 8, 13, 41
and Saladin's siege of Jerusalem 116
See also Muslims; Muslim treatment
of Christian prisoners

Urban II, Pope's calling of First Crusade,
views on
Baldric of Dol 7, 16–19
Fulcher of Chartres 5–6, 12–14
Guibert of Nogent 7–8, 19–22
letter of Alexius to Count Robert 4–5,
9–12
Robert the Monk 6, 14–16
Urban III (Pope), Eraclius' letter
on Hattin 91–2, 99–100
Usamah ibn Munqidh
Baldwin's exemption of his uncle
from indemnity 245
Frank adopting Muslim dietary
laws 247–8
Franks devoid of jealousy 253–4
friendly Frank of 248–9
Muslim and Christian
medicine 249–51
positive reflections of Christian and
Muslim piety 251–2
U.S. News and World Report xiv

Venice 123
Villehardouin, Geoffrey de, crusaders'
plan for division of Constantinople
126, 131

Western internal reform and rise
of crusading xxii–xxiv
Wibald, Abbot of Corvey
letter from King Conrad III 80–1
See also Second Crusade, failure of
William of Tyre 59–60, 80, 125
Baldwin's efforts of
repopulation 242–3
fiasco at Damascus in 1148 63–8
Godfrey's election in
Jerusalem 239–241
massacre of Latins in Constantinople
in 1182 129–30
Richard's execution of Muslim
prisoners at Acre in 1191 216–17
wives 112, 229, 252, 265
Frankish immodesty 253–4
immoral behaviour of Pulani 257–8
marriage law and multiple wives 270
women 229
abuse of Christian women 231–2
as blessing to crusading army 232
as combatants 230–1
execution of Muslim prisoners
by Christian women 214, 216
expulsion of Christian women 233–4
as source of sin and cause of
failure 232–3
Worms, attack against Jews in 25

Zara 123

FIGHTING WORDS

Fighting Words is an innovative and accessible new military-history series, each title juxtaposing the voices of opposing combatants in a major historical conflict. Presented side by side are the testimonies of fighting men and women, the reportage of nations at war, and the immediate public responses of belligerent war leaders. Together, they offer strikingly different perspectives on the same events.

The extracts are short and snappy, complemented by brief introductions which set the scene. They vividly recreate the conflicts as they were experienced. At the same time, they open up new perspectives and challenge accepted assumptions. Readers will question the nature of primary sources, the motivations of the authors, the agendas that influence media reports and the omissions inherent in all of the sources. Ultimately, readers will be left to ponder the question: whose history is this?

Competing Voices from the Crusades
Andrew Holt and James Muldoon

Competing Voices from the Pacific War
Chris Dixon, Sean Brawley and Beatrice Trefalt

Competing Voices from Native America
Joy Porter and Dewi Ioan Ball

Competing Voices from the Russian Revolution
Michael C. Hickey

Competing Voices from World War II in Europe
Harold J. Goldberg

Competing Voices from the Mexican Revolution
Chris Frazer

Competing Voices from Revolutionary Cuba
John M. Kirk and Peter McKenna

14 FEB 182